FORWARD TO PROFESSORSHIP IN STEM

FORWARD TO PROFESSORSHIP IN STEM

Inclusive Faculty Development Strategies That Work

Edited by

RACHELLE S. HELLER
*Department of Computer Science, George Washington University,
Washington, DC, USA*

CATHERINE MAVRIPLIS
*Department of Mechanical Engineering, University of Ottawa,
Ottawa, ON, Canada*

PAUL SALI SABILA
*Chemistry and Physics Program, Department of Science, Technology, and Mathematics,
Gallaudet University, Washington, DC, USA*

AMSTERDAM • BOSTON • HEIDELBERG • LONDON
NEW YORK • OXFORD • PARIS • SAN DIEGO
SAN FRANCISCO • SINGAPORE • SYDNEY • TOKYO

Academic Press is an imprint of Elsevier

ELSEVIER

Academic Press is an imprint of Elsevier
125, London Wall, EC2Y 5AS.
525 B Street, Suite 1800, San Diego, CA 92101-4495, USA
225 Wyman Street, Waltham, MA 02451, USA
The Boulevard, Langford Lane, Kidlington, Oxford OX5 1GB, UK

Notices
Knowledge and best practice in this field are constantly changing. As new research and experience broaden our understanding, changes in research methods, professional practices, or medical treatment may become necessary.

Practitioners and researchers must always rely on their own experience and knowledge in evaluating and using any information, methods, compounds, or experiments described herein. In using such information or methods they should be mindful of their own safety and the safety of others, including parties for whom they have a professional responsibility.

To the fullest extent of the law, neither the Publisher nor the authors, contributors, or editors, assume any liability for any injury and/or damage to persons or property as a matter of products liability, negligence or otherwise, or from any use or operation of any methods, products, instructions, or ideas contained in the material herein.

ISBN: 978-0-12-800855-3

British Library Cataloguing-in-Publication Data
A catalogue record for this book is available from the British Library.

Library of Congress Cataloging-in-Publication Data
A catalog record for this book is available from the Library of Congress.

For Information on all Academic Press publications
visit our website at http://store.elsevier.com/

Publisher: Sara Tenney
Acquisition Editor: Mary Preap
Editorial Project Manager: Mary Preap
Production Project Manager: Chris Wortley
Designer: Christian Bilbow

Typeset by MPS Limited, Chennai, India
www.adi-mps.com

  **Working together
to grow libraries in
developing countries**

www.elsevier.com • www.bookaid.org

Contents

List of Contributors   xiii

Prologue   xvii

1. The Origins of Faculty Development in Science, Technology, Engineering, and Mathematics   1
RACHELLE S. HELLER

Introduction   2
Brief History of Faculty Development   3
Programs for Advancing Women in STEM   5
Resource Development   8
General Design Issues for Faculty Development Workshops   11
Beyond Workshops   13
Conclusion   14
References   14

2. The FORWARD to Professorship Workshop   17
CATHERINE MAVRIPLIS

Introduction   18
Workshop Goals and Design   20
Implementation   22
Results of the FORWARD to Professorship Workshop   35
Paying It FORWARD   36
Acknowledgments   43
References   43

3. Path of Professorship: A Student Leadership Model for Catalyzing Change at MIT   47
SHANNON MOREY, BLANCHE STATON AND BRAD SAN MARTIN

Origin and Goals   48
Successes and Outcomes   49
Impact on Attendees and Organizers   50
Workshop Sessions   54
An Institution-Centered Workshop   55
Graduate Students as Leaders   56

Institutional Leadership   57
Institutionalized Financial Support   57
Challenges and Responses   58
Revisions   59
Lessons Learned   60
Conclusion   61
References   61

4. Jumpstarting STEM Careers   63
D. PAGE BALUCH

Introduction   63
Organizing a Team   65
Creating a Program   65
Jumpstarting STEM Careers Workshops and Symposiums   67
Moving Forward   73
Event Feedback   73
Concluding Remarks   75
Acknowledgments   75
References   75

5. University of Guam: Advancing Female STEM Faculty
in the Western Pacific   77
HELEN THOMPSON

Introduction   77
University of Guam Project   80
Project Evaluation—Successes   82
Project Evaluation—Challenges and Criticism   86
The Difficult Way Forward   87
References   89

6. When and Where I Enter...A FORWARD to Professorship
Workshop   91
LESLEY BERHAN, AMANDA BRYANT-FRIEDRICH, NANCY COLLINS, ISABEL C. ESCOBAR,
CHARLENE GILBERT AND CYNDEE GRUDEN

Introduction   92
Goals   93
Description   94
Challenges   97
Evaluations   99
Outcomes and Successes   101
Lessons Learned   103
Conclusions and Suggestions for Future Workshops   104
References   105

7. Workshop Design for Diversity and Dialogue: Women
in STEM Empowered to Engage Across Difference   107
GERTRUDE FRASER AND MARGARET HARDEN

Introduction   108
Starting with Story   108
Conceptual and Intellectual Framework: Guideposts for the Workshop   110
The Planning Group   111
Designing a Workshop to Facilitate Engagement Across Difference:
    Core Principles and Strategies   111
Pre-workshop Work   114
Workshop Implementation: An Interactive Format   115
The Participants' Perspective   119
The Facilitation Perspective   121
A Few Practical Lessons Learned   124
Recommendations   125
Conclusion   126
Acknowledgments   127
References   127

8. To Tenure and Beyond: Building an Intentional
Career in STEM   129
AMANDA SHAFFER AND SUSAN FREIMARK

Evolution of the NSF ADVANCE Initiatives at CWRU   130
Objectives of TT&B   131
Recruitment of Participants   132
Development of Modules and Customization to Cohort Needs   135
Rationale for Key Curricular Themes: Understanding Career Arc
    and the Intentional Change Model   138
Evaluation and Outcomes   141
Challenges and Ongoing Efforts   142
References   144
Further Reading   145

9. FORWARD Oklahoma State University: Building an
Academic Toolkit for Women at a Land-Grant Institution   147
JEAN VAN DELINDER, SHIPING DENG, JEANMARIE VERCHOT, AMY MADEWELL
AND DAISHA DELANO

Introduction   148
FORWARD OSU   150
Analysis   158
Conclusion and Implications for Future FORWARD Workshops   162
References   163

10. Advancing Toward Professorship in Biology, Ecology, and Earth System Sciences 165

MARIA T. KAVANAUGH, KATE S. BOERSMA, SARAH L. CLOSE, LISA M. GANIO, LOUISA HOOVEN AND BARBARA LACHENBRUCH

Introduction 166
BEESS Research is Unique Within STEM Disciplines 168
Workshop 170
Survey 170
Demographics 171
Workshop Challenges 172
Logistical Lessons 173
Workshop Outcomes 175
Lessons Learned 180
Post-workshop Efforts 182
Acknowledgments 182
References 183

11. Metropolitan Mentors: Building a Network of Women in Mathematics and Computer Science Across New York City: The New York City College of Technology of the City University of New York Workshop 185

PAMELA BROWN AND DELARAM KAHROBAEI

Goals of Our FORWARD to Professorship Project 186
FORWARD to Professorship Workshops: Women in Mathematics and Computer Science Across NYC 189
What was Learned from the First Workshop? 192
Looking Back at the Workshop Series 192
Follow-up Survey 193
Suggestions for a Group Planning to Run a Similar Workshop 194
Institutional History and Why This FORWARD to Professorship Project Was Important for Us 194
Relevance to Other Institutions 196
Conclusion 196
Acknowledgments 197
References 197

12. Career Advancement in a Research Environment 199

SIMERJEET GILL, KRISTINE HORVAT AND TRIVENI RAO

Background 200
CARE 2012 201
CARE 2013A 204
CARE 2013B 206
Conclusions 208
References 208

13. Moving FORWARD in Space: The Temple University
Workshops   211
JENNIFER L. PIATEK AND ALEXANDRA DAVATZES

Introduction   211
Workshop Design and Implementation   213
Different Settings and Different Demographics   214
Participant Feedback   219
Workshop Follow-up   220
Conclusion   221
References   221

14. FORWARD Workshops: Strategies for Inclusion of the
Deaf and Hard of Hearing   223
PAUL S. SABILA, H. DAVID SNYDER AND CHARLENE C. SORENSEN

Gallaudet University   224
Deaf, Hard of Hearing, and the ADA Act   226
The Challenge of Bringing D/HoH into STEM   227
Origins of FORWARD at Gallaudet   228
FORWARD in SEM   229
The FORWARD to Professorship and Pay It FORWARD Projects   232
Evaluations: Participants' Views of the FORWARD Workshops at GU   233
Impact of FORWARD on D/HoH Participants and GU   234
Impact of D/HoH Participants and GU on FORWARD and on "Hearing"
     Participants   239
Strategies for Inclusion of D/HoH Participants and ASL Interpreters
     in Scientific Workshops   240
Acknowledgments   242
References   242

15. The Participant Experience   245
ELIZABETH FREELAND

Introduction   245
Why are Workshops for Women Needed?   246
Pre-conference: Participant Expectations   248
During the Conference: Participant Activities   248
Post-conference: Overall Impressions   251
The Future   252
References   253

16. Speakers Find Value in Workshop Participation   255
LYNNETTE D. MADSEN AND CATHERINE MAVRIPLIS

Introduction   255
Eager Speakers   258

Unanticipated Impact on Presenters   261
Conclusion   264
Acknowledgments   265
References   265

17. Possible Benefits for Workshop Organizers   267
CATHERINE MAVRIPLIS AND LYNNETTE D. MADSEN

Introduction   268
Motivations   269
Benefits to Organizers   273
Drawbacks and Difficulties Encountered   281
Conclusion   283
Acknowledgments   284
References   284
Examples of Intellectual Outcomes   285

18. Evaluation of the Pay It FORWARD Program   289
PATRICIA K. FREITAG AND CATHERINE MAVRIPLIS

Introduction   290
Workshop Leadership Team Training   292
The FORWARD Workshop Model   296
Adaptations of the National Model Workshop   298
Evaluation Methods   300
Pay it FORWARD Results and Follow-up Questionnaire Responses   300
Lessons Learned Through the Evaluation Process   317
Conclusion   318
References   318

19. Fortifying the Pipeline to Leadership: The International
Center for Executive Leadership in Academics at Drexel   319
DIANE MAGRANE AND PAGE S. MORAHAN

Program Design: Strategies for Developing a Community of Leaders   320
Translating the ICELA Model for National Leaders in Engineering
   and Science: Conception, Birth, and Nurturing   326
Multiple Mirrors to Evaluate Outcomes and Guide Improvement
   of Leadership Development Programs   330
Looking to the Future: Diversity, Collaboration Across Programs,
   and Sustaining Alumnae in Leadership Roles   332
References   333

20. Synthesis   337
RACHELLE S. HELLER AND CATHERINE MAVRIPLIS

Faculty Development—How Are Existing Models Faring?   337
How Are Faculty Development Models Evolving?   345

Some New Faculty Development Models Are Evolving to an Online Presence   347
What Is the Future of Faculty Development?   348
References   351

21. Lessons Learned   353

RACHELLE S. HELLER AND CATHERINE MAVRIPLIS

Introduction   353
The Whole Is Bigger than the Sum of the Parts   354
So You Want to Host a Workshop...   355
The Devil Is in the Details   356
Creating a Buzz   358
Watching Your Creation Mature   359
References   362

Appendices   **363**
Index   **405**

List of Contributors

D. Page Baluch School of Life Sciences, Arizona State University, Tempe, AZ, USA

Lesley Berhan Department of Mechanical, Industrial, and Manufacturing Engineering, The University of Toledo, Toledo, OH, USA

Kate S. Boersma Department of Zoology, Oregon State University, Corvallis, OR, USA; Department of Biology, University of San Diego, San Diego, CA, USA

Pamela Brown New York City College of Technology, City University of New York, Brooklyn, NY, USA

Amanda Bryant-Friedrich Department of Medicinal and Biological Chemistry and Chemistry, The University of Toledo, Toledo, OH, USA

Sarah L. Close Department of Zoology, Oregon State University, Corvallis, OR, USA; Dean John A. Knauss Marine Policy Fellow, National Oceanic and Atmospheric Administration, Silver Spring, MD, USA

Nancy Collins Department of Medicine, The University of Toledo, Toledo, OH, USA

Alexandra Davatzes Department of Earth and Environmental Science, Temple University, Philadelphia, PA, USA

Daisha Delano Sociology Department, Oklahoma State University, Stillwater, OK, USA

Shiping Deng Plant and Soil Sciences, Oklahoma State University, Stillwater, OK, USA

Isabel C. Escobar Department of Chemical and Materials Engineering, The University of Kentucky, Lexington, KY, USA

Gertrude Fraser Department of Anthropology, University of Virginia, Charlottesville, VA, USA

Elizabeth Freeland School of the Art Institute of Chicago, Chicago, IL, USA

Susan Freimark Faculty Leadership Development Institute, Flora Stone Mather Center for Women, Case Western Reserve University, Cleveland, OH, USA

Patricia K. Freitag Education Consulting, Potomac, MD, USA

Lisa M. Ganio Department of Forest Ecosystems and Society, College of Forestry, Oregon State University, Corvallis, OR, USA

Charlene Gilbert Department of Women's and Gender Studies, The University of Toledo, Toledo, OH, USA

Simerjeet Gill Brookhaven National Laboratory, Upton, NY, USA

Cyndee Gruden Department of Civil Engineering, The University of Toledo, Toledo, OH, USA

Margaret Harden Institute for Faculty Advancement, University of Virginia, Charlottesville, VA, USA

Rachelle S. Heller Department of Computer Science, George Washington University, Washington, DC, USA

Louisa Hooven Department of Horticulture, Oregon State University, Corvallis, OR, USA

Kristine Horvat Materials Science and Engineering Department, Stony Brook University, Stony Brook, NY, USA

Delaram Kahrobaei New York City College of Technology, City University of New York, Brooklyn, NY, USA

Maria T. Kavanaugh Department of Marine Chemistry and Geochemistry, Woods Hole Oceanographic Institution, Woods Hole, MA, USA

Barbara Lachenbruch Department of Forest Ecosystems and Society, College of Forestry, Oregon State University, Corvallis, OR, USA

Amy Madewell Psychology Department, Southeastern Oklahoma State University, Durant, OK, USA

Lynnette D. Madsen National Science Foundation, Arlington, VA, USA

Diane Magrane Professor of Obstetrics and Gynecology, Drexel University College of Medicine, Philadelphia, PA, USA

Catherine Mavriplis Department of Mechanical Engineering, University of Ottawa, Ottawa, ON, Canada

Page S. Morahan Emerita Professor of Microbiology, Drexel University College of Medicine, Philadelphia, PA, USA

Shannon Morey Massachusetts Institute of Technology (MIT), Cambridge, MA, USA; East Boston High School, Boston, MA, USA

Jennifer L. Piatek Department of Geological Sciences, Central Connecticut State University, New Britain, CT, USA

Triveni Rao Brookhaven National Laboratory, Upton, NY, USA

Paul S. Sabila Chemistry and Physics Program, Department of Science, Technology, and Mathematics, Gallaudet University, Washington, DC, USA

Brad San Martin Massachusetts Institute of Technology (MIT), Cambridge, MA, USA

Amanda Shaffer Office of Faculty Development, Case Western University, Cleveland, OH, USA

H. David Snyder Chemistry and Physics Program, Department of Science, Technology, and Mathematics, Gallaudet University, Washington, DC, USA

Charlene C. Sorensen Chemistry and Physics Program, Department of Science, Technology, and Mathematics, Gallaudet University, Washington, DC, USA

Blanche Staton Massachusetts Institute of Technology (MIT), Cambridge, Boston, MA, USA

Helen Thompson Career Interactive, London, UK

Jean Van Delinder Sociology Department, Oklahoma State University, Stillwater, OK, USA

Jeanmarie Verchot Entomology and Plant Pathology, Oklahoma State University, Stillwater, OK, USA

Prologue

With almost 20 years behind us since we started our journey FORWARD, we are pleased to see the culmination of our efforts and experiences recorded in this volume. Our team formed at a time when the "leaky pipeline" metaphor was being used to address the issue of the underrepresentation of women in science and engineering. Our first FORWARD project aimed to shore up the undergraduate-to-graduate school leak in the pipeline and, with the US National Science Foundation ADVANCE funding program, we tended to the doctoral-to−assistant professor leak.

Today, the leaks are still there, but they are diminishing, and the issues that contribute to those leaks are openly discussed. A plethora of resources exist online and at many institutions to address diversity issues, but face-to-face workshops are still in demand. The value of connecting with others in similar situations cannot be overestimated, as time and time again, we witnessed at our workshops peer-to-peer and near-peer mentorships forming and friendships growing through shared experiences. The resulting empowerment was evident to us on site, in the evaluations, and beyond, as participants shared with us their successes in forging their own career paths.

Our message is simple—with a small amount of resources and serious drive, you can do a lot. It is our hope that you will find this volume helpful in organizing and developing your own career development workshops, as we show through the stories recorded here that it is relatively easy and cost effective to run such events and that the return on investment is immense. We encourage you to read and learn from our experiences as the FORWARD organizers, use our materials, many of which are offered in the appendices to this volume, and network with the other chapter authors who creatively adapted the FORWARD model to their regions, disciplines, or social groups; reflected on their experiences as participants, speakers, or organizers; or developed their own leadership programs to continue the work of increasing and furthering the participation of women and underrepresented groups in STEM.

We thank the US National Science Foundation (NSF) and the National Institutes of Health (NIH) for their financial support for these projects and are especially indebted to their staff for having the vision and perseverance to shape the funding programs that eventually created a community and national movement to reshape the face of academia and its internal workings. Furthermore, we are indebted to all our wonderful speakers, assistants, ELDers, trainees, and new workshop organizers for their enthusiastic and selfless dedication to making our events successful and meaningful experiences.

This book is dedicated to our brave and dynamic workshop participants, from whom we learned so much. They are the way FORWARD!

On a personal note, we thank Dianne Martin, Charlene Sorensen, H. David Snyder, and Yell Inverso for their tremendous contributions that kept us moving FORWARD. Many thanks to Mary Preap and the editorial team at Elsevier for shepherding this project through to completion.

The Origins of Faculty Development in Science, Technology, Engineering, and Mathematics

Rachelle S. Heller

Department of Computer Science, George Washington University, Washington, DC, USA

OUTLINE

Introduction 2

Brief History of Faculty Development 3

Programs for Advancing Women in STEM 5
Early Programs and Movements 5

Resource Development 8

General Design Issues for Faculty Development Workshops 11

Beyond Workshops 13

Conclusion 14

References 14

INTRODUCTION

The United States needs a sustained investment in science education and basic research to spur innovation and successfully compete, prosper, and be secure in the global community of the twenty-first century. A recently released report, "Rising Above the Gathering Storm, Revisited" (National Academy of Sciences, 2010), noted that the climate that produced four over-arching recommendations to meet this need in 2005 has worsened. The report notes that the mission is still to improve education in science and math, increase funding in science research, and encourage more Americans to pursue careers in science, engineering, and mathematics. The challenge is even harder in the face of the "economic recession and the growth of the national debt over this period from $8 trillion to $13 trillion" (p. 4), the report says. Moreover, other nations have been markedly progressing, thereby affecting the relative ability of the United States to compete for new factories, research laboratories, and jobs (p. 4). If science and science education do not diversify their workforce by including women and minority viewpoints, progress will be limited in approach and perspective.

The challenge to bring women into Science, Technology, Engineering, and Mathematics (STEM) is a constant. In an exhibit at the Grolier Club (New York City) and an accompanying textbook, *Extraordinary Women in Science and Medicine: Four Centuries of Achievement* (Smeltzer et al., 2013), the struggles of women to enter and remain in science, stretching from Madame la Marquise du Châtellet to Rosalyn Yalow, are chronicled. A poignant story is told there about the correspondence between Florence Sabin and Helen Taussig. In 1936, Dr Taussig wrote to Dr Sabin that she was concerned about Johns Hopkins's conservative attitude toward women in science, that this atmosphere might stifle her advancement, that she was paid less than her peers, and that her self-respect demanded that the institution in which she worked had confidence in her.

In 1965, Rossi asked the question, "Women in science—why so few?" She noted that, in the age after Sputnik and the 1950s, domestic life did not get the high praise it once had. The President's Commission on the Status of Women (1963) suggested that steps be taken to bring women into the technical and scientific workforce. The climate, then (to perhaps a larger degree than in 2013), was that society believed that women should not pursue a career in science. Rossi did not expect any advancement on the inclusion of women in science until and unless society takes into account that "Most college-educated women are married and living with their husbands and children" (p. 1197). She continues to argue that so long as society permits the pursuit of a science career to exact a toll on the personal life of women, the disadvantages for women cannot be overcome. Rossi goes on to note the barriers to women in science: society's view of the priority of marriage, impact of career interruption (usually due to childbirth), and child rearing.

What Rossi does not talk about, which is the very basis of current-day workshops for faculty development in STEM, are opportunities for women to gather to address these and other impediments to moving ahead in a career in science. Writing about the pipeline and recruiting young minority women to science, a program targeted at high school girls, Martin and Heller (1994) reported on a working conference of 20 experts in addressing the STEM pipeline for women. Using a decision support system, they reviewed the current state of events and ranked the importance of characteristics of programs that were designed to gather young women together and provide the skills and discussions to prepare them to enter and stay in the pipeline. They prepared a list of essential characteristics that ranked the highest (9 out of 10, where 10 is essential) as follows:

1. Follow-up
2. High expectations
3. Role models
4. Career counseling
5. Fun
6. Mentoring.

These can easily be applied to professional development workshops.

The flow within the pipeline for women coming into academia is still slow. Although, overall, more women are obtaining PhDs than men [except in business, engineering, and the physical sciences (American Enterprise Institute, 2015)], a recent study conducted by the American Association for the Advancement of Science (AAAS) reports that they are less likely to enter and remain in scientific careers (AAAS, 2010). The bottom line: "gender still matters with regard to women's being able to be successful and to move ahead in science," as Shirley Malcolm, AAAS director of education and human resources, told a congressional panel on September 23, 2010. Although women have made continual strides in all sectors of academic employment, substantial disparities still exist in salary, rank, tenure, and personal job satisfaction. "New assistant professors who successfully negotiate for the resources that will make them successful and who can recognize environments where they are likely to be successful are more likely to be promoted and tenured" (Chesler et al., 2010, p. 1931). Faculty development plays a large role in preparing new professors.

BRIEF HISTORY OF FACULTY DEVELOPMENT

Faculty development, alternatively called *professional development*, seems to have been named as such in the early 1970s and defined as "any planned activity to improve an individual's knowledge and skills in areas considered essential to the performance of a faculty member in a department" (McLean et al., 2008, p. 555). Early faculty development, not focused on STEM, saw an expansion of activities to include special programs. Models included instructional development and personal development (which others called *faculty development* or *faculty renewal*). In his study, Centra (1978) groups faculty development into four categories: workshops and seminars, assessment procedures, course development, and institutionwide practices.

In their charts on what might be included in academic development, McLean et al. note that others have suggested topics that have expanded the role of a faculty member from teaching personnel to include a focus on research and leadership; these topics include improving institutional culture, grant proposal writing, conducting research, and even organizational development. While the major trends before 2000 focused primarily on teaching and learning, the new century brought additional focus on the expanded and changing role in faculty in higher education (Sorcinelli & Austin, 1992). While their development content focuses primarily on teaching development for medical faculty, McLean et al.'s suggestions around implementation, evaluation, and feedback can provide general guidance for workshops. While they never specifically propose a format for faculty development, they do suggest a list of three things to consider in planning: (i) identifying the problem and general needs; (ii) performing a needs assessment of the target audience; and (iii) setting appropriate goals and measureable outcomes. They urge workshop organizers to ensure that there is sufficient and "protected" time to carry out the development, and to consider interdisciplinary groups and active learning. Finally, they say, "Although evaluation is an important aspect of faculty development, it is probably the most neglected" (McLean et al., 2008, p. 576); hence, they strongly suggest that evaluation and long-term documentation form an integral part of faculty development efforts.

In the book *Creating the Future of Faculty Development* (Sorcinelli et al., 2006), the authors identify five historical stages of faculty development and how the efforts to provide support for faculty were presented within those contexts (see Table 1.1).

Sorcinelli et al. (2006) report on their survey of faculty development program websites which they characterize as part of the stage called "Age of the Network" (p. 14), in which they characterize the programs into seven different categories:

- Individual consultation programs
- New faculty orientation programs across an entire university
- University-run or supported workshops
- Lengthy off-site intensive seminars
- Programs supported by external grants
- Publications and support material
- Programs that are tailored to meet a very local, specific need.

TABLE 1.1 Stages of Higher Education—Related Faculty Development Foci (Sorcinelli et al., 2006)

The age	Years	Focus of support for faculty advancement	Format
The age of the scholar	Mid-1950s to mid-1960s	Improving and advancing scholarly competence[a,b]	Informal and often unstructured
The age of the teacher	Mid-1960s through 1970s	Teaching skills and abilities	Development of teaching and learning centers[a]
The age of the developer	1980s	Renewed excitement about faculty development in a multitude of areas	Centers, staffing, policies, and procedures are created
The age of the learner	1990s	Focus on teaching, learning and the role of technology	Professionalization of faculty development, including the POD Network[b]
The age of the network	2000s	Collaboration among all stakeholders	Collaborative organizations

[a] In 1962, the University of Michigan formed the first Center for Research on Learning and Teaching.
[b] Professional and Organizational Development Network in Higher Education; podnetwork.org.

PROGRAMS FOR ADVANCING WOMEN IN STEM

Early Programs and Movements

Workshops to address the professional advancement of women in STEM in general and in academia specifically were essentially nonexistent before the late 1990s.

The Society of Women Engineers (SWE) was founded in 1950 at the Cooper Union for the Advancement of Science and Art with the intent "to enable women to make their way into a profession that did not necessarily welcome them" (Kata, 2011; SWE, 2012). SWE was, in part, a reaction to the nature of the existing technical societies that seemed to reinforce the masculine nature of the field. SWE members saw the educational value of recruiting and promoting women through sharing and supporting each other as they moved forward in their engineering careers, both inside and outside academia. The members also saw their purpose as educating the public to the fact that women could be engineers. SWE, while conceived as an educational (rather than technical) society, did address issues of career advancement for women. For example, the *SWE Journal* was a place where women could publish and disseminate their work under "their full names as sole authors"

(Kata, 2011). SWE continues to be an advocacy group for women engineers, though not limited to women in academia.

The Women in Engineering Programs and Advocates Network (WEPAN) began in 1990 (WEPAN, 2000), was founded on the notion that there was a need to increase the number of girls and women in engineering and that WEPAN could be a "catalyst for change to enhance the success of women in the engineering profession" (p. 2). The conference held that year in Washington, DC focused on "addressing issues, sharing learning, forging partnerships and setting directions" (p. 5). WEPAN (whose original name was "Women Engineering Program Administrators Network") used regional training seminars to provide support for women advancing in engineering. The original name supported the focus in which experienced colleagues shared what they knew with those just beginning their efforts in workshops and group discussions. The emphasis was on strategies—the "nuts and bolts" of how to get resources and funding, develop precollege programs, consider student needs assessments, implement program evaluation, and engage the industry. In the opening plenary to WEPAN's 1991 Women in Engineering Conference, Jewel Plummer Cobb, a distinguished African American biologist and former president of California State University, Fullerton, gave a presentation entitled "Social Barriers and Strategies for Succeeding in the Technical Sciences." But the WEPAN focus was not exactly on advancing academic women, and a presentation is not a workshop.

Wells (2010, p. 5) suggests that consciousness-raising groups and meetings that were part of the feminist movement of the early 1960s and 1970s provided a place for women to talk about the issues around pursuing science. But consciousness-raising groups are not workshops.

As noted previously, the Age of the Network brought many stakeholders to the table (see, for example, Chapter 19 of this book on Drexel's ELAM and ELATE Executive Leadership programs). And, in 1993, the Association of American Colleges and Universities (AAC&U[1]), together with the Council of Graduate Schools, developed programs and models for graduate student education that included preparation to join academia after completion of advanced degrees (Adams, 2002). In her article, Adams calls for doctoral programs to "enable their students to make an informed decision about choosing an academic career" (p. 10), and that this would include information about teaching, research, academic life, and searching for a position. Others, such as Preparing Future Faculty (PFF; Schneider, 2002) and Penn State's focus on junior faculty (Thorndyke et al., 2006), developed programs for graduate students, not specifically for women and not specifically in the sciences.

---

[1]AAC&U became the home of the Preparing Future Faculty program.

At about the same time, the National Science Foundation (NSF) began to support specific programs targeted toward career advancement for women academics in the sciences through the Visiting Professorships for Women (VPW). Recognizing the importance of promoting women in STEM fields, VPW "enables doctoral women scientists and engineers to undertake research and teaching at host institutions where they can advance their careers and provide guidance and encouragement to young women seeking to pursue research careers" (NSF, 1995). In an email to the author, former NSF ADVANCE program director Alice Hogan pointed out, "I think the VPW program was intended to provide a way for women who might be at less research-intensive institutions to go somewhere where they could do research in a more supported environment. Additionally, one of the issues with the POWRE program was that NSF learned that because these were awards available only to women, they were not considered full awards with respect to tenure decisions. It may be important to note also that the legal framework for government programs that had restricted eligibility was changing in the 1990s and programs that were exclusively available to women were more likely to be challenged in court."

The 1997–2000 NSF program Professional Opportunities for Women in Research and Education (POWRE), targeted at individual women, had the objective "to increase the prominence, visibility, and influence of women in all fields of academic science and engineering supported by NSF, *especially in contexts where women are underrepresented.* By providing opportunities for career advancement, professional growth, and increased prominence of women in science and engineering, more women will be encouraged to pursue careers and achieve leadership positions in science and engineering, and women scientists and engineers will obtain greater visibility and influence in academic institutions and in industry. The Foundation is particularly interested in increasing the participation of minority women and women with disabilities. Members of these groups are especially encouraged to apply" [emphasis in original]. The focus was to support women who already had a career target and would benefit from access to financial support. In this program, women were to identify their career goal and how the activity for which they were seeking support would further that goal (NSF, 1998).

Rosser (2004b, 2006) collected data from roughly 400 women who had been awarded POWRE grants in 1997 through 2000 to investigate the existing barriers to success. The greatest number saw balancing work and family as a major challenge, with concerns for time management, isolation, being seen as credible by colleagues, and dual-career couples as additional challenges. When asked specifically about the laboratory climate, respondents noted a "boys' club" nature, the lack of numbers and funding, and isolation as important barriers to success. These concerns, in part, formed policy considerations for what was to come next at NSF, a program called ADVANCE that was designed to develop model policies and practices to address institutional barriers and discouragements faced by female science, technology, engineering, and mathematics faculty (Rosser and Lane, 2002; Rosser, 2004a).

While the POWRE programs were targeted at individual women already in the academic workforce and ready to be leaders, our ideas for the FORWARD program were directed at groups: from 1996 to 2000, we targeted groups of undergraduate women for the FORWARD to Graduate School workshops and, around 2001, ideas were emerging for targeting groups of women from the postdoctoral to tenure-track stage for the FORWARD to Professorship workshops. The shift from individuals to groups came with the ADVANCE program. The first NSF ADVANCE solicitation for proposals in April 2001 included opportunities for support of individual research (Fellows), as well as institutional transformation (university awards) and leadership programs to develop and implement new strategies for increasing the number of women in STEM fields and to adapt best practices to do so.

In an interview conducted by Danielle LaVaque-Manty, original NSF ADVANCE program director Alice Hogan noted that earlier NSF programs "sought to provide women access to research funding that would allow them to emerge as independent researchers" (LaVaque-Manty, 2007, p. 21). This set-aside approach, she noted, provided too little money to really effect change. Additionally, the programs and focus changed so often that it was difficult for a sustained impact to emerge. And, most telling, without changing the system in which women worked, progress was unlikely. The focus on the academic workplace and its policies and practices revealed the many ways in which institutional factors limited women's advancement. Dr Hogan noted that they "wanted to create a community [sic: drawn from those who submitted proposals] who took the issues seriously and had funding to tackle deep-rooted systemic barriers" (p. 23). The ADVANCE focus moved the problem to interventions within the system, and the outcome of this shift was that "the system of science had a gender problem" (p. 25).

RESOURCE DEVELOPMENT

Few resources existed before 2000 for women academics in general, and women in STEM specifically, although some publications, including booklets, monographs, and even plays, started to emerge at this time. JoAnn Moody's first publication in 1997 aimed to "[d]emystify certain parts of academic careers that typically bewilder not only early-stage faculty (tenure-track, adjunct, clinical, visiting, research, term, physician/faculty, and others)" (Moody, 2001, p. 1), provide ideas on coaching future faculty for success, "spotlight and tell the truth about the special burdens and taxing dynamics often imposed on nonmajority faculty (especially if they are 'one of a few' or the 'only solo')" (p. 1), and coach or prompt current faculty so that they "*grasp in detail* the stresses and confusions experienced by less advanced majority and nonmajority faculty and then, based on their new understanding, [. . .] *take pro-active steps* to reduce those confusions and stressors" (p. 1; emphasis in the original quotes). In a private email to the author, Moody wrote, "This booklet currently still has the same three sections. From the beginning, the Demystifying booklet has been used by a number of campuses. University of New Haven Press, no longer in business, was surprised by how well this small publication did, from the beginning. I was surprised, too. I still receive a few emails from time to time, thanking me. . .and others who shared advice and caveats in that booklet."

While not directed specifically at women in STEM, the Center for Research on Learning and Teaching (CRLT) at the University of Michigan held interactive theater performances concerning issues related to academic life. The powerful scripts addressed "the transformation of the faculty work world—for instance, faculty meetings, hiring, mentoring, and the tenure and promotion process—so that women and faculty of color, who may be marginalized in their departments, are more likely to succeed" (Kaplan et al., 2006, p. 35).

In 1996, the Natural Sciences and Engineering Council of Canada (NSERC) established regional chairs with the goal of increasing the participation of women in STEM. In 2000, F. Mary Williams, inaugural Atlantic region chair, and Carolyn Emerson hosted a conference on the status of women in STEM in Canada. In their book *Becoming Leaders: A Handbook for Women in Science, Engineering and Technology* (Williams and Emerson, 2008), an outcome of the conference that was first published in 2002 by NSERC/Petro-Canada Chair for Women in Science and Engineering and Women in Science and Engineering, they provided a text guide for all women, at all levels, in STEM fields (Figure 1.1). While they identify sections for each level—students, career women, faculty, academic leaders, and business managers, each section provides valuable information for all groups and focuses on key issues for each group. Their chapters for students, for example, provide information on time management, sexual harassment, and the role of mentors. For faculty, they outline the typical pathway,

FIGURE 1.1   The cover of the Becoming Leaders guide book by Williams and Emerson (2008).

balancing work and life, establishing personal networks and mentors, and creating a "woman as leader" mindset. Their chapters for academic leaders focus on the avenues that can be taken to be proactive in promoting diversity and the role of women. Their format includes situations that readers might currently encounter, such as how to respond to inflammatory questions, as well as some that might occur in the future, such as video appearances. While the section with advice for children of such women is a bit humorous (e.g., it reminds children *not* to ask for cookies to be baked the night before they are due, but to plan ahead), it does bring to light in a very concrete manner the types of "work/life" interactions women address on a regular basis.

One offshoot of the *Becoming Leaders* book is the leadership workshop series now part of the Canadian Centre for Women in Science, Engineering, Trades and Technology (WinSETT), which was established in 2003 (WinSETT, 2015). WinSETT, from the outset, had an industry focus. Pilot workshops begun in 2007 were to develop, deliver, and evaluate products and services in areas of recruitment and retention, especially for women in the oil and gas industry. They also focused on construction and trades, information technology, and, of course, on post-secondary education.

In 2005, the COACHE faculty survey program at Harvard was established. In a private email (2013), Cathy Ann Trower said, "Co-founder Richard Chait and I started COACHE in 2005 in response to a market need to better understand the workplace for early career faculty. Our aim was to shed light on factors that lead to satisfaction or dissatisfaction of the faculty that academic leaders could do something about—all COACHE measures are actionable. A second purpose was to help create more transparency about, and equity within, the academic workplace and create a constructive competition among colleges and universities to be a great place to work. Because we provide data by gender and race/ethnicity, across schools and departments, and in comparison to peers, leaders really come to know what is happening on their campuses with respect to the faculty. We started conducting workshops on campuses shortly after we began surveying faculty because we realized that it wasn't enough to merely provide data or even policy suggestions—those alone do not change cultures. But bringing data and policies to life by catalyzing conversations about academic culture and departmental climate do!" It should be noted that COACHE (COACHE, 2015) now also surveys tenured and non-tenure-track faculty.

GENERAL DESIGN ISSUES FOR FACULTY DEVELOPMENT WORKSHOPS

The literature on designing, delivering, and evaluating a workshop is slim, but writers agree on a few points. While his book *The Ultimate Training Workshop Handbook* is not directed toward a specific audience or field (and certainly is not directed toward women in academic STEM fields), Klatt (1999) compiles advice for workshop leadership replete with examples and worksheets ranging from preparing yourself to lead a workshop to presenting the workshop. Workshop design, he says, should include active learning and he provides an "activity smorgasbord," including "[a] list of activities, models, and ideas" (p. 254). He urges leaders to prepare themselves by learning about learning, for which he provides a detailed overview. He likens the leader at the start of a workshop to a pilot—training, reviewing the material, resting, and getting ready to introduce the participants. He provides advice and opportunities for planning and suggests a needs assessment and a plan for evaluation before designing the workshop. Finally, for advice during the workshop, Klatt discusses addressing participant questions, time management, maintaining interest, keeping control of the flow of the workshop, and ending the workshop by reviewing what has been covered and what the next steps might be. Evaluation, he says, has four levels: whether the participants liked the workshop, learned from it, and used the material, and whether the workshop made a difference (see also Kirkpatrick and Kirkpatrick, 2015). All good leaders, he says, should take the time after a workshop to reflect on what has happened.

The Mind Tools website (2015) provides workshop creation guidance: define your goals and target audience; pick the "right" location; create an agenda and have a follow-up plan (Mind Tools, 1996–2014). Creating an active learning workshop is an essential way of getting everyone involved. In summary, they suggest, "The workshop's goal should be at the center of all your planning. Creative exercises will get everyone relaxed and involved, and don't forget to follow up afterward: Although it can be scary to hear what people really thought of all your hard work, it's the only way you'll improve your next event."

In her undated online article, "How to Conduct an Interactive Workshop," Barnet (2014) underscores the need for a goal, and knowing your audience in order to be successful. In addition, she is a major proponent of an interactive workshop and provides a list of many techniques to engage participants, including "brainstorming solutions, working from participants' questions or issues raised, having participants work on problems or answer questions in small groups, sharing solutions with the entire group, and having participants get involved physically, if only to move into and out of groups. Since participants will be actively engaged in the material, it may be difficult for them to take notes," so she urges that "handouts be prepared as the participants (and you) will want to remember the material and refer to it after the workshop is concluded." Finally, she notes, "be on time, introduce yourself and your audience and strongly consider providing handouts."

Sorcinelli et al. (2006) collected data from faculty development professionals to discern the priorities for future faculty development. They asked for the top three challenges facing faculty and facing the institution and noted the movement from teaching and research to issues of work/life balance and academic leadership. They identified the responders as being from research/doctoral, comprehensive, liberal arts, and community college institutions. The leading challenge identified by all individuals across all institutions was balancing multiple roles, both professional and social. Other concerns included the changing role of a full- and part-time faculty member, the demands of teaching (including new paradigms for teaching, assessment and technology), the role of collaborative teams and activities in faculty advancement, and programs for training department leadership.

BEYOND WORKSHOPS

Beyond workshop design, some scholarly and narrative works have focused on professional development for women in STEM, especially in academia. In his text *Tomorrow's Professor: Preparing for Academic Careers in Science and Engineering,* Richard Reis (1997) provides graduate students and postdoctoral scientists with a road map of material for pursuing an academic career in STEM areas. He provides an information timeline from the characteristics of universities (i.e., research oriented, etc.) as well as the application process, how to negotiate an offer, time management to address the many requirements to juggle as a faculty member and as a person, and what you need to know to succeed in a faculty position.

Among the earlier books addressing women's journeys in science and engineering, Ambrose et al. (1997) provide stories of women who serve as role models. The interviews and profiles serve as support, but the text was not intended to provide specific professional development directions. The book *Athena Unbound* (Etzkowitz et al., 2000) does not provide for faculty development; rather, it offers a view from which to look at women's careers in STEM fields by providing data from and analysis of interviews with graduate students, faculty, and even young children on their perceptions of what a scientist is. Except for the chapter on department initiatives for change, the topics provide evidence of the difficulties of advancement and gender inequity but do not offer much guidance for remedies to the issues. They suggest that successful programs have support from the leadership of the institution and a designated nonfaculty director, but also feature faculty and student involvement, adequate funding, and evaluation.

Every Other Thursday (Daniell, 2006) chronicled the biweekly meetings of seven women scientists in California as they wrangled with the issues of academic success and professional advancement. They took the group seriously, planned agendas, and kept the chitchat to a minimum. They did, however, support each other beyond their professional lives. The book provided a road map for other academics to find mentoring and support within their institutions. Other texts were less prescriptive, but they were empowering nonetheless. In their chapter in *The Handbook of Career Counseling for Women* (Walsh and Heppner, 2006), Fassinger and Asay (2006) profile three women from different backgrounds, disciplines, and stages in their career: Tammy (a white graduate from a research university in biology), Beverly (an African American assistant professor in computer science), and Jean (an Asian American working in the chemical industry). The authors provide suggestions for career counseling, ranging from providing support for communication and writing skills for scholarly work and grant submission, to social and professional networking, to self-efficacy, to personal values and prioritization of tasks and work/life integration, to negotiating the chilly climate. The outlined help is made personal to the reader by situating these suggestions within case studies of the three women.

CONCLUSION

The history of faculty development programs provides limited examples of workshops for academic women in STEM. The PFF programs (Schneider, 2002) notwithstanding, in 2001, when FORWARD was proposed, the FORWARD to Professorship workshop model was unique. It addressed postdoctoral women in STEM fields, while PFF targeted a fuller pipeline, with a variety of topic areas relevant to the three general academic requirements of research, teaching, and service. FORWARD was designed to present the advancement policies and practices that existed in academia, and, at the same time, the workshops included the open discussions for and by women around these issues. Moreover, FORWARD to Professorship laid the groundwork for methodologies for adapting and adopting the workshop concept for faculty development.

References

Adams, K., 2002. What Colleges and Universities Want in New Faculty. Preparing Future Faculty Occasional Paper Series. Association of American Colleges & Universities, Washington, DC.

Ambrose, S., Dunkle, K.L., Lazarus, B.B., Nair, I., Harkus, D.A. (Eds.), 1997. Journeys of Women in Science and Engineering: No Universal Constants. Temple University Press, Philadelphia, PA.

American Association for the Advancement of Science (AAAS), 2010. Handbook on Diversity and the Law: Navigating a Complex Landscape to Foster Greater Faculty and Student Diversity in Higher Education, American Association for the Advancement of Science, Washington, DC.

American Enterprise Institute, 2015. Available from: <https://www.aei.org/publication/women-earned-majority-of-doctoral-degrees-in-2012-for-4th-straight-year-and-outnumber-men-in-grad-school-141-to-100/> (accessed 15.01.15.).

Barnet, M.A, 2014. How to Conduct an Interactive Workshop. Available from: <http://faculty.virginia.edu/marva/Teaching%20Workshops/conduct_workshop.htm> (accessed 18.11.14.).

Centra, J., 1978. Types of faculty development programs. J. High. Educ. 49 (2), 151–162.

Chesler, N., Barabino, G., Bhatia, S., Richards-Kortum, R., 2010. The pipeline still leaks and more than you think: a status report on gender diversity in biomedical engineering. Ann. Biomed. Eng. 38 (5), 1928–1935.

COACHE, 2015. Available from: <http://isites.harvard.edu/icb/icb.do?keyword=coache&pageid=icb.page307142> (accessed 15.01.15.).

Daniell, E., 2006. Every Other Thursday: Stories and Strategies from Successful Women Scientists. Yale University Press, New Haven, CT.

Etzkowitz, H., Kemelgor, C., Uzzi, B., 2000. Athena Unbound: The Advancement of Women in Science and Technology. Cambridge University Press, Cambridge.

Fassinger, R.E., Asay, P.A., 2006. Career counseling for women in science, technology, engineering and mathematics (STEM) fields. In: Walsh, W.B., Heppner, M.J. (Eds.), Handbook of Career Counseling for Women, second ed. Lawrence Erlbaum Associates, New Jersey, pp. 427–452.

Kaplan, M., Cook, C.E., Steiger, J., 2006. Using theatre to stage instructional and organizational transformation. Change: Mag. Higher Learn. 38 (3), 32–39.

Kata, L., 2011. The boundaries of women's rights: activism and aspirations in the Society of Women Engineers, 1946–1980. J. Soc. Women Eng. 5, 36–49.

Kirkpatrick, D.L., Kirkpatrick, J.D., 2015. Evaluating Training Programs. Available from: <http://bkconnection.com/static/Evaluating_Training_Programs_EXCERPT.pdf> (accessed 15.01.15.).

Klatt, B., 1999. The Ultimate Training Workshop Handbook: A Comprehensive Guide to Leading Successful Workshops and Training Programs. McGraw Hill, New York, NY.

Lavaque-Manty, D., 2007. Transforming the scientific enterprise: an interview with Alice Hogan. In: Stewart, A.J., Malley, J.E., LaVaque-Manty, D. (Eds.), Transforming Science and Engineering: Advancing Academic Women. University of Michigan Press, Ann Arbor, MI.

Martin, C.D., Heller, R.S., 1994. Attracting young minority women to engineering and science: necessary characteristics for exemplary programs. IEEE Trans. Educ. 37 (1), 8–12.

McLean, M., Cilliers, F., Van Wyk, J.M., 2008. Faculty development: yesterday, today and tomorrow. Med. Teach. 30, 555–584.

Mind Tools, 1996–2014. Planning a Workshop—Organizing and Running a Successful Event. Available from: <http://www.mindtools.com/pages/article/PlanningAWorkshop.htm> (accessed 18.11.14.).

Mind Tools, 2015. Available from: <http://www.mindtools.com> (accessed 15.01.15.).

Moody, J., 2001. Demystifying the Profession: Helping Junior Faculty Succeed. University of New Haven Press, New Haven, CT.

National Academy of Sciences, 2010. Rising Above the Gathering Storm, Revisited. Available from: <http://www.nap.edu/catalog/12999/rising-above-the-gathering-storm-revisited-rapidly-approaching-category-5> (accessed 08.12.14.).

National Science Foundation, 1995. NSF Visiting Professorships for Women Program Announcement and Guidelines. Available from: <http://www.nsf.gov/pubs/stis1995/nsf95113/nsf95113.txt> (accessed 08.12.14.).

National Science Foundation, 1998. Professional Opportunities for Women in Research and Education (POWRE) Program Announcement. Available from: <http://www.nsf.gov/pubs/1998/nsf98160/nsf98160.htm> (accessed 18.11.14.).

President's Commission on the Status of Women, 1963. American Women; Report of the President's Commission on the Status of Women. US Government Printing Office, Washington, DC. Available from: <http://babel.hathitrust.org/cgi/pt?id=mdp.39015016913678;view=1up;seq=3> (accessed 15.01.15.).

Reis, R., 1997. Tomorrow's Professor: Preparing for Academic Careers in Science and Engineering. IEEE Press, New York, NY.

Rosser, S.V., Lane, E.O., 2002. Key barriers for academic institutions seeking to retain female scientists and engineers: family-unfriendly policies, low numbers, stereotypes and harassment. J. Women Minor. Sci. Eng. 8, 161–189.

Rosser, S.V., 2004a. The Science Glass Ceiling: Academic Women Scientists and the Struggle to Succeed. Routledge, New York, NY.

Rosser, S.V., 2004b. Using POWRE to ADVANCE: institutional barriers identified by women scientists and engineers. NWSA J. 16 (1), 50–78.

Rosser, S.V., 2006. Using POWRE to ADVANCE: institutional barriers identified by women scientists and engineers. In: Bystydzienski, J.M., Bird, S.R. (Eds.), Removing Barriers: Women in Academic Science, Technology, Engineering and Mathematics. Indiana University Press, Bloomington, IN, pp. 69–92.

Rossi, A.S., 1965. Women in Science. Why so few? Science. 148 (3674), 1196–1202.

Schneider, C.G., 2002. PFF-the road ahead. Lib. Educ. 88 (3), 2–3.

Smeltzer, R.K., Ruben, R.J., Rose, P., 2013. Extraordinary Women in Science and Medicine: Four Centuries of Achievement. The Grolier Club, New York, NY.

Society of Women Engineers, 2012. The SWE Story. Available from: <http://societyofwomenengineers.swe.org/index.php/membership/history/2454-the-swe-story> (accessed 08.12.14.).

Sorcinelli, M.D., Austin, A.E., 1992. Developing New and Junior Faculty. Jossey Bass, San Francisco, CA.

Sorcinelli, M.D., Austin, A.E., Eddy, P.L., Beach, A.L., 2006. Creating the Future of Faculty Development: Learning from the Past, Understanding the Present. Anker Publishing, Boston, MA.

Thorndyke, L.E., Gusi, M.E., George, J.H., Quillen, D.A., Milner, R.J., 2006. Empowering junior faculty: Penn State's faculty development and mentoring program. Acad. Med. 81 (7), 668–673.

Wells, H.M., 2010. The Personal is Still Political: Women's Access to STEM Majors and Careers in the 21st Century, Paper presented at New York State Political Science Conference.

WEPAN, 2000. The 1st Ten Years. Available from: <http://c.ymcdn.com/sites/www.wepan.org/resource/resmgr/Press/The%201st%2010%20Years.pdf> (accessed 18.11.14.).

Williams, F.M., Emerson, C.J., 2008. Becoming Leaders: A Handbook for Women in Science, Engineering and Technology. ASCE Press, Reston, VA.

WinSETT 2015. Available from: <http://www.ccwestt.org/winsett/tabid/56/default.aspx> (accessed 15.01.15.).

2

The FORWARD to Professorship Workshop

Catherine Mavriplis

Department of Mechanical Engineering, University of Ottawa,
Ottawa, ON, Canada

OUTLINE

Introduction	18
Workshop Goals and Design	20
Implementation	22
Setting the Program	23
Choosing the Speakers	30
Recruitment	32
Setting	33
Funding	33
Management Team	34
Results of the FORWARD to Professorship Workshop	35
Paying It FORWARD	36
Design of Pay It FORWARD	36
Design of the Training Program	37
The Competition for Seed Funding and Training	38
The FWDer Teams	39
ELDers: Experts in Leadership Development	41
The 2010 and 2011 Training Programs	42
Pay It FORWARD Results	43
Acknowledgments	43
References	43

INTRODUCTION

The FORWARD to Professorship workshop was designed in 2001 to address the leaky pipeline (Berryman, 1983; Blickenstaff, 2005; Bennett, 2011) of women in Science, Technology, Engineering, and Mathematics (STEM) academia: it took aim at the critical juncture of doctoral and postdoctoral positions to professorship. Based on previous success with the FORWARD to Graduate School workshop, the organizers conceived a model that would address, much in the same way as FORWARD to Graduate School, the "nuts and bolts" of applying for, securing, and succeeding in a tenure-track assistant professor position in STEM.

The FORWARD in Science, Engineering, and Mathematics (SEM) program, developed in 1996 and 1997 by Rachelle Heller, professor of computer science and then associate dean for academic affairs in the School of Engineering and Applied Science at George Washington University (GW), Catherine Mavriplis, then associate professor of mechanical and aerospace engineering at GW, Charlene Sorensen, then assistant professor of chemistry at Gallaudet University (GU), and H. David Snyder, professor of physics at GU, addressed the leaky pipeline for women and deaf and hard-of-hearing students at the undergraduate to graduate junction in SEM. FORWARD, an acronym for Focus on Reaching Women for Academics, Research, and Development, comprised five activities to strengthen the juncture: a FORWARD to Graduate School workshop, a Summer Research Competition for female graduate students, an interdisciplinary science and engineering course, A Walk on the Moon (Mavriplis et al., 2000), a Deaf STEM education American Sign Language (ASL) tool development project, as well as student support at Hood College, Smith College (both historically colleges for women), Hampton University (a historically black college and university (HBCU)), and the National Technical Institute for the Deaf (NTID) at the Rochester Institute of Technology (RIT). Details on the origins and impetus for the FORWARD in SEM project are given in Chapter 14 from the point of view of GU, the leader in undergraduate education for the deaf and hard of hearing.

FORWARD to Graduate School grew from a small one-and-a-half-day weekend workshop at GW in 1998 to a vibrant workshop for approximately 25–30 women and members of other underrepresented groups, including a substantial number of deaf and hard-of-hearing participants, at GU, which ran for four consecutive years. A significant component of the workshop, preparation for the Graduate Record Examination (GRE) for deaf students, continued at GU beyond the lifetime of the workshop, as described in Chapter 14. The approach taken to designing the workshop was to provide participants with the steps and techniques for finding a STEM graduate program and advisor, applying and launching into a graduate career. As the National Science Foundation Program for Women and Girls funding (NSF 9714729) for FORWARD in SEM drew to a close, the investigators conceived the FORWARD to Professorship workshop, as an extension of the FORWARD to Graduate School workshop, ratcheted up for assistant professor careers. This formed the basis of a NSF ADVANCE Leadership Award (NSF 0123582 and 0123454) in 2001.

In 2001, the statistics showed that although the numbers of women in science and engineering fields were increasing at the undergraduate level (up to 43% in science and 22% in engineering), and at the graduate level (up to 37% in science and 21% in engineering at the master's level, 30% and 12% respectively for PhDs), these students still lacked female role models and mentors as professors: women made up 15% of the senior faculty in science and only 3% in engineering (NSB, 2000; NSF, 1996, 2000). While some argued that the lower percentages at the faculty level were only due to a lag (i.e., the time it takes for the increased female population to creep up into higher echelons of the tenured faculty ranks), it became clear that there was something more systemic at play. In particular, engineering departments had very few women faculty. Looking at the percentage of senior faculty in science, at 15% in 1997, one could look back 17 years prior to get an idea of the pool at the time. The female percentage of science PhDs was 18.7% in 1980. It therefore seems that a large percentage of the graduating science PhDs became faculty. For engineering, the senior faculty only had 3% women, and yet the pool 12 years prior was 6% in 1985. This time frame is roughly equivalent to the time it takes to advance from PhD graduation to the rank of full professor.

In 1998, it was unheard of to bring a group of women together for a workshop that addressed the challenges faced by women and underrepresented minorities, particularly deaf and hard of hearing individuals. By 2001, as mentioned in Chapter 1, some faculty development efforts were starting to appear, but certainly none devoted to the plight of underrepresented groups in STEM. As noted in Chapter 1, faculty development efforts before 2000 were centered on teaching and learning. One of the few references available at the time was Sorcinelli and Austin's edited volume, *Developing New and Junior Faculty* (1992). In this volume, advice emerged for protecting new faculty members from an excess of teaching and service work, advice largely unheeded especially in STEM fields. A recurring theme in the volume is lack of collegiality: new and junior faculty members expressed a great disappointment in the level of collegiality that they experienced and felt isolated according to several studies quoted in the book. Collegiality was also shown to be a predictor for success.

At the same time, sweeping changes were affecting support of women in STEM fields. The year 1999 saw the publicizing of the MIT Report (MIT, 1999), a critical look at inequities among senior women science professors at the Massachusetts Institute of Technology (MIT). Subtle inequities and unconscious bias (Valian, 1998) were emerging as persistent and real hurdles for the advancement of women in all areas, but especially for women in STEM academia as pointed out by the MIT Report. The NSF responded to these changes by restructuring their support programs for women from individual-based funding, such as the Visiting Professorships for Women (VPW) prior to 1997 (NSF, 1995) and the Professional Opportunities for Women in Research and Education (POWRE) (1997–2000) (NSF, 1998) programs (see Chapter 1) to institution-based funding (ADVANCE) as of 2001 (NSF, 2001), with the intent to improve the STEM academic climate and to effect "institutional transformation" (La-Vaque-Manty, 2007). The premise also argued that an improved climate for women would improve climate for all.

Within this context, we developed the FORWARD to Professorship workshop, described next.

WORKSHOP GOALS AND DESIGN

The FORWARD to Professorship workshop was designed to fill a need, that of clarifying the steps to securing and succeeding in a tenure-track professorship. As one participant later stated, it "provides information nowhere else available." Women have been shown to be excluded from crucial formal and informal networks (Becker, 1990; Kemelgor and Etzkowitz 2001; Thomson, 2000) and, in the world of elite academic institutions, networks and personal references are extremely important. As such, we set out to provide what we came to term as "insider information" on our call for participants; i.e., the "nuts and bolts" of choosing the right type of academic institution for oneself, finding positions to apply for, preparing a competitive application package, and, once in a position, securing research funding, becoming an effective teacher, limiting administrative work, and leading a balanced life. This two-tiered approach of addressing the pre-position stage as well as the crucial skills to get off to a productive start in a position aimed to help plug the leak in the pipeline at the doctoral or postdoctoral to assistant professor junction.

The workshop was also designed to provide information, tools, and skills development activities that would be applicable to men or women. The context of the predominantly female group would provide the right atmosphere for addressing issues specific to women or possibly other underrepresented groups without focusing on female-only issues. Men were invited to participate. We felt this was important for the participants in their bid to fit into a male-dominated environment, as well as for ourselves as STEM faculty members: we were ever aware of how our own actions would be perceived by our colleagues and tenure and promotion evaluators. Significantly, we never received any comments or backlash that we were privileging women or engaging in nonserious work. A significant pervasive goal throughout the 17-year FORWARD project that needed to be reiterated often and with conviction was that graduate and faculty development and graduate and faculty development workshops for women are serious, intentional, and constructive steps toward building a successful career. Many of the men who did attend told us they felt they learned so much and were very appreciative.

The workshop was designed to be free. The funding we secured from the NSF (NSF 0123582 and 0123454), and later, the National Institutes of Health (NIH) (NIGMS 1R13GM080942-01) would serve primarily to offer the workshop free of cost to participants, as well as providing travel and subsistence funds for the participants. The idea followed that of the open access to information design goal: to eliminate as many barriers to entry to the profession as possible. Graduate students and postdoctoral researchers were prioritized for travel funds. All participants were encouraged and coached to solicit travel funds from their institutions. As we knew instinctively, and later learned from Women Don't Ask, Babcock and Laschever's (2003) meta-analysis of research on women and negotiation, women in general, and, women in STEM in particular, don't often ask for what they need to be successful and don't feel they have the right to ask in many cases. We therefore wanted to offer the travel funds but also cultivate a habit of asking for support by tutoring them in how to ask.

The workshop was designed to provide information, but also to be an active workshop, where the participants could work on their own skills and leave with some products in hand. Icebreaker activities would be planned to get participants to know each other early on in the workshop. Work assigned before arrival at the workshop would serve to engage the participants in the task ahead: to actively participate rather than only sit back and absorb information. At the workshop, sessions were a mixture of lecture and active work, either alone or in pairs, in small groups, or as an entire group. The last session would serve as a time to work on one's personal career plan so as to leave with a set of goals and a sketch of how to get there.

As part of an active workshop, participants would be encouraged to contribute their questions, comments, and experiences to share with others. We had learned from the FORWARD to Graduate School workshops, where we had invited the FORWARD Summer Research Competition awardees to speak, that near-peers had a special rapport with participants. Often, the answers to participants' questions or suggestions to resolving their difficult situational problems came from other participants rather than from us (older) organizers. This became especially true as the academic and social media environment began to evolve more rapidly. The makeup of the participant body, finishing doctoral students, postdoctoral researchers, and beginning assistant professors, provided the opportunity for near-peer mentoring and support. This peer and near-peer mentoring complemented the built-in near-peer and senior-junior peer interactions with the speakers. The overall open atmosphere of sharing experiences contributes to the positive experience and empowerment of the participants. Informal settings were built into the program to allow for more personal discussion with fellow participants, speakers or mentors, and networking.

By design, the workshop sought to be as comprehensive as possible in terms of topics covered, but also in terms of breadth of types of institutions represented, STEM fields, career levels, underrepresented groups, geographical regions, and lifestyles. As women and members of other underrepresented groups find themselves isolated in STEM places of study and employment, the importance of gathering as broad a range of role models and examples of successful scientists as possible is key to participants' ability to visualize a path for themselves. Until the day when a critical mass (some say 30%; e.g., Etzkowitz et al., 1994) is present, this breadth will remain important. The experience of a single role model, or even a few role models, can been negative: for example, women graduate students reported being turned off from academia after observing the stressful lives of the few female STEM professors in or close to their fields (Thomson, 2000; Mason et al., 2009). Presenting, instead, a wide variety of successful scientists who have found ways "to cope" (Morganson et al., 2010) is far more positive and empowering for pipeline entrants.

IMPLEMENTATION

With a successful application for a NSF ADVANCE Leadership Award, we set about organizing the first FORWARD to Professorship workshop for May 2003. The workshop was held in Washington, DC, at Gallaudet University's Kellogg Conference Center, which provides meeting rooms, auditoriums, overnight hotel accommodations, and banquet facilities, all on the beautiful, grassy, historical campus downtown.

Setting the Program

As we built the first FORWARD to Professorship program, we knew that we needed to address the three components of tenure: teaching, research, and service, while also paying attention to work/life integration, which affects women in particular at the assistant professor career stage. Beyond those components, the possibilities were open. Delving into the mechanics of obtaining a position as we did for FORWARD to Graduate School, we realized that writing was a crucial skill to address: writing an application package for tenure-track positions, but also writing proposals for funding research and journal publications for research scholarship. Tenure requirements also appeared to be nebulous to most participants, whether they were on the tenure track or not. Finally, the subtle differences between men and women in a male-dominated field, such as how to negotiate and how to gain advice from a mentor or an administrator, were also rich ground for exploration. Built into the program, we knew that we would need to have several opportunities for informal discussion and networking, as near-peers and peers can offer particularly pertinent advice and rapport building is an especially appreciated feature of the workshop. Meeting so many women in STEM for the first time in one place for most participants was an unexpected pleasure, as we came to discover. A sample program from 2011 is shown in Appendix C of this book.

An *introductory overview and welcome session*, where we introduce the concepts to be discussed of tenure, promotion, research, teaching, service, and work/life integration, serves to open up the workshop. This session is meant to get participants "warmed up" to the atmosphere of sharing experiences. An *icebreaker activity* is used to get participants to meet each other and discover that they have similar concerns and questions. Later in this session, *the keynote speech*, usually held during dinner right after the overview session, is another opportunity to build rapport. We found that choosing a sincere, open, and thoughtful keynote speaker did more for the atmosphere of the workshop than almost any other component. Over the years, we learned that setting the tone on the first day was key to the success of the workshop experience for participants. We therefore recommend starting with a dinner, sincere keynoter, and icebreaker activity. For us, starting with an evening event with personal experiences being exchanged and then letting participants "sleep on it" was extremely effective in opening up their minds, conversations, and acceptance of the topics to be discussed. In particular, we found that on the first day or evening, the driven PhD female scientist or engineer participants were very eager to "just get the information" but were not very open to share their experiences without these built-in activities. This was learned over time with several implementations of the workshop.

Teaching is a topic most participants are familiar with. Teaching is also the most immediate task of a new professor: on the first day on the job, a new professor must stand in front of a large classroom mostly filled with young ambitious men and deliver the course material. The design of the course must also be done by the first day of class. There is no slack in the time allowance for this task. For these reasons, we start the program with a *session on teaching* after the introductory session and keynote.[1] Participants are able to contribute to the discussion based on their considerable experience in this area. Mindful that most participants have acted as teaching assistants, if not instructors, and had plenty of observations of their own professors, we tailor the teaching session to tips on time management in course and class preparation, classroom management techniques, and learning styles in order to introduce some pedagogy to participants who have none of this training from their STEM graduate school experience. This session therefore also serves to warm up the atmosphere of the workshop.

Paramount in new and aspiring professors' minds is the challenge of securing funding for research. We therefore follow the session on teaching with the *session on research*. There is no need to address how to do research, as most doctoral students and postdoctoral scientists already excel in this area and could probably teach us a thing or two. However, securing funding is daunting, and every year, it seems to get more and more competitive. Participants are particularly anxious about this task. In the same vein, as mentioned previously, that women don't ask or feel they have the right to ask, we felt it best to bring the funding program directors to the participants rather than just encourage participants to contact them. The session on research was therefore designed as a time for participants to hear short presentations from program directors from the major government funding agencies, and to then spend time with them in small groups to ask questions and hear advice. This format worked well and endured throughout the evolution of the project. In some years, we also had a university facilitator for seeking funding from private foundations and a representative from the American Chemical Society, both of which proved extremely useful as well. For the government agencies, it is imperative to include program directors from at least the two major funding organizations: the NSF and the NIH. These were always supplemented by program directors from U.S. Department of Defense agencies such as the Office of Naval Research (ONR), the Army Research Office (ARO), and the Air Force Office of Scientific Research (AFOSR). We also provided our own tips for getting

---

[1]In most years, the teaching session followed the keynote speech on the morning of the second day. However, the timing varied in some years, as in the 2011 example shown in Appendix C of this book.

off to a quick start in research funding. As I had recent experience as a program director at NSF, I was able to offer advice on how to select programs to apply to, contact program directors before and after submitting proposals, and learn by serving as proposal reviewers and review panel members.

To complete the set of three requirements for tenure, *a session on service* is also planned for the workshop. This session can be dealt with in a short (45 min, as opposed to 1, 1½, or 2 hr) session. In the early years, we learned that most participants had no idea what "service" meant. The session therefore defines service, gives examples of committees and outside associations to devote time to, and gives tips on how to avoid spending too much time on service while playing the political game of being seen as an important contributor to the department. Our session came to take on the title "How to Say No."[2] Participants were coached and practiced saying no to service requests that would be detrimental to their success in the early years of the tenure track.

In order to keep the participants active, the research session is followed by a *session on writing*, in which participants are paired with partners to critique each other's writing samples. This session usually comes before lunch, when participant attention span is once again fading after a full morning of receiving detailed information. This session went through several incarnations over the years until we settled on the format of (i) providing writing advice to the whole group for 20 min, then (ii) breaking the group into three subgroups, (iii) having the participants work in pairs within the subgroups for 45 min, (iv) having the subgroup facilitator solicit and summarize tips for the writing task of the subgroup (20 min), and (v) reporting the results of each subgroup to the entire group (20 min). Extra time is allotted for movement of the participants to subgroup tables and back, rounding out to a total of 2 hr for this session on writing.

Writing encompasses many aspects of the tenure track professor's life. We concentrated on research proposals in the early years, but then we realized that many of our participants were more focused on the stage of applying for tenure-track positions. They needed advice on the three major components of an application package: the cover letter, the research statement, and the teaching statement or philosophy. We therefore changed the format to have participants work on their own samples of these three writing assignments. We asked participants to send in, prior to the workshop, samples of one or more of these. As organizers, we would read these texts, critique them, and return the edited samples to the individual workshop participants at the conclusion

---

[2]In the example of the 2011 program listed in Appendix C of this book, note that some of the "saying no" practice work was rolled into the negotiation session.

FIGURE 2.1   "FORWARD to Professorship" workshop participants discuss their writing samples in pairs during the writing session. Source: *Photo permissions: Laura Haya, Hassan Shaban, Sarah Dare, Marianne Fenech, and Lindsay Fitzpatrick.*

of the writing session. In the subgroups (namely, one for cover letters, one for research statements, and one for teaching statements), the participants would pair up and read each other's samples, and then critique them (Figure 2.1). Each subgroup discussion was facilitated by one of the organizers, who solicited suggestions from the subgroup participants and offered overall tips for writing such statements or letters. The results of the discussion were posted on easels for all participants to see for the rest of the workshop.

The engagement of the participants by asking them to submit writing samples was particularly effective, we felt. Participants were especially appreciative for the opportunity to share their samples with someone and to receive advice from senior mentors, as well as near-peers. Many expressed disappointment at not being able to attend all three subgroup discussions. In a limited time allotment, this was simply not possible. We also wanted participants to learn that they can continue this type of exercise back home. We later learned that some had indeed participated in or even organized writing groups after attending the workshop.

Other ways that we attempted to *engage the participants before arriving at the workshop* and at the workshop were to assign readings and solicit discussion on these readings. We suggested that participants might read a biography of a great woman scientist before arriving at the workshop and planned for a lunch discussion at individual tables on the reading. This was particularly effective for some participants. Others felt they had no time to read anything other than work-related research. In some ways, we were trying to instill some culture of work/life integration by asking them to read in their free time and to prepare the way for some of the more delicate discussions at the workshop, such as discussion on the climate of STEM academia and the work/life integration challenges that women face. Choosing biographies of historical women scientists who had struggled with far more daunting challenges than our generation was particularly effective in this regard. The books assigned were Brenda Maddox's *Rosalind Franklin: The Dark Lady of DNA* (Maddox, 2002) and Barbara Goldsmith's *Obsessive Genius: The Inner World of Marie Curie* (Goldsmith, 2005). The same book was assigned to everyone. The different books were used for different years of the workshop.

Every year, we planned *more relaxing activities for this second evening*, off campus if possible, so that participants could relax and share experiences of a kind different from the intensity of the daytime sessions, in a separate and informal environment. In one year, we augmented the reading of the book on Marie Curie's life by a performance of a one-woman play, *Manya—The Living History of Marie Curie* (Frontczak, 2015). The discussion after the performance with the actress and author, Susan Marie Frontczak, added to the engagement of the participants. The play was held after the dinner of the second day. Another year, we hosted the University of Michigan's Center for Research on Teaching and Learning (CRLT) players, with their performance of *The Faculty Meeting*, an interactive play designed under the University of Michigan's NSF ADVANCE Institutional Transformation grant (CRLT, 2014). This performance was held at the Mount Vernon campus of the GW in Post Hall. The room is an elegant ballroom of yesteryear, built for the elite Mount Vernon College for Women, founded in 1875. The play, which presents an extremely accurate view of STEM faculty meetings for deciding on a final selection of candidates for hiring a tenure-track professor in a Computer Science department, resonates well with participants and speakers alike. The interactive aspect, where the audience can ask characters what they are thinking in stop-motion action, was especially effective in continuing our conversation of the challenges and solutions to the challenges of being a minority faculty member in a STEM department. Other outings for the second night of the workshop included a trip to the Marian Koshland Museum (National Academy of Sciences, 2015), a museum dedicated to "stimulat[ing] discussion and shed[ding] light on how science supports [political] decision making." At times, we simply organized smaller group outings to interesting restaurants in downtown Washington, DC, near the government building and museum tourist sights. The outings or informal activities always related in some way to STEM.

The third and final day of the workshop finds the participants in an even more receptive mood to discuss and share as experiences from the past two days have served to bring the group closer together. As such, the participants are ready to be active and seek out peers and speakers with whom to discuss their challenges. In the 2011 program, we started the final day of the workshop with a two hour *session on negotiation*. In the early years, the negotiation session was run by us, the organizers, brainstorming with the group what items could be negotiated. Most participants had no idea they could negotiate for laboratory space, student fellowships, and other perks that could facilitate the launch of a new professor's career. Most only thought of salary as the negotiation topic and were of the opinion that they "were just so grateful to get an offer that they didn't think of negotiating salary" or anything else. Here's where near-peers were critical in the conversation: several participants or speakers recounted their navigation through the hiring process, often in terms of negotiating start dates or pregnancy and maternity situations. They also recounted that they learned the hard way from their male colleagues that by not negotiating, they had missed out on resources that they had no idea existed. As mentors, we, the organizers, sought to inform the participants of the existence of resources and the critical need for them to negotiate for these resources to have a successful start and continued success in their careers. While most women are reluctant to ask for what they need, as mentioned previously (Babcock and Laschever, 2003), we tried to instill in the participants the idea that they would not be taken seriously or seen as effective in their roles if they didn't negotiate for these resources. In later years, we hired negotiation speakers to run a more effective session, including the information just described, but also instructing the participants on the different theories of negotiation and in consultation with us, the organizers, designing role-play scenarios that addressed the challenges of STEM assistant professors. These were particularly effective sessions that kept the participants active and had direct relevance to their experiences.

"Having It All" is our *work/life integration session*, held on the last day, once participants have loosened up quite a bit from the first day. Always an interesting and particularly poignant session, "Having It All" discusses several aspects of work/life integration: the dual-career problem, maternity, being single and pursuing interests outside work, caregiving (whether for children, aging parents, or others), sticky situations, and navigating the fine line between one's personal and professional life. To cover as many of these aspects as possible, we drew upon a number of speakers to share their stories with the participants. It was useful to bring both the woman and the man in a couple who had navigated the dual-career problem or studied it. The majority of speakers and participants have to deal with maternity, including pregnancy and leave issues, so this is always a big part of the work/life integration session. However, we learned early on that single women didn't appreciate the overwhelming emphasis on the topic, so we were careful to devote time to discussions of being single as well. For this session, we always

FIGURE 2.2 "FORWARD to Professorship" activities allow participants time to engage in meaningful conversations with near-peers. Source: *Photo permissions: Sarah Dare and Marianne Fenech.*

rearranged the seating so as to create a more intimate atmosphere and to get the participants up and moving around to stay active. Presenters shared their stories in a limited amount of time (10—15 min), while the question-and-answer period took up the rest of the allotted time, for a total of 90 min. This session was usually held right before lunch to allow conversations to continue over a meal (Figure 2.2).

The last session of the final day of the workshop is devoted to career planning to send the participants off with a tangible product in their hands: a personalized written career plan. The *personalized plan session* gives tips on the importance and elements of a career plan, informs participants of resources for career planning such as several postdoctoral training programs at some universities, and provides a worksheet for participants to work on during the session (Figure 2.3). With their career plan sketches in hand, participants then move to small groups with seasoned STEM administrators to discuss their plans and ask questions and seek advice for navigating the tenure track.

In some years, we varied the program with a *session on communications in a male-dominated field*, which included negotiation tips, or a *stress management session*, which related to work/life integration. Each of these sessions included very active components and audience participation.

As mentioned previously in the writing and service session descriptions, *time budgeting* is important for the flow of the workshop. We were mindful of (i) keeping the participants active, (ii) the relative importance of the subjects treated, (iii) the participants' experience with those topics, and (iv) the process of building rapport between participants and speakers. Certainly, a 2½-day workshop is long. We wrestled with the length of time for the workshop. Treating it as a 3-day experience

FIGURE 2.3 "FORWARD to Professorship" activities allow participants time to work on their professional and personal plans. Source: *Photo permissions: Lindsay Fitzpatrick.*

seemed long to many prospective participants. They didn't feel that they could take time off work. Some asked if it could be on the weekend, as they feared their research supervisors would not let them go or they simply couldn't ask for the time. The participants were also coming from far away, which added to the time needed off from work. We felt, however, as organizers, that we could not adequately cover the material in less than two days. We also wanted to instill the notion that faculty development is important and legitimate, and should be continuous, insisting that it was a serious undertaking in one's career planning and that therefore, it should be done on work days, not on the weekend. We positioned the workshop either at the end or beginning of the week to take advantage of the weekend for travel time.

The time allotted for each session was discussed at length by the organizers. For subjects we felt the participants would be familiar with, an hour would be sufficient, such as teaching, leaving time of course for participation from the audience. Service, as mentioned above, was limited to a 45-min discussion. Most other sessions involved active participation and, as such, required time to introduce the subject, time to get the participants oriented and physically moved to their groups, time for the participant work, and then time to regroup and report on what happened. This requires a minimum of $1\frac{1}{2}$–2 hr per session.

Choosing the Speakers

For the first implementation of the workshop, we, the organizers, did most of the speaking. We soon realized, however, that there were better experts out there. Perhaps it was necessary for us to be the speakers on the first round, to determine what material was most relevant, what length of time was needed for each session, and what the participants wanted to know. Moving forward, we recruited more and more speakers to replace us for the different sessions.

Negotiation, for example, was one topic where we sought experts, although most of them would not commit to any less than half a day. We didn't feel that we could budget half a day in the schedule for this single topic. Negotiation speakers often expected to be paid, and paid well. This was not feasible in the early days of a shoestring budget.

The teaching session was easily handled by the organizers, Charlene Sorensen and Rachelle Heller, as they had more experience in the area, Rachelle having a PhD in education. We had also participated as a team in the University of Wisconsin Oshkosh Women in Science Institute for Curriculum Reform under FORWARD in SEM to design our "Walk on the Moon" interdisciplinary seminar. There, we received training in novel teaching techniques for inclusive approaches in science. Nevertheless, we invited Susan McCahan in later years to handle this session, as she has specialized in engineering education and routinely handled a classroom of over 1300 mostly male engineering students at the University of Toronto. Her classroom and teaching assistant management tips were especially useful for our audience.

Funding agency program directors for the research session were easy to find in Washington, DC, thanks to our experience and contacts with these agencies. Having worked as one at NSF, I had several people in mind who would be open as speakers, as did Rachelle, Charlene, and David Snyder. Program directors are expected to have contact with potential grantees so they were always eager to participate. Government workers cannot be paid either, so they came at no cost.

The writing and service sessions were mainly presented by us, the organizers, although in later years, we experimented with some support from true writers for the writing session: an English professor and a novelist. "Having It All" work/life integration panelists were easy to recruit, given our large network of colleagues from past years. The administrators for the career planning advice were recruited from the greater Washington, DC, area based on our contacts.

When we needed speakers that we didn't already know, we often referred to pertinent articles in the *Chronicle of Higher Education* addressing climate or other issues of STEM higher education, which seemed to become more frequent as the years passed. Today, with social media, the networking is even more accessible. As years passed, we recruited more and more past participants as speakers, and this near-peer approach proved to be extremely successful for both participants and speakers.

Recruiting keynote speakers was a little more challenging. We wanted high-profile women who would deliver a sincere speech about their experiences. Without knowing them personally, it was difficult to judge if they would fit the bill. Also, the higher profile the woman, the harder scheduling became. And you cannot invite several high-profile people in parallel. You must wait to hear from one before moving on to the next (in case they decline). Nevertheless, we had tremendous success in recruiting keynote and other speakers. They were all eager to participate in this seemingly unique opportunity. They were excited to share their experiences with this mostly female, up-and-coming audience. Certainly the energy and high caliber of the participants fed into the speakers' experience.

Most of the speakers were female, but several men participated as well. Especially in the case of the administrator advisors, we purposely invited male speakers so that participants could try out their questions on them before returning to their own male-dominated milieux. We were also mindful of inviting administrators that they would likely not have professional interactions with beyond the workshop, so that they would feel "safe" in asking these confidential questions. Involving administrators also served to effect some systemic change within institutions, by apprising them of the challenges and possible solutions for women and underrepresented groups in STEM professorship.

Recruitment

Recruiting participants was challenging at times, especially in the early days. The world was not as connected then by the Internet and social media. We essentially sought out professional associations of women in STEM or minorities in STEM (through listservs and newsletters of WEPAN-L, WIPHYS, WISENET, WISE, WIS, GWIS, SWE, AWIS, and SYSTERS) and sent them notices of the workshop. We also used our many contacts to disseminate the invitations. We attempted to contact women in industry and national laboratories to recruit women to reenter academia. After the first workshop was delivered, many of our proactive participants shared their experiences with colleagues, so word of mouth became our primary vehicle for recruitment. This we had learned from our FORWARD to Graduate School workshop. The entire FORWARD in SEM program (including the five activities described previously) also formed a pipeline to the new workshop. Every year thereafter, the workshop was oversubscribed. We also inquired several times at NSF as to why ADVANCE grantees other than the Institutional Transformation awardees couldn't participate in grantee meetings. Eventually, these meetings did welcome us, and our yearly presentations there also served to spread the word.

Being mindful of the desired balance of participants from various disciplines, career stages, and geographical location, in subsequent years, we implemented (at the suggestion of a seasoned graduate assistant, Yell Inverso) an application form rather than a straight registration. Since the program had become oversubscribed, this step became necessary. We kept names of those turned down to give them priority the following year. We accepted some male participants. Often, these were spouses of participants.

We attempted to offer child care some years, but this was quite difficult. The most successful year for this effort was one in which we provided names of agencies and caregivers who could provide temporary services in the Washington, DC, area.

Setting

Finally, the workshop was held at GU, an environment for the deaf and hard of hearing, where all interactions are interpreted in ASL. The deaf environment for learning and communication is so different from the mainstream (hearing) world of most participants that, in a context of high-pressure and highly competitive science, participants could appreciate the significant additional challenges for deaf or hard of hearing scientists and reported appreciating this opportunity to learn about deaf culture (as described in Chapter 14). The environment significantly contributed to the openness of the workshop atmosphere.

Funding

The national FORWARD to Professorship workshop was held in May 2003, 2004, 2005, 2007, 2008, 2010, and 2011 at GU in Washington, DC, thanks mainly to sustained funding from the NSF ADVANCE program: in 2001, our first leadership award (NSF 0123582, 0123454) provided $252,170; in 2005, our second leadership award (NSF 0540801, 0540800, 0540016) provided $345,764 for a second version of the workshop and a study of women in career breaks (Heller et al., 2010); in 2007, based on advice from our NIH speaker Jean Chin, we applied for and received a NIH grant (NIGMS 1R13GM080942-01) of $15,000 to add health-related researchers to our participant audience and to provide extra content for them; finally, in 2009, under a new NSF ADVANCE PAID award (NSF 0930126, 0930112) of $536,064, we proposed the "Pay It FORWARD" program to train ten new teams to develop their own workshops based on our FORWARD model: the training took place at the 2010 and 2011 national workshops. In addition, in 2005, at the recommendation of one of our first participants from MIT, we organized and ran an adapted version of the FORWARD to Professorship workshop for MIT (MIT, 2014). MIT then institutionalized the workshop as "Path of Professorship," a popular yearly workshop since 2005, described in Chapter 3.

The funds were spent primarily on participant support. Travel allowances were made for each participant. On-site meeting rooms, materials, and subsistence were paid for by the grants. The proposal had budgeted for ASL interpreters for each workshop. A small amount of travel money was used for dissemination: the organizers presented either mini-versions of the workshop or reports on the workshop at various STEM conferences. The first set of workshops was run on a shoestring budget. In the second round of funding requests, we made the case for paying the speakers a modest honorarium. Too often, as we noted to our participants in our service without overcommitment session and in our grant application, women freely donate their time for work that should really be paid by institutions. We therefore felt that the (overwhelmingly female) speakers, who took the time out of their extremely busy schedules to travel to Gallaudet and prepare a presentation, needed to be recognized, if only by a token honorarium. Funding was also budgeted for the graduate assistant who took care of most of the logistics for the workshop delivery, aided by a few undergraduates, mostly deaf students at Gallaudet.

Management Team

As the creators of the FORWARD program, Rachelle Heller, Catherine Mavriplis, Charlene Sorensen, and David Snyder had worked together since 1996 on programs for women and underrepresented groups in STEM disciplines. We work well together, each member representing and bringing experience from four different scientific disciplines and career attainment levels. We have learned to work well together despite our geographical separation, through email, conference calls, and other distance tools. We certainly benefit from a history of a very close relationship when we were all in Washington, DC, from 1996 to 2003. We have developed a brainstorming method that works well for us. Each member brings different talents and skills, including organizational, creative, communications, administrative, and interpersonal skills. The production of new ideas at every stage was a group effort. All of us contributed equally to the design and development of the workshop and its components. All of us presented several sessions of the workshop and recruited the outside presenters. All of us participated in dissemination, evaluation, and assessment activities. Other tasks were divided up logistically as follows:

- The GU effort was directed at the infrastructure of the workshop. Charlene Sorensen, David Snyder, and later Paul Sabila worked directly with the Gallaudet graduate assistant Yell Inverso, professional assistant Sharron Cargo, and undergraduates on logistics, registration and pre-workshop preparation, and communications. They also concentrated on issues related to deaf STEM professionals, including the hiring of interpreters.

- The GW effort was directed at the evaluation and assessment portion of the project and in dealing with workshop presenters and participant travel. Rachelle Heller worked with Cheryl Beil, executive director of academic planning and assessment, and later Patricia Freitag, as evaluators and several GW graduate assistants on the assessment activities. As an associate dean, and later as an associate provost, Dr. Heller provides strong administrative support and takes a prominent role in the dissemination effort, in particular to high-level administrators.
- Catherine Mavriplis's effort is directed at the overall organization of the project. She is responsible for the overall planning of work and activities, based on program goals and evaluation feedback, for dissemination and reporting.

RESULTS OF THE FORWARD TO PROFESSORSHIP WORKSHOP

By 2009, five 2½-day national workshops had been held in Washington, DC, and two mini-workshops at the 2004 Women in Engineering Programs and Advocates Network (WEPAN) national meeting and the 2007 Society for Advancement of Hispanics/Chicanos and Native Americans in Science (SACNAS) national meeting. We had held a shorter 1½-day workshop for MIT in 2005 (Halber, 2005) and had helped MIT organize their own workshop, "Path of Professorship," which has been institutionalized as an annual event. Overall, 325 women and 20 men, 48% of them from underrepresented STEM groups (including Hispanic, African American, Native American, and deaf people), had been participants in our workshops, in addition to 120 women at MIT by 2009.

Daily formative workshop evaluations and final-day evaluation forms were used to assess the program at each workshop offering. Participants rated the overall workshop experience highly: 4.9/5 (where 1 is poor, 5 excellent). The organization, the selection of speakers, and the activities in relation to meeting the participants' needs and expectations were also rated highly. Detailed comments on the evaluation forms reflect the high approval rating and sense of empowerment that many participants felt; for example:

> Probably the most inspiring and confidence building thing I've ever done as far as science goes.

100% of the evaluation form respondents said they would recommend this workshop to their friends and colleagues. And many did! The following quote is typical of unsolicited emails received after the workshop:

> I must say that the experience has reinforced my decision to enter academia and I feel more knowledgeable about how to proceed. [...] I'll keep you posted on my PhD completion.

A four-year, five-workshop survey of past participants was administered in the summer of 2007, and results were presented at the PROMETEA 2007 Women in Engineering Research and Technology International Conference (Mavriplis et al., 2010). Both workshop evaluations and the survey showed that the participants were very satisfied with the workshop; participants attained a very positive and confident outlook on their careers, in all the key elements of a successful academic career (e.g., teaching, publishing, writing proposals, and obtaining funding). Participants mentioned negotiation training as particularly useful; they successfully and confidently used this skill in subsequent career actions, despite having rated confidence in their negotiating ability quite low prior to the workshop. Further survey results are presented in Mavriplis et al. (2010) and in Chapter 18.

PAYING IT FORWARD

With the experience of six implementations of the FORWARD workshop (in 2003, 2004, 2005, 2007, and 2008 in Washington, DC, and at MIT in 2005), which incorporated several refinements, adjustments and adaptations, and experimented with new elements, we felt the workshop was ready to be launched as a model for new groups to adapt or adopt, in order to further our reach. The Pay It FORWARD program was developed to train ten teams to do just that.

Design of Pay It FORWARD

The goal of Pay It FORWARD was to enable others to create workshop experiences tailored to their constituents, and thus we would "pay it forward." This would enable even more individuals, departments, administrations, and institutions to transform themselves. Under a new NSF ADVANCE initiative, we proposed to train up to ten teams of Future Workshop Developers (FWDers—called the FORWARDers) to develop and run their own workshops. These could be institutional (i.e., within one institution), regional (e.g., within the southwest), or special cohort workshops (e.g., Latinas in STEM academia, deaf people in STEM academia). Teams would ideally include faculty and administration to promote institutional (or greater) transformation. We asked the FWDers to come to the national workshop with a member of their institution's administration so that the commitment to transformation would go beyond an individual faculty member or department. By including both levels, the hosting institution could support not only their expectations of new faculty (and the current expectations those new faculty have), but also significantly reshape their protocol of how new faculty are supported and how their needs are met.

Our proposed activities would provide for bigger and broader audiences, as well as personal transformations (through development of a new cadre of leadership experts) and a basis for institutional change. Our plan was to train the FWDers, provide materials, resources, and seed funding sources, evaluate the impact, and provide mentoring. This would be aided by site visits, evaluations, support, and suggestions provided to the FWDers. To evaluate the impact, there would be an assessment of participant response, FWDers' project activities (including the production of material to be shared with the administration), and institutional adaptation/transformation resulting from new awareness regarding the "face" of new tenure-track job applicants. On an individual basis, we expected to see continued positive outcomes from the participants of this new generation of workshops.

Design of the Training Program

The training was to be conducted at the national "FORWARD to Professorship" workshop in Washington, DC, primarily as a demonstration and training opportunity for the FWDers. The workshops would be held as in the past at GU, the world's only liberal arts university for the deaf and hard of hearing. FWDers would be invited to apply to attend the "national model workshop" as observers, with the understanding that, in turn, with mini-grant support, they would develop and implement workshops targeted to their particular audience at their home institution or in their region. FWDers were expected to seek out at least one other person, and no more than two others, and to apply as a team. Such a FWDer team, ideally made of up a young faculty member, a longtime faculty member, and an administrator, would be able to sustain each other when they return to their home institution, work through the local procedures and policies to implement the workshop, and work well as a brainstorming group.

We expected that each FWDer team would ultimately fully develop a proposal for a local or regional workshop or a workshop for a specified target group (e.g., Latinas in neuroscience). Each FWDer team would be expected to understand the idiosyncratic needs and culture of their particular target audience. The following is a list of attributes that we thought FWDers should possess:

- Understanding of the local/target group issues
- Support from their immediate supervisor to engage in this project
- Interest in engaging people and colleagues
- Evidence of a history of good pedagogy, research, and university service
- Collaborative style, yet assertive enough to "make cold calls" for speakers and resources
- Excellent organizational and communication skills.

The application process would require that FWDers provide a short background on themselves, evidence of the attributes noted previously, a team application if possible (i.e., if they apply with at least one partner or if they ask to be partnered with another applicant), a description of their target audience and its specific needs, the rationale for running such a workshop, experience or previous work in this area or in leadership (if any), and expectations of outcomes.

Once accepted, the groups would be sent materials concerning the issues of mentoring, negotiation, teaching statements, research statements, and quality-of-life issues, as well as a selected set of background literature (e.g., MIT, 1999). FWDers would then attend the workshop to observe. We would provide a half-day pre-workshop briefing/training and a full-day post-workshop debriefing/training for them to consider the whole event and to process and to understand. They could also discuss with the Pay It FORWARD Leadership team how they might adapt or adopt the workshop to their particular institution, region, or targeted group.

The Competition for Seed Funding and Training

Mini-grants of up to $10,000 were made available to FWDers to conduct a workshop with the expectation that an additional $5,000 would be raised locally. $5,000 would be available for their revised workshop, again expecting them to raise additional funds locally. These plans formed a Request for Proposals (RFP) that was sent out to STEM professional associations for women and minorities and contacts from our previous workshops. We promoted the program regionally to special cohorts such as SACNAS, HBCUs, Society of Women Engineers (SWE), National Society of Black Engineers (NSBE), Society of Hispanic Professional Engineers (SHPE), and undergraduate institutions, as well as through the more than 325 former participants of our own national workshops. We also promoted the program to regions with a significant concentration of deaf and hard of hearing individuals, as well as institutions with deaf faculty or that have had deaf graduate students in STEM fields.

The seed funding would be distributed to applicants with proposals that had the best chance of being successful and that served the needs of advancing women, particularly women of underrepresented groups in STEM academia (ethnic, racial, color, and disability (e.g., deaf) diversity). Again, while the leadership team for Pay It FORWARD had experience with many groups, it was expected that the FWDers would have the primary understanding about the needs and culture of their audiences. This amount of funding ($10,000) would be sufficient to launch a major portion of the workshop: participant support for the workshop attendees, including conference expenses and some funding for travel and honoraria for speakers. To cover additional expenses, we would coach the FWDers in negotiating with administrators and seeking other outside funding.

This entire process was presented twice: once in 2009–2012 (Cohort A), and again, with a new cohort (Cohort B), in 2010–2013.

The FWDer Teams

The 2009–2010 competition received five proposals and funded four. Cohort A consisted of:

- The Arizona State University team (see Chapter 4), which proposed a workshop for the southwestern United States
- The University of Guam team (see Chapter 5), which proposed a workshop for women of the Western Pacific
- The University of Toledo team (see Chapter 6), which proposed a workshop for STEMM (the STEM fields as well as medicine-related fields) "women of color" in the Midwest
- The University of Virginia team (see Chapter 7), which proposed a workshop centered on engaging across difference (particularly racial difference).

These Cohort A teams applied for funding in 2010 in response to a late 2009 RFP; attended the 2010 national workshop in Washington, DC, where they received training; and developed their own workshops over the course of the following year, delivering their first workshop in 2011. Some of the teams delivered second workshops in 2012, with Arizona State continuing with the series to date.

The 2010–2011 competition received ten proposals and funded six Cohort B members:

- The Case Western Reserve University team (see Chapter 8), which proposed a longitudinal career development program for central Ohio
- The Oklahoma State University team (see Chapter 9), which proposed a workshop for the state of Oklahoma, and land-grant institutions in particular

- The Oregon State University team (see Chapter 10), which proposed a workshop for women in biology, ecology and earth system sciences, areas requiring fieldwork and public outreach
- The City Tech team (see Chapter 11), which proposed a regional New York City workshop for mathematics and computer science
- The Brookhaven National Lab—State University of New York Stonybrook team (see Chapter 12), which proposed a national laboratory approach in collaboration with a university
- The Temple University—Central Connecticut State University team (Chapter 13), which proposed to tend to the "lone wolves" (isolated women) of planetary sciences.

These Cohort B teams applied for funding in 2011 in response to a 2010 RFP; attended the 2011 national workshop in Washington, DC, where they received training; and developed their own workshops over the course of the following year, delivering their first workshop in 2012. Some of the teams delivered second workshops in 2013.

Although we had encouraged teams to include an administrator from their institution, only a handful of teams were able to do so: Pamela Brown was City Tech's dean of arts and sciences at the time of application, and is now associate provost; and Gertrude Fraser was University of Virginia's vice provost for faculty recruitment and retention at the time. Most teams were composed of women STEM professors, young and more experienced, though many early career women took on large responsibilities for the task. In some cases, these were graduate students and postdoctoral scientists. While a handful of men were mentioned in one of the proposals, as observers and trainers, we did not have any interactions with them. Three of the principal investigators were in the social sciences: Charlene Gilbert in women's studies at University of Toledo, Jean Van Delinder in sociology, and Gertrude Fraser in anthropology. Amanda Shaffer, Susan Freimark, both from Ohio State University, and Maggie Harden at University of Virginia are faculty development professionals.

Three of the projects benefited from previous experience with NSF ADVANCE projects at their institutions: Case Western, Ohio State, and Oklahoma State. Others had very little experience with the literature and trends of research and programs for women in STEM, but plenty of firsthand experience with the issues. These were dedicated women who were passionate about making a difference for their younger colleagues, as we were back in 1996. Some had already established good connections and resources, but most were inexperienced yet eager to learn and create a new structure to remedy a persistent problem that they seemed to understand quite well.

ELDers: Experts in Leadership Development

In order to inform our training program, in March 2010 we assembled a group of experts in leadership development (termed *ELDers*) for a 1-day workshop to synthesize best practices for women's faculty development and leadership development programs. The selection of groups invited was based in part on an effort to balance the diversity of target audiences by discipline, academic status (e.g., ELAM[3] targets senior academics), and ethnic or regional targets (e.g., MIT or Center of Excellence Women and Science (CEWS), Bonn, Germany). Leaders from each of ten groups were invited to attend a 1-day working meeting held at the Mount Vernon campus of GW, the purpose of which was to tease out some of the common themes and problems shared by all of most groups and review nonproprietary lessons learned. Each group's target audience and proprietary materials were judiciously respected. By meeting as a supragroup, networking among the groups was enhanced and provided a level of cooperation and information sharing. The schedule included:

- Pre-meeting sharing of biographies and group profiles
- Presentation of sample programs, processes, and audience profiles at the meeting
- Discussion of issues common to all groups, and what further research is needed
- Facilitated discussions on recruitment strategies
- Facilitated discussion on the needs and preferences of future faculty as seen by participant response in previous FORWARD workshops (the "face" of future faculty)
- Facilitated discussion on the best practices of mentoring
- Discussion of adaptation to the needs of a specific population or institution
- Discussion of personal growth and institutional change.

ELDer attendees were asked to become a mentor for one of the individual FWDers. As a mentor, they would provide support and guidance for the teams as they designed and developed their local workshops. Small honoraria were offered for that effort, and some travel support was available for mentors should they wish to observe the FWDers' workshops.

The recommendations that resulted from the ELDers meeting of 2010 are summarized in the training booklet that was distributed to the FWDers, as well as in Appendix L of this book.

[3]The list of ELDers who attended the 2010 meeting is included in Appendix L of this book.

The 2010 and 2011 Training Programs

The 2010 and 2011 training programs consisted of the following:

- Pre-workshop briefing and training (one half-day in duration) right before the start of the national model workshop
- In-workshop observation and support (two and a half days)
- Post-workshop debriefing (one half-day in duration) on the day following the end of the workshop
- Support in setting up their own workshops (i.e., year-long mentoring on an as-needed basis)
- On-site observation of their workshops and debrief (by one of us, the trainers, and Patricia Freitag, the evaluator)
- Debriefing at the April 2013 meeting and chapter writing (2013–2014).

The FWDer teams were permitted to send two trainees to the national model workshop and training session in Washington, DC. Travel funds were allotted for the trainees above and beyond their seed funding of up to $10,000 for their own workshops. It was interesting to note that not every team sent its principal investigator to the training session. In some cases, only one team member was able to attend. The composition and the leadership of the teams seemed to change from the proposal to final implementation and chapter-writing stages for some teams.

During the pre-workshop training and through the observation of the national model workshop, we offered the FWDers a model to adopt, adapt, or reinvent for their own purposes. What we perceived as the essential elements was offered as a structure from which to build their own implementations. These included the items described earlier in this chapter in the section "Workshop Goals and Design," with emphasis on a great keynoter to set the tone, active sessions, not too many "talking heads," unstructured time, changing the activities, keeping the workshop fresh (revising every year), one-on-one work with writing products, access to decision makers (program directors and academic administrators), a diversity in the composition of participant body and speaker body, and team composition.

The pre-workshop training included instruction on how to observe and analyze interactions, to interpret what the FWDers would be seeing at the workshop in terms of the participant experience, and how, as an organizer, to deliver that participant experience. Observer template sheets and participant interview questions and recording sheets were included in the training booklet for use during the workshop observation.

Finally, as the FWDers headed home after the national model workshop and debriefing, they took with them a sample timeline, budget, and budget justification in the training booklet. These materials are available in the appendices of this textbook.

Pay It FORWARD Results

Between 2011 and 2012, the ten FWDer teams launched their own workshops to great success. The descriptions and outcomes of these ten new formats of the "FORWARD to Professorship" workshop are described in Chapters 4–13. The MIT workshop, which started earlier in 2006 following our tailoring of the workshop to their needs in 2005, is described in Chapter 3. Chapter 17 also reports on these projects with a look at benefits to workshop organizers. Analysis of the entire project, with its training program and outcomes, is reserved for Chapters 20 and 21, and evaluation of the project is found in Chapter 18, so that readers may first hear from the FWDer teams and consider the creative set of different implementations that were organized and executed across the country.

Acknowledgments

Rachelle Heller and I wish to thank our original collaborators, Charlene Sorensen and H. David Snyder of Gallaudet University, for their hard work, creativity, and dedication to the FORWARD program. Many thanks also to Yell Inverso, our longtime graduate assistant, who contributed to the development of the program. The dedication of our undergraduate assistants, ASL interpreters, all our speakers, and participants was also much appreciated and contributed to the success of the program. The FWDer teams did an excellent job of prolonging the reach of our original efforts and we are grateful to them for this work. Thanks also to the ELDers, who provided timely advice and recommendations. Support from GW and GU is also gratefully acknowledged. Finally, we thank the NSF, NIH, and their respective program directors and proposal reviewers for funding this project.

References

Babcock, L., Laschever, S., 2003. Women Don't Ask: Negotiation and the Gender Divide. Princeton University Press, Princeton, NJ.

Becker, J.R., 1990. Graduate education in the mathematical sciences: factors influencing women and men. In: Burton, L. (Ed.), Gender and Mathematics: An International Perspective. Cassell Educational Limited, London, pp. 119–130.

Bennett, C., 2011. Beyond the leaky pipeline: consolidating understanding and incorporating new research about women's science careers in the UK. Bruss. Econ. Rev.—Cahiers Écon. Brux. 54 (2/3), 149–176.

Berryman, S.E., 1983. Who Will Do Science? Trends, and Their Causes in Minority and Female Representation Among Holders of Advanced Degrees in Science and Mathematics. A Special Report. Rockefeller Foundation, New York, NY.

Blickenstaff, J.C., 2005. Women and science careers: leaky pipeline or gender filter? Gend. Educ. 17 (4), 369–386.

Center for Research on Teaching and Learning (CRLT), 2014. Faculty Meeting— Navigating Departmental Politics. Available from: <http://www.crlt.umich.edu/crltplayers/faculty-meeting-navigating-departmental-politics> (accessed 17.01.15.).

Etzkowitz, H., Kemelgor, C., Neuschatz, M., Uzzi, B., Alonzo, J., 1994. The paradox of critical mass for women in science. Science. 266, 51–54.

Frontczak, S.M., 2015. Manya—The Living History of Marie Curie. Available from: <http://www.storysmith.org/manya/> (accessed 17.01.15.).

Goldsmith, B., 2005. Obsessive Genius: The Inner World of Marie Curie. W.W. Norton & Co., New York, NY.

Halber, D., 2005. Workshop offers guidance to help future female academics succeed, MIT Tech Talk, October 5.

Heller, R.S., Yassinskaya, N., Dam, K., Shaw, M., Beil, C., Mavriplis, C., et al., 2010. Mind the gap: women in stem career breaks. J. Technol. Manage. Innov. 5, 140–151.

Kemelgor, C., Etzkowitz, H., 2001. Overcoming Isolation: Women's Dilemmas in American Academic Science. Minerva: A Review of Science, Learning and Policy. 39, 239–257.

LaVaque-Manty, D., 2007. Transforming the scientific enterprise—an interview with Alice Hogan. In: Stewart, A.J., Malley, J.E., LaVaque-Manty, D. (Eds.), Transforming Science and Engineering: Advancing Academic Women. The University of Michigan Press, Ann Arbor, MI.

Maddox, B., 2002. Rosalind Franklin: The Dark Lady of DNA. Harper Collins, New York, NY.

Mason, M.A., Goulden, M., Frasch, K., 2009. Why graduate students reject the fast track. Academe. 95, 11–16.

Massachusetts Institute of Technology (MIT), 1999. A Study on the Status of Women Faculty in Science at MIT.

Massachusetts Institute of Technology (MIT), 2014. Path of Professorship. Available from: <http://odge.mit.edu/development/pop/> (accessed 02.03.15.).

Mavriplis, C., Beil, C., Dam, K., Heller, R.S., Sorensen, C., 2010. An analysis of the FORWARD to Professorship Workshop—what works to entice and prepare women for professorship? In: Godfroy-Genin, A.S. (Ed.), Women in Engineering and Technology Research: The PROMETEA Conference Proceedings, LIT Verlag, Berlin, pp. 443–460.

Mavriplis, C., Heller, R.S., Snyder, H.D., Sorensen, C.C., 2000. A walk on the moon: an interdisciplinary inquiry-based course. Proceedings of the WEPAN 2000 National Conference.

Morganson, V.J., Jones, M.P., Major, D.A., 2010. Understanding women's underrepresentation in science, technology, engineering, and mathematics: the role of social coping. Career Dev. Q. 59, 169–179.

National Academy of Sciences, 2015. Marian Koshland Museum. Available from: <https://www.koshland-science-museum.org/> (accessed 17.01.15.).

National Science Board, 2000. Science and Engineering Indicators. National Science Foundation, Arlington, VA (NSB-00-1).

National Science Foundation, 1995. NSF 95-113 NSF Visiting Professorships for Women Program Announcement. Available from: <http://www.nsf.gov/pubs/stis1995/nsf95113/nsf95113.txt> (accessed 18.11.14.).

National Science Foundation, 1996. Women, Minorities, and Persons with Disabilities in Science and Engineering. National Science Foundation, Arlington, VA (NSF-96-11).

National Science Foundation, 1998. Professional Opportunities for Women in Research and Education (POWRE) Program Announcement. Available from: <http://www.nsf.gov/pubs/1998/nsf98160/nsf98160.htm> (accessed 18.11.14.).

National Science Foundation, 2000. NSF 00-327. Women, Minorities and Persons with Disabilities in Science and Engineering. Arlington, TX.

National Science Foundation, 2001. NSF 01-69. NSF ADVANCE Program Solicitation. Increasing the Participation and Advancement of Women in Academic Science and Engineering Careers. Available from: <http://www.nsf.gov/pubs/2001/nsf0169/nsf0169.htm> (accessed 18.11.14.).

Sorcinelli, M.D., Austin, A.E. (Eds.), 1992. Developing New and Junior Faculty. Vol. 50 for New Directions for Teaching and Learning. Jossey Bass, San Francisco, CA.

Thomson, E.A., 2000. Study Points to Career/Family Concerns Among Women Engineering Faculty, Massachusetts Institute of Technology News Office. Available from: <http://newsoffice.mit.edu/2000/women-0329> (accessed 10.12.14.).

Valian, V., 1998. Why So Slow? The Advancement of Women. MIT Press, Cambridge, MA.

3

Path of Professorship: A Student Leadership Model for Catalyzing Change at MIT

Shannon Morey[1,2], Blanche Staton[1]
and Brad San Martin[1]
[1]Massachusetts Institute of Technology (MIT), Cambridge, MA, USA
[2]East Boston High School, Boston, MA, USA

OUTLINE

Origin and Goals	48
Successes and Outcomes	49
Impact on Attendees and Organizers	50
Workshop Sessions	54
An Institution-Centered Workshop	55
Graduate Students as Leaders	56
Institutional Leadership	57
Institutionalized Financial Support	57
Challenges and Responses	58
Revisions	59
Lessons Learned	60
Conclusion	61
References	61

ORIGIN AND GOALS

In 2004, a student at the Massachusetts Institute of Technology (MIT), funded by the Office of the Dean for Graduate Education (ODGE) and the National Science Foundation (NSF), attended the FORWARD to Professorship workshop in Washington, DC. Upon her return, she emphatically reported to the ODGE that, of all the events she had attended in her academic career thus far, this was the most illuminating and helpful one. Based on this student's enthusiasm, the ODGE asked the FORWARD to Professorship organizers to bring their workshop to MIT, which they did in 2005. The positive feedback from the attendees was overwhelming: "This information is hard to come by," wrote one attendee, "and women at MIT need it to be successful in academia."

Following the success of the 2005 program, MIT's ODGE decided to continue to host its own annual workshop beginning in 2006. Based on the FORWARD to Professorship model, Path of Professorship is a one-and-a-half day event serving MIT's female postdoctoral researchers and graduate students. Funded by the ODGE and the Office of the Vice President for Research, it features a group of panelists composed of approximately 27 female faculty, primarily from New England, with a few from elsewhere in the United States.

Path of Professorship aims to increase the influx of female science, technology, engineering, and mathematics (STEM) professors, as women are continually underrepresented in these fields (Durant, 2004). To provide support to female students in these disciplines, Path of Professorship raises awareness of both general challenges and those specific to women, as they search for a faculty position and enter the tenure process. Through carefully curated panel discussions focusing on a number of key issues, Path of Professorship speakers provide advice and personal stories illustrating ways to overcome or at least manage these challenges. Additionally, the workshop provides ample networking opportunities for attendees within their peer group and with panelists.

MIT's Path of Professorship is organized by a team of graduate students and postdoctoral researchers under the direction of the senior associate dean for graduate education. This organizational structure allows the workshop to cater specifically to the MIT community by providing a number of important resources tailored to the needs of MIT's graduate and postdoctoral women—and giving student organizers invaluable leadership experience.

SUCCESSES AND OUTCOMES

Since 2006, Path of Professorship has had a demonstrably positive effect on the lives and careers of the attendees, panelists, and planning team—and enriched the MIT community at large. As one of MIT's senior officers so graciously put it, "Path of Professorship is one of MIT's crown jewels." When MIT underwent review for accreditation from the New England Association of Schools and Colleges (NEASC) in 2009, the NEASC's resultant report specifically cited Path of Professorship as being a "particularly innovative" workshop for graduate student professional development. Path of Professorship was the only program of its kind to be mentioned. This acknowledgement from NEASC—based on the immediate and long-term impact that Path of Professorship has had on its attendees, panelists, and the MIT community—carries great weight at the institute, and has led to further funding and support from the administration.

Each year, the workshop's merits are first measured by feedback collected via written surveys, which are administered on site to attendees at the end of the workshop (thus leading to a nearly 100% response rate each year). The feedback form asks attendees to evaluate each session on criteria of usefulness, how relatable the speakers were, the relevance of the topics covered, and whether or not the session devoted enough time to the topics at hand. Since 2006, attendees have consistently rated each session—and the overall workshop—highly favorably. A representative selection of quotations from participants, drawn from surveys and correspondence received after the workshops, follows:

I attended the workshop last October, and it was the best experience I have had at MIT. The workshop gave me the confidence to interview, negotiate, and get a job offer. It is my sincere hope that this program will continue at MIT so that other graduate and postdoctoral women can enjoy the same support and positive community that I have had here.

The speakers in this workshop were all so great. It is even difficult to simply describe how inspiring it is for me when these great people I look up to shared their experience and wisdom of how they handle different problems in appropriate ways. It was also just very encouraging to find out that so many people are having similar struggles and questions and there are so many supports out there.

Thank you so much for organizing this wonderful workshop – 10 years of school and 2 years of postdoc brought me across a mere handful of role models, and then I came to Path of Professorship with more than 20 impressive female professors presenting their views. You cannot imagine what a big impact that had on my view of the field, and especially on how I might fit in.

This conference is unique and the experience I obtained is priceless. During this workshop, I had a chance to ask many questions and hear about the different routes

I can choose as a woman in academia. It prepared me for the interview process and gave me a very clear idea of what I should expect as a young faculty member... I wish there were more initiatives like the 'Path of Professorship' workshop that encouraged young researchers and helped them in their career path.

In addition to attendee satisfaction, Path of Professorship's impact on the MIT community can be further measured by the proliferation of events held at the institute that were inspired by feedback from Path of Professorship participants. These have included a conflict resolution workshop, dissertation writing skills workshop, presentation skills workshop, and focus groups with MIT graduate women's groups. Each event has had an estimated attendance of 40–50 students.

IMPACT ON ATTENDEES AND ORGANIZERS

The number of Path of Professorship participants that have obtained faculty positions has been tracked by utilizing online search information. Statistics for each cohort are shown in Table 3.1. It is important to remember that attendees in recent cohorts may still be at MIT or, if graduate students, have gone on to a postdoctoral researcher position at MIT or another institution. The number of attendees that are still in a student or postdoctoral researcher position is also shown in Table 3.1. A comparison of these results is shown in Figure 3.1.

In a 2012 survey of MIT alumni who have graduated in the last three years, 26% of women receiving doctoral degrees and 28% of men

TABLE 3.1   Current Career Status of Path of Professorship Attendees by Cohort Year, Compiled at the Close of 2012

Cohort year	Percentage of attendees in tenure-track positions	Percentage of attendees in other academic positions	Percentage of attendees in graduate student or postdoctoral student positions
2006	44	7	2
2007	27	7	15
2008	27	13	21
2009	24	11	24
2010	21	0	48
2011	2	2	83
2012	0	0	100

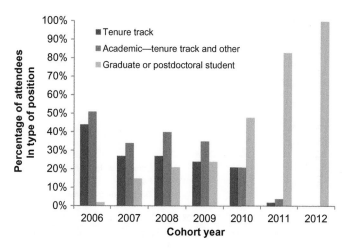

FIGURE 3.1 Comparison of the career status of Path of Professorship attendees by cohort year.

receiving doctoral degrees reported being faculty members. Graduate alumni 5, 10, 15, 20, and 25 years after graduation were also surveyed in 2012, and of the doctoral respondents, 33% of women and 35% of men reported being a college or university faculty member. Additionally, 36% of women and 41% of men reported having held a college or university tenure or tenure-track position since their degree. As the Path of Professorship cohorts continue to progress through their careers, we hope to see a continued increase in the number of female graduate students pursuing an academic career.

The number of women at MIT has also gradually increased in recent years. The number of women enrolled in doctoral programs, awarded doctoral degrees, and in faculty positions in the sciences and engineering are shown in Figures 3.2 and 3.3, respectively. As the number of role models and the community of women at MIT increases, we hope that this growing community will have a positive effect on the career paths of Path of Professorship attendees, and women at MIT generally.

In addition to the effect that Path of Professorship has on attendees, the program provides planning team members and panelists a unique opportunity for professional development outside of the research and lab environment (Bogle et al., 2010). The graduate and postdoctorate students on the planning team gain essential leadership and communication skills, learning to work in teams while growing their professional network with other students at the institute and the professors with whom they communicate. Equally as important, deep friendships have formed and evolved from the shared experience and mutual support nurtured while working together.

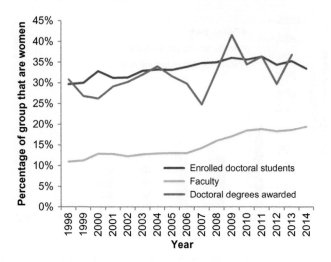

FIGURE 3.2   The number of women enrolled in science doctoral programs, awarded science doctoral degrees, and in science faculty positions at MIT.

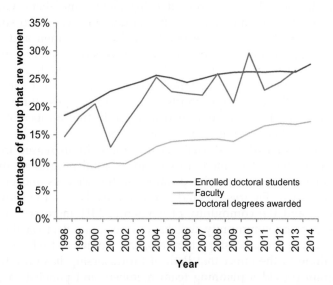

FIGURE 3.3   The number of women enrolled in engineering doctoral programs, awarded engineering doctoral degrees, and in engineering faculty positions at MIT.

When former planning team members were surveyed about their experience working on Path of Professorship, one of the most compelling themes to emerge was a newfound sense of confidence. Organizing the workshop strengthened the team members' desire to continue pursuing careers in academia. One respondent stated, "I haven't given up, when I might otherwise have done so." She also said that the "lasting imprint in my brain and heart [left by Path of Professorship] is one reason I haven't been part of the 'leaky pipeline' phenomenon." Another former planning team member, Sarah Bagby, also commented on how the workshop has inspired her to persevere when faced with challenging obstacles:

> It gave me strategies to cover so many situations, large and small (negotiating for a two-body solution; handling a difficult colleague; successfully attending a conference when you don't know anyone at the beginning), and the simple fact that these strategies can be taught is useful in itself: it's all too easy to tell yourself, when you encounter a situation you don't know how to navigate, that you just don't have what it takes to be successful. Nope. The failure is one of knowledge, not innate skill. You just need to sit down, maybe by yourself and maybe with a mentor or trusted colleague, and work out a strategy. And then you have it, and you can share it.

In addition to a sense of confidence, planning team members mentioned other skills they gained through organizing the workshop, including leadership, organizational, and mentorship skills. Sarah Bagby commented on how she has continued to use these mentorship lessons in her career:

> The planning process and the workshop itself encouraged me to think of myself as a potential mentor, and as a postdoc I have put a good bit of time into learning to mentor the graduate students in the lab. I think I've made a material difference in several students' graduate experiences. That's been very rewarding, and I think the practice will serve me (and, more importantly, my students) well when I become a professor.

The faculty invited to participate as panelists also find the workshop to be a rewarding experience. A valuable networking opportunity, it gives them the chance to interact with dozens of graduate women, post-doctoral students, and both present and future colleagues in academia. In the process, they also gain firsthand knowledge of students' questions and concerns, which helps them become better advisers and mentors.

Select recurring panelists were surveyed. Kristala Prather, an associate professor in chemical engineering at MIT, summarized the benefits to speakers and attendees:

> Path of Professorship provides "face time" with current women faculty, but also allows participants to network and build community with each other. The former can be mentors while supportive peer groups can be assembled from the latter. Both are critical. The information imparted also prompts many attendees to think about aspects of the path to a successful academic career that perhaps they did not previously consider.

Path of Professorship has now been a part of the MIT community long enough that past participants are returning as panelists. In a recent survey, these women stressed the benefits of Path of Professorship, both as an attendee and a panelist. Cara Stepp, currently an assistant professor at Boston University, summarized her experience by saying:

> As a student, I learned so many things it would be difficult to name them all. I didn't know how clueless I was about the process for obtaining an academic position or what it would be like to have that job until participating in the workshop. As a speaker, I've continued to understand where students are coming from by the questions that they ask, and to expand my own understanding of how women at other institutions interact with their universities.

Another attendee that has returned numerous times as a speaker, Professor Dora Carrico-Moniz of Wellesley College, explained why she keeps coming back:

> As a postdoc at MIT several years ago, I had the great opportunity to attend the Path of Professorship workshop. The workshop was so useful and meaningful to me that I was delighted when I was invited to be a speaker. As a college professor now, I am honored to be able to participate in this great workshop and be able to give back some of the wonderful advice I received.

Professor Carrico-Moniz also mentioned the lasting impact that Path of Professorship has had on her, and on how she has helped younger women in their career paths:

> I love meeting with attendees and offering my help. I have had several attendees who have contacted me after the workshop asking for feedback on their job applications, questions about funding or just some advice on how to decide between types of institutions. I am glad I was able to provide some sort of help to some talented women as they begin their academic careers.

WORKSHOP SESSIONS

Over the course of the workshop's one-and-a-half days, attendees participate in a number of sessions addressing issues facing women pursuing advancement in academia. These sessions deal with both personal and professional challenges, with topics including time management and work/life balance, choosing the right institution, building and maintaining professional networks, the application and interview processes, the criteria for promotion and tenure, and more.

One of the workshop sessions that attendees have found most intriguing is "Negotiating the Offer." This discussion explores the ins and outs of negotiating prior to accepting an academic position. This session has proven particularly useful not only for those who eventually enter academia, but for all women starting a career. In many cases, attendees remarked that it empowered them to negotiate—something that women are historically much less likely to do (Babcock and Laschever, 2003). Many are surprised to learn that negotiations can encompass more than just salary. Especially in academia, candidates can make their acceptance contingent on such additional benefits as space (office, classroom, or laboratory), classroom hours, summer schedules and salary, and even employment and research opportunities for spouses.

Each year, the last session of Path of Professorship focuses on delivering interesting, engaging presentations and how body language can be important in one's career. This session is often conducted by Nancy Houfek from the American Repertory Theatre at Harvard University, who uses her experience in the theater to instruct attendees on how best to use their voice and posture to be a compelling candidate during the interview process and aid them as they continue the academic career path. This advice can have a huge impact on attendees for years to come as indicated by a former attendee's experience:

> Years later I worked for a professor who...bullied people working under him.... He tried to intimidate me through verbal abuse and assuming physically threatening positions (puffing up and yelling while at the same time incidentally blocking the only exit from the room with his body). I was able to remember the lessons I was taught about how to use my height (and 3-inch heels on top of that), body language, conversational distance, and posture to my advantage. The next time he came at me in a rage, I simply stood up and asked him to repeat himself. I was taller than he was and standing close to him, so he had no choice but to look up, shrink, and mumble what his issue was. I solved it for him and he never tried that again with me!

AN INSTITUTION-CENTERED WORKSHOP

From its inception, Path of Professorship was specifically designed to meet the needs of MIT graduate students and postdoctoral researchers. Although the demand for this type of workshop extends well beyond the MIT community, having Path of Professorship be MIT-centered is a productive model that has continued to yield positive results. First, it allows for stable funding. As a crucial professional development initiative for community members, we are confident in the institute's continued support. In addition, there is no shortage of demand within the MIT community to fill the workshop. In fact, every year the program has been held, demand has far outstripped supply. While having the workshop open only to MIT students and postdoctoral researchers can limit the perspective of the attendees, the students and researchers come from a wide range of backgrounds and networks, allowing a great deal of stimulating discussion, ideas, and opinions. Furthermore, Path of Professorship has been very important in building relationships within the MIT community. Many of the students and postdoctoral associates involved would not have met each other were it not for this workshop, leading to friendships and professional collaborations that would not have been possible otherwise.

GRADUATE STUDENTS AS LEADERS

There are many skills that graduate and postdoctoral students need to succeed in the professional world, both in academia and elsewhere. Such skills extend beyond proficiency in research and lab environments to include the personal and the professional management capabilities necessary to lead projects in a multitude of contexts, the ability to work as part of a team, and the tools to be able to communicate effectively (Bogle et al., 2010). As Professor Stepp observed previously (see the section entitled "Impact on Attendees and Organizers," earlier in this chapter), these are difficult to develop amid the day-to-day work of a graduate student or postdoctoral student on a demanding academic schedule.

Path of Professorship offers its student organizers the opportunity to help cultivate a transferable skill set essential for the modern workplace. As mentioned previously, the workshop's planning team is led by two MIT Graduate Community Fellows (GCFs), who are advised by the senior associate dean for graduate education. The GCFs head a planning team of approximately five other MIT graduate students and postdoctoral researchers.

This model offers great rewards to both the administration and the student participants. GCFs are given the opportunity to undertake important leadership roles (Bogle et al., 2010) as they helm a planning team of their peers, interact with the institute's administration, and correspond with faculty from numerous institutions. In post-workshop surveys and correspondence, numerous planning team leaders have commented on the leadership skills and confidence they gained through their experience with Path of Professorship. Serving on the planning team also facilitates important networking opportunities for the students involved (Forret and Dougherty, 2004). The GCFs are the primary liaison for all of the invited panelists, allowing them to make connections within the MIT community, the greater New England area, and beyond.

Having graduate students lead the Path of Professorship planning also ensures that the workshop is organized by the community it is serving, allowing more direct insight into the needs and concerns of the workshop's student attendees. Trusting GCFs and graduate students with this responsibility has the added benefit of easing the responsibilities of MIT faculty and staff.

INSTITUTIONAL LEADERSHIP

The unwavering support of the Office of the Dean for Graduate Education, particularly the support of Senior Associate Dean Blanche Staton, has been one of the key components of Path of Professorship's continuing success. Dean Staton has led the Path of Professorship program from its infancy, and she continues to lend her guidance and expertise each year to the planning team, enabling them to grow both personally and professionally. Through her leadership, generations of planning teams have embraced her vision for greater representation of women in STEM fields and made it their own. By fostering relationships between the planning teams, attendees, and panelists, she has assured the success of Path of Professorship for many years to come. When planning team members were surveyed about their experience organizing Path of Professorship, they invariably commented on the importance of Dean Staton's guidance. One former planning team member, Sarah Bagby, described her leadership by saying:

> I don't know how Dean Staton did it, but she was the perfect mentor: she managed to give us the framework we needed and alert us to potential pitfalls, while still giving us ownership of the project.

INSTITUTIONALIZED FINANCIAL SUPPORT

The Path of Professorship workshop has grown into a vital program for MIT, and it receives support from the highest levels of the institute. The acknowledgment of the accreditation committee in 2009 was instrumental in garnering this support (see the section entitled "Successes and Outcomes," earlier in this chapter). Funding is provided by the Office of the Dean for Graduate Education (ODGE) and the Office of the Vice President for Research. The ODGE supports the graduate students attending the program, while the Office of the Vice President for Research provides funding for the postdoctoral associates.

Because it is supported solely through funds from MIT, the program is not forced to comply with any other requirements and can instead be designed to focus specifically on the needs of the students attending. Additionally, because the institute is funding the program, it is more committed to the success of Path of Professorship.

CHALLENGES AND RESPONSES

Path of Professorship organizers face numerous challenges. However, many of these can be overcome by careful planning, listening attentively to the community, and utilizing the many skills and resources of the planning team.

One issue that has been raised is the fact that Path of Professorship is open only to the MIT community. All of the planning team and attendees are either MIT students or postdoctoral researchers. This limits the perspective of the attendees, as their immediate experience is centered on the MIT environment. Also, attendance is open only to students in STEM fields, to the exclusion of other MIT disciplines (including humanities, economics, urban planning, etc.). Additionally, all of the planning team is from MIT, and their network consists mostly of people within the MIT community—making the identification of potential faculty presenters difficult. Unlike the FORWARD to Professorship workshop and other conferences, Path of Professorship does not foster exchanges with peers at local or nonlocal institutions.

With this issue in mind, the Path of Professorship team has opted to use the inherent limitations of the workshop to the advantage of the community, creating a program that is of tremendous relevance to MIT graduate students in STEM disciplines. By reviewing feedback and acting accordingly, the organizers have custom-fitted the material presented to the expressed needs of the attendees, giving them a uniquely local insight unavailable at more wide-ranging programs. Also, the proportion of presenters hailing from MIT rarely exceeds 50%, giving attendees a variety of perspectives from beyond the institute. The presence of postdoctoral students, many of whom have experience at universities other than MIT, helps to diversify the pool of attendees. They also often suggest presenters from other institutions.

Another difficulty encountered is the scarcity of time and labor. The ODGE is a small office with finite resources, and is already committed to a number of existing programs and initiatives. The Path of Professorship team therefore relies heavily on students, in the form of the aforementioned pair of paid GCFs and a planning team of approximately five members. As these students are engaged in a demanding research environment, not every student can attend every planning meeting. This is overcome via electronic communication (email, voicemail, text messaging, etc.) and careful structuring, ensuring that important developments are transmitted in a timely manner and responsibilities can be coordinated with a minimum of face-to-face contact.

Recruiting new student organizers in an active setting like MIT can prove challenging. At this point, however, Path of Professorship is well established on campus, and students are increasingly aware of the valuable opportunities for networking and professional growth that planning this workshop offers them. Also, the GCFs generally serve for two years: The first year, they assist senior team members; the second year, they assume a more senior role and mentor incoming teammates.

Although hosting the workshop on an annual basis is taxing on ODGE staff and student organizers, doing so gives Path of Professorship a stronger presence on campus and creates a continuous legacy as attendees ascend into new roles in academia. As the workshop's reputation has grown, applications have increased noticeably. In 2011 and 2012, there were two or more times as many applicants as openings available. However, limited resources—including time, venue availability, funding, and the identification of additional panelists—prevent the workshop from taking place more than once a year. Finite space and funding also prohibits the Path of Professorship workshop from lasting more than one-and-a-half days.

While attendees initially expressed the concern that being away from their duties for the duration of the workshop would have a negative impact on their research, over time it has become apparent to most that the opportunities presented by the workshop are worth the sacrifice. Conversely, a day and a half is still a very brief amount of time to convey a great deal of information, and the earliest Path of Professorship workshops found many sessions ending abruptly, with much material still to cover. This has been corrected by focusing less on time-consuming, hands-on work (editing of individual CVs, teaching statements, etc.) and more on panel discussions highlighting the presenters' experiences. The ODGE has also created separate events to address issues that cannot be covered during Path of Professorship due to time constraints (see the section entitled "Successes and Outcomes," earlier in this chapter).

REVISIONS

With every iteration of Path of Professorship, changes and improvements have been strongly influenced by prior attendee feedback and time limitations. Space prohibits listing every change made during the course of the workshop's seven-year history, but one of the most important revisions was moving the "Finding the Time to Do it All" session to the very beginning of the workshop, as students were asking questions pertaining to this topic during earlier sessions, taking time away from other valuable subjects. In addition, an entire session on funding was added to the workshop based on attendee feedback. The "Applying" session used to include time to edit application materials, with attendees required to do some work ahead of time. This session was shortened to a standard panel session in order to cover more topics. Furthermore, the final session, which focuses on presentations, has changed its emphasis from year to year.

Aside from changes to the program format, a $20 deposit became mandatory for attendees in order to discourage students from skipping the workshop after signing up. The deposit is returned upon receipt of an attendee's feedback forms, guaranteeing a nearly 100% response rate. The deposits have allowed us to keep attendance high and gain significant insight into the thoughts of our attendees.

LESSONS LEARNED

Certain sessions, particularly "Finding the Time to Do it All," bring out strong opinions in the panelists and attendees. Each year, a diverse group of panelists is gathered at the workshop, but even with over 20 different speakers, it is impossible to address every attendee's particular case. In some cases, panelists have thoughts or advice that some attendees do not agree with, which is mentioned in their feedback. However, the institute cannot control what panelists say; they are simply sharing their own experiences. It is also impossible to tailor the workshop to everyone. The planning teams have come to the realization that it is not beneficial to endlessly rework controversial sessions such as "Finding the Time to Do it All." This panel, which is concerned with striking a healthy balance between the personal and the professional, proves particularly challenging because participants invariability have different ideas of what constitutes a fulfilling personal life. For some, this includes children and a family; for others, it involves time to dedicate to other pursuits. Addressing everyone's unique experience and priorities is simply not possible.

The importance of collecting feedback from attendees after the workshop cannot be overstated. The time that is taken to fill them out and summarize the feedback significantly improves the quality of future events. In addition, the feedback provides ideas for other events conducted throughout the year.

Also, it has been discovered that having a planning team consisting of both postdoctoral and graduate women allows a greater diversity of experience and widens the available networks of the planning team, leading to a better event.

CONCLUSION

Following Path of Professorship's inception and first staging, Claude Canizares, then MIT's vice president for research and associate provost, expressed a willingness to increase the workshop's capacity (committing increased financial support), and, upon hearing that the program would be continued, wrote, "I am delighted that this is happening again...the program looks terrific." In a relatively short amount of time (especially considering the institute's vast history), Path of Professorship has established itself as a vital, dynamic workshop with a positive, far-reaching impact. It has done so by staying true to the two basic goals that first inspired its creation: first, to increase the number of women faculty members in STEM fields; and second, to serve the needs of MIT women graduate and postdoctoral students by offering guidance specifically suited to their unique challenges. By listening openly to feedback from panelists, attendees, and student planners while fostering an ever-growing network of students and professors, Path of Professorship has proven to be a valuable tool, capable of informing, enriching, and furthering the careers of all involved.

References

Babcock, L., Laschever, S., 2003. Women Don't Ask: Negotiation and the Gender Divide. Princeton University Press, Princeton, NJ.

Bogle, D., Dron, M., Eggermont, J., Willem van Henten, J., 2010. Doctoral degrees beyond 2010: training talented researchers for society. League of European Research Universities. http://www.grc.uzh.ch/coordinators/quality/LERU_beyond_2010.pdf.

Durant, E., 2004. Plugging the leaky pipeline. Available from: <http://www.technologyreview.com/article/403094/plugging-the-leaky-pipeline/>.

Forret, M.L., Dougherty, T.W., 2004. Networking behaviors and career outcomes: differences for men and women? J. Organ. Behav. 25, 419–437.

4

Jumpstarting STEM Careers

D. Page Baluch

School of Life Sciences, Arizona State University, Tempe, AZ, USA

OUTLINE

Introduction	63
Organizing a Team	65
Creating a Program	65
Jumpstarting STEM Careers Workshops and Symposiums	67
Forward to Professorship: Jumpstarting STEM Careers Workshop #1	67
Jumpstarting STEM Careers Workshop #2	69
JSC Symposium #1: Communication	71
JSC Symposium #2: The Business of Science	72
Moving Forward	73
Event Feedback	73
Concluding Remarks	75
Acknowledgments	75
References	75

INTRODUCTION

Many universities, including Arizona State University (ASU), have similar struggles in establishing equal representation in their professorship and administration for women within science, technology, engineering, and mathematics (STEM). Employers within institutions of higher education have improved their recruitment of women into academia, but in addition to increasing their representation, it is becoming important to provide career preparation so these women can help fill the predicted shortage of qualified professionals. New statistics from the US Department of Education report that only 16% of American high school seniors test at a proficient level in mathematics, placing the US ranking at 25% in the world for mathematics and 17% in science (Carnevale et al., 2010; Hanushek et al., 2011). To make matters more complex, a recent study by Georgetown University found that STEM field careers are the second-fastest-growing occupations (behind health care), and that by 2018, the nation is expected to have 8.6 million STEM jobs available, with 60% requiring skills possessed by only 20% of the workforce (Glenn, 2000; Beede et al., 2011). Over the last decade, the US government has invested $3 billion a year in 220 programs across 13 different agencies to improve the STEM education system in order to create a sustainable pipeline of trained professionals (Holdren, 2013). Utilizing this federal support, some of these groups have initiated programs to not only address the future shortage of STEM professionals, but also ensure that women are well represented in this workforce.

Most colleges and universities offer career training. A recent poll in the United Kingdom asked 8000 postdoctoral fellows questions about their preparation for a STEM career. The results revealed that 75% had been encouraged to engage in career training, but less than 20% actually took advantage of the programs offered at their institution (Pain, 2013). It is, in fact, not uncommon to see many campus organizations throughout the world host seminars or workshops in an effort to provide career training for STEM professionals. Many resources have been developed that describe how to create a career training seminar or workshop on popular topics such as funding, writing, or teaching (Macdonald et al., 2004; Mavriplis et al., 2005). When creating a program, it is important for new workshop organizers to research what is currently offered through their professional societies and at their institution. A workshop will attract more attendees if it enhances or takes a fresh approach to the efforts that are already underway.

Many of the chapters in this book will provide unique perspectives on how to create a practical workshop to address the needs of students pursuing an academic career. In 2010, an evaluation of female representation in STEM tenure-track positions at ASU identified that less than 20% of those who held the rank of full professor were women, especially in the fields of physics, mathematics, and engineering. Often referred to as the "leaky pipeline," studies have shown that while nearly half of STEM graduate degrees and early academic careers are held by women in the biological sciences, and as they advance in their careers, their numbers will sharply decline (Pell, 1996). Many believe that one way to correct this problem is to offer female STEM graduate students, postdoctoral researchers, and early faculty additional opportunities for career training. An added benefit to providing training is that these opportunities also bring together new and established STEM professionals to foster the formation of local networks, collaborations, and mentoring relationships (Gray and Drew, 2008). Individuals once isolated in departments can now connect with colleagues who might share similar struggles and obstacles.

ORGANIZING A TEAM

The Arizona team was one of the first five groups selected in 2010 as part of the Pay It FORWARD project to replicate the FORWARD to Professorship Workshop at ASU. This original team was comprised of a diverse mix of individuals who were all based at ASU. Having a contribution from individuals at various career levels proved to be very helpful in establishing a well-rounded program. Initially, the team included two tenure-track professors who were at the assistant and associate level, one research faculty, one departmental staff, and two graduate students. Over the years, the team has shifted and currently has one tenure-track faculty at the assistant professor level, one research faculty, one postdoctoral researcher, two graduate students, and two undergraduate students. Only two individuals remain from the original team. Why does this matter? After many years of hosting career-building events, experience shows that those who volunteer their time to help are usually seeking more training themselves to advance their own career. Individuals who are employment stable, satisfied with their positions, have supportive mentors, and a well-laid-out career path are less likely to volunteer time to organize events. With this in mind, it is best to determine if your workshop will be a one-time event or if the intent is to create an ongoing, yearly program. If the intent is to establish an ongoing program, then it will be important to also develop a succession plan or incorporate the event into a departmentally supported program that has dedicated staff coordinating the planning.

CREATING A PROGRAM

The program developed by the Arizona team was very similar to the FORWARD to Professorship model for the first 2 years, but was then modified to fit the needs of local attendees and projected budgeting support. Similar to the FORWARD program, the initial event was set up as a workshop and scheduled for two-and-a-half days, which would run Thursday through Saturday. The half-day activities were informal and intended to invite attendees to meet with speakers ahead of the workshop. Many local and national speakers were invited to present at the workshop, so additional time was allotted during the half-day so that a few speakers could give research-based seminar talks and interact with attendees during a dedicated luncheon. Because the workshop presentations were based on career development, the added opportunity allowed the speakers to share their research with attendees and interested faculty from the university. The next two full days were divided into multiple sessions, which focused on topics such as careers in STEM, teaching, research funding, writing, negotiation, lab management, and work/life balance. Each themed topic had multiple speakers and included some type of physical activity. Meals were catered on Friday and Saturday and included breakfast, lunch, an afternoon snack, and beverages that would be available throughout the day. A dinner buffet was provided on Friday night at a local restaurant that was within walking distance from the conference center. There were a few out-of-state attendees, but the majority were from Arizona, so housing accommodations were not an issue or budget concern. The Friday-night dinner became a great team-building event because it brought together people who were from various STEM fields who did not know one another, but were able to network and make new connections, as well as relax after the all-day event.

The first 2 years of the Arizona program were funded by the Pay It FORWARD grant, which enabled the Arizona team to host two full days (with catering) and to invite speakers from outside the region. Although there was a great selection of speakers to choose from within the university community, it was felt that potential attendees would be more committed to attend if well-known professionals from outside the community came to speak. It has been the experience of the Arizona team that seminar attendees see less value in a speaker who is a peer than someone who comes from outside their community. This can be achieved by inviting speakers from other departments, regional experts, as well as nationally and internationally known speakers and researchers. Because the target audience was primarily women in STEM, the organizers were committed to recruit mainly females as the primary and keynote speakers. To help identify these speakers, the team used speaker lists from professional societies who have committees whose focus is to provide programs and support to women in STEM. One of these groups, Women in Cell Biology, which belongs to the Association for Cell Biology, has a well-known speaker list that features female STEM professionals who are available as speakers for upcoming conferences and workshops (American Society for Cell Biology, 2014). This list is often used to recruit speakers for the Keystone, Gordon, and national society conferences.

JUMPSTARTING STEM CAREERS WORKSHOPS AND SYMPOSIUMS

Forward to Professorship: Jumpstarting STEM Careers Workshop #1

Using the FORWARD to Professorship model developed by the Pay It FORWARD team, the organizers at ASU developed a two-and-one-half-day workshop in 2011 geared toward graduate students, postdoctoral researchers, and early faculty to provide career training to increase the success of women, minorities, or those with disabilities seeking a career in STEM. This event featured more than 30 speakers from ASU and local colleges and businesses, in addition to speakers from other universities, federal agencies, industry, and STEM-based professional societies. Registered attendees were a diverse group of primarily graduate students and postdoctoral researchers from STEM departments at ASU (Figure 4.1). Because the event was widely advertised, it also attracted attendees from neighboring states and other Arizona-based colleges and universities. The event took roughly 6 months to plan and required a team of volunteers who utilized a successful timeline model to assemble all elements of the event (Figure 4.2). The workshop was divided into modules, covering topics such as careers in STEM, funding, teaching, and writing (Figure 4.3). These primary topic modules were divided into subcategories and paired with speaker panels and workshop activities. The module system was needed to break apart large generalized topics and ensure that the topic would apply to any STEM discipline.

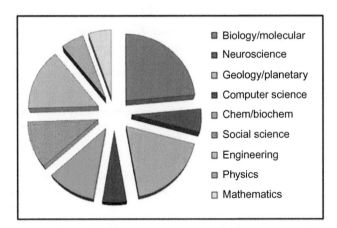

- Biology/molecular
- Neuroscience
- Geology/planetary
- Computer science
- Chem/biochem
- Social science
- Engineering
- Physics
- Mathematics

FIGURE 4.1   **STEM disciplines represented at ASU FORWARD to Professorship workshops.** The FORWARD to Professorship Workshop, The Jumpstarting Careers Workshop, and JSC symposium attracted participants across many disciplines.

**Top 10
Timeline Planning Tips**

1. Assemble a workshop team
2. Identify funding sources
3. Reserve venue(s)
4. Recruit/confirm speakers
5. Arrange catering
6. Plan workshop activities
7. Purchase workshop supplies
8. Host workshop
9. Send out thank yous
10. Conduct follow-up surveys

FIGURE 4.2   This list provides a useful timeline guide for creating a career-training workshop or symposium.

Workshop modules

Category	Subcategory
Careers in STEM	Academia, liberal arts colleges, industry
Teaching	Strategies, tools, techniques
Funding	University grant system, federal, foundation, private
Writing	Grants, applications, publications
Communication	Interviewing, negotiation
Lab management	Setting up a lab, mentoring
Work-life balance	Dual careers, family timing

FIGURE 4.3   **Workshop modules.** Many topics are typically covered during a multiday workshop. Dividing these topics into subcategories makes it easier to break up the material into multiple presentations and activities.

Much of the success of this event was due to the diverse set of speakers who gave presentations. The initial 2011 workshop was kicked off by the president of ASU, Michael Crow. Dr Crow is well known and respected throughout the country and is also a great motivational speaker. Having him start off the workshop provided instant credibility to the program and energized the attendees for the upcoming sessions. The event was enriched further by having Dr Elizabeth Gould, a leading neuroscientist known for her work in understanding the relationship between stress and adult neurogenesis, as the keynote, and Dr Joan Herber, president of the National Association for Women in Science (AWIS), as the concluding speaker. Another favorite speaker was Elizabeth Pennisi, reporter and editor from the journal *Science*, who worked in conjunction with Dr Duane Roen, assistant vice provost for university academic success programs and professor of English, to edit preassigned writing samples. Attendees were excited to hear about how the editing process is conducted at *Science* and to see examples of how complicated text can be transformed into an easily readable format for nonscientists. It is important that female speakers be included in your program. In addition to being successful STEM professionals, these speakers should be actively involved in helping women advance in their careers because it provides confidence and encouragement to other women who are just beginning their own journeys.

Each session included an activity component to break up the series of talks and encourage discussion among the participants. At each table was a faculty mentor who moderated the discussions and activities. The tables were organized so that fellow attendees would be at the same career level and would therefore have similar challenges and goals. Various exercises were used to diversify the program. These included activities such as discussions on assigned topics that were shared with the group; mock interviews, where participants played the role of both interviewer and interviewee; an open panel discussion; and team activities, where they evaluated one another's proposals or curriculum vitae. The personal development plan was an activity originated by the FORWARD team, which provided a multiquestion survey that asked the attendees to self-evaluate where they stood in their professional development, what their goals were, and what they planned to accomplish in the next year to achieve these goals. Two copies of the "1 year goals" section were made, such that the second copy could be mailed to the attendees a year later and they could reexamine the goals they had set for themselves.

Jumpstarting STEM Careers Workshop #2

In 2012, the workshop was offered again and renamed "Jumpstarting STEM Careers (JSC)" to embrace the diverse career opportunities available to STEM professionals. The general format was retained, but the workshop module topics were fine tuned in response to feedback from the first event. Strategies from the prior year that worked well were retained, and those with poor reviews were modified. For example, as already mentioned, one of the highlights of the 2011 workshop was *Science* reporter and editor Pennisi, who presented guidelines on how to write for a general audience. Due to the popularity of this presentation, the speaker and topic were retained in 2012. However, the module on teaching did not get as high reviews in 2011, so for the 2012 conference, the teaching module was modified to introduce the newest tools and trends for interactive teaching. In addition to updating the teaching module focus, the addition of interactive demonstrations increased audience participation and allowed attendees the opportunity to test-drive new educational tools. This example underscores the importance of sculpting content to meet the needs of the audience members. Another issue to consider is if the attendees equally represent many STEM disciplines, then the corresponding speakers and distribution of topics should match these more diverse interests. Likewise, organizers should recognize that funding opportunities might vary among disciplines, as well as startup package requirements. Taking this into account, the second workshop included a more diverse representation of granting agencies and potential funding opportunities.

For the 2012 JSC workshop, the organizers again recruited many nationally recognized speakers to help more fully develop the workshop and increase participation. The keynote was Dr Zena Werb, National Academy member and past president of the Association for Cell Biology, and the concluding speaker was Janet Koster, CEO of AWIS. Both provided inspirational talks to the attendees and participated in a student luncheon and seminar on the day prior to the workshop. Another item that had been requested from the first workshop was to provide information about alternate careers. Realizing that not all STEM graduates will acquire a tenure-track position, organizers included speakers who represented liberal arts and community colleges, as well as those who were from national laboratories such as the US Department of Agriculture (USDA). This session was very well received and has since influenced the decision to add similar seminars throughout the year that address alternate careers.

It can be challenging to keep attendees engaged during multiday events. The workshop format is useful because there is typically an interactive component that breaks up the sessions. Many of the more popular activities used in the first workshop, such as interactive mock interviews and discussion groups, were retained for the 2012 workshop, but the challenge remained to reduce the stress of participating in a multiday event. To help alleviate the physical fatigue that occurs after sitting for long periods of time, a stretching and breathing exercise was incorporated during the "Work/Life Balance" session. One of the table mentors was a yoga instructor who led a series of exercises to rejuvenate the group. To help attendees concentrate, pay attention, and retain the information presented during the funding opportunities presentation, the organizers incorporated a *Jeopardy!* game to test the participants' knowledge. Freely available online are Microsoft PowerPoint programs that can be loaded with various questions and answers to simulate the game show *Jeopardy!* Each table competed with the others on their knowledge of different grant programs and funding opportunities. Similar to year one, the final session ended with the preparation of a personal development plan, which received high reviews the previous year.

JSC Symposium #1: Communication

Going into the third year, the Arizona team had to reevaluate the program because workshop funding would no longer be available through the Pay It FORWARD grant, and competing career development programs were continuing to develop rapidly at the university. An unexpected development, partially caused by great reviews in the local press, was that many of the workshop topics were being used for seminars hosted by other organizations (i.e., Faculty Women's Association, Graduate and Professional Students Association, and Grad Student Clubs; Baluch, 2010, 2012, 2013; Coulombe, 2010, 2011; Grobmeier, 2012; Leander, 2013). Another challenge that became apparent after the 2012 workshop was that on campus, there is a limited population of graduate students and postdoctoral researchers that slowly turns over every few years. This meant that organizers would be working with a limited audience and the pool of potential attendees would be rapidly depleted if the full workshop were offered every year. Based on these reports, the team opted to change the workshop's format to focus on only one topic per year.

The first 2013 JSC topic-centric symposium was developed to focus on communication. The format began with an informal lunch and followed with presentations by three speakers. Realizing that the choice of speakers could make or break an event, a large amount of effort was invested in selecting top speakers that well represented the topic of communication for STEM. The final decision was to choose two faculty members from ASU and a well-known local expert who could speak about public communication. Dr Jess Alberts, from the Hugh Downs School of Human Communication at ASU, spoke about "Asking for What You Want"; and Dr Steve Neuberg, from the department of psychology, described "The Art of Persuasion" and how it can work for you. Although these speakers were local (both from ASU), they have a past history of great presentations and are frequently asked to speak on these topics by other professional groups. The "celebrity" speaker was Kari Lake, a news anchor at TV Fox 10, who explained how STEM professionals should communicate their science to people at a level that the general public could understand.

Attendance for the first JSC Symposium increased 60% over the previous year's workshop. This improvement can be attributed to many factors such as the shorter duration of the event; the quality of the speakers; speakers who were well-known public figures; the venue; or the program's reputation for hosting quality career-building events. It was assumed that a shorter event with excellent speakers would attract attendees, but including a well-known local celebrity also drew a lot of attention. The 2013 symposium venue changed from using a general university conference room to the ASU Biodesign Auditorium. The Biodesign building is well known in the research community within the Phoenix metro area and may have increased the event value merely by its prominence. Another potential factor that improved attendance is that the Arizona team had developed a reputation over the past 2 years so that they now had a following.

JSC Symposium #2: The Business of Science

The 2014 symposium was held using the half-day format that again concentrated on a specific theme: the business of science, a topic that is attracting a lot of interest. STEM professionals must realize that research laboratories are actually small businesses that require managing employees (trainees, technicians, and research associates), budgeting (lab expenses), establishing and maintaining income (grants), and producing a final product (papers and presentations). Without having the proper training to run a lab (small business), the long-term efficiency and research goals will be affected.

For the second year, there was again a big focus on recruiting excellent speakers who would attract a larger and more diverse crowd. Past events have shown that speakers from business or educational institutions other than ASU attract more attendees. This encouraged the team to expand their recruitment to include STEM professionals from the industry sector. The final speakers chosen were Tracy Lea, assistant VP of economic development and corporate engagement from SkySong, Scott Holman, senior human resources consultant from Intel, and Dr Jennifer Nahrgang, faculty from the ASU WP Carey School of Business. Their presentations were formatted to fit academic STEM professionals and provided guidance on topics ranging from how to develop a business plan to effectively managing employees.

MOVING FORWARD

The JSC program has become a successful yearly event and has built a reputation and gained support from ASU. Key factors that led to the success of this event are collaboration, research, communication, and financing. A major supporting mechanism that JSC has in its favor is that the event organizers all belong to the Central Arizona chapter of AWIS. AWIS Central Arizona hosts monthly career-building seminars throughout the year, which provides the symposium organizers with insight related to the needs and trends of students, faculty, and staff. This information allows organizers to focus on training topics that are current and in high demand. As a program becomes established, the network of contacts throughout STEM disciplines at both the local and regional level continues to develop. Communication is important in not only advertising an event, but also reporting its successes. After many years of hosting JSC, workshop organizers have found that the more people are aware of the benefits and quality of your event, the more likely you are to recruit top speakers, increase attendance, and receive sponsorship. The Arizona team has established an impressive network of contacts to recruit speakers and promote their annual event. In an effort to network at the national level, organizers also created posters to present at various scientific conferences to share their experience with others who might want to host a similar event at their institution or who may be interested in speaking at a future JSC workshop (Baluch et al., 2012, 2013; Cease et al., 2013; Sweazea et al., 2013). Sustainability is another major concern for anyone who hosts an event that includes catering, venue, and invited speaker expenses. The long-term success of a program depends on establishing financial support for your event. The 2014 symposium was sponsored by eBiosciences, a biochemical supply vendor. This was the first time that the JSC program was sponsored by a business rather than a grant or the university. Financial support is not the only benefit in sponsorship; it also implies that the business supports your training efforts to prepare the future workforce.

EVENT FEEDBACK

Feedback from an event can be collected in many forms. One of the most useful formats is the evaluation form that is provided at the conclusion of an event. This is helpful whether you have a 1-hour seminar or multiday event. Participant feedback from both the speakers and attendees will give insight into what attracted an individual, why the person stayed, and if he or she will come back. Hosting a workshop or symposium is a service-oriented event. If the customer (attendee) does not like the product (workshop/symposium), he or she will not come back and will not promote the event to colleagues, even if it is free. The evaluation form is one of the easiest ways to get feedback, but it requires that the organizer carefully compose a list of questions that take full advantage of this resource. Another useful way to get feedback is to randomly select individuals during an event and ask questions pertaining to the catering, speakers, venue, and content. This could be done verbally or as a follow-up email. Many believe that an honest response will be more likely if collected anonymously through a survey, but through past experience, the Arizona team has found that most STEM professionals are very open and direct about their opinions, so both methods work very well.

Evaluating the effectiveness of an event requires not only obtaining the immediate responses of recent attendees, but also following up with past attendees and organizers to determine how this training has affected their career development. An unfortunate component of the program is that the majority of attendees are in a transitional stage of their career and will likely move to the next level within a few years. This makes it difficult to follow up with those individuals in order to ask how the program had helped them prepare. Follow-up surveys with past attendees of the JSC program reported that all participants who responded had obtained careers in academia, national laboratories, or industry. Many of these past attendees and organizers have also sent additional comments and compliments with regard to the program. Dr Carolyn Weber, past attendee and now assistant professor at Idaho State University, credited her success to the "value in workshops like the NSF [National Science Foundation] ADVANCE program (JSC)." Many responses from our evaluations were similar to that made by Dr Karen Sweazea, assistant professor at ASU, who stated, "I really enjoyed the F2P (Forward to Professorship) workshop! The sessions were very helpful and offered practical advice for both trainees interested in pursuing an academic career as well as people already in a tenure-track position. I would encourage more of these events to help prepare trainees and early career investigators for academic careers." Geri Lamble, currently a research scientist at the Ames Research Center of the National Aeronautics and Space Administration (NASA), stated that "programs such as the JSC are critical to the success of women in STEM because they provide not only training, but the network and support of caring individuals." As the format changed to a half-day symposium, the feedback was again positive, indicating that this was especially helpful for postdoctoral researchers and lower-level faculty because it offered more specific information and guidance needed at this career level. As the event continues to move forward, feedback will be important to adjust the content and format because it is rare that one program type will fit the needs of all people.

CONCLUDING REMARKS

All professions require career development training, but this is especially necessary for those entering a STEM field. By 2020, there are expected to be increases as high as 62% in jobs such as bioengineering, which require a post-secondary education (Holdren, 2013). It should come as no surprise that entering a more technologically advanced age requires more advanced STEM training for those shaping this future. At the same time, it is also important to recognize the shifting demographics in our nation and to support diversity and the contributions of those presently underrepresented. The Arizona team is committed to providing training and mentorship to help ensure that women are well represented in the future STEM workforce.

Acknowledgments

The success of Jumpstarting STEM Careers is due to the contributions of many people. The first group of people that enabled the program to be established at Arizona State is the FORWARD team: Rachelle Heller, Catherine Mavriplis, Charlene Sorensen, Yell Inverso, Patricia Freitag, and Paul Sabila. Their encouragement and support not only initiated the program, but also has been a huge resource of advice and guidance. The next group of individuals who created the foundation of this program at ASU includes the original and newer organizers who have joined the team. These include Page Baluch, Valerie Stout, Karen Sweazea, Peggy Coulombe, Kirsten Traynor, Arianne Cease, Susan Holechek, Jennifer Glass, Sandra Leander, Karla Moeller, Melinda Weaver, Kim Pegram, Rebekah Brubaker, Elizabeth Nieves, Sandra Kavuma, Leanne Harris, Terri Hedgepeth, and Ashleigh Gonzales. Another critical set of individuals whom we must thank are all of the speakers who have volunteered their time to speak at one of our past JSC events. Lastly, we must thank our supporters at the university, which includes in kind and financial support from the School of Life Sciences, the Biodesign Institute, and the College of Liberal Arts and Sciences. It is through the contributions of many people that we have experienced the formation of a successful program, and we look forward to continuing this event for many years to come.

Special thanks go to Dr Karen Sweazea, assistant professor in the College of Nursing & Healthcare Innovation, and Peggy Coulombe, College of Liberal Arts and Sciences Director of Communications, for their consultation and review of this chapter.

References

American Society for Cell Biology, 2014. Women in Cell Biology Speaker Referral List. Available from: <http://www.ascb.org/wicb-speaker-referral-list/> (accessed 08.10.14).
Baluch, D.P., 2010. Looking for a few good women. AWIS Mag. 41 (3), 10–12.
Baluch, D.P., 2012. Moving forward with AWIS-Central Arizona. AWIS Mag. 43 (3), 45.
Baluch, D.P., 2013. AWIS-central Arizona heats up. AWIS Mag. 44 (2), 48.
Baluch, D.P., Traynor, K., Cease, A., Coulombe, M., Stout, V., Sweazea, K., 2012. Jumpstarting STEM careers. Mol. Biol. Cell. 23 (suppl), Abstract No. 985.

Baluch, D.P., Kavuma, S., Harris, L., Gonzales A., 2013. Career Training for Aspiring Neuroscientists. 23.13SA/MMM22.2013 Neuroscience Meeting Planner. Society for Neuroscience, San Diego, CA. [online].

Beede, D., Julian, T., Langdon, D., McKittrick, G., Khan, B., Doms, M., 2011. Women in STEM: a gender gap to innovation, Executive Summary. USDCESA. Available from: <http://www.esa.doc.gov/reports/women-stem-gender-gap-innovation> (accessed 08.10.14).

Carnevale, A.P., Smith, N., Strohl, J., 2010. Help Wanted; Projections of Jobs and Education Requirements Through 2018. Georgetown University's Center on Education and the Workforce. Available from: <http://survey.csuprojects.org/uploads/j-/ul/j-ul01tOShATFY88Kw3B7g/Georgetown-Center-on-Education-and-the-Workforce-jobs-projections.pdf> (accessed 08.10.14.).

Cease, A., Traynor, K., Coulombe, M., Stout, V., Sweazea, K., Baluch, D.P., 2013. Jumpstarting STEM Careers. Poster Presented at 2013 SICB Conference. 3–7 January, San Francisco, CA.

Coulombe, M., 2010. STEM workshop set to advance women, minorities. EurekAlert. Available from: <http://www.eurekalert.org/pub_releases/2010-12/asu-sws120810.php> (accessed 08.10.14).

Coulombe, M., 2011. Jumpstarting STEM Careers workshop provides training, support. ASU News. Available from: <https://asunews.asu.edu/20111114_jumpstartSTEM> (accessed 08.10.14).

Glenn, J., 2000. Before it's Too Late: A Report to the Nation from the National Commission on Mathematics and Science Teaching for the 21st century. US Department of Education. Available from: <http://www.weirdsciencekids.com/files/Before_It_s_Too_Late.pdf> (accessed 08.10.14.).

Gray, P., Drew, D.E., 2008. What They Didn't Teach in Graduate School: 199 Helpful Hints for Success in Your Academic Career. Stylus, Sterling, VA, p. 26.

Grobmeier, D., 2012. STEM Workshop Geared Toward Women. The State Press. Available from: <http://studentmedia-dev.jmc.asu.edu/2012/01/16/stem-workshop-geared-toward-women/> (accessed 08.10.14.).

Hanushek, E.A., Peterson, P.E., Woessmann, L., 2011. Teaching math to the talented. Education Next. Available from: <http://educationnext.org/teaching-math-to-the-talented/> (accessed 08.10.14.).

Holdren, J.P., 2013. Federal Science, Technology, Engineering, and Mathematics (STEM) Education 5-Year Strategic Plan. Committee on STEM Education, National Science and Technology Council. Available from: <http://www.whitehouse.gov/sites/default/files/microsites/ostp/stem_stratplan_2013.pdf> (accessed 08.10.14.).

Leander, S., 2013. Jumpstarting STEM Careers symposium supports women, minority students. ASU News. Available from: <https://asunews.asu.edu/20130125_STEMcareers> (accessed 08.10.14).

Macdonald, R., Manduca, C.A., Mogk, D.W., Tewksbury, B.J., 2004. On the Cutting Edge Professional Development Program: Workshop and Web Resources for Current and Future Geoscience Faculty. EOS Trans. AGU, Fall Meeting Supplement, Abstract ED23B-0095 85(47).

Mavriplis, C., Heller, R., Sorensen, C., Snyder, H.D., 2005. The 'FORWARD to Professorship' Workshop. Proceedings of the 2005 American Society for Engineering Education Annual Conference and Exposition, Portland, OR, pp. 6537–49.

Pain, E., 2013. A wake-up call for postdocs. Sci. Careers J. Sci. Available from: <http://sciencecareers.sciencemag.org/career_magazine/previous_issues/articles/2013_09_12/caredit.a1300197> (accessed 08.10.14).

Pell, A.N., 1996. Fixing the leaky pipeline: women scientists in academia. J. Anim. Sci. 74 (11), 2843–2848.

Sweazea, K., Baluch, D.P., Traynor, K., Cease, A., Coulombe, M., Stout, V., 2013. Jumpstarting STEM careers. FASEB J. 27, 740.1.

5

University of Guam: Advancing Female STEM Faculty in the Western Pacific

Helen Thompson

Career Interactive, London, UK

OUTLINE

Introduction	77
University of Guam Project	80
Project Evaluation—Successes	82
Project Evaluation—Challenges and Criticism	86
The Difficult Way Forward	87
References	89

INTRODUCTION

The objective of the University of Guam project "Advancing Female STEM Faculty in the Western Pacific" was to provide information, resources, and a network of support to junior female faculty in Science, Technology, Engineering, and Mathematics (STEM) fields across the Western Pacific region. The University of Guam team recruited 25 participants from the 2- and 4-year post-secondary institutions in the Western Pacific—College of Micronesia in the Federated States of

77

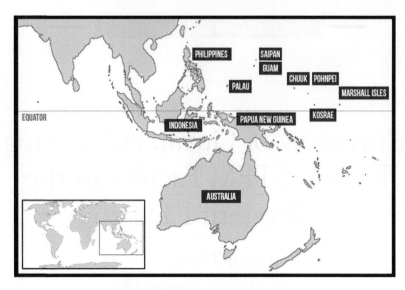

FIGURE 5.1   Map of the region of the Western Pacific.

Micronesia (Pohnpei, Kosrae, Yap, and Chuuk), Northern Marianas College in Saipan, Palau Community College, University of the South Pacific in the Marshall Islands, University of Guam, and Guam Community College—and gave them funding to come to Guam for an initial 2-day workshop and then continued the dialogue through an online forum (Figure 5.1).

Guam is a US unincorporated territory in the Western Pacific, and the Federated States of Micronesia (FSM) is connected to the United States via a Compact of Free Association (COFA). The population of this region consists of Asians and Pacific Islanders, an underserved minority population within the context of US demographics.[1] The campuses of these institutions are small, and early-career female faculty often find themselves heavily recruited into service work. These institutions also require large teaching loads, resulting in limited time for research and networking with other female faculty across the campuses. Most of the female faculty lack terminal degrees, because in order to earn a PhD, students have to leave their island homes and travel to the United States, Australia, or New Zealand. Given women's roles in Pacific Island cultures, relocating for educational purposes is much more of a challenge for women than for men.

[1]Pacific Islanders constitute a complex demographic group and are the dominant population on their respective islands. They are only a minority population when factored into US demographics.

Recent research by the American Association of University Women (AAUW) in their publication *Why So Few?* (Hill et al., 2010, p. 17) suggests that women's participation in STEM careers has improved over time but varies considerably by field. More women are seeking doctorates in biology, for example, than in physics and math. The research report also points out that "the climate of science and engineering departments is closely related to satisfaction of female faculty and that providing effective mentoring and work-life policies can help improve job satisfaction and, hence, the retention of female STEM faculty." Some of the most significant reasons that women are not progressing in academic careers in the STEM fields are that they do not receive the kind of encouragement that they need, they are not exposed to successful female role models, and, once in the field, they feel isolated and outnumbered.

While a useful benchmark for understanding the barriers that women on the US mainland face when pursuing careers in STEM, this study does not provide a complete picture of women living in the Pacific, who belong to cultures where women's work extends beyond the limits of the Western nuclear family and who sometimes have to negotiate their roles in ways that are far more challenging.

Within the Western Pacific region, women are keepers of the extended family, the predominant kinship system. Family name and filial connections to others provide the foundation of Pacific island cultures; if a person has no family, he/she has no power and no social position. This means that women are less likely to enter STEM fields because of the demands of research that would often take them away from the many family obligations that they are expected to honor. For example, women are expected to care for elderly family members whether they are working, studying, or both. While traditionally, many Pacific island cultures were matrilineal, and women still are respected as important keepers of land and family, the influence of Western cultures through colonization has changed the dynamic such that women are expected to work as well as maintain the family network. Gender socialization and family obligations create a significant stumbling block for women who want to sustain an academic career in STEM. Additionally, these family obligations can make it difficult for women to progress within their careers, as they try to negotiate work demands that go beyond regular business hours, such as caregiving in their own and extended families.

Within some Pacific Island traditions, such as Chuukese culture, women and men are separated as much as possible in order to protect the sanctity of family from the incest taboo. According to Moral (1998), Chuukese women, when in the presence of men, may not speak and draw attention to themselves because of potentially creating sexual tension in the group. Hence, their communication methods must be circuitous and carefully orchestrated. These kinds of interactions do not work in the male-dominated STEM workplace, so women who follow these traditional cultural practices are essentially barred from following a STEM career path. Workplace conflicts, ranging from simple disagreements to sexual harassment, become real obstacles for Pacific island women to deal with because of the gendered communication barrier in place. Also, within Pacific cultures, those with seniority (usually men) are to be respected and not challenged. Given that island communities are small and personal and professional affiliations are blurred, thus significantly reducing the possibility of privacy at work and at home, women's actions can be scrutinized more stringently. Therefore, female workers within male-dominated workplaces must behave themselves and not complain if their male counterparts do not follow suit.

The Pacific is often considered an "amorphous, homogenous entity," according to Berno and Jones (2001, p. 93), rather than a plethora of distinct cultures across the different island nations. While Westerners often have little concrete knowledge of this geographic region, they are not, according to White and Adinkrah (2007, p. 93) "devoid of any content;" instead, perceptions of the Pacific are infused with mythical impressions of a tropical paradise, and therefore a retreat from the complexities of modern life. Pacific Island women bear the brunt of this representation because, like the landscape, they are seen as exotic, beautiful, and inviting. With grass skirts and coconut bras highlighting their voluptuous figures, presented for the specific pleasure of the male gaze, Pacific island women are an important part of the alluring image of the tropics. Schellhorn (cited in Berno and Jones (2001) p. 96) describes how "Women of the South Pacific have been employed as 'geographical markers' in the task of creating and maintaining tourist motivations to visit the South Pacific Islands." They also endorse a history of mythic constructions of the Pacific islands, from the early "discoverers" through contemporary popular media. In this scenario, women are premodern, willing and available, exotic, and valued for their physical appearance. These women, adorned with flowers and sarongs, do not have complex lives and are not scientists.

UNIVERSITY OF GUAM PROJECT

"Advancing Female STEM Faculty in the Western Pacific" was designed with these specific barriers in mind. Our interventions were designed to facilitate discussion of the challenges of family and community facing Pacific island women progressing in STEM. Not only did we aim to bring women together from across the region to offer a supportive network and community that would empower them to strengthen their credentials, but also we wanted to make gender concerns more visible on their campuses. Hence, our workshop offered the opportunity to improve upon the climates of our science programs by empowering female faculty and sustaining the support of administrators, faculty governance, and the union to recognize and eliminate gender bias in these programs. With the kinds of support that the workshop and mentoring provided, we hoped that current female faculty would be more likely to achieve seniority, and their visibility would empower their female students to embark on careers in STEM.

In order to fully support our participants, we designed the workshop around the following outcomes:

Upon completion of the 2-day workshop series, participants will have successfully:

- Networked with other female STEM faculty from Western Pacific institutions of higher education
- Comprehended the particular challenges faced by fellow female STEM faculty
- Developed strategies for overcoming the particular challenges faced by female STEM faculty
- Prepared plans for advancement in their particular institution in the areas of instruction, research, and service where relevant
- Devised methods for a healthy balance of personal and professional responsibilities
- Prepared themselves for constructive professional relationships with colleagues and administrators.

The University of Guam is the only 4-year tertiary institution in the Western Pacific, and it has strong STEM programs.[2] We therefore felt perfectly situated to influence the recruitment and promotion of future indigenous female faculty in Pacific institutions of higher learning. With typically limited resources to support female faculty in STEM fields in this region, the participants' home institutions are unable to offer gender-specific guidance and mentoring toward seniority; therefore, the workshop we designed was a benchmark not just for female STEM faculty, but also for supporting female faculty in other academic fields.

Since the individual programs at the University of Guam are typically small, cross-disciplinary collaboration was important for the success of our project. The workshop team was diverse in terms of disciplines, ethnicity, and seniority. Such a mix provided a richness of experience since all of us brought something unique to the project.

[2]The university supports the NIH Rise Program, Western Pacific Tropical Research Center, Guam Aquaculture Development Training Center, Marine Laboratory, Water and Environmental Research Institute of the Western Pacific (WERI), Cooperative Extension Services, and the Planetarium.

Our team consisted of administrators, research faculty, and teaching faculty from a variety of STEM and non-STEM disciplines. Our team also represented faculty at different stages in their careers and from different nationalities and cultures. Importantly, our project was supported by the upper university administration, with the chair of the Faculty Senate and the senior vice president of academic and student affairs serving on the organizing committee.

This workshop extended another project being directed by two management team members, Andrea Hartig and Helen Thompson, on encouraging girls in middle and high school and women in college to study STEM subjects. Funded by two separate grants from the AAUW,[3] a student-based team created a 45-min film, *Portrait of a Scientist as a Young Girl*, based on interviews with female scientists at the University of Guam and women working in STEM fields in Guam. The student team also wrote creative vignettes to tackle some of the misconceptions about girls entering STEM. The project was funded for another year and ran in conjunction with the faculty workshop project. For the planned second-year project, the team of students created an evening event to promote girls' participation in STEM subjects.

PROJECT EVALUATION—SUCCESSES

While the project implementation faced the challenge of recruiting faculty from programs across the University of Guam campus from both non-STEM and STEM departments, the diversity of the management team actually became one of the strengths of the project. The project had more visibility because of the wide reach of the organizers, and the team was able to draw upon the resources of multiple colleges in order to make the project viable. For example, additional support was generated from the dean of the College of Natural and Applied Sciences, the dean of the College of Liberal Arts and Social Sciences, the dean of the School of Education, and the senior vice president's office. This kind of cross-disciplinary support created opportunities for faculty and administrators to find common ground and develop productive relationships that went beyond our typical roles within the university infrastructure. Instead of competing with faculty in other colleges for limited resources, or commiserating when administrators are forced to chip away at those resources, we bridged the gap and

[3]Namely, these were 2010 and 2011 AAUW Campus Action Project Grants, each for $5000. In 2010, the grant was awarded for making the film *Portrait of a Scientist as a Young Woman*; in 2011, the grant funded an evening event for girls, parents, and teachers to support girls' STEM studies.

worked together for the success of the project. In addition, we gained knowledge of how different members of the university community work within our infrastructure. These insights helped to develop allegiances across the divisions of discipline and job function.

We also received support from the neighboring Guam Community College, as well as the administrations of all of our participant institutions. Participants were allowed administrative leave to attend the workshops—a significant commitment given the heavy teaching load of the participants and the difficulties of finding substitute faculty. Also, the interinstitutional support was significant given the sometimes competitive relationships between the 2-year Pacific institutions and the University of Guam that tend to inhibit collaboration. In fact, a network of contacts was developed within the faculty and administration of the tertiary institutions in the Western Pacific region—a formidable accomplishment given the distance between the islands and the difficulties in maintaining effective communication.

The workshop also became a model for the dean of the College of Liberal Arts and Social Sciences, who expressed interest in using the workshops as a model for all new faculty orientation. The system of providing resources to new faculty during the first weeks of the semester had been criticized for being more informative and less supportive, leaving new faculty feeling overwhelmed and without effective mentoring. The dean believed that the workshop structure established for the female STEM faculty could be a useful model for all faculty, regardless of discipline or gender.

As a result of the workshops focusing on female junior faculty in 2012, the senior vice president for academic and student affairs established a Women's Leadership Initiative (WLI). The WLI was described as a project "designed to assist in... mentoring, encouraging, supporting, and tracking the careers of women (all women employees) at the University of Guam. This is meant to provide a forum to discuss issues specific to women at the University of Guam and to help find solutions."[4] The initiative offered support to all female faculty and staff at the University of Guam.

Participant responses also suggest that the workshop was effective in a variety of ways. The management team provided pre- and post-questionnaires evaluating the general effectiveness of the workshop. Out of 12 respondents (from a total of 25 attendees to the final evaluation of the workshop process), 50% found the workshops "very useful"; and 100% found the workshops between "very useful" and "somewhat useful." The feedback also indicated that 100% of respondents ($n = 12$) answered "yes" to the question, "Have you met someone at the

[4]Email communication, February 27, 2012.

workshops from a different institution with whom you plan to stay in touch?" Out of 12 respondents, 11 answered "yes" to the question, "Are you interested in participating in an online forum at www.academia.edu with other participants from the workshops?" One respondent self-reported that she is going to create a women's group for women in higher education at her institution and planned to ask for the support of her dean.

The project's effectiveness can also be gauged through assessment of the project outcomes.

Networked with Female STEM Faculty in the Western Pacific

In addition to the results already reported, feedback confirmed that the contacts made during the campus tour indicate that the workshops have facilitated a continuing network of STEM faculty within the region.

Comprehended the Particular Challenges Faced by Female STEM Faculty

Dr Rachelle Heller's initial presentation and the sessions on balancing work and family and service without overcommitment offered workshop participants an understanding of the experiences of women in STEM. This presentation presented the participants with new experiences, as well as validating their own particular circumstances through the kinship they felt with the stories of the women who had family obligations and had difficulty turning down service work. However, the participants did not have sufficient opportunity to discuss their own unique circumstances, and they sometimes felt alienated by the constant listening to speakers rather than dialoguing informally.

Developed Strategies for Overcoming the Particular Challenges Faced by Female STEM Faculty

Comments from the overall workshop evaluation indicate that many participants felt emancipated from aiming for perfection and taking on too many tasks. They found the panel on "Service Without Overcommitment" (see Appendix C for program elements) particularly empowering because they recognized that they were not alone in this struggle, and that there are ways out of this kind of overcommitment.

Prepared Plans for Advancement in Their Particular Institution in the Areas of Instruction, Research, and Service Where Relevant

Some participants recognized the need for a career plan, something they had not previously considered. The "Personalized Plan" segment of the workshops helped participants focus on their particular needs, and it was specifically mentioned in the overall evaluation as one area that helped them think about their own futures and shaped them with the planning advice offered by the grant team and the group of participants. However, the overall feeling was that more time should have been accorded to this portion of the workshop because the hands-on experience was limited to just one session, which was not sufficient.

Devised Methods for a Healthy Balance of Personal and Professional Responsibilities

Interestingly, many of the strategies cited by workshop participants concerning the balance of family and work life came from the panel "Service Without Overcommitment," rather than "Having It All—Balancing Work and Family." When participants were asked what strategies they found helpful in balancing work and family life, they cited the importance of saying "no," creating time for themselves, recognizing that perfection is not necessary all the time, and choosing service commitments.

Prepared Themselves for Constructive Professional Relationships with Colleagues and Administrators

When asked about strategies for better engaging with colleagues and administrators, many participants drew upon the philosophical strategies offered by Dr James Sellmann in his presentation on effective communication. Some of the strategies cited were: learning the art of negotiation, active listening, and differentiating between long- and short-term goals in order to compromise.

In addition to the overall assessment, each workshop session was evaluated by the management team, which was able to track the effectiveness of each session, as well as the workshop experience as a whole, with pre- and post-questionnaires. Participants appreciated a variety of sessions, as demonstrated by the following responses:

- "Dr Heller gave a great and inspiring presentation. Women have come a long way to where they are in terms of obtaining careers they want; however, we still have few representatives in STEM fields. Dr Heller gave some great tips in terms of how to get into the field." (Keynote Presentation)
- "We should have more presentations/workshops like this! Very true and interesting! I wish we had an all-day session with Dr Nabobo-Basa." (Culturally Sensitive Teaching Strategies)
- "Good facilities. It would be great if other campuses could collaborate with University of Guam (UOG) to have their students sent here for a week or even longer to get a chance to work with other students and faculty (get exposed to the technologies UOG has)." (Campus Tour)
- "Picked up some useful tips on grant writing." (Research)
- "All of the stories told by each panelist were interesting—can relate to my own experience—kids, husband, work, and service—best advice, learn to say "no" and no one is perfect—also learn to let go and it is okay." (Service Without Overcommitment)
- "This I was looking forward to the most, as it is the area where I need the most work. I am good at influencing others, but a horrible, Horrible, HORRIBLE active listener. And though I am good at

influencing others, I am not always happy with my approach or tactics in this regard." (Effective Communication)

After 2 days of working together in the workshop, participants left with a 1-year membership in the Association for Women in Science, a thumb drive containing articles and resources relating to women in STEM fields, and a copy of *Becoming Leaders: A Practical Handbook for Women in Engineering, Science, and Technology* (Williams and Emerson, 2008). The participants also received instructions on joining www.academia.edu to create a forum for continuing support.

PROJECT EVALUATION— CHALLENGES AND CRITICISM

While the project enjoyed a great deal of success, there were areas where the workshop could have been more useful to the participants. Despite the brief that they were given by the management team, some of the presenters focused only on procedures at the University of Guam; they did not consider differences at other institutions. While academic environments share many similarities, they are also quite different, especially if they are not 4-year institutions. The team had not anticipated the difficulty of translating experience from one institution into more general advice. The workshop sessions would have been more effective had we drawn upon presenters from different institutions to provide information that is more diverse to a group who had diverse needs. Indeed, some of the sessions were less valuable to participants because of different requirements at their home institutions and the status of their employment. For example, most of the participants were mostly evaluated on their teaching, and less so on research. They had little need to write large, multiyear grant proposals and, even if they had the desire, they had limited means because of the size of the institution. Similarly, most of the participants did not have a terminal degree but were looking for ways to fund a PhD program. We did not provide this kind of advice because of grant restrictions, so we could not offer them the help they most needed.

One of the most prevalent criticisms was that the workshops did not give participants enough opportunities to interact. Participants felt bombarded with information and not given enough sessions in which to process what they had heard. The workshop would have benefited from a different structure whereby on the second day, when participants were getting to know each other better, they had the opportunity to talk rather than just to listen. The participants would have benefited greatly from a third day where no presentations took place and they got a chance to talk to each other and brainstorm their future plans and current challenges. As one participant said on the evaluation sheet, "A must-have—a meeting of each other and sharing of our experiences—was missing."

Beyond talking to each other, some participants wanted hands-on sessions where they created and revised documents such as a teaching statement or course syllabus. Also, in areas such as technology in the classroom, some participants called for breakout sessions where demonstrations of these strategies could take place, and they could practice and develop these ideas under the guidance of the workshop conveners. It was suggested that if participants had copies of the handouts and Microsoft PowerPoint presentations before they arrived, they could have been better prepared, and the management team could have found more time in the schedule for interactive sessions in which participants produced their own documents.

Some participants pointed out that they had limited access to technology on their campuses, making the use of technology in the classroom less effective. Also, with power outages and slow Internet connections (if they even existed) due to less developed infrastructure in the Pacific, electronic communication after the workshop would be difficult for some participants. Hence, our plan to maintain an electronic forum for future communications was not a realistic plan for all attendees.

A favorite session of many of the participants, "Culturally Sensitive Teaching Strategies," was also controversial. Some participants pointed out that the viewpoint on what was culturally sensitive did not represent all women at the workshops, and some felt the focus was too much on "traditional" roles for women. Hence, a need was identified for more diverse understandings of what "culture" means for women in the Pacific, and that in choosing an education specialist from Melanesia, we were not considering the variety of approaches to culture in Micronesia, the area where our participants lived and worked. Also, some participants wanted the culturally sensitive approach to address not just STEM content in the classroom, but also how to interact in meaningful ways with Pacific Island students.

THE DIFFICULT WAY FORWARD

Perhaps the most challenging aspect of this project has been its sustainability. The 2-day workshop was organized with minimal logistic support and with a small group of dedicated faculty who also had full-time teaching and research obligations, as well as families—in essence, the same barriers to professional development that the workshop participants faced. The work was relentless and rewarding to the management committee, but it was unsustainable over the long term. The management committee had hoped to take the workshops in the second year to the College of Micronesia in Pohnpei and to create more interactive sessions in response to participant feedback. However, after the first-year project concluded, the team was not able, given a myriad of additional commitments, to follow up and provide a second year of support. Hence, "Advancing Female STEM Faculty in the Western Pacific," despite its promise, was not sustainable, like so many needed projects for women that are funded on small grants.

A revised version of the management team did write a proposal for an opportunity to compete for naval grant funds on STEM. For the Sponsoring Scholars in Science Funding Initiative, through the Office of Naval Research, the team designed a STEM Advocacy Kit. The core of the proposal was to design and deliver a seminar (online and *in situ*) on scientific, empirical research skills for university and community college faculty and middle and high school teachers in STEM fields and STEM-related social studies in the Western Pacific region. Throughout the yearlong seminar, participants would enrich their research skills and knowledge, practice them, and apply these skills within their unique cultural environments to the development of scientific activities and learning experiences for their students. Ultimately, they would be able to share these experiences via a website and handbooks created as part of the kit. We proposed that at the conclusion of the project, the Western Pacific STEM Advocacy Kit would include an updated version of the AAUW-funded STEM film, *Portrait of a Scientist as a Young Girl*, including segments on STEM career opportunities and effective teaching strategies for classrooms of Pacific Island boys and girls, an interactive website, a series of learning experiences focused on STEM fields that are culturally and gender appropriate, and a specialized handbook created by the grant team for distribution throughout the region. The need for culturally and gender appropriate learning materials in regional schools—including both pedagogy and content—is significant. Additionally, the network of STEM professionals would continue to work together through these media to promote and sustain the development of girls and women in STEM fields across the region.

Unfortunately, the University of Guam team was not successful in securing naval funding, and the team members moved on to different responsibilities, some of which took us to other paid positions, further ensuring the difficulty of sustaining this worthwhile project.[5] In small

---

[5]As of August 2013, only three of the original seven members of the management team still live and work in Guam. The rest have relocated to the US mainland, Hawaii, Australia, and the United Kingdom.

island institutions such as the University of Guam, burnout rates are high, and faculty turnover is a regular fact of life. Leaving island is not like moving to another state, so continued collaboration rarely happens because of geographic restrictions.

Yet, the project designed to support island women in STEM disciplines can be replicated in Pacific institutions and adapted for the needs of minority women in the diverse communities on the US mainland and beyond. The second year of this project could take place in Fiji or Fresno, and with modifications, offer a different group of women support and strategies for advancement in STEM work at their institutions.

References

Berno, T., Jones, T., 2001. Power, women and tourism development in the South Pacific. In: Somnez, S., Timothy, D.J., Astolopoulous, Y. (Eds.), Women as Producers and Consumers of Tourism in Developing Regions. Praeger, Santa Barbara, CA, pp. 93–119.

Hill, C., Corbett, C., St. Rose, A., 2010. Why So Few? Women in Science, Technology, Engineering and Mathematics. AAUW, Washington, DC.

Moral, B., 1998. Changes in women's status in Micronesia: an anthropological approach. In: Vinding, D. (Ed.), Indigenous Women. The Right to a Voice. IWGIA, Copenhagen, pp. 65–74.

White, C., Adinkrah, M., 2007. Mythical realities: college students' constructions of the South Pacific. Coll. Stud. J. 41 (1), 99–111.

Williams, F.M., Emerson, C.J. (Eds.), 2008. Becoming Leaders: A Practical Handbook for Women in Engineering, Science, and Technology. ASME Press.

6

When and Where I Enter...A FORWARD to Professorship Workshop

Lesley Berhan[1], Amanda Bryant-Friedrich[2], Nancy Collins[3], Isabel C. Escobar[4], Charlene Gilbert[5] and Cyndee Gruden[6]

[1]Department of Mechanical, Industrial, and Manufacturing Engineering, The University of Toledo, Toledo, OH, USA [2]Department of Medicinal and Biological Chemistry and Chemistry, The University of Toledo, Toledo, OH, USA [3]Department of Medicine, The University of Toledo, Toledo, OH, USA [4]Department of Chemical and Materials Engineering, The University of Kentucky, Lexington, KY, USA [5]Department of Women's and Gender Studies, The University of Toledo, Toledo, OH, USA [6]Department of Civil Engineering, The University of Toledo, Toledo, OH, USA

OUTLINE

Introduction	92
Goals	93
Description	94
Organizing Committee	94
Attendee Application and Profiles	94
Opening Dinner	94
Day 1	95
Planning and Funding Research	95
Writing in the Profession	95

Lunch   96
Dinner   96
Day 2   96
Funding   97

Challenges   97
  Organizational Challenges   97
  Operational Challenges   98
  Personal Challenges   99

Evaluations   99

Outcomes and Successes   101

Lessons Learned   103

Conclusions and Suggestions for Future Workshops   104

References   105

INTRODUCTION

In 1892, Anna J. Cooper, the fourth African American woman to receive a doctoral degree in the United States, wrote, "Only the Black Woman can say 'when and where I enter, in the quiet, undisputed dignity of my womanhood, without violence and without suing or special patronage, then and there the whole *Negro race enters with me'.*" (Cooper, 1892, p. 31). This well-known passage illustrates a conceptual framework for social change rooted in the experiences of underrepresented women that can result in expanded opportunities for a larger community, whether it be defined in racial, ethnic, or gender terms. Cooper's rallying cry became the impetus for the design of a FORWARD to Professorship workshop called "When and Where I Enter..." hosted by The University of Toledo (UT). This workshop is for those in the STEMM faculty pipeline in the US Midwest, with specific emphasis on women of color. This population is significantly underrepresented in the science, technology, engineering, mathematics, and medicine (STEMM) disciplines. The addition of women in medicine came upon our realization of the challenges faced by these women, post the merger in 2007 of the UT with the Medical University of Ohio.

In a survey of science, engineering, and health doctorate holders employed by universities, black and Hispanic women were 2.3% of the tenure track faculty and only 1% of the tenured faculty (NSF, 2013).

This group of women is subjected to multiple levels of discrimination, stereotyping, and bias based on the double bind (Malcom et al., 1976) of their race/ethnicity and gender. In addition, women of color STEMM faculty in the Midwest often face challenges related to geographic isolation when they accept positions in small, midwestern cities and towns with limited ethnic and racial diversity. The layered and specific challenges faced by this community of women STEMM faculty necessitates targeted strategies that speak to the unique and structural obstacles they routinely encounter.

The "When and Where I Enter...." workshop was the collective attempt of a small group of women faculty to address this very specific need. Our planning group was diverse and included black, white, and Hispanic women, as well as women from different life stages and sexual orientations. We focused on women of color because we believe, as Cooper did, that through removing the obstacles for this community of women, we will not only serve women of color, but we will also identify strategies that may improve the field for the entire STEMM community, regardless of race, ethnicity, or gender. We believe that consideration of the specific nature of the experiences of women of color STEMM faculty is often missing from the larger dialogue on women in STEMM. The fundamental purpose of our "When and Where I Enter...." workshop was to provide women of color in the STEMM faculty pipeline in the Midwest with (i) professional development training, (ii) a safe place to share their experiences in their respective STEMM disciplines, and (iii) strategies for self-care and professional excellence that would assist women in their efforts to negotiate hostile work environments.

GOALS

"When and Where I Enter...." targeted pre-tenure and senior graduate students in STEMM fields who are women of color (i.e., women of African descent, Latinas, Native Americans, and Pacific Islanders) since these populations are often academically and socially isolated. Asian women, while not always identified as underrepresented in STEMM, were also allowed to apply, based on the social and cultural obstacles they face. The workshop goal was to support advancement through training and social networking in the areas of teaching, service, and scholarly activity. A significant dimension of this $2^1/_2$-day workshop was a focus on the fusion of productive and healthy professional and personal development.

Our goal was to seek participation of women of color at the pre-tenure stage throughout the Midwest. We used the FORWARD grant to pay for hotel, travel, and meals for attendees during the workshop. The activities of the workshop were designed to provide skills and information to the participants and to connect them with each other and national networks. The workshop aimed to provide safe spaces and opportunities for women of color to have conversations among and between themselves about their experiences, lessons learned, and strategies for success.

DESCRIPTION

Organizing Committee

Six faculty women from the Colleges of Engineering, Pharmacy, Medicine, and Arts and Sciences organized "When and Where I Enter…" in Toledo, Ohio, at the Hilton Hotel/Dana Conference Center on the UT Health Science campus. The committee was a multicultural/multiethnic group, which included three women of African descent (two African American and one Trinidadian), one Latina (Brazilian), and two of European descent. The committee met at least once a month for the 12 months prior to the workshop to design a 2½-day workshop specifically tailored to the needs of women of color in STEMM from the Midwest. Committee members were responsible for specific tasks, and interactions were harmonious. An additional 10 women were invited to serve on panels and address the group during the course of the workshop. These facilitators came from a range of institutions and environments to offer expertise in their specific areas of employment and intellectual endeavor. The overwhelming majority of these women came from groups underrepresented in STEMM.

Attendee Application and Profiles

A total of 24 applications were received from women seeking to participate in the workshop, with 20 accepting and 19 attending. Participants included postdoctoral researchers, graduate students, faculty members, a research scientist, and a woman from the private sector hoping to return to academia. The workshop was composed of a series of panels, oral presentations, and group breakout discussions organized around the following topics: "Planning and Funding Research," "Writing in the Profession," and "Having it All: Creating Strategies for Work/Life Satisfaction."

Opening Dinner

The tone of the workshop was set during the opening dinner and keynote address by Dr Vivian Pinn, then associate director for research on women's health and director of the Office of Research on Women's Health at the National Institutes of Health (NIH). The opening session served multiple purposes, including, but not limited to, the following:

- Establishing a warm and welcoming venue for the workshop attendees and other participants to meet each other in a relaxed environment
- Highlighting a veteran woman of color in STEMM to share her wisdom from a multifaceted career spanning several decades
- Providing an opportunity for the workshop sponsors to be recognized and interact with attendees and other participants
- Encouraging senior university leadership to meet our facilitators, several of whom were well-known and accomplished women of color in STEMM
- Increasing the impact on the local community by arranging for Dr Pinn's full presentation to be filmed for broadcast by WGTE Public Media.

    This can be viewed at the Knowledgestream website: (http://www.knowledgestream.org/presentations/womens-health-in-usa).

Day 1

The first full day of the workshop was composed of a series of panels on professional development organized around two broad topics: "Planning and Funding Research" and "Writing in the Profession."

Planning and Funding Research

This panel was designed to provide attendees with vital information on the grant preparation and submission process and to familiarize them with the internal workings of the grant process at federal agencies. The panel was composed of women from diverse ethnic backgrounds representing. Dr Joan Fry represented the National Science Foundation (NSF), and Dr Christine Chow, the associate dean for research and graduate studies at Wayne State University, represented the academic perspective. Presentation slides were made available by all facilitators. The panel discussion was also videotaped, as requested by the dean of the College of Engineering, to present to early-career faculty at UT.

Writing in the Profession

Female faculty members (two Hispanic and one African American) with experience in job searching, tenure, and promotion and the preparation of publications provided information pertaining to the documents needed at various stages of an academic career.

These panels were followed by breakout sessions where participants could ask specific questions and explore topics in-depth, with smaller focus groups led by a facilitator. A sage or senior faculty member was also present in each group to provide detailed explanations on key points.

Lunch

The lunch period was used as an opportunity for informal networking and a brief address by Dr Patsy Komuniecki, the dean of the UT Graduate School and past president of the NW Ohio chapter of the Association for Women in Science (AWIS), who shared her experiences as the sole woman faculty member in the department of biological sciences when she moved to the Midwest.

The afternoon sessions focused on service, effective communication, teaching, and negotiation, addressing the specific issues that were particular to women of color (i.e., the "burden of being a double minority"). Six of the eight women presenting were from groups underrepresented in the sciences. Dr Kelly Mack, who was at the time program director of the NSF ADVANCE program, presented an exceptionally insightful session on the current state of minority women in academic STEMM.

Dinner

The Toledo Zoo was chosen as the venue for the evening meal, where a prominent local woman in science, Dr Anne Baker, then served as director. The zoo provided a relaxing outing that facilitated more informal networking, sharing, and connection. Dr Christine Grant, associate dean of faculty development and special initiatives at North Carolina State University, delivered a motivational talk regarding her professional and personal journey as a woman of color in STEMM. The attendees marked her presentation as one of the highlights of the conference.

Day 2

The final day was designed to be a safe place where participants could discuss the very specific and personal challenges they face as women of color in STEMM under the title of "Having it All: Creating Strategies for Work/Life Satisfaction." The first session was an open forum specifically designed to provide a safe place where participants could safely share powerful and often previously undisclosed stories about the complex ways in which gender, race, and ethnicity had affected their professional lives. The session was both painful and inspiring. Due to the unique nature of this session, all members of the organizing team and guests who were not women of color were excused from the room. This provided an environment free of perceived or actual judgment or intimidation. The second half of the day was focused on brainstorming strategies to deal with the myriad of challenges, with each woman sharing ideas, strategies, resources, and insights from her own perspective.

The closing session provided participants with a template to develop personal plans for professional development and success based on the lessons learned during the entire workshop.

Funding

In addition to funds obtained from FORWARD to Professorship, local funds were needed to cover the costs of the workshop. The UT community responded enthusiastically. Specifically, funds were provided by the President's Lecture Series on Diversity, the Ohio Space Grant Consortium, and the UT Colleges of Engineering, Natural Sciences and Mathematics, Pharmacy, and Medicine.

CHALLENGES

The challenges faced by the organizers can be classified as *organizational, operational,* and *personal.*

Organizational Challenges

The first major organizational challenge was reaching out to and identifying the target audience. The underlying rationale for the workshop (namely, that there are few women of color in STEMM in the Midwest) meant that participants were hard to locate. Although we cast a wide net using personal, professional, and electronic networks, the number of applicants was small, leading to a relaxation of the geographic and career-level requirements. Eventually, the source of participants extended beyond the Midwest to both coasts of the United States, and many applicants from a more junior level were admitted than had been in the original plan. The second major challenge was choosing and prioritizing the topics to be covered. While our focus was on professional development and self-care, there were many powerful, wideranging aspects to these topics. Committee discussions were spirited and engaging, but in the end, we were faced with the prospect of choosing from among competing topics and wondering if the time allotted was sufficient to do them justice. Also, our goal of creating a safe space for individual sharing required time and trust, which could not be hurried. It is possible that our choices of exact topics impacted and set the stage for the challenges discussed next. Finally, in executing the workshop, we found that the participants identified to a highly variable degree with the category of "women of color," with cultural or ethnic identities, or both, such that individual presentations, by necessity, needed to cover a broad range of experiences. This finding has important implications for future workshops.

Operational Challenges

Although all committee members were experienced in workshop and meeting organization in their respective disciplines, we encountered some unique operational issues. The committee members are primarily "hard" scientists (engineers and basic and medical scientists), so we were inexperienced in designing metrics and analyzing social science data collected from a small number of participants. Support and examples of analytical tools and personal plans from the FORWARD national team were helpful, but anxiety remained as to the validity of our analysis. Along with the FORWARD observers, we found certain components of the workshop to be problematic:

- Most presentations were in a lecture format, so more interactive sessions should be included in future workshops. For example, the writing in the profession session did not include any actual writing strategies or practice.
- There was unintended overlap between sessions. Individual presenters were not aware of the content of other presenters' talks.
- While constructing individual personal plans was a powerful idea and well received by participants, actual plan writing should have been allocated more time. Also, if the aim of writing personal plans had been introduced earlier in the program, the participants might have listened with a more attuned ear and produced better products.
- Crucially, at the post-workshop stage, we discovered that we should have planned for, and given more thought to, setting up and executing community building activities. Creating community post-workshop was more time consuming than anticipated; even though bonding between individuals occurred during the workshop. Contact with participants via Facebook was disappointing.

Finally, as the organizers went back to their standard professional activities, not enough attention was paid to follow-up, such that the proposed February 2012 surveys were not sent out. This resulted in a lack of data on the lasting effect on the participants and whether they passed on the mentoring advice they received.

Personal Challenges

Ironically, given the topic of the workshop, the organizers' multiple commitments to their own careers and lives competed with the time necessary to organize the workshop. It soon became apparent that more secretarial and operational administrative support was needed for the committee during the preparation stage and in the crucial follow-up communication with participants. Though individual departments and the university gave support for workshop activities, it was not enough to offset the cost in time and energy to the organizers. The positive effects on the organizers of working with a multicultural team composed of trusted colleagues cannot be overstated. Team members had worked with each other on several previous women's programs, forging friendships, respect, and good working relationships. During the workshop organization, we became increasingly sensitive to each other's life experiences. This laid the groundwork for the decision that one of the sessions on the final day would be organized specifically as a safe space for women of color.

EVALUATIONS

Assessments were prepared and distributed to workshop participants daily. The assessments distributed during the first day of the workshop provided demographic and contextual details such as job description (Table 6.1), length of employment, challenges that participants face in the workplace, and motivations for attending the workshop. Most of the workshop participants (8 of 19) were postdoctoral researchers. In addition, the vast majority of the participants (15 of 19) had been in their position for 0–3 years.

TABLE 6.1 Job Description of Workshop Attendees

Current position	No. of attendees
Graduate student	3
Postdoctoral researcher	8
Faculty position, tenure track	5
Faculty position, other	1
Research scientist	1
Consultant	1

The reason for attending the workshop varied among individuals. Some women (6/19) attended the workshop to gain insight into challenges faced by women of color in STEMM, while others (7/19) were facing a period of transition, including a job change or impending decisions on promotion and tenure.

Information was also collected on the efficacy of the application and communication process prior to the workshop, which was evaluated as excellent by 11 of 19 participants and good by 7 of 19 participants. Since identifying eligible and interested participants was a significant challenge that we faced in the planning process, we also inquired about how participants learned of the workshop. We found that 9 of 17 participants were contacted directly by a mentor or an organizer rather than a written communication (e.g., email or a newsletter). As such, it was not entirely surprising that over half of the respondents (8 of 15) indicated that they had a very effective or adequate network.

The assessments were also designed to provide the workshop organizers with both formative and summative assessment of the workshop content, with opportunities for feedback on specific presenters and an identification of lessons learned. Attendees were asked to provide feedback on a scale of 1–5 (excellent to poor) for each session. In 14 sessions, 9 received a score of excellent by at least 10 participants, indicating that they were effective, and 5 sessions received evaluations that were evenly distributed between excellent and good/average. It is our interpretation from the assessments that these 5 sessions, "Planning and Funding Research," "The Job Search," "Creating Your Network," "Communication in the Classroom," and "Negotiation," could be improved.

Throughout the assessment process, a number of challenges for workshop attendees were identified. Those that were identified by four or more participants in the assessment process are listed in Table 6.2. Many of these challenges were addressed in individual sessions. Interestingly, being asked to participate in an excessive

TABLE 6.2   Challenges Identified by Workshop Attendees

Challenge	No. of attendees
Communication in majority-dominated environment	13
Grant writing	12
Balancing family/work (research/teaching)	5
Being a woman of color (access)	4
Publications	4

TABLE 6.3 Take-Home Messages from Participants

Take-home message	Category	No. of attendees
I am not alone	Belief	6
I can overcome adversity	Belief	5
Know yourself/know your value	Affirmation	4
Build/use a network	Action	3
Develop a plan/follow goals	Action	2
Be confident	Affirmation	2

amount of service was identified as a challenge for a minority of participants (7 of 19). This can be attributed to the fact that most were post-doctoral researchers at the time of the workshop.

The vast majority of the sessions were focused on *actions* that would promote the advancement of the workshop participants. Some examples include "Planning and Funding Research," "Publish or Perish," "Developing a Personal Plan," and "Negotiation." However, the workshop sessions also addressed *beliefs* and *affirmations* (e.g., "Having It All"). All three categories were identified by participants as take-home messages from the workshop (Table 6.3).

When participants were asked immediately following the workshop, "What information that you gained at this workshop will you implement immediately when you return to work? What about in the next calendar year?" the responses were action items including getting my house in order (complete unfinished work, updating CV, etc.), writing grants and publications, and developing a personal plan. In future workshops, participants would like to see more discussion of family, health, and workplace issues. Specifically identified topics included motherhood, relationships, family balance, time management, and health and nutrition. In addition, some participants (3) requested more concrete examples of negotiation scenarios. We hope that there will be a sufficient number of responses to the FORWARD follow-up surveys that we will be able to include these data in future discussions.

OUTCOMES AND SUCCESSES

Two years after the completion of the workshop, a survey was sent to the participants in order to assess whether the workshop had any long-term impact on their professional or personal development, and to determine the current career status of participants. Respondents were also asked to provide suggestions for possible ways to improve future workshops.

A total of 50% of the participants responded to the survey. Of the respondents, two had left academia to start their own businesses. The remaining respondents had remained in academia, with several having advanced to the next stage of their careers (e.g., from assistant to associate professor or graduate student to postdoctoral researcher or assistant professor).

All the respondents, including those who have since left academia, reported that the workshop had been a positive experience for them, and the consensus of most participants was that the information shared at the workshop helped them to better understand and navigate academia and to better position themselves for the next stage of their careers. The session on negotiating for an academic position, in which participants were able to see a mock negotiation and a debriefing of the interactions, was singled out by several participants as being especially valuable. The session in which participants shared their personal stories and experiences was described as being both humbling and empowering. The personal plan was also thought to be an excellent self-evaluation tool.

The workshop was seen as both a source of self-empowerment and a vehicle to build networks, as evidenced by the following quotes from survey responses:

> Even now, I still believe the workshop was profoundly beneficial to me. I've found a greater strength and belief in myself that has allowed me to stand up for myself when needed...
> I believe the workshop provided the women in STEM with a strong network of support to navigate the rigors of the academic environment. The workshop helped solidify my passion for diversity and inclusion work in higher education, particularly for those in STEM.

One recommendation for improving future workshops was the inclusion of a discussion of the psychology of why women of color may not follow through during the negotiation process, and how they might develop strategies to overcome psychological or emotional barriers. Another participant suggested that talks should be made available online for later viewing by anyone who might be interested in the topics discussed.

The organizers also reflected on the workshop experience 2 years after its conclusion. While the team was originally assembled just to organize "When and Where I Enter," the group remains in close contact and continues to collaborate on other initiatives for the advancement of women of color in STEMM in academia. The diversity of the group is one of its greatest strengths. The following quotes from some of the group members reflect the tremendous sense of inclusion and collaboration shared by the team members:

> All members of the FORWARD group were friends and close, which always gave an easy dimension to interactions. However, many interactions/collaborations with friends have been frustrating for me in the past, but the FORWARD group was very like-minded. Our FORWARD group work ethic and dynamics were trusting, empowering and supportive to all members, from my perspective. I looked forward to our meetings because individuals were getting tasks done, so the project kept moving forward.
>
> Planning and executing the workshop gave me time to focus on the needs of women of color in the academy. Seeing the needs of my colleagues at my own institution as well as those from other parts of the country made me aware of how similar our experiences can be even if we are in vastly different types of institutions and geographical locations. I also enjoyed working with a multidisciplinary and diverse group of women who are driven by the same motivations as I am. This effort gave me renewed energy to work to make the issues of women of color in the academy known broadly. I have taken on other responsibilities within this arena which I would not have considered before the workshop. It greatly added to my career and my sense of self.
>
> At the start, I was surprised when my offer to be on the committee was accepted. I am European-American and a generation older than the other organizers. I lived through and remember with high emotion the Civil Rights movement and the second wave of American feminism, so the opportunity to work with young women of color in science was powerful but intimidating. My experience spanned years before most of the participants were even born, so I feared that my language or opinions would be out of date, insensitive, or offensive. Consequently, I was quieter, more tentative, and listened harder than I normally do. I am profoundly grateful to my wonderful UT colleagues for their teaching, patience, and acceptance of me as I stretched my mind and soul in ways I had not foreseen.

LESSONS LEARNED

As can be expected, the organization of a conference for women of color was an eye-opening experience that resulted in a great deal of self-reflection. The team of six women who came together to build upon the concept created by Charlene Gilbert, a professor of women's and gender studies as well as theater and film, was comprised of those who live the intersectionality of race, gender, and sexual orientation as women in STEMM disciplines, not just as scholars studying this complex topic. The need to dissect the term "women of color" and how we fit or do not fit into this group was one of the greatest lessons learned during this process. Women of color and their needs, viewpoints, and desires within the academy are as varied as the racial, ethnic, religious, social, and cultural backgrounds from which they originate. The organization of a one-size-fits-all workshop to address the needs of this unique and diverse population of women requires a high degree of sensitivity to this point. Finding a means to express and contemplate this fact resulted in the heightened sensitivity and awareness of differences and similarities required to create the FORWARD Workshop.

During the execution of the workshop, it became clear that the challenges and experiences encountered by women of color on their journey through the academy have been both physically and emotionally taxing. The impact of bias, both conscious and unconscious, isolation, work-life conflict, and merely existing as an underrepresented minority in a sometimes overwhelmingly hostile environment became recurring themes during closed sessions of the workshop. It is our belief that sessions such as these dealing with emotionally draining topics should be carefully and thoughtfully planned. Follow-up and the creation of a sense of community are keys to assisting all involved in dealing with the weight of participation in such a workshop.

It became clear during the course of the workshop that mainstream topics were appreciated by the participants, but topics such as work-life satisfaction, personal planning, and exchanging experiences were key in creating the unique and powerful overall feel of the workshop experience. These topics should have been expanded and more time allocated to interactive sessions to facilitate discussion and the synthesis of ideas. The need for increased time in these areas was not initially clear to the organizers of the workshop and, as mentioned earlier, the need to cover many topics sometimes detracted from much needed areas.

The lessons learned during the planning and execution of the FORWARD workshop are many and diverse. The camaraderie developed among the workshop organizers provided a sense of community for this microgroup, which strengthened our relationships. It also provided important support that each of us needed, especially when we are working to eradicate problems related to the retention and advancement of women, women of color and minorities in STEMM disciplines. Recognition of the importance of mutual support to effect change of the status quo for women of color in STEMM is one of the most important lessons gleaned from participation in this project.

CONCLUSIONS AND SUGGESTIONS FOR FUTURE WORKSHOPS

After the workshop was finished, the organizers met to discuss recommendations for future workshops based on their experience and participant comments. Based on participant suggestions, the workshop should be increased to three full days and redesigned by adding sessions on time management, job search strategies, and dealing with burnout. Participant suggestions also included more time to develop personal plans. Based on the organizers' experiences, administrative support would be needed for logistics, and presenters should be fully briefed prior to the workshop to avoid unnecessary overlap in content.

Two suggestions are made with respect to policy regarding women of color in the academy. First, there has been much work with respect to storytelling, by collecting stories and testimonials from women and sharing these with other women in similar situations. However, this collection of stories needs to be extrapolated and shared with administrators, since they are in positions to make policy changes. Furthermore, pipeline resources need to be used by hiring committees: for example, networking opportunities for people in decision-making positions to know the talent and pipeline, as was done at our opening dinner. Finally, we suggest organizing similar workshops for other members of the academic community whose decisions can help change the climate for women of color on the importance of the role of an ally in academia and industry.

We believe that the "When and Where I Enter..." workshop was successful in assisting women of color in STEMM to become more successful and in sustaining members of the academy, by providing them with the tools needed to recognize factors contributing to their isolation and to increase their ability to navigate the complex academic landscape.

References

Bilimoria, D., Joy, S., Liang, X., 2008. Breaking barriers and creating inclusiveness: lessons of organizational transformation to ADVANCE Women Faculty in Academic Science and Engineering. Hum. Resour. Manage. 47, 423–441.

Blackwell, L.V., Snyder, L.A., Mavriplis, C., 2009. Diverse faculty in STEM fields: attitudes, performance and fair treatment. J. Divers. High. Educ. 2 (4), 195–205.

Cooper, A.J., 1892. A Voice from the South with an Introduction by Mary Helen Washington. Oxford University Press, New York, NY.

Hill, C., Corbett, C., Rose, A.S., 2010. Why So Few? Women in Science, Technology, Engineering and Mathematics. AAUW, Washington, DC.

Hunt, V.H., Morimoto, S., Zajicek, A., Lisnic, R., 2012. Intersectionality and dismantling institutional privilege: the case of the NSF ADVANCE Program. Race, Gend. Cl. 19 (1-2), 266–290.

Institute for Women's Policy Research, 2013. Accelerating Change for Women of Color Faculty in STEM: Policy, Action, and Collaboration. Washington, DC.

Mack, K.M., Rankins, C.M., Winston, E.C., 2011. Black women faculty at historically black colleges and universities: perspectives for a national imperative. In: Frierson, H.T., Tate, W.F. (Eds.), Beyond Stock Stories and Folktales: African Americans' Paths to STEM Fields (Diversity in Higher Education, Volume 11). Emerald Group Publishing Limited, Bingley, UK, pp. 149–164.

Malcom, S.M., Hall, P.Q., Brown, J.W., 1976. The Double Bind: The Price of Being a Minority Woman in Science. American Association for the Advancement of Science, Washington, DC.

National Science Foundation, Division of Science Resources Statistics, 2009. Women of color in STEM education and employment. (CEOSE Mini-symposium on Women of Color in STEM, Joan Burrelli). Arlington. Available from: <http://www.nsf.gov/od/iia/activities/ceose/mini-symp-pres/Women_of_color_stem_Oct2009/Oct27/JoanBurrelliv2.pdf> (accessed 30.07.13).

National Science Foundation, 2013. Survey of Doctorate Recipients. Available from: <http://www.nsf.gov/statistics/wmpd/2013/minwomen.cfm> (accessed 30.07.13).

Ong, M., Wright, C., Espinosa, L.L., Orfield, G., 2011. Inside the double bind: a synthesis of empirical research on undergraduate and graduate women of color in science, technology, engineering, and mathematics. Harv. Educ. Rev. 81 (2), 162−172.

Rosser, S.V., 2004. The Science Glass Ceiling: Academic Women Scientists and the Struggle to Succeed. Routledge, New York, NY.

Rosser, S.V., 2007. Leveling the playing field for women in tenure and promotion. NWSA J. 19 (3), 190−198.

Rosser, S.V., Lane, E.O., 2002. Key barriers for academic institutions seeking to retain women scientists and engineers: family-unfriendly policies, low numbers, stereotypes, and harassment. J. Women Minor. Sci. Eng. 8 (2), 161−190.

Sonnet, G., 1995. Gender equity in science: still an elusive goal. Issues Sci. Technol. 12, 53−58.

Towns, M.H., 2010. Where are the women of color? Data on African American, Hispanic, and Native American faculty in STEM. J. Coll. Sci. Teach. March/April 2010, 6−7.

Turner, C.S.V., Gonzalez, J.C., Wong, L.K., 2011. Faculty women of color: the critical nexus of race and gender. J. Divers. High. Educ. 4(4), 199−211.

Valian, V., 1998. Why So Slow? The Advancement of Women. MIT Press, Cambridge.

Workshop Design for Diversity and Dialogue: Women in STEM Empowered to Engage Across Difference

Gertrude Fraser[1] and Margaret Harden[2]

[1]Department of Anthropology, University of Virginia, Charlottesville, VA, USA [2]Institute for Faculty Advancement, University of Virginia, Charlottesville, VA, USA

OUTLINE

Introduction	108
Starting with Story	108
Conceptual and Intellectual Framework: Guideposts for the Workshop	110
The Planning Group	111
Designing a Workshop to Facilitate Engagement Across Difference: Core Principles and Strategies	111
Pre-workshop Work	114
Workshop Implementation: An Interactive Format	115
The Participants' Perspective	119
The Facilitation Perspective	121
A Few Practical Lessons Learned	124

Recommendations   125

Conclusion   126

Acknowledgments   127

References   127

INTRODUCTION

This chapter describes an innovative workshop, "Engaging Across Difference," jointly planned by colleagues from three Virginia universities, funded by the National Science Foundation (NSF) FORWARD to Professorship program, and convened for a day and a half in the summer of 2010 at the University of Virginia (U.Va.). The workshop created an environment for a diverse group of women in science, technology, engineering and math (STEM) to learn from one another. Instead of featuring invited experts, planners designed a workshop to leverage the collective knowledge, experience, and heterogeneity of participants themselves, including their discipline, race/ethnic identity, generation, institutional affiliation, and individual experiences. The relative brevity of the workshop demanded focus and specificity. In advance, applicants were asked to describe challenges faced in their STEM careers and their hopes for the workshop. Their responses helped determine the focus for small-group sessions (sharing stories, defining challenges, discussing approaches) and collective sessions (debriefing and reflecting on emerging patterns). Participants fostered collective exploration, common purpose and insight, caring, playfulness, and community. To tell the story of the workshop from conception to impact, this chapter includes voices of the planners, facilitators, program consultant, and participants. For readers who may wish to orchestrate a similar workshop, we include a section on lessons learned and key recommendations.

STARTING WITH STORY

Gertrude Fraser: "I am an African American woman, an anthropologist and faculty member at the University of Virginia, a predominantly white institution. My administrative duties placed me at the hub of institutional efforts to recruit and retain diverse STEM faculty. These various roles involved me in many discussions about improving gender diversity in STEM. Among white women colleagues in STEM, I often noticed limited facility and expressed discomfort in discussing matters of race, ethnicity, or other dimensions of difference within gender.

"There are very few women of color in STEM at the University of Virginia. In focus groups of white STEM women faculty exploring their career experiences at U.Va., participants skillfully navigated such topics as gender and science, research funding, work/life issues, and other pertinent matters. They were less comfortable and expansive when asked why there are so few women of color in STEM. Beyond acknowledging the unfortunate absence of under-represented women colleagues and noting that these women would be uncomfortable in majority white departments, focus-group members had few insights into the experiences of women of color in STEM. Many participants had never had a woman of color as a professor, teaching assistant, or graduate-student peer. It was striking to note the level of hyper-segregation even within a small, marginalized population such as women in STEM. Few everyday opportunities exist for white women in STEM to get to know, and listen to, women of color. Further, the one or two women of color in STEM may have been reluctant to discuss their specific experiences with their white women colleagues. Differences beyond gender rarely emerged in the focus-group dialogues, and when they did, the energy in the room shifted. I would describe it as awkward, somewhat tense, with less head-nodding in recognition of shared experiences. Perhaps there was less resonant agreement that differences can bring value to group discussion of common solutions, and a sense that bringing those who are different into the conversation might create conflict or discomfort.

"Gender is a conventional vehicle for articulating shared experiences of marginality and generating action within the patriarchal STEM academy. In the U.Va. focus groups, other discursive frameworks—whether for articulating difference or areas of commonality—were avoided. The term 'avoided' suggests an aversion that may not be an accurate description of the phenomenon. Rather, white women faculty in STEM at U.Va. appeared unaccustomed to discussing the situation of women in STEM through any dimension of difference, whether of race and ethnicity, social class, nationality, or hierarchies of professorial rank and tenure. If homogeneity, understood as consensus on gender, provided the conditions for engagement, then any conflict or potential cleavages may have been experienced as detracting from the women's project. I can readily understand how one could come to that conclusion if heterogeneity seemed to threaten ties of communal affiliation."

Based on these insights, our goal was to develop a workshop focused on career advancement that would also encourage dialogue among and leverage the benefits of bringing together a diverse group of STEM women. We know that differences, that diversity, can have a profoundly positive impact—even though it also makes us uncomfortable—so we designed a program to highlight skills to build coalitions across difference, and not coalitions that erase or make difference invisible, or displace or ignore it, but that draw upon it as a strength, that put diversity at the center rather than at the margins. The "Engaging Across Difference" workshop positioned diversity and learning in diverse teams as assets, and conveyed the message that awareness of similarities and differences in the STEM academic workplace is a critical skill in charting and accomplishing career success.

CONCEPTUAL AND INTELLECTUAL FRAMEWORK: GUIDEPOSTS FOR THE WORKSHOP

Within organizations, individual and group processes often reinforce preferences for homogeneity and congruency, whether related to visible attributes such as gender, race/ethnicity, age, and disability, or to deeper factors such as values, beliefs, knowledge, and skills (Page, 2007). The normative preference for homogeneity helps explain why women in majority-male STEM fields face multiple challenges to their full incorporation: their difference may be perceived as inherently problematic. It also explains why women of color in STEM face distinct experiences of marginalization and lack of access to career opportunities when compared to white women (Ong et al., 2011).

For the workshop, we wanted to build heterogeneous groupings. We wanted to create engaging and safe spaces and activities so that diverse women from different career and life stages could discuss their experiences in STEM and collectively solve problems. We did not assume that shared gender would inherently disrupt the normative preferences for homogeneity and congruence. The research literature guided us to create "exploration-rich" activities that would foreground and encourage openness to differences within the shared identities of gender and STEM.

In a meta-analysis of the organizational and social psychology literature, Mannix and Neale (2005) reviewed studies to ascertain what variables moderated the preference for homogeneity and predicted organizational effectiveness when two conditions held: (i) an increasingly diverse workforce; and (ii) internal and external pressures for employees to work in cross-functional, heterogeneous teams. The main finding in this comprehensive review is that heterogeneous teams generate two types of conflict. Negative conflicts emerge from relationship or personality dynamics that ultimately undermine team goals. Team members become conflict averse and blame diversity as the problem. By contrast, learning-based conflict is characterized by vigorous and open exchange of differing and opposing ideas among diverse team members. But there is an additional, somewhat counterintuitive conclusion based on the research literature: Heterogeneous teams are successful and improve their ability to solve complex problems when attributes and commitments held in common, rather than differences, are emphasized. Diversity-effective organizations are able to foster conditions of "being different, yet feeling similar" and thereby encourage social integration that recognizes the value brought to the group by "uniquely experienced individuals" (Mannix and Neale, 2005, p. 47). The workshop format would take on the challenge of leveraging the power of heterogeneity while creating a sense of community and collective purpose.

THE PLANNING GROUP

The planning group was composed of seven faculty members holding positions at U.Va., Virginia Commonwealth University, and Norfolk State University (a historically African American institution). Everyone had experience creating and implementing professional development programs for faculty and/or graduate students. Six of the seven faculty members held administrative appointments. Although our faculty planners were relatively senior in rank and career stage, we were otherwise quite diverse. Four of our faculty came from engineering, two from the humanities (history and German), and one from social science (anthropology). Three of the seven planners identified themselves as African American and two as Hispanic. Further, two of the seven were immigrants to the United States. Jeff Galbraith, a U.Va. PhD in educational psychology, worked closely with the planning group as a consultant on the dialogue process.

DESIGNING A WORKSHOP TO FACILITATE ENGAGEMENT ACROSS DIFFERENCE: CORE PRINCIPLES AND STRATEGIES

As a group, the planning committee was very committed to creating a positive, mutually supportive, engaged community with a strength-based approach to diversity. We knew that several key issues would be a challenge for us. We knew, from our own lived experiences and from research, that there existed very real, culturally determined hierarchies and divisions based on race and ethnicity, faculty rank, and institutional prestige that we could not and did not want to ignore. In order to accomplish this "engaged community," our planning team used a variety of specific strategies, from the application and acceptance processes to the structure and pedagogy of the workshop itself, to encourage engagement across differences without erasing or delegitimizing those differences.

At every step of the planning process, we prioritized diversity combined with engagement. Not only did we want the participant group as a whole to be broadly diverse, but we also wanted participants to really engage and interact with each other across various culturally and socially constructed boundaries. Accordingly, when we drafted the proposal for our program, we specifically defined our target participants as diverse "women in STEM fields who are either finishing doctoral programs or have obtained a PhD, whether or not they are (1) postdoctorates, (2) unemployed, having recently obtained a PhD or finished a postdoctorate appointment, (3) in the early stages of a tenure-track or non-tenure-track academic position, or (4) employed outside academia." Being this broadly inclusive was not without risk. There was some trepidation in the planning group as to whether we could create a program that would actually work for such a diverse group of women. How helpful would a session on networking really be for women at such different career stages? Could we have useful conversations about the various challenges that these women were facing when those challenges would likely vary tremendously? Would this workshop really be effective for all of the participants? Would we even be able to establish a strong sense of community and connection (not to mention safety) within such a brief span of time?

Accordingly, we sought to encourage a high level of interaction. Exercises were designed to generate multiple viewpoints, surface participants' narratives of career challenges, create an evolving sense of mastery and comfort with sharing experiences among small diverse groups, and establish a sense of trust in giving and asking for advice. A workshop is but a brief configuration in time and space. This is an inherent limitation. At the same time, a national workshop provides opportunities to maximize heterogeneity, whereas it is rare to find such heterogeneity in a single institution or STEM department. We invited women faculty, postdoctoral researchers, and graduate students from different institutional types, disciplines, racial and ethnic identities, and cultural backgrounds. We organized the workshop around small, heterogeneous dialogue groups, each with a facilitator. Group members could, in turn, share their differing perspectives, listen, pose questions, and suggest alternative strategies or approaches to address career challenges. This format encouraged "task-focused conflict," which, according to Mannix and Neale (2005, p. 42), establishes the necessary conditions for exploration-centered problem solving.

There are many known approaches to narrative-based and dialogue-based work with heterogeneous groups (Deturk, 2006; Innis and

Booher, 2003; Nagda and Gurin, 2007; Sannino, 2008; Zuniga et al., 2002). Our consultant, Jeff Galbraith, adapted a framework he created while working with individual faculty members and corporate clients. This approach guides participants through an exploration of career challenges, isolating a few core elements that are then used to structure the small-group dialogue. Questions include: What is my current academic setting? What are its expectations and goals regarding values, beliefs, skills, and style of behavior? How do I fit and not fit? What is my level of confidence? What action(s) do I want to take? This approach seeks to encourage flexibility and awareness of options and perspectives in organizational environments that are complex and intellectually challenging.

Jeff Galbraith: "Any inquiry that is human-centered is narrative. Narrative knowing is situated and relational and iterative. The structured-dialogue process allows people to see themselves as situated and related to others within a given context. By describing the situation and its people within a narrative format that is somewhat structured, participants have a common frame that allows them to easily talk to each other even if they disagree as to the particulars. Over the course of the small group dialogue sessions, participants can then begin to make sense of things, develop possibilities, and envision next action steps. These action choices can over time lead to better work patterns and, in this case, the betterment of women's STEM career experience."

We sought to be as clear as possible—on our website and in all distributed materials—that a major focus of the workshop would be meaningful engagement across difference and that participants should come prepared to listen deeply and reflect thoughtfully on their own experiences and the experiences of others. As part of the application process, we elicited personal demographics, including highest degree, institutional affiliation, race/ethnicity, field of study, subfield, desired career position in the next five years, and, in 200 words or fewer, a statement expressing career constraints and reasons for attending the workshop. This open-ended question gave us further insight into each applicant's perceptions of career challenges and priorities as well as the range of issues across the group. Below are selected responses, edited to preserve anonymity. They convey a good sense of differences and similarities.

Faculty member at a teaching institution: "I have been quite fortunate, in my role as an assistant professor, to have very few or relatively minor constraints or barriers. I have fortunately experienced few obvious/highly constraining barriers in my academic path. This is due in great part to being mentored by several intelligent and passionate female scientists. However, if I had an opportunity to change one aspect of my academic career, I would reduce the number of courses I teach per semester to one, so that I could invest more time in research."

PhD candidate: "I am a first generation PhD, really a first-generation college student. My department is run by an all-male staff and comprised of mostly male students. My challenge is often with specific individuals. This environment sometimes affects my confidence level, particularly in group settings. Women tend to work together to solve problems, but I have found that males are more competitive. I occasionally take comments regarding my ideas too personally, and then I hold back from adding my input in future discussions."

Faculty member at a research institution: "I am trained as a biostatistician, but my home department is in psychology. It has been fun talking to psychologists—we share a common goal. However, I am feeling often a little alone because I also need stimulus and conversation from people who are trained with similar mathematical and statistical rigor. I am eager to meet other women in science and engineering to start building a community for me."

Postdoctoral scientist: "As a minority female in engineering fields, I find that the higher I go in postbaccalaureate work and positions, the less diversity I see. While it is very imperative at that stage to be self-sustaining, it is also beneficial to have some points of guidance … Throughout my engineering background, I have struggled to embrace culture among the STEM population at a university setting."

We selected applicants primarily on the concreteness of their reasons for applying. We funded all those accepted to attend the workshop. Regrettably, high travel costs prevented some individuals who were selected from participating. Considering application information, we created six-person teams containing various viewpoints, racial/ethnic identities, institutional affiliations, career stages, and other salient features. We made each team as heterogeneous as possible, but with sufficient overlap to allow some "attributes and commitments held in common" (Mannix and Neale, 2005), such as kinds of conflict, STEM field, institutional type, race/ethnicity, and social class of origin.

PRE-WORKSHOP WORK

A month prior to the workshop, we sent participants detailed program information and an assignment for "pre-work." Specifically, we explained that participants would explore similarities and differences in their experiences, identify their own effective efforts to collaborate, develop their ability to work with difference, disagreement, and conflict, and define actions they might take individually or in alliance to advance the participation and integration of women in STEM fields. Their previous application responses helped us design pre-work with high salience.

We asked each participant to think of a specific situation and challenge. We provided worksheets with the core elements organized around a circle. We also provided instructions and an example based on topics that had surfaced in the open-ended application responses. First, each participant was asked to write in the circle her view of herself as a participant in her academic setting. Then she was to shift perspectives and map how others, such as a colleague, an ally, a mentor, a student, a boss, or an antagonist, would see himself or herself in the same situation. For example, the participant might note that she prefers a cooperative, open style of departmental interaction, but her workplace is competitive. Further, although she has a high level of confidence about her science, she feels unsupported by her laboratory colleagues. She might then map an antagonistic lab mate, perhaps noting that he, in his final year of a postdoctoral appointment, lacks organizational skills and is competitive rather than cooperative, and so on. We provided participants with the emails and phone numbers of the consultant and team members who could answer questions and provide guidance to help them accomplish the pre-work meaningfully. They were to bring their written pre-work to the workshop, not for reading by workshop planners or other participants, but for their own reference during team dialogue.

Completing the pre-work primed participants and was the beginning of a process that would continue through dialogue at the workshop. Participants arrived already having defined their specific professional situation, identified key actors and actions, and reflected on their stake and the stake of colleagues. They were already beginning to share common language and visual tools, anchors for initial workshop dialogue. This pre-work thus lessened the time required in the opening session to elicit each participant's narrative. Indeed, as the dialogue groups convened, participants eased fluidly into animated conversation, producing just the sort of noise we had wanted.

WORKSHOP IMPLEMENTATION: AN INTERACTIVE FORMAT

The workshop itself included 15 h of highly structured programming over a day and a half. In order to facilitate community building, we deliberately organized relatively routine activities to downplay possible social and prestige hierarchies, mediate the perception of boundaries and create a sense of safety. For us, matters as simple as how participants were welcomed, where they would sit and how they would be introduced were taken very seriously. For example, at the outset, we wanted participants, upon arrival in their rooms, to feel comfortable, strong, and appreciated. Since they would be staying in dormitories, without hotel amenities, we made up small, inexpensive gift bags containing a few essentials and a warm note of welcome. To ensure a safe, relaxing environment for nurturing vulnerability and growth by way of open talk about work and life purpose, we gave much thought to setting, process, and, of course, food. During the first workshop session, participants were asked to sit with their *a priori* constructed heterogeneous groups. The first welcome was brief, and introductions were made within groups according to a specific protocol whereby participants shared only their names, strengths, and opportunities. Excluded from the protocol were title, rank, and institution. Each group facilitator ensured adherence to this protocol. The introduction was designed specifically to exclude possible signifiers of status and to ease participants into the actual work of generative dialogue, which tran-spired from 4:30 to 6:30 p.m. on the first day. This small group and the facilitator stayed together for three sequential dialogue sessions. They came to know one another well.

After a recuperative break and informal mingling, came dinner. Each conferee was greeted at dinner with a collection of inspirational quotes. One was from Audre Lorde: "When I dare to be powerful—to use my strength in the service of my vision, then it becomes less and less important whether I am afraid." Another was from Zen master Thich Nhat Hanh: "Once there is seeing, there must be acting. Otherwise, what is the use of seeing?" Over dinner, each conferee then introduced herself to the room, with her name, her favorite quote (from the list or somewhere else), and a brief statement about why she chose the quote and how it represents her. We deliberately inverted the conventional workshop practice of starting introductions with disciplinary and insti-tutional credentials so we could highlight each woman's sense of self and purpose. Not until the closing session on day two did participants collectively share information revealing social and prestige hierarchies, such as title, rank, and institution affiliation.

On the second workshop day, two morning sessions involved small-group dialogue with participants moving from description to analysis as they shared their challenges and strengths. Each facilitator guided participants in developing awareness of their own current situation, identifying individual strengths and challenges, testing possible solu-tions, and then in thinking as a group about emergent strategies and actions. Solutions often surfaced when participants began to see simi-larities and differences between themselves and antagonists in their stories. The morning ended with a moderated plenary discussion of insights gained and important themes emerging.

After lunch, participants attended one of two concurrent workshops, two and a half hours in length each, for which they had specified a preference in advance. One, "Critical Conversations," focused on critical/difficult conversations. The other, "Community and Connectivity," focused on networking and mentoring. We chose these two topics for two reasons. First, issues of mentoring, networking, and voice were among the most common issues mentioned in the workshop application (i.e., "Networking is a part of my academic life that is missing so far..." and "At my university, it's tough to have a voice..."). Second, marginalized people, such as women of color and white women in STEM careers, need multiple specific strategies for connecting with diverse allies, creating supportive communities, and empowering themselves to speak their own truth.

"Critical Conversations" started with a whole-group discussion eliciting basic principles for success in difficult conversations. Participants were highly participatory and eager to share their own thoughts and experiences. A subset of the planning team used the participant experiences to highlight principles mirrored in the works of Stone et al. (1999), Fisher and Shapiro (2005), Fisher et al. (1991), and Davidson (2011). Next, groups of six worked with a facilitator to role-play and discuss particular cases chosen in advance by a subset of the planning team based on issues raised by the participants in their applications. The content was thus relevant and immediately applicable. Although the cases involved only two to three roles, within the small groups, multiple participants would play one role. For example, for a case that involved a department chair and an assistant professor, three participants would take the role of the chair and three would take the role of the assistant professor. During the actual role-play, they were allowed to confer and interrupt each other. In this way, they could (and did) draw on each other for expertise and accountability. Finally, participants gathered for debriefing and questions. During the debriefing, participants indicated that having multiple participants play one role allowed them to experience and thus experiment with the impact of differing perspectives on the framing and course of a difficult conversation. However, due to participant interest, the question-and-answer session ended up focusing almost exclusively on specific conversations that participants were planning to undertake back home. In fact, participants were very open and specific about issues that they were facing, indicating a high level of comfort and sense of safety within the group. They shared advice among themselves, drawing on principles discussed in the opening session and additional insights gained in workshop dialogue. If we were to do this again, we would consider including a panel during this final debriefing to provide additional perspectives.

"Community and Connectivity" involved an interactive theater exercise, a drawing session, and an expert panel of successful women professionals, with each panelist speaking for 10 min. To start the session, we continued the practice of shifting convention to create a sense of exploration and reveal hidden strengths. As participants entered the room, they divided into two teams for a game of invisible kickball. The facilitator tossed the invisible ball between the teams, and play erupted with jumping, dodging, catching, hurling, and squealing with laughter. Invisible kickball was created by a pioneer in improvisational theater, Viola Spolin, who says that such games energize participants (especially useful after lunch!). Spolin et al. (1999) theorize that as participants play with and track the invisible ball, they begin to give shape to the invisible, interact with one another in a different way, and develop greater access to the intuitive aspects of self. (See also the actor Alan Alda's use of these exercises in his work with scientists at SUNY Stony Brook's Alan Alda Center for Communicating Science, 2009.) Participants played along with much glee but were not necessarily sure of the reason for the tomfoolery.

After about 15 raucous minutes, we addressed the topic of networks and community. The panel moderator provided a brief discussion of networks and why they were important to career success. Participants then sat on the floor next to a large piece of poster paper and colored markers. They were to draw their networks. Besides experiencing the wonder of scientists and engineers sitting on the floor, drawing with markers, borrowing colors from one another, and searching for their inner artist, participants represented their strengths as they envisioned them. A few asked for specific directions about how to draw networks, but after the initial hesitancy, all started to create visual, colorful representations of their connections and resources. With network drawings affixed to the walls, participants explained their drawings, and panelists pointed out interesting themes or connections and asked questions. Participants had depicted many types, shapes, and categories of networks within their disciplines: volunteer, research, religious, childcare, and athletic, for example. Most, but not all, had placed themselves at the center and then depicted their types of networks around that central figure.

The wall of network drawings generated expansive, energetic discussion and reflection. As one participant put it, "The session was very useful. It helped to visually map our current network and to think about how the network will change." Participants could see others' drawings as exemplars to emulate. Viewing and discussing so many network maps, participants were bound to gain increased awareness of strengths and weaknesses in their own system. Some participants spoke about areas where they had dense networks and areas where they could develop additional ties. If someone's system lacked adequate research networks, she could point to her expansive volunteer networks and imagine how the skills and knowledge used to develop those connections might be used to form networks with

Fellow researchers. A few noted that they were overnetworked and might cut back.

For the final hour of the session, the panelists convened at the front of the room to tell their stories, offer their network expertise, comment further on the drawings, and respond to questions and comments. Panelists included an African American chemical engineer, a white chemical engineer, an African American executive director of a non-profit, grass-roots community organization (who created it from the ground up), and a white chemistry professor (who worked to connect multiple scientists and humanists). Each panelist described her own network, outlined her process for creating community, and offered advice to participants for building their career and personal networks, followed by a rich question-and-answer period.

THE PARTICIPANTS' PERSPECTIVE

Before departing from the workshop, each participant completed a paper evaluation that considered overall organization; facilitation; acquisition of information and skills, including ways to increase connectivity; and sense of community and inclusion. The survey included 13 five-point Likert-scale items and 6 open-ended questions. In addition to looking at overall averages, the evaluator did some basic statistical analyses on the Likert-scale questions to look for both consistency and variation across demographic differences. Data from the open-ended responses were analyzed for specific skills, community, and inclusion, as well as for post-workshop intentions. One conferee left early, but 31 surveys were distributed and all were returned.

Overall the survey results were very positive. Workshop sessions were well received. Participants scored the "Structured Dialogue" and "Community and Connectivity" sessions 4.1 and 4.4, respectively, for overall effectiveness and relevancy. A total of 77% of respondents indicated that they either agreed or agreed strongly with the statement "I am now more aware of my own strengths." In addition, over 90% of respondents indicated that they either agreed or agreed strongly with the statement "I now feel more confident dealing with difficult interpersonal issues." All respondents endorsed the statement that they would recommend the workshop to a colleague. Participants gave high marks to the structured-dialogue facilitators (4.4 out of 5; Table 7.1) and slightly lower marks (4.1 and 4.2) to the moderators for the concurrent sessions. Some participants who had attended the "Critical Conversations" session also rated the cases less relevant, with a 3.9 out of 5 rating. Having spent considerable time delving into their own circumstances, participants may have wanted to continue on that path rather than explore hypothetical

TABLE 7.1　Individual Session Ratings for U.Va.'s Engaging Across Difference Workshop

Individual session ratings for "Engaging Across Difference"			
Session →	Structured dialogue*	Critical conversations[†]	Community and connectivity[‡]
Overall effectiveness	4.1	3.9	4.4
Effectiveness of the facilitator	4.4	4.1	4.2
Discussion	4.3	4.0	4.4
Relevancy of subject matter	4.1	3.9	4.4

*31 Responded
[†] 15 responded
[‡] 16 responded
Scale: poor = 1, excellent = 5.

cases. The tool used to frame their challenges proved unhelpful to a few participants. In addition, there were some critical comments that the workshop was not long enough to cover everything in sufficient depth, and that participants wanted more unstructured time either for informal conversations with one another or to mentally refresh themselves, especially after the intense dialogue sessions.

Every respondent named at least three things that she learned from the workshop. In addition, when asked whether they intended to take any specific actions post-workshop, almost all participants indicated that they intended to strategically broaden their current social network, resolve a specific conflict, and/or improve a specific relationship. The most dominant themes in the written responses related to networking, being in community ("I am not alone"), and reframing (trying to understand the perspective of others). Beyond those themes, there was much variety. Here are some verbatim answers, both within and beyond those primary themes:

- I guess one of the most key things was that I was validated, I was allowed to listen, and to speak, and to realize the struggle is not just my own.
- I have much strength that I can use to solve problems. I am not alone in the problems I face.
- I learned about issues that I face on the road towards tenure that I hadn't considered. How to negotiate more effectively. That I am all right and my situation is temporary.
- I learned more about graduate work in science and engineering at other institutions. I also learned a framework for considering my position and other's [sic].
- I learned to use "the circle" to assess a situation, my role, and the role of other players. I learned how to develop strategies that will help me step back and deal with conflict.
- I met other scientists who have had both similar and very different career paths—good to hear personal/specific situations.

THE FACILITATION PERSPECTIVE

Overall, the activities, content, and structure of the workshop were consistent with program design specifications regarding generative dialogue and best practices in adult education. For example, generative dialogue requires a broad focus where the primary conversational material emerges from the group. One sign of this is whether the facilitator is asking questions or making statements and how often the facilitator speaks as compared to the group. Post-workshop reflections from the facilitators and observations from non-participating management-group members indicate that there was a high degree of interactivity, with participants dominating the conversations, and that specific topics emerged from the participants rather than being introduced by the facilitators. Because topics were identified by participants and thus focused on the participants' opportunities and strengths, the discussions were deemed consistently applicable to their own lives.

Jeff Galbraith on facilitator training: "It's important that the facilitators as a group go through the dialogue process with a similar, real problem of their own. This group practice, done in a round-robin format, allows facilitators to play both the participant and facilitator roles. Engagement at this level helps them understand the process from the inside out. They will then more fully grasp the idea that everyone—facilitators and participants—cannot only own the problem but also the possibilities and choices to solve the problem. The key idea stressed here is that everyone is a leader, and leaders get out of their own comfort zone and expand their own response range rather than forcing others to do so."

Maggie Harden: "As a facilitator, I found ample evidence of at least short-term success. Over the course of the workshop, the participants seemed to bond with and trust each other. Although there was some initial hesitancy within the group that I facilitated, this dissipated rapidly such that, by the end of the first day, participants were engaging and discussing and beginning to problem solve around deeply personal issues that were adversely impacting their professional lives. On the second day, when we took participants outside for a group picture, the participants themselves pushed us as organizers to take small group pictures. Despite the heterogeneity of the groups we had constructed, the individuals within those groups seemed to feel very connected to each other and wanted to create and take home a visual representation of that connection. Perhaps even more importantly, the individuals in my group were able to explicitly identify and then draw on their own strengths, from various and compartmentalized sections of their lives, in order to begin to problem-solve. There are two aspects of this that I think it is important to stress. First, the structure of the facilitated conversations helped disrupt the false dichotomy between personal and professional lives. Participants were able, through the discussion, to bring the various parts of their lives and their identities together. Second, participants were very actively engaged in recognizing their own strengths and perspectives in addition to the strengths and perspectives of other group members, and this in turn led to the creation of shared knowledge and shared problem solving. For example, on day one, there were two members of my group who shared very similar stories from opposing viewpoints. The basic story involved the sharing and withholding of information and credit. At first, these two participants sympathized with each other, but seemed unable to recognize the similarities in their stories. By the end of the second day, not only could they see and discuss those similarities, they could also extrapolate and be more open minded about possible opposing viewpoints."

Juliet Trail: "Beginning with the facilitator training and planning discussions, we were consistently trained towards a dynamic where the participants would speak far more than the facilitators. The goal was to enable a multipart conversation where the participants could understand the boundaries and goals for each small-group dialogue, in the midst of bringing forward their stories and insights, while being guided lightly by the facilitator towards recognizing a wider array of personal strengths and interpersonal opportunities that could be used in their professional settings. The lens for this progression was that of sharing a specific professional situation that had brought them great challenge or conflict. Each of the small-group sessions contained goals allowing each participant to: share their situation; reflect more deeply on conditions of culture, inclusion, and difference within the situation; explore in depth the possible perspective of the other party with whom they experienced the challenge or conflict; and then examine tools and opportunities for positive resolution from all segments of their life, including personal activities and relationships alongside their professional ones. By understanding these goals clearly within and across the three small-group sessions, the facilitator could offer probing questions to assist the participants by inviting expansion, reflection, and/or sharing towards each of these various goals. This approach, of understanding clearly the goals of each session and playing the role of a quiet, gently-questioning facilitator, proved to be very effective. It enabled each participant to become her own coach, gaining deeper insights and discovering new possibilities for resolving conflicts through greater utilization of her own existing skillset from across all domains of her life.

"Another effective element of the facilitator training and practice that came through during the workshop was guiding participants to connect through empathy, but not to judge or direct one another during the discussions. Participants were thus encouraged to notice similarities between one another's stories, and between the elements of culture, inclusion, and difference that played out in those stories, but not to respond with statements such as 'You know what you *should do* here is xxx.' Thus, the facilitator served throughout the dialogues to remind participants to act as listeners and supporters of the speaker and to offer helpful questions, much as the facilitator did, in order to offer the potential for the speaker to gain new insights, but without imposing their own judgment onto the speaker. In my group, this approach worked very well. I had at least one very strong personality among my heterogeneous groups of participants, so the setting of boundaries around reflecting or probing versus judging others in the circle was very important. By the end of the workshop, this approach proved extremely effective, and the participants were able to trust and to openly share their stories, skills, and insights freely with one another without needing to worry about being told who they 'should be' or what they 'should do' in a given situation. Instead, they began to connect with one another across stories and personal qualities, building a mutually supportive dynamic. Further, they became advocates for each other as they explored each woman's skills and personal traits towards identifying potentially positive insights or actions. They would encourage the speaker to have belief in her ability to transfer a positive experience or conflict-resolution trait from another setting into the professional situation that was the focal point of the workshop dialogues."

Wraegen Williams: "Reflecting back on the group of six women that surrounded the table where I served as a facilitator, I recall that they spanned from the graduate level to postdoctoral, and even the professoriate. The diversity of their backgrounds was not only unique and intriguing, but also provided different avenues for me as the facilitator to connect with the group and for the women to connect with one another. With this in mind, I originally found that the graduate students were more comfortable sharing their issues. As time progressed over the day and a half- long workshop and all realized they were in a 'safe environment,' I noted that the women who were more advanced in their careers let down their guard and began to think critically about solutions to the personal issues that were affecting advancement to the next level. Looking back on the initial hesitancy, one could perceive this situation as the natural hierarchy inside the ivory tower and within the STEM disciplines in academia. Needless to say, this initial tentativeness impeded the progress to plausible solutions and next steps for the more advanced women. Although this may be seen as an undesirable result, I trust that they left feeling empowered by the fact that they were able to impart experience-based wisdom to women following similar career paths. As a result of their willingness to share and bond with others in the group, I believe that the graduate students grew drastically with respect to how they viewed their issues. More importantly, I appreciated the fact that the graduate students were able to discover undisclosed strengths that they could use to bridge the differences they were experiencing. This is extremely significant as they have now recognized strengths that they can continue to draw upon for the rest of their lives, no matter what path they choose."

A FEW PRACTICAL LESSONS LEARNED

STEM women want to talk with and learn from one another. Pre-workshop work should be expected from each participant as the currency for workshop success. Workshop size is a primary consideration. Small-group dialogue works best, with no more than seven participants and a facilitator. Hence, it seems essential to learn about each participant and use that information to guide program planning. Ask people what their issues are beforehand; don't assume that you know. The workshop experience confirms our initial guiding principle that participant diversity across many dimensions is critical to workshop success. Each individual brings wisdom and an important point of view. Open-structure opportunities to talk and reflect must be balanced with organized sessions. Resist the urge to overprogram. It is important to convene a diverse group with varied experiences, knowledge, and career pathways. At the same time, based on participant feedback, it may be important to offer some sessions where people at similar career stages, especially faculty, have an opportunity to brainstorm and interact. Starting off with dialogue in small groups and keeping those groups together to build cohesion will encourage all to participate.

To create an environment of trust and willingness to share, context must be designed. Rooms need to have a human scale and should not be too imposing. Round tables create a sense of informality. It is better to place people relatively close together, and yet the noise generated during intense conversations must not interfere with overall effectiveness. The choice of room can make a lot of difference. Good food matters, too, with options for dietary needs. Early on and throughout the workshop, breaks should be integrated into the program design and respected. No issue is trivial. In the evaluations many respondents complained that the rooms were too cold. We tried to adjust the air temperature during the sessions but were unsuccessful. Next time, we will test room temperature beforehand, will monitor it, and will remind participants to bring a sweater or shawl, even in the dog days of summer in Virginia.

Jeff Galbraith: "Good dialogue design requires setting up a narrative that respects the participants; it must be relevant and at their current level of inquiry. Participants can then quickly accept the process, engage in the dialogue, and get on to the harder work of making sense, developing possibilities, and making action choices. Good dialogue design also requires that something be in place that helps participants take the dialogue process back to their own settings. Perhaps that is why designing a dialogue that is particularly relevant is so crucial, since participants can begin to learn how to take a stand and strategize around that stance. Practicing in this way produces the confidence needed to effectively carry through on newly developed ideas for action, once the participants return to their everyday lives."

RECOMMENDATIONS

Our recommendations focus on a few pragmatic matters. Workshop costs are a primary consideration. The FORWARD to Professorship grant supported about one-third of total costs. The remaining costs were borne by the U.Va. program budgets. Faculty and staff time (in terms of planning and implementing the workshop) was a considerable in-kind (and thus less visible) expense. In addition, travel and housing were the most expensive budget items. The workshop also funded food and drinks. How such an expensive event will be paid for must be decided early. One early decision point for us was that participants would not bear any portion of these costs. Although our participants paid no fees, other groups may want to consider nominal fees, allocating a portion of the expenses to the participants, and/or reducing travel expenses by limiting participation regionally.

A year to plan and deliver is a minimum time frame. The planning committee must work well together and be able to commit their time, as well as themselves, to this endeavor. But consider the meaning of "work well together," and the theme of heterogeneity and networking. Also consider the documented benefits when quite diverse people learn to work together for a common purpose. Committee members must be willing to commit to each other and to the workshop. When it comes to planning, the contributions of all of the team members are important. Each person brings very different and sometimes divergent views to the table. The planning team will sometimes disagree and may challenge each other. But in the end, what gets created out of those disagreements and discussions will be stronger than what any one individual might create on their own. Members of the planning team with administrative positions and resources can be especially helpful in navigating the institutional landscape. Because support staff are invaluable in such an undertaking, at least one member of the planning team ought to have a personable working relationship with those who arrange furniture, monitor temperature, serve food, clean up, and the like.

Early and sustained communication with workshop participants is invaluable. We were lucky to have the superlative logistical and planning expertise of trusted colleague Sherri Barker, executive coordinator at the U.Va. She took charge of communicating with applicants on logistical matters, organizing travel, planning committee schedules, coordinating facility setup, overseeing workshop registration, and the marshaling of colleagues to help with final workshop details. Barker was also the go-to person for participants' last-minute requests before and during the workshop. If you are not as fortunate, then it may be essential to include professional workshop/event planners in the budget.

CONCLUSION

We took a risk in organizing a STEM career development workshop whose engine would be participants' own stories, experiences, and perspectives. Our approach departs radically from conventional, didactic career development workshops, especially in our instrumental use of personal narrative to inform participants' assessment of their own and others' strengths and weaknesses. This approach generated individual and collective conceptions of viable strategies for action. We integrated heterogeneity into the program's format, into the process of selecting participants, and into the conceptual underpinnings, believing that exploration-rich activities best result from diverse teams or groups working through and with conflict. With deliberate purpose, we directed attention to similarities and differences as a way to approach challenges and solutions. After all, similarity and difference, challenge and solution, and a host of other seemingly opposing forces are dynamic, normative features of complex organizations such as universities. We achieved most of the goals set for the workshop as measured by the participants' responses to evaluation questions and by their informal feedback during the workshop. As one participant put it, "The most rewarding part of the workshop was meeting diverse women who have very similar interests to mine and learning from their experience." Facilitators' descriptions of the richness of small group exchanges provide additional evidence that participants benefited from their engagement with one another.

Our workshop story offers a model that is quite different from how STEM career development workshops are usually organized. Our model, as presented here, is not intended as an effective long-term tool for resolving structural variables that now produce demographic inequities in the STEM workforce. However, we do suggest that bringing some of these concepts into departments and institutions has the potential for systemic impact. All of us STEM faculty and administrators must learn skills and attitudes of collaboration, especially collaboration with those who seem different. We all must learn to work well in heterogeneous teams and contexts. Finding ways to see, understand, and engage difference (Davidson, 2011; Page, 2007) is critical, not only for the career advancement and well-being of women in STEM, but also for the development of transformative STEM leaders, not to mention the positive impact of such efforts on faculty interaction with undergraduates, graduate students, and support staff.

Acknowledgments

A successful workshop depends on many hands and minds working together. We were very fortunate to have a tremendously intelligent team of diverse people who consistently brought their whole selves—their experiences, knowledge, creativity and energy—to this workshop, both in the planning and the execution.

Our thanks to the team who helped plan and implement the workshop. Rosalyn Hobson Hargraves, associate professor of electrical and computer engineering at Virginia Commonwealth University, gave freely and consistently of her time and her expertise. She attended the FORWARD to Professorship "train-the-trainers" workshop in Washington, DC, facilitated multiple workshop sessions, and continues her work with us on this important endeavor. Suely Black, professor of chemistry at Norfolk State University, and Carolyn Vallas, director of the Center for Diversity in Engineering, and Roseanne Ford, Cavalier Distinguished Teaching Professor and Chair, Chemical Engineering, both at U.Va, all shaped the workshop as members of the planning committee. Our colleagues facilitated sessions, served as advisors to participants, and provided their STEM diversity expertise. Jeff Galbraith, PhD, served as project consultant. He developed the Nimble Journeys method, which formed the basis for the structured-dialogue sessions. With 30 years of experience as an executive and career coach and instructional designer, he helped us tailor the process to the participants' specific experiences and profiles, and train dialogue facilitators. Our thanks to Juliet Trail, research assistant, and Wraegen Williams, research associate, formerly affiliated with the Center for Diversity Engineering. Both donated many hours to training, helping with planning, and most of all serving as exemplary facilitators during the structured dialogue sessions.

We are also grateful to Dawn Hunt and Sherri Barker for bringing a high level of thoughtfulness, organizational acumen, and attention to detail in terms of getting us organized and off the ground.

References

Alda, A., 2009. Improvisation for scientists workshop. Available from: <http://www.centerforcommunicatingscience.org/improvisation-for-scientists/> (accessed 09.06.14.)

Davidson, M., 2011. The End of Diversity As We Know It: Why Diversity Efforts Fail and How Leveraging Difference Can Succeed. Berrett-Koehler, San Francisco, CA.

DeTurk, S., 2006. The power of dialogue: consequences of intergroup dialogue and their implications for agency and alliance building. Commun. Q. 54 (1), 33–51.

Fisher, R., Ury, W., Patton, B., 1991. Getting to Yes: Negotiating Agreement Without Giving. Penguin, New York, NY.

Fisher, R., Shapiro, D., 2005. Beyond Reason: Using Emotions as You Negotiate. Penguin, New York, NY.

Innes, J., Booher, D., 2003. Collaborative policymaking: governance through dialogue. In: Hajer, M., Wagenaar, H. (Eds.), Deliberative Policy Analysis: Understanding Governance in the Network Society. Cambridge University Press, Cambridge, pp. 33–59.

Mannix, E., Neale, M., 2005. What differences make a difference? The promise and reality of diverse teams in organizations. Psychol. Sci. Public Interest. 6 (2), 31–55.

Nagda, B., Gurin, P., 2007. Intergroup dialogue: a critical-dialogic approach to learning about difference, inequality, and social justice. New Dir. Teach. Learn. 2007 (111), 35–45.

Ong, M., Wright, C., Espinosa, L.L., Orfield, G., 2011. Inside the double bind: a synthesis of empirical research on undergraduate and graduate women of color in science, technology, engineering, and mathematics. Harv. Educ. Rev. 81 (2), 172–209.

Page, S., 2007. The Difference: How the Power of Diversity Creates Better Groups, Firms, Schools, and Societies, New ed., 2008. Princeton University Press, Princeton, NJ.

Sannino, A., 2008. Experiencing conversations: bridging the gap between discourse and activity. J. Theory Soc. Behav. 38 (3), 267–291.

Spolin, V., Sills, C., Sills, P., 1999. Improvisation for the Theater: A Handbook of Teaching and Directing Techniques. third ed. Northwestern University Press, Evanston, IL.

Stone, D., Patton, B., Heen, S., 1999. Difficult Conversations: How to Discuss What Matters Most. Viking, New York, NY.

Zúñiga, X., Naagda, B., Sevig, T., 2002. Intergroup dialogues: an educational model for cultivating engagement across differences. Equity Excell. Educ. 35 (1), 7–17.

8

To Tenure and Beyond: Building an Intentional Career in STEM*

Amanda Shaffer[1] and Susan Freimark[2]

[1]Office of Faculty Development, Case Western University, Cleveland, OH, USA [2]Faculty Leadership Development Institute, Flora Stone Mather Center for Women, Case Western Reserve University, Cleveland, OH, USA

OUTLINE

Evolution of the NSF ADVANCE Initiatives at CWRU	130
Objectives of TT&B	131
Recruitment of Participants	132
Development of Modules and Customization to Cohort Needs	135
Module 1: Self-Awareness	*136*
Module 2: Power, Politics, and Influence	*137*
Module 3: Developing the Career Plan	*137*
Rationale for Key Curricular Themes: Understanding Career Arc and the Intentional Change Model	138
Evaluation and Outcomes	141
Challenges and Ongoing Efforts	142
References	144

*A Pay It FORWARD Project at Case Western Reserve University.

EVOLUTION OF THE NSF ADVANCE INITIATIVES AT CWRU

For the last 10 years, Case Western Reserve University (CWRU) has been at the forefront of furthering the National Science Foundation (NSF) ADVANCE program goal to "increase the workforce participation of women at all levels in academic science and engineering careers by transforming institutional structures and culture." These efforts began with the NSF ADVANCE Institutional Transformation award called Academic Careers in Engineering and Science (ACES, 2003–2008; Bilimoria and Liang, 2012), continued with the Partnerships for Adaptation, Implementation, and Dissemination (PAID, 2009–2013) award called Institutions Developing Excellence in Academic Leadership (IDEAL), and are also supported by the 2011 Pay It FORWARD award (2011, 2012), "To Tenure and Beyond: Building an Intentional Career in STEM."

Pay It FORWARD, a joint program of The George Washington University in and Gallaudet University in Washington, DC, was funded by a NSF ADVANCE PAID award. It was a project to fund teams to develop new workshops to advance women and other underrepresented minorities in Science, Technology, Engineering, and Mathematics (STEM). In spring 2011, Pay It FORWARD funding was awarded to Amanda Shaffer, director of faculty development at CWRU, to support the creation of "To Tenure and Beyond: Building and Intentional Career in STEM" (TT&B), a regional career development workshop series for pre-tenure women professors in STEM in northern Ohio.

TT&B was designed to work concurrently with the CWRU-led IDEAL project, an innovative 3-year partnership to foster gender equity and institutional transformation at six research universities in northern Ohio: CWRU, Bowling Green State University (BGSU), Cleveland State University (CSU), Kent State University (KSU), the University of Akron (UA), and the University of Toledo (UT). The goal of the IDEAL partnership grant, the first such collaboration in Ohio, was to enhance the depth and effectiveness of leadership on each of the respective campuses and establish a collaborative institutional community of formal and informal academic leaders to serve as a community resource—a powerful force for cultural transformation and an incubator of innovation (Holly, 2004; see also Richlin and Cox, 2004; Hansen et al., 2004).

IDEAL, as a NSF PAID project, adapted and disseminated the successful academic leadership development and institutional transformation methods developed by CWRU during its earlier 5-year NSF ADVANCE IT initiative, ACES. The well-documented contemporary issues facing women and minorities in science and engineering (e.g., Burke and Mattis, 2007; the National Academies, 2007; Rosser, 2004), as well as the institutional solutions initiated by NSF's ADVANCE IT program to redress them (Stewart et al., 2007), provided the framework for ACES, IDEAL, and subsequently TT&B.

IDEAL had three major objectives: (i) to create a regional learning community, (ii) to develop leadership for senior faculty, and (iii) to encourage institutional commitment to the advancement and participation of women faculty at the partner universities. These objectives were accomplished through leadership development workshops, an annual plenary conference, and the design and launching of annual change projects by change leader teams at each university. The change projects communicated a university-specific institutional theme around the participation and advancement of women faculty.

Midway through year two of the grant, all six of the partner universities were independently working on aspects of creating mentoring and faculty development programs for their universities. After discussions with IDEAL change leaders, TT&B was conceived as a pilot mechanism to formally launch faculty development efforts for women faculty in STEM and to provide additional momentum for the further institutionalization of faculty development activities at the partner universities. The TT&B workshop design leveraged IDEAL faculty change leaders and co-directors to engage senior administrative leadership as panel experts and in the recruitment of pre-tenure faculty.

OBJECTIVES OF TT&B

TT&B was conceived initially as a mechanism to pilot collaborative, regional faculty development efforts with the partner universities involved in IDEAL to increase the participation of women in academic STEM by increasing their efficacy, persistence, and potential to become future leaders (Buse et al., 2013). Developing a scalable model for faculty development that provided targeted, professional career coaching, strategic skill building, and career plans emerged as a compelling opportunity.

- Objective 1: Develop a model for untenured faculty development that stresses tenure as a career milestone, not an end goal, to encourage future leadership.
  Strategy: Assess strengths and gaps; provide means for long-term career planning as well as skill development for targeted areas of concern identified on a pre-assessment survey.

• Objective 2: Create a learning community and reduce isolation by leveraging IDEAL relationships and building cross-institution networks.

Strategy: Administrators and faculty involved with IDEAL were instrumental in promoting the workshops and facilitating details.

• Objective 3: Utilize the CWRU career coaching model as an essential support.

Strategy: Engage longtime CWRU coaches to work at 60% of their usual rate during a pilot supplemented by TT&B trainers who are also career coaches.

• Objective 4: Provide evidence that faculty development should be institutionalized.

Strategy: Pre- and post-assessment, evaluations, external marketing.

RECRUITMENT OF PARTICIPANTS

The target population for both TT&B consisted of a pool of 85 pre-tenure women STEM faculty (based on 2009–2010 data in Table 8.1) identified as pre-tenure STEM faculty at six northern Ohio research universities (the IDEAL partners): CWRU, BGSU, CSU, KSU, UA, and UT. In the spring and summer of 2011, the IDEAL co-directors obtained the names of pre-tenure women faculty in the NSF fundable departments at their universities and approached the appropriate deans to participate in nominating three to four members of their respective faculties. Each institution was encouraged to nominate multiple participants to develop or increase the peer network for women faculty, who are often isolated in their home departments.

TABLE 8.1   To Tenure and Beyond Round 1 (2011) Female STEM Faculty Participation. Number in Tenure-Track Pool, Number Nominated and Corresponding Percentage of the Pool, Number Attended and Corresponding Percentage of those Nominated, by Participating Institution

Female STEM faculty in IDEAL 2009–2010	2009–2010 Tenure-track pool	2011–2012 Nominated for TT&B		2011–2012 Attended TT&B	
	N	N	%	N	%
BGSU	7	1	14	0	0
CWRU	22	9	40	6	66
CSU	15	4	26	1	25
KSU	22	4	18	2	50
UA	10	5	50	4	80
UT	9	0	0	0	0
Total	85	23	27	13	56

Of the 23 nominated faculty, 17 accepted the nomination and completed a pre-workshop assessment survey. Then 4 participants withdrew for personal reasons, leaving 13 assistant professors representing multiple disciplines: engineering (biomedical, civil, chemical), biological sciences (biology, physiology/biophysics), medical sciences (genetics and infectious diseases), psychology, and geology.

The total lack of participation by the pre-tenure faculty at BGSU and UT (Table 8.1) was attributed to the distance required to attend and lack of networks for carpooling; however, administrations at both universities remained eager to offer this opportunity to their faculty in 2012–2013. A 2012 no-cost extension for unexpended funds from the 2011 award was used to provide TT&B at BGSU and UT (referred to as "TT&B West") by having the trainers travel to the locations, with administrators subsidizing the cost of the trainer travel.

The TT&B West tenure-track pool of 73 women faculty was based on 2009–2010 data (Table 8.2). A total of 12 faculty members were nominated by their dean to participate, with 1 faculty member subsequently exiting her university prior to the start of TT&B. All of the 11 participants were assistant professors from a range of disciplines, including medical sciences (physiology, pharmacology, biochemistry, cancer biology), biology, chemistry, psychology, bioengineering, and statistics.

In 2011, the FORWARD funding covered all associated costs for participants. The 2012 renewal award (Round 2), however, provided only 50% of the previous budget, necessitating a small fee per participant. Participants were drawn from the four geographically close research universities: CWRU, CSU, KSU, and UA.

Building on the pilot experience, Round 2 benefited from word of mouth, with a total of 31 STEM faculty nominated by their deans and

TABLE 8.2 To Tenure and Beyond West (2012 No-Cost Extension) Female STEM Faculty Participation. Number in Tenure-Track Pool, Number Nominated and Corresponding Percentage of the Pool, Number Attended and Corresponding Percentage of those Nominated, by Participating Institution

Female STEM faculty in IDEAL departments 2009–2010	2009–2010 Tenure-track pool	2012–2013 Nominated for TT&B		2012–2013 Attended TT&B	
	N	N	%	N	%
BGSU	7	4	57	4	100
UT	9	4	44	4	100
UT/SOM basic science	57	4	7	3	75
Total	73	12	16	11	91

Abbreviations: SOM, School of Medicine.

TABLE 8.3   To Tenure and Beyond Round 2 (2012) Female STEM Faculty Participation. Number in Tenure-Track Pool, Number Nominated and Corresponding Percentage of the Pool, Number Attended and Corresponding Percentage of those Nominated, by Participating Institution

Female STEM faculty in IDEAL departments 2009–2010	2009–2010 Tenure-track pool	2012–2013 Nominated for TT&B		2012–2013 Attended TT&B	
	N	N	%	N	%
CWRU	22	20	91	10	50
CSU	15	4	27	4	100
KSU	22	3	14	3	100
UA	10	4	40	4	100
Total	85	31	36	21	67

TABLE 8.4   To Tenure and Beyond Round 2 (2012) Female Non-STEM Faculty Participation. Number in Tenure-Track Pool, Number Nominated and Corresponding Percentage of the Pool, Number Attended and Corresponding Percentage of those Nominated, by Participating Institution

CWRU non-STEM female tenure-track faculty 2012–2013	2012–2013 Tenure-track pool	2012–2013 TT&B nominated		2012–2013 TT&B Attended	
	N	N	%	N	%
MSASS	3	2	67	2	66
WSOM	6	6	100	2	33
SDM	2	0	0	0	0
FPBSON	4	0	0	0	0
Total	15	8	53	4	50

21 accepting the nomination (see Table 8.3). Round 2 continued to forge a regional learning community and peer network among junior women faculty in STEM, and extended experimentally into four schools at CWRU that were not previously eligible to participate in the IDEAL project. The Mandel School of Applied Social Sciences (MSASS), School of Dental Medicine (SDM), Frances Payne Bolton School of Nursing (FPBSON), and Weatherhead School of Management (WSOM). Two of the schools chose not to participate. Eight non-STEM pre-tenure women faculty were nominated and four accepted (see Table 8.4). Because of their non-STEM status, the costs for these participants were not

subsidized by NSF funds, resulting in a slightly higher participation fee for the corresponding deans who were sponsoring their faculty. A total of 25 STEM and non-STEM faculty participated in TT&B Round 2.

Because of the range of the increase in eligible participants, the 25 Round 2 faculty more broadly represented the academic disciplines, including biological sciences, chemistry, economics, engineering (civil and electrical), geography, health sciences, humanities (sociology, psychology, and anthropology), marketing, organizational behavior, physics, social work, and statistics.

DEVELOPMENT OF MODULES AND CUSTOMIZATION TO COHORT NEEDS

Faculty who accepted the nomination to participate in TT&B were sent an online self-assessment that measured perceptions about their personal efficacy and interpersonal awareness and their satisfaction with their academic support and career planning. Participants were also able to indicate areas of interest for skills or competencies that they would like to develop or improve. The self-assessment, administered prior to the first session, allowed for content to be somewhat customized to the needs of the cohort.

The workshop content consisted of three modules; "Self-Awareness," "Power, Politics, and Influence," and "Developing the Career Plan," with two to three units per module tailored to fit the skill development needs of the cohort. The units were delivered with a variety of methods, including skill-building presentations, large- and small-group discussions, exercises, case studies, and expert panels of senior faculty. The workshops were also designed to include interaction with a variety of administrators to reinforce institutional commitment and networking.

TT&B was developed to encourage the participants to view their academic life not as a static entity, but as a protean career path (Hall, 2004). The protean career is one that is ongoing, and where all experiences (whether education, training, volunteer opportunities, and work in different settings) become important as they are called upon at different times. The skills, experiences, and knowledge gained from myriad settings work together to assist the individual to recognize strengths, capabilities, likes, and dislikes. For instance, developing a new skill while serving as a committee member might introduce the individual to a new responsibility that, in turn, becomes fulfilling and part of one's larger career plan. Participants were supported to develop a vision of the future based on their own experiences and expectations that would go beyond the goal of achieving tenure.

Creating a space where participants can dream and imagine their ideal career arc, TT&B asked the participants to forget the word *should* (e.g. "I *should* answer this way") and to resist suppressing their reactions in order to engage in "visioning" and self-assessment activities that allowed individuals to internalize criteria for goal setting, meaning, and self-defined success. The development plan, based on self-assessment and self-awareness, was a path crafted by the individual to facilitate increased confidence efficacy, and ultimately optimism about achieving academic milestones such as tenure.

Module 1 focused on self-assessment and individuals identifying their career and professional development needs. Modules 2 and 3 provided information and activities concerning how individuals are affected by and in their environments. Based on the feedback from evaluations in 2011–2012, the 2012–2013 iteration of TT&B included units on "Building Social Capital," "Emotional Intelligence," "Managing Students in the Lab," and "Negotiating." The 2-year evolution of the TT&B program has allowed the designers to develop a core of modules and units that can be formatted to meet the needs of each individual cohort. The pre-assessment continues to provide information as to the specific developmental issues of the cohorts, which then enables fine-tuning of existing units or the creation of new units.

Module 1: Self-Awareness

The first module focused on self-awareness and launched the process of intentional change, with a five-step model involving (i) creating a personal vision of one's desired future; (ii) assessing one's current state relative to that vision, articulating strengths and gaps; (iii) developing a plan of learning and action to move from the current to the desired state; (iv) experimenting with and practicing new behaviors as outlined in the learning and action plan; and (v) drawing on trusting relationships that help, support, and encourage each step of the process. Prior to the second module, the "Self-Awareness" module introduced the concept of executive coaching and charged participants with the assignment of developing specific, measureable, attainable, realistic, time-bound goals, known as *SMART goals* (Doran, 1981). Work/life integration topics included self-awareness of time management and boundary setting with students and service obligations.

Module 1 objectives included:

- Understanding concepts: Intentional change, self-awareness, role models, SMART goals
- Establishing group cohesion: Icebreakers, working in pairs, small- and large-group discussions
- Preliminary career planning activities: Work/life integration inventory, role model attributes, values inventory, identifying short-term SMART goals.

Module 2: Power, Politics, and Influence

Module 2 emphasized understanding the dynamics of power, personal comfort with power and politics, and emphasizing the value of influence without authority (Goleman, 2006; see also Patterson et al., 2007). Participants engaged in social networking mapping to better understand the power dynamics within their department. To encourage a broad vision for a career plan where tenure is a single milestone, the launch panel was asked to describe their career trajectory, especially branch points where a new direction was added in research, professional engagement, or service. Faculty members experienced with promotions and tenure committees informed participants how they might monitor and develop the tools (Garand et al., 2010) necessary for the academic process.

Module 2 objectives included:

- Understanding concepts: Power, negotiation, emotional intelligence, and social capital
- Deepening group cohesion: Group accountability on homework, SMART goal successes and challenges
- Career-planning activities: Panel of faculty in leadership, insights from recently tenured peers, mapping networks.

Module 3: Developing the Career Plan

In this final session, participants engaged in visioning for the final stage of their career plan, outlining steps to accomplish long- and short-term goals, and exploring the value of sponsorship for women (Ibarra et al., 2010). Skill building included best practices for managing, training, and advising students, with adaptable tools for successful lab management. Participant role-playing between a department chair and an unproductive student, a common area of concern repeatedly raised by participants, was based on a video scenario of the limiting climate and barriers to advancement women that frequently face that depicted successful negotiation and self-promotion in an academic setting (Tracy et al., 2007).

Module 3 objectives included:

- Understanding concepts: Vision, mentoring, sponsorship, social capital, mentoring, negotiation
- Skill building: Student management and productivity, framing difficult conversations, senior researchers with mentoring reputation
- Career-planning activities: Developing a mission statement, long-term career goals, completion of a summation document of participant learning.

RATIONALE FOR KEY CURRICULAR THEMES: UNDERSTANDING CAREER ARC AND THE INTENTIONAL CHANGE MODEL

Becoming clear about oneself and how others experience us is difficult and takes courage. **Richard Boyatzis**

A core theme for the development of TT&B was that intentional change, with its framework of individuals' proactive steps, assists in building a solid, satisfying career. The theory of intentional change was developed by Richard Boyatzis (Boyatzis and McKnee, 2006). Boyatzis's theory is that all sustainable change is intentional and conscious, and that with self-awareness and acceptance of one's true needs and wants, change becomes more intrinsically motivated and long-lasting.

Due to the nature of the academic structure, pre-tenure faculty have extrinsically set career goals (i.e., achieve tenure and promotion). Intentional change as a foundational theory was used to make conscious the short-term and long-term goals and choices that are often buried when a career is propelled by the momentum of external expectations. It is a less-than-optimal setting for long-term success and intrinsically motivated satisfaction to be swept along on a pre-set career path that moves an individual from one step to the next, with little opportunity to consciously evaluate personal needs.

Many of these pre-tenure individuals additionally carry the mixed reward of following in their mentor's footsteps with their own research agenda. They have had success in working from this platform and feel confused as to how to break into their own research direction. Starting with the premise of externally set goals and mixed motivation on a research agenda, the participants are introduced to the intentional change model. The five steps of this model (Figure 8.1), numbered for the purposes of TT&B, are

1. Discovering the Ideal Self
2. Discovering the Real Self
3. Creating a Learning Agenda
4. Experimenting with and Practicing New Behaviors
5. Developing Trust Relationships.

The concept of the "Ideal Self" is a foundation piece of the intentional change process. The Ideal Self is comprised of the individual's meaning and interpretation of success, fulfillment, and expertise. It is one's personal vision of excellence and what one hopes to achieve in career and life. With this image in mind, the individual is optimistic and motivated that there is a meaningful goal to pursue. The vision of excellence and potential achievement is outlined in an exercise where participants describe the attributes of people that they admire in the areas of

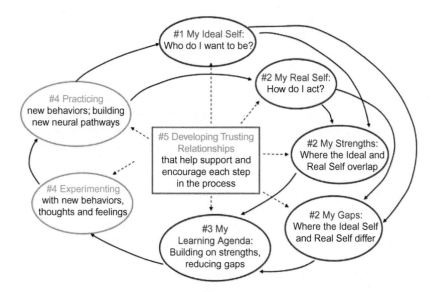

FIGURE 8.1   Intentional change model (Boyatzis and McKnee, 2006).

research, teaching, and service—the three components of the tenure track package. They address the following questions:

- Who do you admire in the area of [teaching service, research]?
- What are their strengths?
- What actions do they exemplify?

Mapping the collective strengths and actions of a range of role models in a large-group discussion provided additional input for the preliminary sketch of the "Ideal Self" that participants had completed prior to this exercise. This resulted in a more comprehensive profile of their "Ideal Self."

In order to move to Step 2 of the intentional change model, "Discovering the Real Self," participants need to be able to objectively assess their own strengths and gaps in the areas of research, teaching, and service. A simple 360-degree assessment was used for the 2011 cohort, but many of the outside respondents were reluctant to provide any negative feedback, making the results unhelpful. In the second cohort, the activity changed to self-assessment with the question "How would your colleagues describe you?" The question solicited information that could be used in the exercise as the "Real Self," which was then added to the working diagram. Using the diagram, the skills or attributes that were identified as overlapping the Ideal and Real Selves were placed in the center and viewed as strengths because they were desired *and* present. Those skills and attributes remaining in the "Ideal Self" section became goals for the learning agenda—the conscious, intentional effort to change or grow (Step 3, "Creating a Learning Agenda").

Participants are now equipped with a meaningful learning agenda of skills, experiences, or attributes that they would like to pursue. By articulating the learning agenda, the participant is laying the groundwork for objectively assessing her performance, while coupling her internally focused goals with the externally imposed goals of the tenure track path.

Step 4 of the change model, "Experimenting with and Practicing New Behaviors," is explored in individual coaching sessions. Working with a coach one on one, the individual can explore risks or obstacles in implementing change and determine safe realistic settings in which to practice new behaviors or skills. The coaching relationship is part of Step 5, "Developing Trust Relationships," as it is essential that trust is established between a coach and coachee as the coach serves to support and encourage discovery.

The coaching component, a distinguishing feature of the TT&B program, provides the participant with two 1-h coaching sessions throughout the duration of the program. The coach and coachee examine the learning agenda produced during the workshop as a draft personal development plan where strengths, weaknesses, time commitments, and realistic goals are articulated. In this confidential setting, the coach guides the coachee in refining her plan and identifying concerns, obstacles, or challenges to implementation. Some challenges that surfaced in coaching sessions dealt with assertiveness, political climates of departments, difficulty in developing new ideas, work/life balance and the impact on research activities, student supervision, lack of self-confidence, team management, sexual harassment, discrimination, time management, feelings of isolation in the department, setting boundaries, need for intellectual stimulation, and reluctance to engage in risk or decision making.

The development plan is a catalyst for uncovering real issues that are affecting the individual's long-term career goals. The individual often has initial concerns about confidentiality, but once trust is built, the coaching relationship enables her to share deeply held fears or concerns. The coaching provides the format for discovering the realities and assumptions of those concerns, how they may be affecting her career, and steps for addressing the concerns.

Role-playing is often used to help the coachee practice new behaviors before implementing changes. These five steps combined with coaching empowers the individual to plan for and "intentionally change" behaviors in pursuit of goals.

EVALUATION AND OUTCOMES

A number of changes were made to the second series of workshops. The first major adjustment was in the timing. Participants in the 2011 cohort recommended that the entire series be held in a single semester rather than being spread over two semesters. This change to the one-semester structure permitted more noticeable group cohesion to occur, as the time between sessions was closer and allowed more familiarity and recognition. The challenge in this format was for the organizers of the program and the coaches. As each workshop in the series was customized to the preassessment survey of a particular cohort, the reduced preparation time between workshops taxed the program organizers and made scheduling coaching sessions more challenging.

Another revision centered on the feedback from colleagues of the participants. This information was to be used as part of the formation of the "Real Self" exercise. Some colleagues who were asked to provide information about a participant's skills, abilities, and emotional intelligence in a 360-degree format did not complete the assessment, while others, in an effort to support the participant, provided only positive feedback. Because the results were not helpful to the participant in forming a sense of the Real Self, in 2012, the activity was changed to participant self-assessment via the question, "How would other people describe you?" While this solicited more helpful information for the outlining of the Real Self, this activity remains under revision.

Workshop evaluations were used to monitor effectiveness of content and delivery and remained at 3 or above on a 4-point scale across all sessions (Table 8.5).

The key results of the post-workshop survey indicated that intentionality is a key tool in faculty development. An analysis of what is (Real Self) and what is desired (Ideal Self) is foundational for personal growth and the development of SMART goals, which drive and shape action. Participants also valued the investment of time for "thinking rather than doing," developing clarity around what questions to ask and what career steps to take; for example:

> The workshop really helped me organize my work and gave me ideas that have greatly enhanced my productivity... I've made back the time I put in through working more efficiently and by negotiating for what I need.

The shift from external goal (achieving tenure) to internal goal (career arc) increased optimism and helped participants feel "motivated," "energized," and "more strategic":

> [TT&B] helped me realize that I already know much of what I need to do—I just need to do a better job of setting goals and working toward them...helped me think toward tenure, but where I want my career to end up.

TABLE 8.5   2012 TT&B Workshop Evaluations

	Provided helpful information	Provided useful strategies	Provided useful opportunities to network across universities	Group discussions were useful	Overall, the session was effective
ROUND 2 (CWRU, CSU, KSU, UA)					
Workshop 1 (N=20) September 14, 2012	3.50	3.60	3.05	3.65	3.55
Workshop 2 (N=15) October 18, 2012	3.53	3.60	3.13	3.60	3.60
Workshop 3 (N=17) December 11, 2012	3.41	3.58	2.82	3.47	3.58
TT&B WEST (BG/UT)					
Workshop 1 (N=10) August 15, 2012	3.65	3.55	3.20	3.33	3.60
Workshop 2 (N=17) October 8, 2012	3.42	3.57	3.00	3.42	3.64
Workshop 3 (N=10) November 14, 2012	3.90	3.90	3.30	3.60	3.88

Scale: 4, Excellent; 3, Good; 2, Fair; 1, Poor; 0, No answer.

Several of the participants reported an increased optimism about achieving tenure at their institution after completing the program.

Structured to build community and reduce isolation through a cross-discipline, cross-university cohort participants reported new relationships with peers at their own and other universities: "[I] developed a network of women going through the profession at the same time"; "meeting female faculty from different institutions is invaluable." The cross-discipline efforts highlighted that some development issues for STEM and non-STEM faculty vary, with participants noting: "Many of us don't have a lab... It might be better using a subgroup in some cases" and "other schools work very differently for tenure and grants... helpful to have a few session by 'groups'; e.g., school of management or medicine." This feedback will be integrated into future cross-discipline workshops.

CHALLENGES AND ONGOING EFFORTS

One challenge to the program is the issue of attendance. Participants were asked to reserve the three scheduled dates of the workshops, but the inconsistent attendance of some of the participants negatively affected the group cohesion and minimized the overall impact on the individuals. The curriculum was designed to build cumulatively on each module, giving participants a full picture of who they are, what they want, and how they might plan to achieve their long-term career goals. While some of the information missed could be recaptured in the individual coaching sessions, participants lose the richness of the group discussion and peer mentoring. In the future, we may examine the attendance data issue to see anecdotally if there is any correlation between attendance and career progression. The participant time commitment in the TT&B framework (three $6\frac{1}{2}$-h days, two 1-h coaching sessions, and travel time of up to 60 min), whether spaced over one semester or an academic year, is significant for an untenured faculty member.

The recruitment of faculty through nomination by academic deans and provosts created understandable delays in faculty enrollment and the administration of the pre-survey, which in turn shortened the amount of time for curriculum design. Because the project was a pilot "in addition to regular duties," staff time was stretched by survey development, evaluation, website updates, and report writing, in addition to the development of new content and resources.

Logistics such as dietary restrictions, allergies, and tepid tea water, as well as parking and the temperature of the room, are eternally challenging for organizers and participants. However, the most significant challenge remains funding. TT&B utilized executive coaching as part of the intentional change model, which is expensive to provide on this scale. The external coaches participating in the project, all previously associated with NSF ADVANCE–related programs at CWRU, generously accepted only 60% of their usual rate. The workshop trainers, who are both professional coaches, also provided some of the coaching services for participants to help offset costs.

A somewhat less significant challenge is an undercurrent of faculty member bias against receiving training or tenure-related guidance from trainers who do not hold faculty positions. When this type of bias is encountered, the amount of experience or depth of expertise of the trainer is usually irrelevant. The reputation and personal integrity of the trainers often enables word-of-mouth testimonials to undermine the bias, but that is an unnecessary ongoing obstacle to implementing faculty development initiatives. Additionally, despite extensive research outlining the barriers to women's advancement in STEM disciplines outside and within academia, some women faculty have stated that they are not interested in gender-specific programming because of the implied remediation or perceived stigma.

Also, while TT&B focused on the issues specific to pre-tenure women faculty in STEM, a different set of professional development issues face posttenure faculty. To address these issues, the three workshops with individual coaching TT&B structures were adapted to create a new program. A total of 19 women faculty participated in the pilot of "What's Next?" in 2013, which offered modules on leadership in the academy and in one's discipline, emotional intelligence, development of a leadership development plan, the social psychology of gender and its presence in the academy, and development of individual and organizational strategies for effecting change.

For the next iteration of TT&B, the Office of Faculty Development, in collaboration with the Flora Stone Mather Center for Women, will pilot a curriculum that is broadened to address the needs of both male and female STEM and non-STEM faculty.

References

Bilimoria, D., Liang, X., 2012. Gender Equity in Science and Engineering: Advancing Change in Higher Education. Routledge, New York, NY.

Boyatzis, R., McKnee, A., 2006. Intentional change. J. Organ. Excell. 25 (3), 49–60.

Burke, R., Mattis, M., 2007. Women and Minorities in Science, Technology, Engineering and Mathematics: Upping the Numbers. Edward Elgar, Northampton, MA.

Buse, K., Bilimoria, D., Perelli, S., 2013. Why they stay: women persisting in US engineering careers. Career Dev. Int. 18 (2), 139–154.

Doran, G.T., 1981. There's a S.M.A.R.T. way to write management's goals and objectives. Management Review (AMA Forum) 70 (11), 35–36.

Etkowitz, H., Kemelgor, C., Neuchatz, M., Uzi, J., 1994. The paradox of critical mass for women in science. Science New Series. 266 (5182), 51–54.

Garand, L., Matthew, J.T., Courtney, K.L., Davies, M., Lingler, J.H., Schlenk, E.A., et al., 2010. A tool to guide junior faculty in their progression toward promotion and tenure. J. Profess. Nurs. 26 (4), 207–213.

Goleman, D., 2006. Emotional Intelligence: Why It Can Matter More than IQ. Bantam Books, New York, NY.

Hall, D.T., 2004. The protean career: a quarter-century journey. J. Vocat. Behav. 65, 1–13.

Hansen, S., Kalish, A., Hall, W., Gynn, C.M., Holly, M.L., Madigan, D. 2004. Developing a statewide faculty learning community program. New Directions for Teaching and Learning. (97), 71–80 (Chapter 6).

Holly, M.L., 2004. Learning in community: small group leadership for educational change. Educar 34, 113–130.

Ibarra, H., Carter, N., Silva, C., 2010. Why men still get more promotions than women. Harv. Bus. Rev. 88 (9), 80–85.

National Academies, 2007. Beyond Bias and Barriers: Fulfilling the Potential of Women in Academic Science and Engineering. The National Academies Press, Washington, DC.

Patterson, K., Grenny, J., Maxfield, D., McMillan, R., Switzler, A., 2007. Influencer: The Power to Change Anything. McGraw-Hill, USA.

Richlin, L., Cox, M. 2004. Developing scholarly teaching and the scholarship of teaching and learning through faculty learning communities. New Directions Teaching Learning, 97, 127–236.

Rosser, S.V., 2004. The Science Glass Ceiling: Academic Women Scientists and the Struggle to Succeed. Routledge, New York, NY.

Stewart, A.J., Malley, J.E., LaVaque-Manty, D. (Eds.), 2007. Transforming Science and Engineering; Advancing Academic Women. University of Michigan Press, Ann Arbor, MI.

Tracy, E., Singer, L.T., Singer, M. 2007. presentation "Gender Issues in the Path to Academic Leadership", to the Council on Social Work Education Leadership Seminar, February 2007, Phoenix, Arizona, AZ.

Further Reading

Bilimoria, D., Joy, S., Liang, X., 2008. Breaking barriers and creating inclusiveness: lessons of organizational transformation to advance women faculty in Academic Science and Engineering. Hum. Resour. Manage. 47 (3), 423–441.

Boyatzis, R., Akrivou, K, 2006. The ideal self as the driver of intentional change. J. Manage. Dev. 25 (7), 624–642.

Committee on Maximizing the Potential of Women in Academic Science and Engineering, 2006. Beyond Bias and Barriers: Fulfilling the Potential of Women in Academic Science and Engineering. National Academies Press, Washington, DC.

McCracken, D., 2000. Winning the talent war for women: sometimes it takes a revolution. Harv. Bus. Rev. 78 (6), 159–167.

Meyerson, D., Fletcher, J., 2000. A modest manifesto for shattering the glass ceiling. Harv. Bus. Rev.127–136.

Ely, R., Thomas, D., 1996. Cultural diversity at work: the effects of diversity perspectives on work group processes and outcomes. Adm. Sci. Q. 46 (2), 229–273. Available from: <http://www.jstor.org/stable/2667087> (accessed 24.08.15).

Ely, R.J., Thomas, D.A., 2001. Cultural diversity at work: the effects of diversity perspectives on work group processes and outcomes. Adm. Sci. Q. 46 (2), 229–273. Available from: < http://www.jstor.org/stable/2667087 > (accessed 24.08.15.).

FORWARD Oklahoma State University: Building an Academic Toolkit for Women at a Land-Grant Institution

Jean Van Delinder[1], Shiping Deng[2], Jeanmarie Verchot[3], Amy Madewell[4] and Daisha Delano[1]

[1]Sociology Department, Oklahoma State University, Stillwater, OK, USA
[2]Plant and Soil Sciences, Oklahoma State University, Stillwater, OK, USA
[3]Entomology and Plant Pathology, Oklahoma State University, Stillwater, OK, USA [4]Psychology Department, Southeastern Oklahoma State University, Durant, OK, USA

OUTLINE

Introduction   148

FORWARD OSU   150
  The Setting: OSU as a Land-Grant Institution   *151*
  Science, Gender Segregation, and the Land-Grant Mission   *152*
  Tool #1: Effective Mentoring and Networking   *153*
  Tool #2: Developing Negotiation Skills   *154*
  Tool #3: Balancing Family and Career—Strategies to
    Face Stereotype Threat in a Negative Work Climate   *156*

Analysis   158
  Pre-conference Survey   *158*
  Experience, Competence, Effectiveness, and Self-Efficacy   *158*
  Exploring the Myth of Work/Family Balance in Academe   *160*

   147

Conclusion and Implications for Future FORWARD Workshops 162

References 163

INTRODUCTION

The two-day FORWARD Oklahoma State University (OSU) workshop was held in March 2012 on the OSU campus, beginning with a keynote speech by Dr Henrietta Mann, president of the newest land-grant college in Oklahoma, the Cheyenne and Arapaho Tribal College in Weatherford. As a Tsistsistas (Cheyenne), Dr Mann shared how her cultural roots shaped her career in higher education (Figure 9.1).

Dr Mann described as her inspiration her great-grandmother, White Buffalo Woman, who survived two massacres, one at Sand Creek in what is now Colorado in 1864. Soon after moving to Oklahoma Territory in 1868, she survived then-Lieutenant Colonel George Armstrong Custer's assault on her village on the banks of Washita Creek. Despite these traumatic events, her great-grandmother endured and thrived because of her resilience and the support of her community. Dr Mann's message was that although Native peoples were haunted by their history, it is "acceptable to be indigenous" even while pursuing a career in higher education. Echoing the words of George Cajete in *Native Science: The Natural Laws of Interdependence* (1999), unlike the Western scientific method, native thinking does not isolate an object or phenomenon in order to understand it but perceives it in terms of relationships. Indigenous peoples have a lot to contribute to traditional Western academic thinking. Science is an endeavor not undertaken in isolation but only made better by collaboration. Women and underrepresented groups can make important contributions, and our voices will be heard only if we learn to successfully navigate the culture of academia. Her inspiring words set the tone for the workshop to impart practical information for academic success while acknowledging the challenges that women face.

The next morning the conference convened at 8:30 a.m. with a welcome and opening remarks by Dr Sheryl Tucker, dean of the OSU Graduate College and professor of chemistry. A panel discussion on reappointment, promotion, and tenure (RPT) processes and criteria was led by Dr Bob Miller, Regents Professor, Department of Microbiology and Molecular Genetics at OSU. Other panelists included Dr Katherine Kocan, Regents Professor and Sitlington Distinguished Professor, Department of Veterinary Pathobiology at OSU, and Dr Estella

FIGURE 9.1 Dr Henrietta Mann, president of Cheyenne and Arapaho Tribal College, served as an inspiring keynote speaker for the FORWARD OSU workshop.

A. Atekwana, Regents Professor and Clyde Wheeler Sun Chair Professor of Hydrogeology, Department of Geology at OSU. This session was followed by breakout discussions on the RPT process, evaluation, and criteria. The discussions were led by panel members and grouped by discipline. The breakouts provided an opportunity for participants to ask questions in a small-group setting. In the first afternoon session, Dr Linda Watson, professor and head of the OSU Botany Department, discussed the topic of "defining productivity." After a short break, a panel roundtable on how to balance family and a career life opened up discussion to the entire group. Panelists included dual-career couples. One panelist remarked, "...this was the best part of the conference for me. I will never forget the kindness of the couple sharing such personal moving experiences—it definitely gave me something to think about and to share when advising graduate students." The final session was on when and how to say yes to service and committee assignments.

A graduate student who was single commented, "I am preparing to graduate and am currently interviewing for faculty positions. The workshop was very timely for me and has helped me tailor the interview questions that I have as well as to know what to expect when going through the tenure process."

Forward OSU was planned around the issues women and minorities often struggle with in setting personal and professional boundaries, creating opportunities for networking, and the visibility required to succeed. Faculty at land-grant institutions need to show accomplishments in extension and outreach, classroom teaching, and research to build a portfolio of success toward promotion and tenure. In this regard, networking needs to be on several practical levels: (i) associations with colleagues within the department, the scientific community, and grant agencies; (ii) commanding leadership in the classroom and scientific discipline; and (iii) building good relationships with university administrators, state commodity groups, and extension clientele.

Extension and outreach focus on practical education for professionals, businesses, and communities in order to develop problem-solving skills. University extension and outreach programs are geared to help businesses and communities through a range of educational programs that are designed to: (i) support business productivity and competitiveness, (ii) strengthen community economic development, nutrition, and health, and (iii) support agriculture and natural-resource management. Extension programs often operate away from the university campus and can be less formal than departmental or other events on campus. Meeting and interacting with stakeholders and individual clientele also involves exclusive informal relationships that are quite different from collegial relationships within the department or scientific discipline. Gender and cultural differences can affect success in these informal relationships.

FORWARD OSU

The workshop sessions suggested tools that foster skill development in four key areas for women scientists: (i) promotion and tenure process at a land-grant institution; (ii) defining productivity and outputs; (iii) balancing family and career; and (iv) developing negotiation skills to handle negative stereotype threats. The tools included (i) effective mentoring and networking; (ii) developing negotiation skills; and (iii) strategies to face stereotype threat in a negative work climate. These tools are key for women to be successful in higher education. Expanding on Swidler's (1986) notion of culture as a toolkit that people selectively draw on to inform their behavior and decision-making, successfully navigating academic culture requires its own specialized toolkit. The ideologies and traditions embedded in the institutional culture of higher education simultaneously constrain and enable certain types of behaviors that reinforce certain negative gender norms as "common sense"—such as "women do not belong in STEM fields" (Alexander, 2003; Hays, 2000; Xie and Shauman, 2003).

Drawing on previous research and a pre-workshop survey (discussed later in this chapter) about attendees' current career status and expectations, we identified difficulties that women face with regard to career advancement and developed sessions to help participants tailor their academic toolkit to succeed through the promotion and tenure process. In particular, the workshops sought to help women to thrive in academic careers by effectively dealing with stereotype threats that can easily arise in science, technology, engineering, and mathematics (STEM) disciplines, where gender and racial segregation is more the norm. A successful science career requires women and minority scientists to recognize and appropriately handle gender and racial behavior stereotypes that might hinder their ability to be taken seriously as scientists (Steele et al., 2002). This makes the institutional structure of academic work in research-intensive universities, including land-grant institutions, less than ideal family-friendly places to work. This lack of accommodation for family responsibilities accounts for one of the largest leaks in the pipeline for women scientists (Mason et al., 2010). Therefore, with FORWARD to Professorship, it is important for women scientists to develop a personal academic resource toolkit to skillfully build a productive career while establishing the boundary between work and family.

The Setting: OSU as a Land-Grant Institution

Unique to the United States, land-grant institutions were established by the Morrill Act in 1862 to create a system of higher education to meet the growing demand for technical expertise in agriculture and engineering (ALPU, 2012). These institutions flourished with the emergence of the "mechanic arts" in agriculture and engineering and the institutional development of graduate education to help support the expansion of scientific research. Land-grant colleges quickly adopted the German model of scientific training using research groups rather than the more individualized tutorial approach found within the English system (Van Delinder and Tucker, 2014). This emphasis on technological and scientific research facilitated the development of an institutional culture at land-grant institutions that was implicitly masculine. Though land-grants provided women with unprecedented access to higher education, those interested in science were steered toward emerging subjects in the home economics disciplines rather than engineering (Thorne, 1985). The resulting gendered segregation of university curriculum and faculty facilitated a dominant culture and ideology defining women's competence within the domain of the domestic arts. Such negative stereotypes persist today at these institutions, questioning women's innate abilities related to careers in science and engineering (Eccles, 1994).

Established as part of the second land-grant legislation, the Morrill Act of 1890, OSU's academic culture is firmly anchored in agriculture and engineering, and women faculty and students are more likely to pursue education and home economics professions than STEM fields of study. Since institutional culture is part of the "cultural equipment" people use to "make sense of their world" (Milkie and Denny, 2014), in order for people to accept new meanings and adopt new practices, they need to retool—that is, acquire a new cultural toolkit. In institutions where there are few women in science and engineering, a paradigm shift in institutional culture depends upon administrators and female professors recognizing how to lift the curtain of stereotypical gender norms that obscures these women's competence.

Science, Gender Segregation, and the Land-Grant Mission

Some researchers suggest that the academic pipeline in STEM fields is gendered, with a more protective and supportive work climate for men but a chilly and somewhat ambiguous work climate for women (Halpern et al., 2007). One particularity of land-grant institutions is the requirement of faculty members to be engaged in extension and outreach as well as research and teaching. The dynamics of a gendered STEM work climate are complicated by the land-grant mission, in which one must also interact with community officials and the general public. Identifying and understanding the varied cultural practices that produce an institutional climate of gender disparity may provide a better understanding of key factors that ultimately lead to advancing the representation of women in science and academia at land-grant universities.

As part of the preparation and planning for this workshop, we reviewed data collected on differences between STEM and non-STEM women's perceptions of the effect of gender equality, personal/professional life balance, and departmental support for family responsibilities at OSU (Madewell et al., 2012). Data were collected from 418 male and female faculty members made up of 131 STEM male and 26 STEM female, 136 non-STEM male, and 125 non-STEM female. STEM and non-STEM women at OSU reported significantly lower perceptions of departmental gender equality than STEM and non-STEM men, with

STEM women reporting the lowest level of gender equality. One woman faculty member stated that the cultural environment in her department does not promote gender equity, which is, in part, reflected by the way her students interact with her: "In the classroom, students often call me 'Ms.' or 'Mrs.' rather than 'Dr' as they call my colleagues; I rarely correct them because I feel it makes me look 'touchy'." She chose to avoid being perceived as too emotional ("looking touchy")—a negative stereotype about women's emotional makeup—because she was concerned about not being perceived as if she belonged if she asked for the same respect as her male colleagues. This quote illustrates the conflict between socially legitimized behavioral options consistent with predominant gender norms and those associated with being a successful faculty member.

The survey results showed that non-STEM men reported the highest level of perceived gender equality within their department. These findings suggest that the women in our sample experienced lower levels of support, equality, and balance than the men in our sample, regardless of discipline. Furthermore, 54% of women and only 3% of men reported gender discrimination by students, graduate students, and staff.

To extend these preliminary findings, we evaluated faculty perceptions of the hiring process and discrimination. In 2009, we asked STEM and non-STEM male and female faculty to complete a Campus Climate Survey I (CCS-I), which asked about job-related discrimination experienced in the last five years (e.g., race, gender, and religious affiliation) (OSU, 2010a). Out of 96 respondents to this question, 17 faculty members reported gender discrimination during the hiring and promotion-to-tenure process, 45 faculty experienced gender discrimination in terms of salary, and 17 reported gender inequity in department resources, access to staff, and access to graduate student assistants. Finally, 40 faculty members reported gender discrimination occurring between faculty members, 11 reported racial discrimination, sexual orientation discrimination, and religious discrimination by other faculty members at OSU. Interestingly, all faculty who reported gender, racial, or sexual inequities were from a minority group.

Tool #1: Effective Mentoring and Networking

The first tool presented was about the importance of formal and informal mentoring opportunities. Mentoring involves the transmission of information and knowledge not readily available but relevant to work, career, or professional development. Mentoring involves building a relationship with a more experienced person who is perceived to have greater relevant knowledge, wisdom, or experience. Since women and minorities in STEM often feel isolated and are reluctant to initiate mentoring relationships for fear of being perceived as inadequate, the first discussion focused on how to make mentoring work for them to be successful in their careers. The FORWARD OSU workshop benefited from the results of a previous National Science Foundation (NSF) ADVANCE OSU program (NSF #0820240) that created and maintained a mentoring program for both male and female STEM faculty (OSU, 2010b). Faculty mentors were trained to work with junior faculty on developing individual career development plans to help them meet tenure requirements in their departments. Mentors met regularly with their mentees and attended organized workshops and lunches to share experiences and knowledge and provide support. While STEM men who reported having a mentor in their field did not report gender discrimination as a reason for working with a mentor, STEM women with a mentor reported more gender discrimination than any other group. As in the findings of Halpern et al. (2007), women seeking a mentor were more likely to report reduced levels of job satisfaction when they became more informed of departmental inequities. A total of 35% of women with a mentor and 17% of women without one reported gender discrimination in salary.

As one of the tools needed to master the first skills, "Making the Most of Mentor Relationships" was addressed in one of the workshop sessions. An important initial step is to find appropriate professional mentors or dissertation advisers. Mentoring is a lifelong endeavor. Effective mentoring is built on mutual trust and confidentiality where a person seeks guidance but also learns how to positively use criticism to correct less-than-desirable actions. For postdoctoral researchers and junior faculty, effective mentoring is also crucial to building professional networks. It is important to seek a mentor who is willing to share her specialized knowledge on developing a productive and successful career.

Tool #2: Developing Negotiation Skills

The second set of tools presented at the workshop was to facilitate the development of negotiation skills. Success, productivity, and resource allocation are inseparable. Research productivity in STEM is ultimately tied to resource requirements and availability, which are, in turn, tied to institutional support. New faculty may not know what is negotiable and how to negotiate while maintaining positive relationships with their colleagues. Unlike social science disciplines that are more theoretical in nature, being a faculty member in STEM fields often requires significant laboratory space and expensive, specialized equipment (Duch et al., 2012). Negotiation skills enable faculty to compete for funding, supporting the acquisition of major equipment (Duch et al., 2012). Access to resources, especially institutionally granted resources or institutional support, is essential to jump-start an academic career, secure large grants, and pave the road to success. Researchers who have already received some institutional support are able to secure further research resources to strengthen and increase productivity. Therefore, having the tools to negotiate a competitive startup package is crucial to launching a successful academic career. However, many women are not adept at asking for what they need, especially as junior faculty. In a field where access to resources is vital to success, possessing good negotiation skills is crucial. This is an instance where professional norms conflict with gender norms such as being supportive, cooperative, or submissive. Yet, the successful launch of an academic career depends on the ability to assert needs independently, which can cause anxiety because women may misperceive this behavior as aggression.

Other aspects of academic work include skills in negotiating: (i) teaching schedules and load; (ii) extension and outreach commitments, including the clientele organizations that you work with; and (iii) service committees for the department, college, and university. One of the main reasons for negotiating these areas is time and workload management. Any non-tenured faculty member, whether male, female, or minority, will be apprehensive about negotiating these job components because they are less familiar with their own needs to succeed in these areas. Often, graduate school and postdoctoral training does not include training in these aspects of the job. While faculty are often allowed to set their own research agendas so long as they conform to their job description, extension and outreach, teaching, and service commitments can often change dramatically on the road to tenure and can create time- and workload-management issues.

The challenges in effectively negotiating academic workload are being able to set boundaries and being able to distinguish between being a team player and saying no to participating in activities that do not necessarily advance one's career. The general advice offered by career coaches is that requests should never be met with an unconditional yes and should include provisions. Women who are new to negotiations or are pre-tenure approach them with a sense of apprehension or subordination, which can cause them to lose their sense of purpose. In these situations, women are less consistent in their behavior with regard to knowing how and when to be assertive, how to communicate with the appropriate body language, and how to maintain a focus on actionable issues.

STEM faculty members are trained to be strategic in securing external grants to establish their research career, but they often overlook the importance of being just as strategic in service assignments. Service is typically committee work for the department, college, university, professional society, government agencies, or scientific journals. The goal of such service is to raise professional stature, grow a professional network, gain skills and insight into organizational structure and function, and improve decision-making. Identifying a strategy for service means to identify goals for participating in certain committees. For example, in department-level committees, women may be drawn to or asked to participate in services that involve hosting visitors or student nurturing in order to be perceived as a "team player." However, this choice might not be as strategic as committees that enable professional growth and development, such as colloquia or laboratory committees.

Women often do not usually think about negotiation skills as important tools to apply, not only to their academic research, but also to their departmental committee assignments. Women and underrepresented groups are not always aware of the resources available to them. Some universities now have offices of postdoctoral study to help young scientists design an individual professional development plan. Such programs will help STEM women better prepare for the academic workforce.

Refining and developing negotiation skills were discussed in three sessions. These sessions were all led by senior faculty. The first session, "Leadership: How to Say 'No' While Also Inspiring People," addressed how to develop negotiation skills and why it is sometimes difficult for women to put their career needs first. This session emphasized being positive while saying "no" to tasks that deviate from productivity for tenure and promotion. Discussions were extended to evaluating a person's tone and body language while speaking. One strategy is to offer alternatives that are manageable within one's workload. This session was an important foundation to the succeeding sessions: "The Clock is Ticking: Promotion and Tenure" and "Defining Productivity: Scholarship, Teaching, Service, and Outreach."

Tool #3: Balancing Family and Career—Strategies to Face Stereotype Threat in a Negative Work Climate

A negative departmental climate can contribute to poor job performance and overall lower life satisfaction. The third instrument for this academic toolkit is how to develop strategies to identify and appropriately respond to stereotype threat or negative racial or gender stereotypes. When the work environment supports stereotypical gender roles, women are more likely to engage in behaviors that affirm their roles as mothers or caregivers and deemphasize their scientific research (Smith et al., 2013). Battling stereotype threat is linked to lower life satisfaction (De Welde and Laursen, 2011), lower job satisfaction (Hagedorn, 2000), and burnout (Singh et al., 1998), and could, in part, explain why fewer women scientists matriculate through the academic pipeline. One study found that while STEM women faculty performed poorly when discussing research with male colleagues, they performed well when discussing research with female colleagues (Holleran et al., 2010). Holleran et al. (2010) found workplace conversations focusing on research rather than family life as an implicit environmental cue on a positive social identity that affirms women as professionals rather than caregivers or mothers. These group differences were not significant in same-sex conversations or among men conversing with women.

Often, women and minorities struggle with their treatment, as it requires a candid discussion of social issues with people of senior rank who may not be receptive to the conversation (Steele and Aronson, 1995). One finding from our previous research was the importance of training graduate students and postdoctoral Fellows to develop strategies of action, or an alternative cultural toolkit, to better recognize obstacles. In the United States, there is increasing recognition of the importance of creating a more equitable and supportive academic climate inclusive of women and minorities (De Welde and Laursen, 2011). However, behavioral and communication tools, as well as the body language and presentation skills needed to successfully navigate their departmental climate, are often overlooked in favor of focusing on flaws in academic preparation.

Mentoring and negotiation are important skills when developing strategies to effectively invalidate actions or behaviors that are at risk of confirming negative stereotypes about faculty members' gender or racial group. Especially for those who find themselves as the only or one of a few women or minorities in their department, this is key to continued success in an academic career. For women and minority members who are constantly under the pressure to effectively deal with negative stereotypes, it is especially important to recognize such behaviors by paying careful attention to the behaviors and language of others, and to maintain a mindset of independence, self-control, and discipline. These strategies can help maintain a positive image with regard to others' views of stereotype confirmation. Many workshop participants reported feeling isolated or out of place because of their gender or minority status. Stereotype threat remains detrimental to the careers of many women and minorities, and the elimination of its underlying issues should be prioritized in order to promote equality in the STEM fields.

To ameliorate the threat of stereotype confirmation in situations where stereotype threat is recognizable, it is important to be observant, analyze situations, and keep mental notes regarding the manner in which situations play out. The aim was to provide workshop participants the skills to recognize potentially threatening situations when navigating their career advancement. Women often build networks with other women, which can be beneficial in creating relationships of support and mentorship. However, the group social identity created by this type of network can reinforce perceived stereotypes for professionals outside the group. The sessions on this third tool provided information on how to be strategic in selecting mentors who are career minded, do not take advantage of others, provide objective and useful advice, and understand the importance of keeping confidential information private. Any individual who is at risk for the possibility of stereotype threat should be sure to pay attention to other people's motives in interactions, recognize the stereotype association, and be strategic in working against the assumed negative behavior.

ANALYSIS

Pre-conference Survey

Prior to attending the workshop, 35 female participants were asked to fill out a pre-conference survey. FORWARD OSU participants identified goals including (i) obtaining a postdoctoral research position (20%); (ii) obtaining a tenured or a tenure-track position at a research or academic institution (45%); and (iii) obtaining a job in the private sector (15%). Specific professional objectives included (i) planning to finish their dissertation (45%); (ii) conference presentations (45% were very likely to present, and 35% stated that they had already achieved this goal); (iii) publishing (55% were very likely to publish, and 30% had already achieved their goal of manuscript preparation and publication); and (iv) securing research funding (40% planned to obtain funding for their research, and 15% stated that they already had funding).

Experience, Competence, Effectiveness, and Self-Efficacy

Before the conference, workshop participants were also asked to rate aspects of negotiation, writing, and teaching. To assess their experience, the participants were asked to rate their level of faculty experience on a scale of 0 (never) to 3 (more than three times) on the topics of research and teaching (Table 9.1).

To evaluate group differences, the participants were grouped into several categories: (i) graduate students and postdoctoral Fellows, (ii) assistant faculty, and (iii) associate faculty members. Similar to *experience*, when assessing level of *competence*, participants reported significant differences in their level of competence with salary negotiation

TABLE 9.1 Teaching and Research Experience Means and Standard Deviations

Item	Graduate student/ postdoc ($n = 14$)	Assistant professor ($n = 4$)	Associate professor ($n = 2$)
Negotiate a salary[a]	0.29 (0.61)	0.75 (0.50)	3.00 (0.00)
Negotiate a research package[a]	0.07 (0.27)	0.75 (0.50)	3.00 (0.00)
Write a grant proposal[a]	0.57 (1.01)	1.75 (1.50)	3.00 (0.00)
Write a teaching statement	0.86 (1.03)	1.75 (0.96)	2.50 (0.71)
Write a research statement	1.07 (1.21)	1.75 (0.96)	2.50 (0.71)
Teach	2.21 (1.19)	2.75 (0.50)	3.00 (0.00)

[a] denotes a significant difference between groups.
Note: Participant scores ranged from 0 (never) to 3 (more than three times).

TABLE 9.2 Teaching and Research Competence Means and Standard Deviations

Item	Graduate students/ postdoc ($n = 14$)	Assistant ($n = 4$)	Associate ($n = 2$)
Negotiate a salary[a]	2.29 (0.61)	2.29 (0.50)	6.00 (0.00)
Negotiate a research package[a]	2.07 (0.27)	2.75 (0.50)	6.00 (0.00)
Write a grant proposal	0.57 (1.01)	1.75 (1.50)	3.00 (0.00)
Write a teaching statement	0.86 (1.03)	1.75 (0.96)	2.50 (0.71)
Write a research statement	1.07 (1.21)	1.75 (0.96)	2.50 (0.71)
Teach	2.21 (1.19)	2.75 (0.50)	3.00 (0.00)

[a] denotes a significant difference between groups.
Note: Participants were asked to rate their level of competence on a scale of 0 (not at all competent) to 7 (very competent).

(F (2, 17) = 6.93, $p = 0.006$), with graduate students, postdoctoral Fellows, and assistant faculty reporting low levels of competence when negotiating their salary and research package negotiation (F (2, 17) = 6.85, $p = 0.007$). When reporting on their *competence* with writing a grant proposal, teaching statement, research statement, and teaching, they all reported similar levels of competence (Table 9.2).

Participants were asked to report the *effectiveness* of their current network in helping them obtain their five-year goals. The scale was from 1 (not at all effective) to 7 (very effective). All participants reported similar scores ($M = 3.60$, $SD = 1.50$), which may suggest that the faculty do not perceive their rank to be an impediment to their career goals.

Moreover, we asked the graduate students, postdoctoral Fellows, and faculty to respond to a series of questions regarding intrinsic factors that affect their self-reported rates of *self-efficacy*. The scale ranged from 1 (strongly disagree) to 5 (strongly agree). The participants scored relatively similarly on all the self-efficacy items (Table 9.3).

Exploring the Myth of Work/Family Balance in Academe

Work/life balance was an important goal for 70% of the participants, whereas 15% stated they had already achieved this balance. When asked about taking time off for childrearing, more than 40% of the participants said they did not have children. Less than 20% of the participants stated they plan to take time off in the next five years to spend with family. Finding a way to create work/family balance in academic careers can be particularly challenging for women in STEM, especially where laboratory and field work restricts their ability to optimize their schedules. Having work flexibility conflicts with hegemonic cultural norms of the "ideal worker" constructed "around masculine norms of someone who devotes their time and energy to their job and not the household, while the feminine, or 'marginalized worker,' maintains the family life" (Sutherland, 2008, p. 214). The notion of any type of flexibility also contradicts the cultural value of work devotion and dedication, which is "the cognitive belief, moral commitment, and emotional salience of making work the central focus of one's life" (Williams et al., 2013, p. 211). Balancing work and family responsibilities affects both men and women, since the "family devotion schemas mandate that mothers' primary focus should be to care for their children" and that men should be devoted to their work (Williams et al., 2013, p. 214).

STEM faculty often have experiments ongoing, which means that failure to tend to plants, organisms, or petri dishes could result in loss of work for weeks, months, or even years. Unfortunately, the reason behind the failure can sometimes be undeniable or impossible to prevent, such as a major snowstorm, family sickness, power failure, or instrument failure. As a tenured STEM faculty member who attended the workshop noted, "The bottom line is, we do not always have the luxury of setting our own schedule most of the time."

Within a week after the conference, the participants were asked to complete a final assessment of their level of experience and perceived competence in areas related to teaching and research. These same questions were asked as those prior to the conference; responses were

TABLE 9.3 Self-Efficacy Means and Standard Deviations by Academic Rank

Item	Graduate student/postdoc ($n = 14$)	Assistant professor ($n = 4$)	Associate professor ($n = 2$)
I set a high standard for myself and others	4.14 (0.86)	4.50 (0.68)	5.00 (0.00)
I am not highly motivated to succeed	1.50 (1.09)	1.67 (0.58)	1.00 (0.00)
I excel in what I do	4.00 (0.78)	4.00 (0.82)	3.50 (0.71)
I have a lot to contribute	4.00 (0.96)	4.00 (0.82)	3.50 (0.71)
I get stressed out easily	2.71 (1.14)	3.75 (0.96)	2.50 (0.71)
I am not easily bothered by things	3.21 (0.80)	2.00 (0.82)	2.50 (0.71)
I become overwhelmed by events	2.71 (0.91)	3.00 (1.15)	2.50 (0.71)
I readily overcome setbacks	3.71 (0.91)	3.50 (.58)	4.00 (1.14)
People can achieve whatever they set out to accomplish in their careers	3.57 (1.22)	3.75 (.50)	4.00 (1.41)
People who work hard will be successful in their careers	3.86 (1.29)	3.50 (0.58)	3.50 (0.71)
Career success is usually a matter of good fortune	3.15 (1.14)	2.00 (0.00)	3.00 (0.00)
When it comes to career success, who you know is more important than what you know	3.46 (0.97)	3.00 (.82)	3.00 (0.00)
Achieving success in your career is often out of your hands	2.36 (1.08)	2.25 (0.96)	2.50 (0.71)
It is more challenging for women to receive respect in my field	3.36 (0.93)	3.75 (0.50)	3.00 (1.41)
It is challenging to have a family and meet career demands in my field	3.57 (0.85)	4.25 (0.50)	4.00 (1.41)
There is not a great deal of support for women in my field	2.50 (0.94)	3.25 (0.96)	3.00 (1.41)
I have been very successful in achieving the goals I have set for myself in the past	3.64 (1.15)	3.75 (0.50)	4.00 (1.41)
I am inspired by what I do in my field	4.00 (0.78)	4.50 (0.58)	4.00 (1.41)
I value the contributions that my field provides	4.14 (0.86)	4.50 (0.58)	4.50 (0.71)

Note: Participant score options ranged from 1 (strongly disagree) to 5 (strongly agree).

TABLE 9.4 Post-conference competence Means and Standard Deviations with Teaching and Research

Item	All respondents (*n* = 16)
Negotiate a salary	3.63 (1.59)
Negotiate a research package	3.69 (1.82)
Write a grant proposal	4.44 (1.55)
Write a teaching statement	5.06 (1.48)
Write a research statement	5.06 (1.40)
Teach	5.56 (1.32)

Note: Participant scores ranged from 0 (having no experience) to 7 (having much experience).

evaluated using a pre-post comparison at the end of the evaluation. Among the participants who completed both the pre-assessment and post-assessment, the average score was 5.06 on the post-conference survey but no one above 3 on the pre-conference survey. The aggregate ratings are in Table 9.4.

CONCLUSION AND IMPLICATIONS FOR FUTURE FORWARD WORKSHOPS

The value of the FORWARD program is the cooperation among STEM and non-STEM faculty in a national outreach that sponsors workshops in different regions in the United States. The FORWARD program is timely and needed. Graduate students entering the workforce, as well as postdoctoral Fellows and junior faculty, all found the workshop to be informative and extremely useful and timely. Conference participants were given all the conference presentations plus additional articles and materials on a universal serial bus (USB) drive. The topics detailed in this chapter will transform their success. Such efforts could be further strengthened with regular discussions and through disseminating the developed toolkits. If these toolkits were adopted by university administrations, we could experience profound change in professional training for women and minority scientists. One of the future goals for FORWARD OSU would be to develop a packet using the developed toolkits for professional development addressing extension and outreach activities common at land-grant institutions.

When we discuss discrimination on the road to tenure, we try not to specify where this discrimination comes from. Obviously, the groups that affect success prior to tenure are department chairs, promotion and tenure committees, service committees, and extension/outreach clientele. Students do not play a significant role in the tenure decision of a faculty member, except that professors do require positive teaching evaluations. Furthermore, professional societies play a key role in young faculty developing national recognition through speaking engagements, service on journal editorial boards, service on national committees, and national networking. While the FORWARD OSU workshop was geared toward empowering women and minorities, future programs could focus on changing the cultures of committees, department heads, and professional societies.

The goals of mentoring programs and workshops are to ensure engagement or reverse disengagement. Did we learn whether it was possible to reverse disengagement? A critical step to being engaged is the ability to set goals, take charge of your career and success, be confident that you are succeeding, and, when speaking with administrators, be strategic and identify and embrace opportunities in fulfilling the land-grant mission of the institution.

References

Alexander, J.C., 2003. The Meanings of Social Life: A Cultural Sociology. Oxford University Press, New York, NY.

Association of Public Land-Grant Universities (APLU), 2012. The Land Grant Tradition—celebrating 150 years of public higher education. Available from: <http://www.aplu.org/document.doc?id=780/> (accessed 09.01.14.).

Cajete, G., 1999. Native Science: The Natural Laws of Interdependence. Clear Light Books, Santa Fe, NM.

De Welde, K., Laursen, S.L., 2011. The glass obstacle course: informal and formal barriers for women Ph.D. students in STEM fields. Int. J. Sci. Technol. 3, 571–595.

Duch, J., Zeng, X.H.T., Sales-Pardo, M., Radicchi, F., Otis, S., Woodruff, T.K., et al., 2012. The possible role of resource requirements and academic career-choice risk on gender differences in publication rate and impact. PLoS One. 7 (12), e51332. Available from: http://dx.doi.org/10.1371/journal.pone.0051332.

Eccles, J.S., 1994. Understanding women's educational and occupational choices. Psychol. Women Q. 18, 585–609.

Hagedorn, L.S., 2000. Conceptualizing faculty job satisfaction: components, theories, and outcomes. New Dir. Inst. Res. 27, 5–20. Available from: http://dx.doi.org/10.1002/ir.10501.

Halpern, D.F., Benbow, C.P., Geary, D.C., Gur, R.C., Hyde, J.S., Gernsbacher, M.A., 2007. The science of sex differences in science and mathematics. Psychol. Sci. Public Interest. 8, 1–51. Available from: http://dx.doi.org/10.1111/j.1529-1006.2007.00032.x.

Hays, S., 2000. Constructing the centrality of culture and deconstructing sociology. Contemp. Sociol. 29, 594–602.

Holleran, S.E., Whitehead, J., Schmader, T., Mehl, M.R., 2010. Talking shop and shooting the breeze: a study of workplace conversation and job disengagement among STEM faculty. Soc. Psychol. Pers. Sci. 2, 65–71. Available from: http://dx.doi.org/10.1177/1948550610379921.

Madewell, A., Schumacher, K., Van Delinder, J., Bailey, L., Page, M., 2012. Addressing academic climate: effects of stereotype threat on perceptions of gender equality, professional and personal balance, and departmental support of family responsibilities among tenure-track faculty. Manuscript submitted to *Review of Higher Education*.

Mason, M.A., Goulden, M., Frasch, K. 2010. Keeping women in the science pipeline. Paper Presented at Workplace Flexibility 2010, Georgetown Law School, 29–30 November, Washington, DC.

Milkie, M.A., Denny, K.E., 2014. Changes in the cultural model of father involvement: descriptions of benefits to fathers, children, and mothers in Parents' Magazine, 1926–2006. J. Fam. Issues. 351, 225–253.

Oklahoma State University (OSU), 2010a. ADVANCE OSU Summary of Climate Survey. Available from: <http://advanceosu.okstate.edu/images/documents/exec_report_100927.pdf> (accessed 11.12.14.).

Oklahoma State University (OSU), 2010b. ADVANCE OSU Mentoring Program. Available from: <http://advanceosu.okstate.edu/mentoring-program> (accessed 11.12.14.).

Singh, S.N., Mishra, S., Kim, D., 1998. Research-related burnout among faculty in higher-education. Psychol. Rep. 83, 463–473. Available from: http://dx.doi.org/10.2466/pr0.1998.83.2.463.

Smith, J.L., Lewis, K.L., Hawthorne, L., Hodges, S.D., 2013. When trying hard isn't natural: women's belonging with and motivation for male-dominated STEM fields as a function of effort expenditure concerns. Pers. Soc. Psychol. Bull. 39, 131–143. Available from: http://dx.doi.org/10.1177/0146167212468332.

Steele, C.M., Aronson, J., 1995. Stereotype threat and the intellectual test performance of African-Americans. J. Pers. Soc. Psychol. 69, 797–811. Available from: http://dx.doi.org/10.1037/0022-3514.69.5.797.

Steele, C.M., Spencer, S.J., Aronson, J., 2002. Contending with group image: the psychology of stereotype and social identity threat. Adv. Exp. Soc. Psychol. 34, 379–440. Available from: http://dx.doi.org/10.1016/S0065-2601(02)80009-0.

Sutherland, J., 2008. Ideal Mama, ideal worker: negotiating guilt and shame in academe. In: Evans, E., Grant, C., (Eds.), Mama, PhD: Women Write about Motherhood and Academic Life. Rutgers University Press, Piscataway, pp. 213–221.

Swidler, A., 1986. Culture in action: symbols and strategies. Am. Sociol. Rev. 51, 273–286.

Thorne, A.C., 1985. Visible and Invisible: Women in Land-Grant Colleges, 1890–1940. Utah State University Press, Logan, UT.

Van Delinder, J., Tucker, S.A., 2014. Graduate academic experience. In: Sternberg, R.J. (Ed.), The Modern Land-Grant University. Purdue University Press, West Lafayette, IN, pp. 153–168.

Williams, J.C., Blair-Loy, M., Berdahl, J.L., 2013. Cultural schemas, social class, and the flexibility stigma. J. Soc. Issues. 69, 209–234. Available from: http://dx.doi.org/10.1111/josi.12012.

Xie, Y., Shauman, K.A., 2003. Women in Science: Career Processes and Outcomes. Harvard University Press, Boston, MA.

Advancing Toward Professorship in Biology, Ecology, and Earth System Sciences

Maria T. Kavanaugh[1], Kate S. Boersma[2,3],
Sarah L. Close[2,4], Lisa M. Ganio[5],
Louisa Hooven[6] and Barbara Lachenbruch[5]

[1]Department of Marine Chemistry and Geochemistry, Woods Hole Oceanographic Institution, Woods Hole, MA, USA [2]Department of Zoology, Oregon State University, Corvallis, OR, USA [3]Department of Biology, University of San Diego, San Diego, CA, USA [4]National Oceanic and Atmospheric Administration, Silver Spring, MD, USA [5]Department of Forest Ecosystems and Society, College of Forestry, Oregon State University, Corvallis, OR, USA [6]Department of Horticulture, Oregon State University, Corvallis, OR, USA

OUTLINE

Introduction	166
BEESS Research is Unique Within STEM Disciplines	168
Workshop	170
Survey	170
Demographics	171
Workshop Challenges	172
Time Commitment	172

Logistical Lessons   173
    Engaged Participation   173
    Food and Drink   173
    Conference Supplies   174
    Participant Lodging and Travel   174
    Securing a Venue   174
    Publicity Materials   175
    Institutional Approval for Survey (Use of Human Subjects)   175

Workshop Outcomes   175
    Qualitative Successes   175
    Highlight on Field Work   176
    Quantitative Successes   177
    Pre-workshop Survey   177
    Perceptions Through Time   177

Lessons Learned   180
    Work/Life Balance is Individually Defined   181

Post-workshop Efforts   182

Acknowledgments   182

References   183

INTRODUCTION

Despite advances toward equal representation at the graduate level, women scientists are underrepresented at every stage along the tenure track. The National Science Foundation (NSF) 2011 digest on Women, Minorities, and Persons with Disabilities in Science and Engineering reports that the proportion of female PhD recipients in the sciences has steadily increased over the past decade (NSF, 2011); however, there are obstacles at each career transition from PhD to full professor (NRC, 2009). This is especially true in the biological sciences, where the percentage of PhDs awarded to women has increased to 45%, but the proportion of female applicants in tenure track positions has dropped to 26%. Only 20.8% of tenured faculty are women.

In the sciences, the fields of ecology and earth systems sciences (which includes geology, oceanography, atmospheric sciences, and hydrology, amongst others) are similar to other STEM disciplines in terms of attrition, perceived productivity, and representation. In ecology, women have a long history of participation and achievement (Damschen et al., 2005); however, they are still underrepresented in top positions, are paid less (Sakai and Lane, 1996), and publish less than their male counterparts (Primack and Stacy, 1997). Oceanography and other geosciences still lag behind the biological sciences in percentage of PhDs awarded to women (<30%, but climbing); however, the post-PhD attrition pattern is similar: only 10% of full professors in oceanography or other geosciences at PhD-granting institutions are women (O'Connell and Holmes, 2005).

The reasons underlying these rates of attrition are complex and merit ongoing scrutiny. Recent work by Ceci and Williams (2011) suggests that, in some cases, women in science may not face overt discrimination, but rather a constrained suite of career choices compared to their male counterparts, particularly those associated with maintaining balance between productive careers and personal life choices. Others suggest that subtle unconscious bias (Moss-Racusin et al., 2012) stemming from cultural stereotypes may affect the perceptions of the competence of women scientists by their senior colleagues. In a nationwide double-blind study of biology, chemistry, and physics professors, researchers submitted identical job applications with male and female names for a lab manager position. Female applicants were consistently offered reduced starting salaries and less access to mentoring than male applicants. The reduced financial security and access to career mentoring (Moss-Racusin et al., 2012) may combine with the constrained suite of choices (Ceci and Williams, 2011) to increase the attrition of women from an academic career path. Indeed, in a recent synthesis of the graduate exit surveys from the University of California (Mason et al., 2013), decreased financial means was cited as a reason why women scientists opted out of their chosen professions more frequently than female physicians.

Sitting across a café table, two Oregon State University (OSU) graduate students (one community ecologist, one oceanographer) and two tenured professors of forestry met during the spring of 2010 to discuss why there were so few examples of women in senior positions in their departments, and whether there was anything that could be done. They were soon joined by a postdoctoral researcher and graduate student in marine ecology. As scientists, we recognized that multiple factors might combine to elicit a behavior or pattern within a population. Certainly, cultural stereotyping and financial insecurity may play roles, or even interact with gender to prompt women to opt out of careers as tenure track faculty. We also suspected that there were additional characteristics in our natural science disciplines that contributed to the attrition of women from academic science careers. We coined the term *biological, ecological, and earth systems sciences (BEESS)*, to describe this set of natural science disciplines in academia that involve field work and interactions with a broad range of stakeholders, stressors that add to the list that affect other academics. We realized the potential value of providing women with practical tools to navigate these common career hurdles in BEESS disciplines. We began planning a workshop for an at-risk population—postdoctoral and tenure track, but pre-tenured scientists—who may not already have access to targeted professional development. We focused on issues such as job interviews, negotiation, and mentoring. Recognizing that there are factors driving these patterns of attrition that are unique to BEESS careers, we also attempted to interweave skills directed at these factors, including how to structure a successful interdisciplinary research program, communicate with multiple stakeholders, and manage field work. Importantly, these factors are not typically addressed in professional development programming for academic scientists.

BEESS RESEARCH IS UNIQUE WITHIN STEM DISCIPLINES

BEESS research addresses complex systems, such as conservation genetics of populations, community or ecosystem dynamics, or climate effects on biogeochemical cycles. The nature of this complexity generally requires an interdisciplinary approach. More and more, individuals are seeking graduate training that spans multiple disciplines in order to address interdisciplinary questions and structure interdisciplinary careers. However, despite being at the cutting edge of science, interdisciplinary research is associated with increased investment costs (e.g., Cummings and Kiesler, 2005; Rhoten and Parker, 2004) and potentially decreased disciplinary prestige (Metzger and Zare, 1999). Interdisciplinary applicants may exhibit lower apparent research productivity, perhaps due to the amount of time large, complex projects with multiple collaborators take to come to fruition. Recent PhDs who conduct interdisciplinary research are more likely to be in academia and produce more publications than their counterparts, but for unknown reasons they occupy fewer tenure track positions within academia (Millar, 2013). Hiring committees may seek applicants whose research neatly fits within the bounds of a traditional discipline. Interdisciplinary researchers may have higher rates of opting out during their early careers. Natural affinities for collaboration may increase women's interdisciplinary participation (Rhoten and Pfirman, 2007), but limited access to powerful informal networks and subsequent opportunities (Corley and Gaughan, 2005; Fox, 2001) may increase the likelihood of their leaving.

BEESS research requires communication with a diverse stakeholder community. Natural resources research often requires communication with diverse stakeholders from industry, government, politics, the press, and the general public. How well individual researchers foster and manage relationships among stakeholders is often viewed as a value of the added role of an institution in the community, and thus may be considered in the tenure and promotion process. While it has been argued that women may have natural affinities toward multistakeholder management (Edmunds and Wollenberg, 2001), women scientists may have limited opportunities to build such professional relationships. In general, women academic scientists are under-represented in university-affiliated, multistakeholder research centers (Corley and Gaughan, 2005), consulting and entrepreneurial activities (Haeussler and Colyvas, 2011; Murray and Graham, 2007), and corporate science advising boards (Ding et al., 2012). At least for the latter, demand-side gender-stereotyped perceptions and the unequal opportunities embedded in social networks appear to explain some of the gap (Ding et al., 2012). Thus, the combination of low percentages of experienced female colleagues, the supply-side perceptions, and the mandate of multistakeholder networking may pose a particular challenge for women in BEESS disciplines.

Research in BEESS disciplines is often field-based, associated with necessary work at sea, wilderness areas, remote field sites, or field stations. Field work presents particular hurdles for academics with families, who must negotiate child or elder care and caregiver time-sharing. For ecologists, fieldwork is associated with increased productivity for men, but not for women (McGuire et al., 2012). Women conducting tropical ecology research receive a greater number of grants, but are awarded less total grant money compared to their male counterparts, suggesting an imbalance in the time devoted to writing funding proposals compared to the relative pay-off (McGuire et al., 2012). Women ecologists are more likely to have a spouse in a demanding career, bring their children and family to field stations, hire assistants to watch children at field stations, and spend less time in the field actively collecting data. Indeed, family responsibilities were among the top three reasons cited for women leaving field-based research positions, with other common reasons being a change of interest or more lucrative endeavors elsewhere (McGuire et al., 2012). While difficult to quantify directly, fieldwork blurs the divide between personal and professional identity, requiring women to reconcile their perception of their own competence with the public's action-hero, male-based stereotype of a field scientist.

Throughout the workshop design and planning process, we returned to these BEESS-unique factors: interdisciplinary research, multistakeholder communication, and fieldwork. We conducted a 2-day professional development workshop, entitled "Advancing Toward

Professorship in Biology, Ecology, and Earth Systems Sciences (ATPinBEESS)," for assistant professors, postdoctoral scientists, and advanced graduate students designed to provide skills to help participants succeed and thrive as academic scientists. We also conducted longitudinal research to determine the perceptions of career preparation and challenges of our participants as well as to quantify any effect our programming had on those perceptions.

WORKSHOP

Our workshop began on Monday, April 9, 2012 at 5 p.m. with appetizers and a meet-and-greet activity, which were followed by welcome remarks by the ATPinBEESS committee and an opening address by Angelo Gomez of OSU's Office of Equity and Inclusion. On Tuesday, April 10, 2012 OSU faculty offered professional development sessions from 8:30 a.m. until 5 p.m.; these included a mock tenure panel. After dinner, Dr Laura Huenneke of Northern Arizona University gave our campuswide keynote address, entitled "Degrees of Freedom: The Seemingly Random Walk of an Academic Ecologist's Career Path." Following the keynote, participants were encouraged to utilize the newly-gained networking skills with audience members. A half-day of sessions on Wednesday ended with lunch and concluding remarks at 1 p.m. (Table 10.1).

SURVEY

During early planning sessions, we identified three factors unique to BEESS research, including challenges involved with structuring a successful interdisciplinary research program, communication with multiple stakeholders, and fieldwork (as described previously). We hypothesized that these factors may interact with gender and work/life decisions to constrain career choices available to women in BEESS disciplines. While our priority was to conduct a successful professional development workshop, we sought an additional intellectual product to formalize and further legitimize our efforts. Thus, we augmented the FORWARD to Professorship survey questions with ATPinBEESS-specific questions and established a longitudinal study in which we polled participants before, immediately after, and 8 months after the workshop. Survey participants provided written feedback regarding their progress and perceptions of current and future success in their current career trajectories.

TABLE 10.1 General Program: Advancing Toward Professorship in Biology, Ecology, and Earth System Sciences

Evening 4/9/2012	Check-in
	Welcome:
	Angelo Gomez, Interim Executive Director Office of Equity and Inclusion, OSU Icebreaker and Informal Networking
Morning 4/10/2012	Interactive Session Themes:
	1. Fostering Productive Collaborations 2. Networking and Preventing Isolation 3. Mentoring 4. Managing Expectations
Afternoon 4/10/2012	Interactive Session Themes:
	1. Effective and Progressive Management Skills 2. Fieldwork Challenges 3. Parenting: Knowns and Unknowns 4. Tenure Panel
Evening 4/10/2012	Dinner and Keynote:
	Dr Laura Foster Huenneke Vice President of Research Northern Arizona University
	Putting skills to work:
	Public networking session
Morning 4/11/2012	Interactive Session Themes:
	1. Interviewing 2. Negotiating 3. Work/Life Balance
	Workshop close and next steps

For more specific information regarding session format, leaders and biographies, please see http://atpinbeess.forestry.oregonstate.edu/.

DEMOGRAPHICS

We initially targeted newly hired assistant professors and sent direct invitations to contacts from departments related to the BEESS disciplines at colleges and universities across the Pacific Northwest. We advertised on a number of list-servs, including Ecolog, and Earth Science Women's Network. Interestingly, the overwhelming response was not from assistant professors, but rather from postdoctoral scientists who found it challenging to advance to tenure track or equivalent positions

Position level

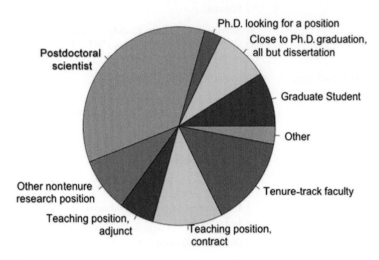

FIGURE 10.1   Demographics of ATPinBEESS workshop participants.

(Figure 10.1). Thus, we modified our programming to include skills to navigate the transition from postdoctorate to assistant professorship, as well as pre-tenure strategies for tenure track faculty (Table 10.1). Participants came from 14 academic institutions in eight US states and Canadian provinces, and from a range of current academic appointments (Figure 10.1). The mean participant age was 34.6 years.

WORKSHOP CHALLENGES

Time Commitment

Time commitment is a concern for any academic service activity. However, our committee benefited from its diverse membership, comprised of academics at different stages in their careers, who had experience organizing conferences and/or special sessions. Our committee consisted of three graduate students, a research associate, and two faculty members. While time commitments varied by committee member and by week, the workload was substantial, with graduate students reporting an average of 10 h per week and faculty members reporting approximately 4 h per week over the 8 months. All committee members contributed intellectually and communicated with academic participants (e.g., attendees, workshop leaders, departmental and institutional leaders, and keynote speakers). It was necessary for faculty members to take on fiscal management roles, although graduate students took on additional logistical roles. It is important to note that the ATPinBEESS specific longitudinal survey was created in part because we wanted to better serve this unique constituency, but also because we wanted to further legitimize our service activity with a scholarly product.

LOGISTICAL LESSONS

Between the six of us, we had experience planning special sessions at meetings, small scientific meetings/workshops (of approximately 30 attendees), and moderately sized professional development meetings (100–150 attendees). However, these efforts tend to be sporadic throughout one's career, so the lessons learned from individual planning events often go undocumented. Each workshop goal and target audience is unique and brings its own logistical challenges. We list some of our lessons learned next.

Engaged Participation

In their applications, scientists were asked to describe their career goals, their professional preparation, and the relevance of attending the workshop. In addition to evaluating their curricula vitae, we wished to understand their personal motivation for applying. We also wanted to ensure that scientists, once selected, were serious about their participation. Often people commit to a free workshop, only to back out at the last minute when personal logistics become challenging. Last minute drop-outs result in lost opportunities for other scientists. We asked selected participants to send us a small deposit in the form of a check ($50), which we refunded on their arrival. All participants agreed. Only one participant who was selected opted out, but did so prior to sending the check.

Food and Drink

Catering logistics go beyond ordering enough food for 30–50 people and staying within budget. These logistics included making decisions on what food to have, where and when (e.g., what choices might lend themselves to networking among participants), to maintaining variety for those with individual dietary requirements (e.g., vegetarian, vegan, gluten-free, kosher), and making calls when snacks were insufficient. During the 3-day workshop, we had a few mishaps with food that required someone to be designated as the catering contact during every service. We recommend that organizers set aside meals for those with special dietary requirements prior to serving and distribute them to the participants directly. We also recommend that the catering contact verify the quantity of specialty foods (e.g., gluten free).

Conference Supplies

We spent time identifying, ordering, and maintaining conference supplies, including items to be distributed to participants and general programming materials. The former included name tags, scratch paper, pens, a folder containing participant contact information, local resources for travel and dining, and workshop schedules. The latter included easels, large notepads, whiteboards, audio-visual preparation, and handouts. This required a priori planning once the main workshop venues were secured. These logistics also required communication and flexibility from the organizers and the participants. For example, we amassed a library of resources to share with participants, but did not wish to print and distribute the materials. Initially, we considered posting Microsoft PowerPoint slides and journal articles on our website, but ran into time and budgetary constraints. Ultimately, we housed the materials on a laptop that was made available during break times for participants to transfer resources via flash drive. An alternative would be to provide a flash drive to all participants with the conference materials already loaded.

Participant Lodging and Travel

Our proposal did not include travel allowances for participants, although we fully subsidized participant lodging. We provided participants with letters to their department heads describing the nature of the workshop to facilitate provisioning of travel support from departmental funds to workshop participants.

Securing a Venue

With the exception of the keynote address, the entire workshop took place at one location in the College of Forestry at OSU. We worked with the college's administrative staff to review potential venues. Two of our committee members worked with the College of Forestry and the general scheduling desk at OSU to reserve rooms that would meet our needs. These committee members were responsible for reserving rooms, coordinating with classes, as well as shifting needs based on food and beverage delivery, break out groups, and potential audio-visual needs.

It is important to note that two committee members worked within the College of Forestry and thus were able to navigate known resources efficiently, rather than search across the campus.

Publicity Materials

We benefited from the internal administration at OSU that managed brand identity in our advertisements and were fortunate to obtain pro-bono assistance of a freelance designer who developed a logo for our workshop. University templates were available to design bookmarks, flyers, and posters. These templates were used on the workshop's website (http://atpinbeess.forestry.oregonstate.edu/), recruitment email, posters around campus and town, as well as participant materials, including coffee mugs. It is important to note that while we advertised the keynote address widely to the public, the workshop itself was limited to accepted participants.

Institutional Approval for Survey (Use of Human Subjects)

In order to conduct a survey of workshop participants, OSU required that we submit survey materials to the Institutional Review Board (IRB) before the workshop. In addition to the longitudinal survey materials, OSU's IRB required review and approval of materials developed by the FORWARD to Professorship program. While we developed the survey materials early in the workshop planning process, we did not initiate the formal IRB process until February 2012, 2 months before the event. We were able to complete the approval process in the time allowed; however, we would suggest initiating much earlier.

Additionally, the IRB requires that researchers complete an online ethics training module. This 4- to 6-h training helped us design, implement, and analyze our survey data. Regardless of the requirements of individual institutions, we recommend that at least one committee member complete this informative process to maintain standards for implementing survey materials.

WORKSHOP OUTCOMES

Qualitative Successes

All sessions received positive comments and elicited candid discussions. The welcoming address provided a historical perspective on advancing participation by women in academia and was well received, and the participants enjoyed the initial ice-breaker activity. A mock promotion and tenure (P&T) committee discussion elicited many comments, including that the P&T process "is obviously the scariest," but that the session was "helpful," and without it, "it may have taken a year or so into my position to clue into." The keynote speaker's personal story was "reassuring," and enabled participants to better envision success in their own career progression. Overall comments about the workshop were extremely positive, including one participant's comment that "so many questions that I didn't even know to ask were answered!" indicating that there is a great need for the type of information our workshop provided.

The evaluations also provided suggestions for improving the workshop. Participants felt that the second day, which included an evening talk and networking session, was too long, and would have preferred a workshop evenly distributed between 2 and 3 days, with more breaks, built-in networking time, and more question and answer time. Some participants commented that fieldwork was not necessarily part of their work, and that the session on parenting may not apply to them, reflecting the diversity in BEESS scientists. Topics suggested for future workshops included strategies for self-promotion, overcoming geographic constraints in the job hunt, dual hires, non-academic careers, conflict resolution, and addressing power differentials.

Highlight on Field Work

A particularly relevant session on fieldwork challenges resonated with many of the participants. The session presider outlined a hypothesis that, in part, the challenges faced by people with fieldwork-heavy careers may be a symptom of a larger but character-related syndrome: (i) women who choose careers involving fieldwork are additionally choosing to prove they can succeed; and (ii) this need for validation translates to saying "yes" more often than necessary in other parts of the job and life to show competence. As a codicil, (iii) this need to show competence can challenge one's feelings about one's femininity. The first premise is built on the feeling that when one imposes her fieldwork onto people with whom one typically collaborates (whether family members, colleagues at the office, or people in other parts of her life), we then feel that, in order to prove that the imposition was necessary, one has to succeed. The second premise is built on our own observations that many of us do work very hard to project competence—which we can show by doing difficult fieldwork well, and by agreeing and coming through on a multitude of projects requested from various sources (from colleagues, friends, and family, to department heads and deans). Many workshop participants thought this profile was apt, and it generated animated discussions.

There were several participants who said they worried that their "pheno-type" of femininity would make them appear less competent than they were, and others who felt that they had to adopt a less feminine "pheno-type" in order to project their competence.

Quantitative Successes

Workshop participants were a highly-motivated, self-selected group, with a generally high degree of self-confidence. A total of 28 partici-pants completed the pre-workshop survey, and 23 each completed the post-workshop survey and the 8-month survey. Their motivation was reflected in their responses to survey questions regarding their per-ceived confidence and competence to achieve key career outcomes. Confidence reflects a belief in either one's innate ability to succeed or a high likelihood of success based on the vicarious experience of peers; competence may reflect concrete examples in their personal history where their skill set contributed to success.

Pre-workshop Survey

Pre-workshop survey results suggest different career trajectories based on confidence (Figure 10.2). These pre-workshop surveys show that the confidence to achieve a tenured position was positively corre-lated with the confidence to write grant proposals ($r_{1,22} = 0.47$, $p < 0.05$) and also with the participant's experience doing so ($r_{1,22} = 0.47$, $p < 0.05$). However, confidence to achieve a tenured position was nega-tively correlated with time spent teaching ($r_{1,22} = -0.69$). Responses from those who aspired to work in doctoral-granting research institu-tions were negatively correlated with responses from those who aspired to liberal arts universities ($r_{1,22} = -0.56$).

Perceptions Through Time

The results of longitudinal analyses responses reflected that partici-pants' confidence in their ability to successfully navigate career transi-tions was variable (Figure 10.3). Participant confidence increased somewhat post-workshop, and then fell to near pre-workshop levels at the 8-month post-workshop survey. However, participants' sense of competence rose dramatically after the workshop, and maintained their relative gain even 8 months afterward. This gain could be generated by multiple processes: the workshop experience may have been formative, the participants may have continued to seek professional development opportunities after the workshop, or a combination of both.

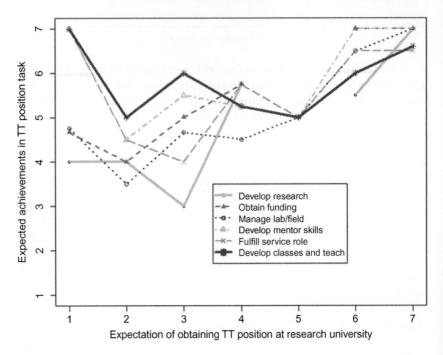

FIGURE 10.2 Mean pre-workshop confidence. Participants were asked to rate their confidence in achieving various career benchmarks, and their expectation of obtaining a tenure track position at a research institution. Response maximum score was 7 ("Very likely") and minimum 1 ("Not at all"). Lines connecting points were included to facilitate interpretation and do not represent responses intermediate to the categorical responses. No participants responded with a score of 5 for "Develop research" or "Obtain funding."

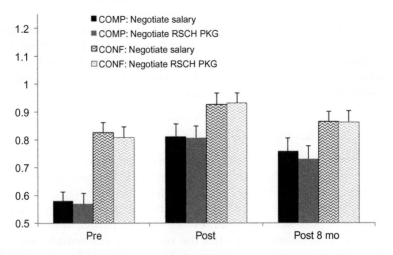

FIGURE 10.3 Mean (+standard error) perceptions of confidence (CONF) and competence (COMP) of workshop participants in successfully negotiating their salary and research packages (RSCH PKG). Participants were surveyed before the workshop (Pre), immediately following the workshop (Post), and 8 months later (Post 8 mo). Several categories were queried across research and teaching skill sets. Normalized response score maximum ("Very much") was 1.2, minimum 0 ("Not at all"), with the mean across all questions being approximately 0.8 for confidence, and 0.7 for competence.

Importantly, workshop participants may have formed professional and or personal networks, whereby peer-to-peer interaction resulted in a significant and sustained positive effect.

The benefits of mentorship and positive role models in all fields of STEM cannot be underestimated. Prior to the workshop, 43% of participants had a mentor at their home institution. Eight months later, 65% of participants responded that they had a mentor. Informal peer networks (IPNs) can also fulfill some mentorship roles, such as access to critical information, as well as providing emotional and social support. We cannot know whether participants sought mentorship outside of a transparent, formal relationship, or whether their IPNs fulfill all of these critical roles. However, there was an increase in perceived effectiveness of current networks immediately following the workshop (Figure 10.4A), suggesting that participants made valuable personal contacts or shifted their perspective on existing relationships at their institutions.

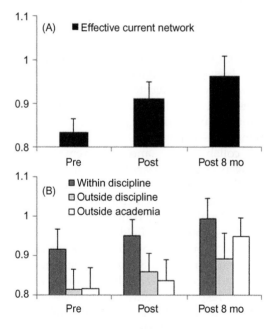

FIGURE 10.4   Mean (+standard error) effectiveness of personal network (A) and breadth of professional network (B). Time periods are as in Figure 10.4. Participants were asked to rate the effectiveness of their current network in helping them achieve their career goals. They were also asked to rank their level of comfort in approaching experts within their discipline, outside their discipline and outside of academia. Normalized response maximum score was 1.2 ("Very effective or Very comfortable") and minimum 0 ("Not at all").

Participants, in general, were quite confident in communicating with people within their discipline (Figure 10.4B), much less outside their discipline, and even less with non-academics. Given the multi-stakeholder nature of BEESS research, this pattern was concerning. However, immediate post-workshop scores increased moderately, with larger increases 8 months post-workshop, particularly with non-academics. Future workshops may wish to solicit presentations from agency leaders as well as non-governmental organizations (NGOs), not simply as career alternatives, but to recognize the growing community of potential collaborators that may be encountered in a successful career. Incorporating communications training, such as those provided by the American Association for Advancement of Science (AAAS; http://www.aaas.org/communicatingscience) or the COMPASS (http://www.compassonline.org), may go a long way toward improving participant confidence in communicating with different audiences.

LESSONS LEARNED

Participants' chosen research topics were motivated more by intellectual curiosity and less by the challenges and travel requirements of fieldwork. Participants were asked to rank the categories of factors that will shape their research over the next 5 years (Figure 10.5). These categories included: intellectual curiosity, strategic decisions to secure funding, P&T requirements, teaching load, fieldwork or travel requirements, requirements of collaborators, and requirements of stakeholders. Decisions regarding research appeared to be internally driven. External factors such as collaborator or stakeholder requirements ranked relatively low and are not shown. When compared with pre-workshop surveys, post-workshop results revealed increases in influence of P&T and teaching requirements, but not fieldwork. Fieldwork requirements ranked relatively low compared to intellectual curiosity, funding, and other job requirements until the 8-month post-workshop surveys, in which all factors tended to increase. Importantly, at least within the pre-workshop survey responses, fieldwork scores were negatively correlated with intentions to start families and the relative importance of maintaining personal relationships. We recognize that the relative importance of personal relationships and decisions regarding reproduction may shift dramatically in time, especially relative to life stage and career. Our results suggest that researchers are making complex decisions and sacrifices in order to balance the demands of field work with other career requirements.

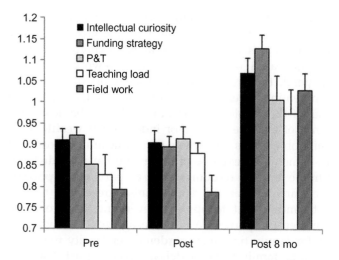

FIGURE 10.5 Importance (mean + standard error) of different factors in driving research questions over the next 5 years. Time periods are as in Figure 10.4. Participants were asked to rate the importance of several factors in driving their research questions, including intellectual curiosity, strategies to secure long-term funding, promotion and tenure requirements ("P&T"), teaching loads, travel and field work requirements, and requirements by collaborators or stakeholders (data not shown). Normalized response maximum score was 1.2 ("Very much") and minimum 0 ("Not at all").

Work/Life Balance is Individually Defined

Our programming had three sessions that fell under the category of work/life balance, as determined by initial feedback from participants in the pre-workshop survey. The first was directed toward managing intrinsic and extrinsic expectations, the second was a specific session on parenting in academia, and the last was a broader session on work/life balance, both in terms of social structures within academia, and institutional and national policy. The first addressed, at least partially, how to manage one's schedule with many concurrent obligations. This session also covered strategies of how to overcome the imposter syndrome, or the tendency for high achieving women to feel like they do not deserve or belong in their positions. The second session facilitated a discussion of strategies to manage the conflicting demands of parenting and field research, travel, and academic obligations. The last session was designed to give participants a sense of what "family-friendly" policies were already in place at academic institutions and how participants might gauge the climate of future home institutions or effect positive change in their own institutions.

While all sessions were well received, unexpected discussion emerged from the parenting session. Session leaders brought their own parenting philosophies, co-parenting and assistance (nannies, grandparents, etc.) strategies, and shared them with the group. However, some workshop participants had no plans to have children and some had experienced increased workloads due to a co-worker's family obligations. In general, the group wanted to see work/life balance defined outside of parenting. Questions that arose included: can academia honor the interests of the whole person? Can "balance" be achieved without the assistance of extended family or independent wealth? Does recognizing family obligations and whole-person health of those with family obligations come at the expense of those who have decided not to have children? In the end, we recognized that all parts of the phrase, "work/life balance," are self-defined. Participants agreed that the concept of work/life balance ought to apply to everyone, and consider faculty without children or spouses. We also recognized that while unwritten allowances for family time may burden other faculty members, formal policies (such as family leave or delayed tenure clocks) within departments and across institutions will be ultimately helpful for all, regardless of how one individually defines "work/life balance."

POST-WORKSHOP EFFORTS

In addition to preparing this chapter, post-workshop efforts have included analyses and presentation of survey results at scientific meetings, manuscript preparation, coordination of networking and reunion activities of workshop participants, and a social media presence. We identified key characteristics of BEESS disciplines and collected information from workshop participants regarding their experience and perceptions on how these characteristics interplay with other career choices through time. In 2012, our group presented a summary of the pre-workshop responses at the Ecological Society of America (ESA) meeting (Boersma et al., 2012). Results from the pre-workshop analyses and from our longitudinal study are also included in this chapter, and a peer-reviewed article describing our findings is in preparation.

Participants continue to network and have had gatherings at subsequent ESA and American Geophysical Union meetings. These gatherings were coordinated primarily through an open Facebook page. Participants currently continue to post articles of interest and provide social support to one another.

Acknowledgments

We thank the FORWARD to Professorship Program for providing the funding and training for us to conduct the Advancing Toward Professorship in Biology, Ecology, and Earth

Systems Sciences (ATPinBEESS) workshop. In particular, we acknowledge Catherine Mavriplis, who provided input to our planning process and engaged participation in the workshop itself. Additional funding was provided by the OSU College of Forestry, Office of Equity and Inclusion, and Office of Women's Advancement and Gender Equity (WAGE). We would like to acknowledge the efforts of several people who led sessions, coordinated activities, or provided other logistical support for the workshop, including Roger Admiral, Sona Andrews, Kelly Benoit-Bird, Donna Champeau, Pat Cordova, Dan Edge, Forestry Computing Services, Tiffany Garcia, Alix Gitelman, Angelo Gomez, Patricia Gregg, Emma Hess, Selina Heppell, Laura Huenneke, Anna Jolles, Pat Kennedy, Janet Lee, Ricardo Letelier, David Lytle, Bruce Menge, Jessica Miller, Sujaya Rao, Beth Rietveld, Rick Spinrad, Barb Taylor, Steve Tesch, Anne Trehu, Terralyn Vandetta, Virginia Weis, and Penny Wright. Co-authors and several individuals mentioned were supported by the Oregon University System and specific academic units across Oregon State University including College of Forestry; College of Earth, Oceanic, and Atmospheric Sciences; the Departments of Zoology, Crop and Soil Science, Horticulture, and Fisheries and Wildlife; and the Women Studies Program.

References

Boersma, K.S., Kavanaugh, M.T., Ganio, L.M., Hooven, L.A., Close, S.L., Lachenbruch, B., 2012. Advancing toward professorship in biology, ecology, and earth systems sciences: Perceptions of confidence in early career scientists. Ecological Society of America Annual Meeting, Portland, OR. Available from: <http://eco.confex.com/eco/2012/webprogram/Paper39715.html> (accessed 09.06.14.).

Ceci, S.J., Williams, W.M., 2011. Understanding current causes of women's underrepresentation in science. Proc. Natl. Acad. Sci. 108 (8), 3157–3162.

Corley, E., Gaughan, M., 2005. Scientists' participation in university research centers: what are the gender differences? J. Technol. Transfer 30 (4), 371–381.

Cummings, J.N., Kiesler, S., 2005. Collaborative research across disciplinary and organizational boundaries. Soc. Stud. Sci. 35 (5), 703–722.

Damschen, E.I., Rosenfeld, K.M., Wyer, M., Murphy-Medley, D., Wentworth, T.R., Haddad, N.M., 2005. Visibility matters: increasing knowledge of women's contributions to ecology. Front. Ecol. Environ. 3 (4), 212–219.

Ding, W., Murray, F., Stuart, T., 2012. From bench to board: gender differences in university scientists' participation in corporate scientific advisory boards. Acad. Manage. J. 56 (5), 1443–1464. Available from: <http://dx.doi.org/10.5465/amj.2011.0020>.

Edmunds, D., Wollenberg, E., 2001. A strategic approach to multistakeholder negotiations. Dev. Change 32 (2), 231–253.

Fox, M.F., 2001. Women, science, and academia: graduate education and careers. Gend. Soc. 15, 654–666.

Haeussler, C., Colyvas, J.A., 2011. Breaking the ivory tower: academic entrepreneurship in the life sciences in UK and Germany. Res. Policy 40 (1), 41–54.

Mason, M.A., Wolfinger, N.H., Goulden, M., 2013. Do Babies Matter?: Gender and Family in the Ivory Tower. Rutgers University Press, Rutgers, New Jersey, USA.

McGuire, K.L., Primack, R.B., Losos, E.C., 2012. Dramatic improvements and persistent challenges for women ecologists. BioScience 62 (2), 189–196.

Metzger, N., Zare, R., 1999. Interdisciplinary research: from belief to reality. Science 283, 5402–5403.

Millar, M.M., 2013. Interdisciplinary research and the early career: the effect of interdisciplinary dissertation research on career placement and publication productivity of doctoral graduates in the sciences. Res. Policy 42 (5), 1152–1164.

Moss-Racusin, C.A., Dovidio, J.F., Brescoll, V.L., Graham, M.J., Handelsman, J., 2012. Science faculty's subtle gender biases favor male students. Proc. Natl. Acad. Sci. USA. 109 (41), 16474–16479.

Murray, F., Graham, L., 2007. Buying science and selling science: gender differences in the market for commercial science. Ind. Corp. Change 16 (4), 657–689.

National Research Council, Committee on Gender Differences in the Careers of Science, Engineering and Mathematics Faculty, 2009. Gender Differences at Critical Transitions in the Careers of Science, Engineering and Mathematics Faculty. National Academy Press, Washington, DC.

National Science Foundation, Division of Science Resources Statistics, 2011. Women Minorities and Persons with Disabilities in Science and Engineering: 2011. Special Report NSF 11-309. Arlington, VA. Available from: <http://www.nsf.gov/statistics/wmpd/> (accessed 09.06.14.).

O'Connell, S., Holmes, M.A., 2005. Women of the academy and the sea. Oceanography 18 (1), 12–24.

Primack, R.B., Stacy, E.A., 1997. Women ecologists catching up in scientific productivity, but only when they join the race. BioScience 47 (3), 169–174.

Rhoten, D., Parker, A., 2004. Risks and rewards of an interdisciplinary path. Science 306 (5704), 2046.

Rhoten, D., Pfirman, S., 2007. Women in interdisciplinary science: exploring preferences and consequences. Res. Policy 36 (1), 56–75.

Sakai, A.K., Lane, M.J., 1996. National Science Foundation funding patterns of women and minorities in biology. BioScience 46 (8), 621–625.

Metropolitan Mentors: Building a Network of Women in Mathematics and Computer Science Across New York City: The New York City College of Technology of the City University of New York Workshop

Pamela Brown and Delaram Kahrobaei

New York City College of Technology, City University of New York, Brooklyn, NY, USA

OUTLINE

Goals of Our FORWARD to Professorship Project   186

FORWARD to Professorship Workshops: Women in Mathematics and Computer Science Across NYC   189

What was Learned from the First Workshop?   192

Looking Back at the Workshop Series   192

Follow-up Survey 193

Suggestions for a Group Planning to Run a Similar Workshop 194

Institutional History and Why This FORWARD to
Professorship Project Was Important for Us 194

Relevance to Other Institutions 196

Conclusion 196

Acknowledgments 197

References 197

GOALS OF OUR
FORWARD TO PROFESSORSHIP PROJECT

Through our FORWARD to Professorship project, we offered a series of workshops to support women who were doctoral students near graduation, postdoctoral scientists, and faculty members, in mathematics and computing, in the metropolitan New York area. One particular focus was the 24 campuses of the City University of New York (CUNY), which range from public community colleges to professional and doctoral-degree granting institutions. All are located within the five boroughs of New York City (Figure 11.1). The plan was to leverage the workshops to help participants form networks and create local support structures, not only to combat the isolation that may be felt as a member of an underrepresented group, but also to promote research collaborations and advance scholarship. This approach takes advantage of the close proximity of the many institutions. College faculty could get to know talented graduate students and postdoctoral researchers and target their recruitment for tenure-track positions. Senior faculty wishing to pursue new directions in their scholarship could serve as mentors while collaborating with assistant or associate professors at other campuses. Faculty at multiple campuses could develop horizontal peer-mentoring networks to help navigate both professional and personal issues. This was an adaptation of the approach used by Karukstis et al. (2010) to establish a horizontal peer network of senior women chemists and physicists at private liberal arts institutions, but with the modification that a range of institution-types and participants at

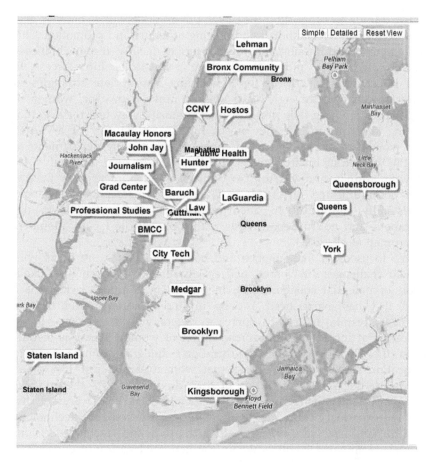

FIGURE 11.1 Map of CUNY campuses.

various stages of their careers would be included. They employed multiday gatherings, mechanisms for regular follow-up, and tailored professional development activities to promote leadership skills. This network had a significant impact on the career development of the 20 senior women participants, who were the only women senior faculty members in their departments. Direct benefits included additional attention to professional goals leading to enhanced leadership, visibility, and recognition on participants' campuses (Karukstis et al., 2010). We also chose to offer a series of workshops rather than a single workshop, so that relationships could develop over time, rationalizing that, as in many other types of efforts to promote change, "one-shot interventions…do not work" (New Jersey Task Force on Child Abuse and Neglect, 2003).

In addition to supporting the development of networks, another goal was to provide information on advancing to tenure and promotion. This was done by addressing the three types of faculty responsibilities—teaching, research, and service, along with leadership. Access to this information is critical for developing appropriate strategies in order to advance through the academic ranks. However, women in departments where they are a distinct minority may feel they are not getting the information they need. In a recent survey of 877 men and women from chemistry and chemical engineering departments at 29 PhD granting institutions in the US, 93% of men, but only 74% of women answered yes to, "Are criteria for tenure at your institution communicated effectively?" The gender discrepancy was only statistically significant in departments with fewer female faculty members, and not in departments with more female faculty members (Chapman et al., 2011).

We focused on mathematics and computing which are areas with similar challenges for women, and closely related, enhancing the likelihood of potential collaborations. In particular, computer science is a field that has experienced a drop in undergraduate enrollment of women, despite efforts to increase diversity and previous initial successes at increasing the representation of women. Analysis of data from the US Department of Education's Integrated Post-Secondary Education Data System revealed that women earned just 18% of all bachelor's degrees in computing in 2012, down from 27% the previous decade (Change the Equation, 2013). Lewis et al. (2007) argued that women experience more gender stereotypes in information technology which, "spill over very directly into curriculum and teaching decisions in male dominated faculties where the gendered nature of curriculum and teaching needs to be considered." Professional support for women faculty in mathematics and the computer sciences will not only help them to achieve their potential, but will also allow them to serve as role models for female students and contribute to a more gender-inclusive curriculum and pedagogy (Lewis et al., 2007).

Another rationale for the focus on mathematics and computer science is the opportunity to provide support for women who may be a small minority in their departments. As of 2006, women in computer science comprised 17.4% of full professors and 21.2% of tenured/tenure-track faculty (Burrelli, 2008). In mathematics, women comprised 8.6% of full professors and 17.4% of tenured/tenure-track faculty (Burrelli, 2008). A study of university physics programs, another discipline where women are underrepresented, found a strong correlation between the number of women on the faculty and the likelihood that they would remain, rather than leave academia for employment in the private sector or government (Whitten et al., 2003). Additional studies have suggested that an underrepresented group needs to reach a critical mass, at least 15–20% of membership, to move from being isolated and at risk to more fully participatory and advocates for improvements in policies relevant to their needs (Etzkowitz et al., 2000; Committee et al., 2007). It is also noteworthy that despite their reputation of being the more collaborative gender, women faculty in science and technology are "somewhat more likely than their male peers to work alone, have fewer partners when they do collaborate and collaborate with other women less frequently than expected (Steffan, 2006)." The opportunities for collaboration created by these workshops may help to reverse this situation for participants.

FORWARD TO PROFESSORSHIP WORKSHOPS: WOMEN IN MATHEMATICS AND COMPUTER SCIENCE ACROSS NYC

The concerns that our project was designed to address include:

- Women in STEM often feel isolated, lacking opportunities for collaboration (Montgomery and Barrett, 1997).
- Women faculty members in STEM are more likely to leave academia than their male counterparts (Burke and Mattis, 2007).
- Women faculty members in STEM don't progress as fast as their male colleagues. For each year after earning tenure, male professors are more likely to be named full professors (Burke and Mattis, 2007). Within the professorial ranks in CUNY, the percentage of women decreases as the rank increases above assistant professor, as shown in Table 11.1.

TABLE 11.1   CUNY Full-Time Faculty in Professorial Ranks by Gender[a]

Rank	Male	% Male	Female	% Female
Einstein Professor	3	100	0	0
Distinguished professor	96	71	39	29
Professor	1227	61	780	39
Associate professor	964	52	903	48
Assistant professor	913	44	1,181	56
Total	3203	52	2903	48

[a] *CUNY WORKFORCE DEMOGRAPHICS BY COLLEGE, ETHNICITY AND GENDER: Fall 2013 Instructional and Classified Staff. <http://www.cuny.edu/about/administration/offices/ohrm/reports-forms/aadsb/Fall2013CUNYWorkforceDemographicsbyCollegeEthnicityandGender.pdf> (accessed August 2015).*

A brief description of the five workshops follows. More details are available on the New York Women in Mathematics and Computing Network website (New York Women in Mathematics and Computing Network, 2014):

1. FORWARD to Professorship (March 2012)—a full-day workshop held on a Saturday, with panel discussions on: (i) teaching, (ii) publishing, (iii) grant writing, offered by program officers from various federal agencies, and (iv) women in STEM, including discussions on balancing professional responsibilities and home life. The poster session was an opportunity for panelists and participants to share their research.
2. Leadership in Higher Education (April 2012)—a panel discussion by women college presidents and provosts.
3. Communication in a Male Dominated Discipline (November 2012)— A workshop presented by Communications Professor Jenepher Lennox Terrion, from the University of Ottawa. Topics ranged from using diplomacy for conflict resolution to awareness of body language.
4. Teaching and Leadership (March 2013)—Dr Karen Wosczyna Birch, executive director of the Regional Center for Next Generation Manufacturing at the University of Connecticut, led a seamless pathway program in engineering and technology between all 12 public 2-year colleges, six universities, and secondary schools. She offered two presentations: a workshop on how to recruit and retain underrepresented populations in STEM disciplines; and another on how women faculty can develop their leadership skills to lead initiatives and achieve their professional goals.
5. FORWARD to Professorship (May 2013)—a full-day workshop held on a Friday. Activities included presentations on international academic scholarly activities; home life and gender bias; a discussion by a panel of program officers on funding opportunities; conversations by a panel of women leaders in mathematics and computer science on their career paths, followed by an opportunity for questions; and a poster session for attendees to present their scholarship, network and share ideas.

In order to encourage attendance, flyers describing the FORWARD to Professorship workshops were emailed to the provosts of New York City campuses. Workshops were also advertised by word of mouth and other venues such as the Feminist Press' online publication, "Under the Microscope." A website was set up for conference registration (Figure 11.2).

FIGURE 11.2   Workshop flyer.

WHAT WAS LEARNED FROM THE FIRST WORKSHOP?

As a series of workshops was planned, the survey results from our first workshop guided the development of subsequent workshops:

1. Popular components of the first FORWARD to Professorship workshop (March 2012), such as the panel discussion by program directors and the poster session, were repeated in the subsequent FORWARD to Professorship (May 2013) workshop. Sample survey comments from the first workshop included:

> I really liked how (the presenters) talked about leadership and team building skills, noticing that it is not what is typically part of our training.
> The presentations exceeded my expectations, and the presenters were very knowledgeable.
> Excellent exchange with program officers.
> Excellent (poster session) but perhaps allow just a bit more time or, better yet, a bit longer breaks to allow for conversation so then there will be more time to actually look at posters during poster session, and most people were really nice and willing to talk, and I thought I would have time to see/talk to everyone, but … then time flies. I was surprised at how fast it went.

2. Three smaller, targeted events were offered—a panel discussion on leadership, a workshop on communication skills, and presentations on teaching and leadership. These events were intended to be of interest to all STEM women faculty in order to promote professional development and extend opportunities for networking. Promotion was through the project website and outreach to CUNY campuses through the provosts and other venues.

LOOKING BACK AT THE WORKSHOP SERIES

Some of the lessons learned were:

1. Participants enthusiastically enjoyed the workshops and found them valuable. One participant commented in the first workshop survey, "Beyond excellent! I got so much useful and relevant information and a plan for how to proceed. I can't wait to start writing up my next proposal."
2. Involving graduate students in workshop planning made the work easier and helped to develop their leadership skills. Another survey respondent noted, "I was expecting fewer participants, was impressed to see many graduate students involved—great opportunity for them."

3. The college's recruitment efforts were supported by the workshops—four workshop attendees were subsequently hired by our mathematics department.

FOLLOW-UP SURVEY

As several of the goals of the workshops were long-term, a follow-up survey was sent in November 2013, to those who attended at least one of the FORWARD to Professorship Workshops ($N = 74$). This was 6 months after the last workshop and 20 months after the first. There were 12 responses, a rate of 16%. For respondents, it was learned that (Note: parentheses indicate the number with that response out of the total responses):

1. 58% (7/12) attended both workshops, 17% (2/12) attended the 2012 workshop only, and 25% (3/12) attended only the 2013 workshop.
2. 67% (8/12) felt that the conference material helped them better understand the grant funding process.
3. 33% (4/12) have submitted a proposal since attending the workshop(s).
4. 42% (5/12) plan on submitting a proposal in the near future.
5. 80% (8/10) felt the conference material about networking was helpful.
6. 42% (5/12) developed collaborations from networking at the workshop.
7. 64% (7/11) have plans to collaborate with conference participants in the future.
8. 33% (4/12) have assumed leadership positions since attending the conference and indicated that the material presented at the conference helped them secure those positions.
9. 50% (5/10) of the respondents developed new teaching strategies based on workshop materials.
10. 9% (1/11) indicated that the conference materials helped them obtain a promotion.
11. 50% (6/12) got ideas for new research at the poster session. One respondent commented, "I got a lot of feedback on my poster and some interesting ideas."
12. Four of the respondents were graduate students when attending the conference; three have found employment (one part-time).
13. When asked to look back on what had been the most useful component of the workshop(s), 33% (4) reported the proposal writing information, 17% (2) the networking opportunities, 8%

(1) each the poster session, information on professorial responsibilities, and teaching strategies.

While results are skewed by the self-selection of the respondents, they suggest that there were perceived long-term benefits to attending the conferences, including increased familiarity with the proposal writing process, opportunities for collaboration and networking, development of leadership skills, and new teaching strategies. Our next challenge is to sustain the momentum. A proposal to fund more workshops was submitted.

SUGGESTIONS FOR A GROUP PLANNING TO RUN A SIMILAR WORKSHOP

Those considering offering a similar series of workshops may benefit from lessons learned, which include:

1. Start early. Offering a multi-campus workshop requires a lot of planning and coordination.
2. Recruit speakers with an international/national reputation to attract more participants.
3. Focus on activities designed to address evidence-based impediments.
4. Program directors from funding agencies will accept offers to present at a regional, multi-campus event, but usually not for a single campus event. These individuals are also a good draw to increase attendance.
5. The poster session is an effective networking technique, and will also increase attendance.
6. Develop a workshop website and use multiple venues to advertise the event. Maintain a list of contacts.
7. Utilizing graduate students for workshop planning and implementation has multiple benefits.

INSTITUTIONAL HISTORY AND WHY THIS FORWARD TO PROFESSORSHIP PROJECT WAS IMPORTANT FOR US

Like many institutions, our campus, the New York City College of Technology, a branch of CUNY, is undergoing a shift in its culture, making support for women in STEM even more critical. A tenure-line faculty member hired 15 years ago, in fall 1998, had a teaching assignment of 27 annual workload hours (equivalent to one semester teaching five three-credit sections and another teaching four three-credit sections), and no "start-up" package to establish a research agenda. While the college offered selected bachelor's degrees, its culture was firmly imbedded in its community college roots. While scholarship was included, the expectations for tenure and promotion were more focused on teaching and service. In the last 9 years under new leadership, the college evolved to a more comprehensive model of serving undergraduates. Since 2004 new baccalaureate degrees in bioinformatics, applied mathematics, mathematics education, nursing, radiological technology, emerging media technologies, electrical engineering technology, construction management, and mechanical engineering technology have been developed, and more are planned. Once the first and only community college in New York City, the number of bachelor's degrees awarded by the City College of Technology is now approaching 50% of all degrees (847 baccalaureate degrees and 1074 associate degrees were awarded in 2011–2012).

A tenure-line faculty member hired in fall 2014 will have an annual teaching assignment of 21 workload hours, reduced even further by a start-up package, which includes a 24 workload hour reduction spread out over 5 years. This is effectively a 40% reduction in teaching responsibility during the first 5 years as a faculty member compared to someone hired 15 years earlier. With this comes an increased expectation of research and scholarship. This change in the institutional focus has contributed to a generational gap between more seasoned and recently hired faculty, as evidenced by results of a faculty climate survey, COACHE (COACHE, 2014). Analysis of responses to a Spring 2009 survey administration suggests that many pre-tenure faculty feel a lack of department collegiality (Gitman et al., 2009a). Women pre-tenure faculty, in particular, expressed a need for effective formal mentoring— likely, in part, because senior faculty did not experience the same challenges they are facing. The pre-tenure faculty members also expressed concern that service expectations were excessive given their need to establish productive research agendas (Gitman et al., 2009a). Faculty hired within the last 9 years have a better understanding of the current expectations for tenure and promotion than their more senior colleagues, and are thus more likely to understand the challenges of balancing service, teaching, and scholarship. They are in a good position to serve as mentors for faculty that will be hired in the near future. A challenge here is how to best groom these faculty mentors for mentoring roles without adding yet another burden to their responsibilities, while in turn providing them with appropriate mentoring. Another group that could benefit from support is mid-career faculty, those still rising in the ranks, but hired before the increased emphasis on scholarship. Many feel pressured because they now face the same expectations for research and scholarship in order to be promoted as their more recently hired counterparts, but with fewer institutionalized resources (i.e., the release time offered to new faculty) to rejuvenate their research agendas. Analysis of responses to the COACHE survey for tenured faculty (Gitman et al., 2009b) revealed that only 40% of women felt scholarly expectations for promotion were reasonable, compared to 56% of men. The college thus faces the challenges of providing junior and mid-career faculty with very different types of support.

Our FORWARD to Professorship workshops were intended to help address these issues by creating networking opportunities and providing information about the grant writing process. At least for survey respondents, there was some measure of success.

RELEVANCE TO OTHER INSTITUTIONS

In addition to addressing the isolation that may be felt by under-represented groups or members of small departments, offering cross-campus workshops may help to address other situations where opportunities to collaborate or receive mentoring are lacking. For example, the mission of many colleges is changing. A case in point is the increasing number of community colleges offering bachelor's degrees. Currently, 20 states allow community colleges to offer bachelor's degrees and more are considering this change (Fain, 2013). This kind of shift in results in the evolution of the college's purpose, and may set the stage for a generation gap between faculty hired before and after this shift has occurred. If expectations for faculty in terms of teaching, scholarship, and research evolve as well, there may not be suitable mentors.

Another shift in academia is the increasing percentage of courses taught by adjunct faculty. US colleges went from 45% of instructional faculty being tenured or tenure-track in 1975, to 24% in 2009 (Andrews, 2012). In many institutions the only expectation of adjunct faculty is teaching, shifting the responsibility of other departmental and college-wide activities for students—that is, advisement, curriculum development and review, peer evaluations, accreditation reporting, etc.—to the full-time faculty. This results in an even greater demand for service from full-time faculty, thus adding to the "juggling act."

CONCLUSION

This project took advantage of the close proximity of women in mathematics and computer science at different institutions and at different stages of their careers, and gave them an opportunity to meet, develop collaborations, discover new knowledge, and otherwise feel supported. Surveys taken immediately following workshops and several months later suggest that many participants valued the experience, reporting positive impacts on teaching, leadership, and professional development. A commitment to increasing the participation of underrepresented groups helps the vibrancy of any organization by assuring different perspectives are represented, leading to comprehensive and creative growth. Our nation's colleges and universities, charged with preparing the next generation, are an important venue in which to practice this philosophy through activities such as the FORWARD to Professorship workshops.

Acknowledgments

Thanks are extended to CUNY graduate students Valia Mitsou, Lisa Bromberg, Ha T Lam, Bianca Sosnovski, Elizabeth Vidaure, Gulustan Dogan, as well as Al Vargas, Lina Garcia, and Cinda Scott for assisting with the organization of the workshops; and Bren Cavallo for conducting post-workshop surveys. We also want to acknowledge Provost Bonne August, as well as Fellow faculty members Nadia Benakli, Victoria Gitman, Janet Liou-Mark, and Hong Li, and program manager A.E. Dreyfuss, with whom we had thoughtful discussions which helped to frame our thinking on the workshops and this chapter. Special thanks are due to Rachelle Heller and Catherine Mavriplis for supporting us with the FORWARD to Professorship awards through their National Science Foundation (NSF) grant which supported the workshops, as well as their thoughtful input on both the workshops and book chapter. We also wish to acknowledge New York City College of Technology's NSF-ADVANCE-IT-Catalyst planning grant (NSF HRD 0811192), which supported the COACHE survey and other activities on our campus. Any opinions, findings, and conclusions or recommendations expressed in this material are those of the authors and do not necessarily reflect the views of NSF.

References

Andrews, M., 2012. Adjunct Nation. Inside Higher Ed, March 21. Available from: <http://www.insidehighered.com/blogs/stratedgy/adjunct-nation#ixzz2p5TpOe00> (accessed 04.03.14.).

Burke, R.J., Mattis, M.C. (Eds.), 2007. Women and Minorities in Science, Technology, Engineering, and Mathematics: Upping the Numbers. Edward Elgar Publishing, Inc., Northampton, MA.

Burrelli, J., 2008. Thirty-Three Years of Women in S&E Faculty Positions. National Science Foundation, Directorate for Social, Behavioral and Economic Sciences InfoBrief. Available from: <http://www.nsf.gov/statistics/infbrief/nsf08308/> (accessed 04.02.14.).

Chapman, S., Dixon, F.F., Foster, N., Kuck, V.J., McCarthy, D.A., Tooney, N.M., et al., 2011. Female faculty members in university chemistry departments: observations and conclusions based on site visits. J. Chem. Educ. 88, 716–720.

Change the Equation, 2013. Half Empty: As Men Surge Back into Computer Science, Women are Left Behind. Vital Signs, Reports on the condition of STEM Learning in the U.S. Available from: <http://changetheequation.org/sites/default/files/CTEQ_VitalSigns_Half%20Empty.pdf> (accessed 04.02.14.).

Collaborative on Academic Careers in Higher Education. (COACHE) at the Harvard Graduate School of Education. Available from: <http://isites.harvard.edu/icb/icb.do? keyword=coache&pageid=icb.page385671> (accessed 04.02.14.).

Committee on Maximizing the Potential of Women in Academic Science and Engineering; Committee on Science, Engineering, and Public Policy (COSEPUP), Institute of Medicine (IOM); Policy and Global Affairs (PGA); National Academy of Sciences, National Academy of Engineering, 2007. Beyond Bias and Barriers: Fulfilling the Potential of Women in Academic Science and Engineering, National Academy of Sciences, Washington, D.C. Available from: <http://www.nap.edu/catalog.php? record_id=11741> (accessed 04.02.14.).

Etzkowitz, H., Kemelgor, C., Uzzi, B., 2000. Athena Unbound: The Advancement of Women in Science and Technology. Cambridge University Press, NY.

Fain, P., 2013. California's Evolving Master Plan. Inside Higher Education. Available from: <http://www.insidehighered.com/news/2013/09/27/two-year-colleges-california-mull-bachelors-degrees> (accessed 04.03.14.).

Gitman, V., Kahrobaei, D., Dreyfus, A. E., 2009a. "Collaborative on Academic Careers in Higher Education" (COACHE) Survey of New York City College of Technology (CUNY) Pre-Tenure Faculty. Available from: <http://www.citytech.cuny.edu/advancecitytech/docs/PreTenureFacultyResults.pdf> (accessed 04.03.14.).

Gitman, V., Kahrobaei, D., Dreyfus, A. E., 2009b. "Collaborative on Academic Careers in Higher Education" (COACHE) Survey of New York City College of Technology (CUNY) Full-time Tenured Faculty. Available from: <http://www.citytech.cuny.edu/advancecitytech/docs/TenuredFacultyResults.pdf> (accessed 04.03.14.).

Karukstis, K.K., Gourley, B., Rossi, M., Wright, L., Hunter, A.B., 2010. Development of a horizontal peer mentoring network for senior women chemists and physicists at liberal arts colleges. In: Karukstis, K.K., Gourley, B.L., Rossi, M., Wright, L.L. (Eds.), Network Mentoring Strategies to Facilitate the Advancement of Women Faculty. American Chemical Society Publications, Washington, DC.

Lewis, S., Lang, C., McKay, J., 2007. An Inconvenient Truth: The Invisibility of Women in ICT Australasian Journal of Information Systems 15(1), 59–76. Available from: <http://dx.doi.org/10.3127/ajis.v15i1.479>.

Montgomery S., Barrett M.C., 1997. Undergraduate Women in Science and Engineering: Providing Academic Support. Available from: <http://www.crlt.umich.edu/pub-links/CRLT_no8.pdf> (accessed 04.02.14.).

New Jersey Task Force on Child Abuse and Neglect, 2003. Standards for Prevention Programs: Building Success through Family Support. Available from: <http://www.state.nj.us/dcf/documents/about/commissions/njtfcan/Standards Prevention.pdf> (accessed 04.02.14.).

New York Women in Mathematics and Computing Network, Available from: <https://sites.google.com/site/nywmcnet/> (accessed 04.02.14.).

Steffan, N., 2006. Advancing women faculty through collaborative research networks. In: Proceedings of the 2006 WEPAN Women in Engineering Programs and Advocates Network. Conference. Pittsburgh, PA. Available from: <https://ojs.libraries.psu.edu/index.php/wepan/article/viewFile/58448/58136> (accessed 04.02.14.).

Whitten, B., Foster, S., Duncombe, M., 2003. What works for women in undergraduate physics? Phys. Today. 56 (9), 46–51.

12

Career Advancement in a Research Environment

Simerjeet Gill[1], Kristine Horvat[2] and Triveni Rao[1]

[1]Brookhaven National Laboratory, Upton, NY, USA [2]Materials Science and
Engineering Department, Stony Brook University, Stony Brook, NY, USA

OUTLINE

Background   200

CARE 2012   201
  Topics   201
  Organization   202
  Outcomes   203

CARE 2013A   204
  Topics   204
  Organization   205
  Outcomes   205

CARE 2013B   206
  Topics   206
  Outcomes   207
  Workshop Organization Advice   207

Conclusions   208

References   208

BACKGROUND

When women are a minority where they work, they are more likely to be judged by their gender rather than their merits, which means that the overwhelming male majority in most research institutions inhibits female growth (Valian, 1998). Steffen-Fluhr (2006) proposed "the creation of small interdisciplinary communities within which women faculty can do collaborative research with each other and select male peers from a position of numerical strength". We believe that more workshops and networking events at research institutions could help facilitate the formation of such communities for the advancement of women and minorities.

At Brookhaven National Laboratory (BNL), less than 10% of tenured positions are held by women, yet approximately 30% of postdoctoral scientists are women. In order to address this discrepancy, in 2010, upon invitation by the laboratory director, a Committee on the Status of Women in Physics (CSWP) of the American Physical Society (APS) conducted a site visit to BNL. Their objective was to review the laboratory's environment for women and to make recommendations on how to recruit, retain, and advance women. Some of the recommendations to BNL were to "place a priority on attracting and promoting women and underrepresented minorities to scientific management positions," "ensure that there is no stigma associated with taking advantage of family-friendly policies," "establish an expectation of effective mentoring and provide visible rewards and encouragement for effective mentoring," and "review and evaluate the tenure procedures, practices, and outcomes in each department" (CSWP, 2010).

In the past 3 years, there have been a number of independent initiatives at BNL, including a concerted effort to increase the interaction between the Stony Brook University (SBU) and BNL faculty and an increased awareness of the need for a mentorship program. There has also been recognition of the great need for women and minorities in Science, Technology, Engineering, and Mathematics (STEM) fields to network and form collaborations with other women and minorities. Brookhaven Women in Science (BWIS) (Available from: http://www.bnl.gov/bwis/.) of BNL and Women in Science and Engineering (WISE) (Aveni, 2014) at SBU submitted a joint proposal to FORWARD to Professorship in 2011 for conducting workshops to explore the common concerns faced by early career women and underrepresented minority researchers at both of these institutions. Given the awareness and CSWP recommendations, upper management was highly receptive to organizing these workshops. For the first time, a program specifically targeting the needs of early career women and underrepresented minorities was implemented at BNL through a series of three workshops, CARE (Career Advancement in a Research Environment). The first was a fact-finding workshop where a broad variety of topics were discussed and feedback was obtained from participants to determine the topics of greatest interest to the early career participants. The subsequent two workshops addressed the specific needs expressed by the first workshop's participants.

CARE 2012

Topics

The objective of the CARE 2012 workshop was to provide an overview of topics of interest to early career women and minorities at both BNL and SBU, such as mentorship, work/life balance, the tenure process, and obtaining research funding. The goal of this workshop was to extract one or two topics of greater interest to those at both institutions for future activities.

The workshop consisted of 2 days of lectures, panel discussions, and breakout sessions with career expert speakers from BNL, SBU, Columbia University, and various funding agencies and consulting firms. Day 1 was devoted to the tenure process and grant proposal writing, while Day 2 was about mentorship and work/life balance. See Appendix D for a detailed agenda of CARE 2012, including names of speakers and organizers.

During the tenure session of CARE 2012, the differences between the tenure processes in the two institutions were brought into sharp focus. A university and a national laboratory have many common interests, but they have vastly different policies. Most notably, the tenure processes at both institutions are very different. At BNL, the tenure process starts about 7 years after an assistant scientist appointment along the tenure track. Emphasis is placed on either exemplary scientific contributions or important contributions to the facility, and accomplishment over the entire career is also considered. The timeline for the two contributions can be significantly different, since the impact on the facility takes a much longer time to become evident. Contributions to teaching or community service are not very relevant since BNL is not a teaching institution. At SBU, there are two academic colleges with STEM disciplines: the College of Arts and Sciences and the College of Engineering and Applied Sciences. Even within these two academic colleges, however, there are different paths for tenure approval. In the College of Arts and Sciences, the tenure clock begins when one is appointed as an assistant professor, and this person's case comes to the tenure committee after 6 years. Tenure candidates are judged by their academic excellence, teaching, and community service, along with their research accomplishments. In the College of Engineering and Applied Sciences, mentoring and supporting graduate students are given high priority, in addition to teaching, scholarship, and research accomplishments. Usually, tenure is considered after 6 years, though the process can be accelerated for deserving candidates. Only achievements after the last promotion are taken into account. This session was very informative to the majority of the attendees.

In the grant proposal writing session, four program managers from the Army Research Office, Department of Energy (DoE), and National Institutes of Health/National Institute of General Medical Sciences (NIH/NIGMS) discussed various funding options from their agencies and the criteria by which grant applications are judged. Proposal writers were urged to pay attention to details (spelling, grammar, etc.) in their proposals and to keep in contact with program managers throughout the proposal writing process.

Speakers at the mentorship session advised having multiple mentors to get a variety of perspectives and to keep in touch with them. Discussions among workshop participants concluded that early career scientists need to be proactive and to seek out mentors. Participants expressed a strong desire for a formal mentorship program at BNL.

In the work/life balance session, human resources representatives from BNL and SBU discussed the various programs available to employees to help maintain a healthy work/life balance. Speakers at the session emphasized the importance of creating a sharp distinction between your work and your home life by scheduling your day to separate both aspects of your life. It is important to not burn yourself out by striving for perfection; there is nothing wrong with paying for help with household tasks or not having a perfectly clean home.

Organization

Information about the workshop was disseminated through institutional newsletters, a Web site, posters at strategic locations at both institutions, and targeted letters to department chairpersons. Registration for the event was open to all interested candidates via the Web site. Potential attendees were asked to complete a questionnaire to establish their career status, career path, field of expertise, field of interest, and rationale for attending the workshop. In order to promote interaction among the attendees and with the speakers, attendance to the workshop was by invitation only. Attendees were selected from the registrants based on their responses to the questionnaire. Every effort was made to achieve a balance between

SBU and BNL candidates and very early career and early career candidates, as well as including a wide variety of fields of expertise. Although 30 attendees were invited for the workshop, there were also a number of drop-ins, swelling the participants to nearly 50.

Table 12.1 lists the accepted attendees' positions and affiliations. The field of expertise of a majority of the attendees (11 people, all female minorities) was physics, but others had backgrounds in chemistry, biochemistry, biology, electrical engineering, materials engineering, nuclear engineering, mathematics, computer science, manufacturing, and oceanography.

The organizing committee consisted of two SBU personnel and nine BNL personnel. Planning for CARE 2012 began 6 months in advance, with the organizing committee meeting once a week. BNL provided administrative support and space free of charge to hold the workshops. Each of these four sessions was chaired by two of the organizers. Scribes were assigned to each session for note taking, and a report of the session was provided by the chairs. In order to evaluate the efficacy of the workshop, the attendees completed questionnaires consisting of both multiple-choice and expository questions. Answers to the multiple-choice questions were used for statistical feedback, while the expository questions were used as feed-forward for future sessions. The session chairs were also responsible for providing statistical analysis of the responses to the questionnaires. The final report was a compilation of session reports and the analysis of the data.

Outcomes

There were several successful outcomes from this first workshop. CARE 2012 was recognized by the DoE on December 13, 2012, in one of its reports, *Fiscal Year 2012 Performance Evaluation Report of the Brookhaven Science Associates for Management and Operations of Science and Technology at the Brrokhaven National Laboratory for the Period October 1, 2011 to September 30, 2012*. The report found that "[s]upport enabling Brookhaven Women in Science to continue its numerous outreach and

TABLE 12.1 CARE 2012 Accepted Attendee Job Positions and Affiliations

Accepted applicant pool	BNL	SBU
Assistant scientist or higher	11	4
Postdoctoral Fellows	7	5
Senior graduate students	N/A	2
Engineer	1	N/A
Total	19	11

scholarship activities that provide encouragement and support to women entering or pursuing careers in science" was a notable outcome for FY2012. In addition, the overall feedback received from these workshops was positive. Upper BNL management strongly supported the organization of the CARE workshops and has begun to follow up on recommendations from the workshops. For example, as a result of CARE 2012 recommendations, BNL is working to establish a mentoring program that will be accessible to all BNL staff.

CARE 2013A

Topics

Attendees of CARE 2012 expressed overwhelming interest in two topics: grant proposal writing and mentoring. Since members of BWIS were involved in the BNL effort to establish a formal mentoring program, it was decided to focus the CARE 2013 workshop on grant proposal writing. The objectives of CARE 2013 were (i) to encourage the participants to establish long-standing collaborations and submit proposals and (ii) to train a cadre of young scientists to run future workshops. The goal for grant proposal writing was to help attendees align their proposals with three specific components: their strengths, the research focus of the institution, and directions from the funding agency. The main objectives were to provide participants with one-on-one interaction time with program managers and to give them insight into the processes involved in writing, editing, and submitting a proposal.

During the first day of the 2-day workshop, a technical grant proposal writing workshop was conducted by a professional who was experienced in training the scientific research community. The speaker used mini-lectures, extensive question-and-answer sessions, and several hands-on exercises to explain good proposal writing techniques. The attendees were encouraged to submit short abstracts of their proposals, which were then analyzed for further improvement.

In the morning session of the second day, the attendees were exposed to the research directions and funding opportunities at both SBU and BNL. In the afternoon, the participants broke out into focus groups to interact with program managers and subject experts in their specific fields. Focus group topics were:

1. Photon/Particle Detectors and Instrumentation,
2. Theory and Computation in Basic Sciences,
3. Development of Teaching and Learning Tools in STEM Fields and Engineering and Engineering Applications in STEM,
4. Nuclear Engineering and Materials,

5. Life Sciences, Structural Biology, and Environmental Sciences, and
6. Industrial Grants: Search, Benefits and Limitations.

These topics were chosen by volunteers who organized their group's session. Since these volunteers were fully responsible for their session, from advertising the session and selecting attendees, to recruiting guest speakers/program managers and writing reports, CARE 2013 proved to be a training ground for a new cadre of organizers. Video-conferencing was offered as an option to minimize travel time and cost and to maximize participation by program managers. For most participants, this was their first opportunity to speak with program managers, so attendees greatly enjoyed breaking into focus groups to hear from program managers specific to their areas of interest. Focus groups provided to be an easy forum for scientists from SBU and BNL to network and share ideas with one another.

Organization

Appendix E shows an image of the poster that was used to advertise CARE 2013, which was similar to that for CARE 2012. Attendance at the CARE 2013 workshop was expanded to include approximately 50 participants of both genders. Table 12.2 lists the accepted attendees' positions and affiliations. A total of 42 people were accepted to attend, but many walk-ins increased the participation to 38 men and 29 women from fields aligned with the focus group topics. Due to timing constraints, the planning stage was very short (only 2 months).

Outcomes

There were several positive findings from this workshop as well. Video-conferencing was crucial for discussions with program managers and other long-distance speakers. It increased the number of program managers who could participate in the CARE workshop significantly. Since they were primarily participating in the focus groups, the

TABLE 12.2 CARE 2013 Accepted Attendee Job Positions and Affiliations

Accepted applicant pool	BNL	SBU	Other
Assistant scientist or higher	15	N/A	N/A
Postdoctoral Fellows	15	2	2
Senior graduate students	N/A	7	N/A
Engineer	1	N/A	N/A
Total	31	9	2

attendees were able to get one-on-one time with them—for the first time ever for a number of attendees. In addition, workshops with a focus on grant proposal writing are a great return on investment for institutions. The more knowledgeable staff and faculty are in writing quality proposals, the more grant money the institution is likely to receive from funding agencies. The authors are aware of at least one proposal to NIH and another to the DoE early career award that have been submitted as a result of these workshops. A number of participants expressed interest in following up on the collaborations established and fine-tuning the ideas developed during the workshop.

CARE 2013B

Topics

The goal of the CARE 2013B workshop was to give another venue for the focus groups created during the CARE 2013A workshop to discuss grants and further explore the mentoring program developed at BNL. There were approximately 60 attendees, including walk-ins. Guest speakers explained the different resources available to scientists to help with grant proposal writing, including BNL's proposal center. Further grant proposal writing advice was given, including seeking out grants at www.grants.gov. Most important, proposal writers were advised to align their research with the funder's mission, goals, and priorities.

Focus groups created during CARE 2013A gave updates of their accomplishments and sought out new group members. Several focus groups organized or planned follow-up activities, such as BWIS-sponsored networking lunch meetings, in order to foster enthusiasm for networking and collaboration and to share valuable resources and experience on research, grant applications, and career development. New focus group topics were also discussed as new focus group volunteers expressed interest in forming new networks. Interest was expressed in forming at least two new focus groups.

In the afternoon, a mentorship panel was held where panelists ranging from graduate students to senior scientists discussed their mentorship experiences and described their ideal mentor-mentee relationship. Panelists concluded that a mentee needs to receive guidance from someone they trust, particularly guidance on funding directions and opportunities. Supervisors should have a primary responsibility for mentoring, and they should make sure that early career scientists are writing journal articles, giving presentations, and improving their skills. Throughout their entire career, scientists should seek mentors and keep asking for advice.

Outcomes

Perhaps the most positive outcome of all these workshops was an increased exchange of ideas, networking, and collaboration among SBU and BNL scientists. While BNL has been co-managed by SBU for the past decade, in recent years, there has been an increased effort to strengthen the bond by establishing new funding opportunities, joint appointments, adjunct professorships, and research collaborations between the two institutions. Communication among postdoctoral staff and junior researchers at both institutions has greatly increased, and a majority of attendees formed new networks or collaborations. Many participants of the CARE 2013 workshop also expressed their intention to submit joint proposals and attend meetings to further collaborations between these institutions. Aside from different institutional perspectives and research capabilities, such joint efforts open up new support avenues; for example, funding from the National Science Foundation (NSF), which is not normally open to researchers at a national lab, is now accessible for BNL-SBU collaborations (within the limits of their policies). In addition, joint appointments afford BNL scientists an opportunity to participate in teaching. At least two of the CARE 2012 workshop participants have had an opportunity to teach classes for WISE undergraduates at SBU and gain valuable teaching experience unavailable at BNL.

Workshop Organization Advice

We developed a number of practices that were successful from an organizational perspective. With the mailing list developed for these workshops, effective dissemination of information on seminars and lectures at both SBU and BNL is now possible. It can also be used for following up with participants to understand the lasting benefits of their experience.

When organizing a workshop, it is beneficial to train new organizers each year to help run future workshops. Organization is vital to workshop success, and training new organizers each year ensures that future workshops will run smoothly. Since new volunteers were trained to help organize these workshops, the pool of trained organizers has increased from 2 to 19 SBU and BNL staff members. Allowing at least 6 months of workshop planning is absolutely necessary to provide enough time to advertise and for participants to respond.

When creating workshop documents for the organizing committee, using a document-sharing Web site to centralize all documents can help minimize miscommunication and prevent information from falling through the cracks. In addition, for each workshop session, an organizing committee member was assigned as a scribe to take notes, which provided excellent and immediate feedback for documenting the success of the workshop and suggesting recommendations for institutional changes or new programs.

The home institutions of guest speakers, especially for those from government agencies, may have restrictions on the video platforms that can be used with their computers at work. Hence, it is essential to communicate with the speakers well in advance, decide on a suitable platform, ensure that the infrastructure has sufficient bandwidth if parallel sessions are in progress, and test it prior to the workshop to iron out any wrinkles.

The focus group sessions with program managers were by far the participants' favorite part of CARE 2013A. One overwhelming request from participants was to have more time for one-on-one conversations with program managers. Similar sessions at regular intervals will be very beneficial to both the institution and the scientists.

CONCLUSIONS

Keeping momentum going so that similar workshops can be held at regular intervals, especially in the face of diminishing resources, can be a challenge. Collaborations were formed between SBU and BNL attendees, and they need to be fostered so that joint proposals can be submitted. As a follow-up for these workshops, regular networking sessions are being held to help increase the reach, collaboration, and exchange of ideas between institutions. Periodic workshops to update staff, as well as to inform new staff of funding agency focuses, are also under consideration. SBU and BNL are working to continue to help early career scientists and to encourage networking. Recently an additional successful one-day CARE 2015 workshop was held with a focus on career exploration and success through career planning and goal setting.

Without a doubt, the organization of workshops to help further women and minorities in STEM is necessary and beneficial. The CARE 2012, 2013A, and 2013B workshops not only provided valuable information and advice, but also helped establish collaborations between two research institutions that, despite having different atmospheres, share the same goal of furthering science and technology. The workshops herein described can be applied to most research establishments, particularly those that wish to strengthen collaborations among varying institutions.

References

Aveni, D., 2014. Women in Science & Engineering. Available from: <http://www.wise.sunysb.edu/> (accessed 02.09.15.).
Brookhaven Women in Science. Available from: <http://www.bnl.gov/bwis/>.

CARE, 2012. Career Advancement in a Reseach Environment. Available from: <http://www.bnl.gov/care/> (accessed 02.09.15.).

CARE, 2013A. Career Advancement in a Research Environment. Available from: <http://www.bnl.gov/care2013/> (accessed 02.09.15.).

CARE, 2013B. Career Advancement in a Research Environment. Available from: <https://www.bnl.gov/care2013b/> (accessed 02.09.15.).

Committee on the Status of Women in Physics of the American Physical Society, 2010. Report from the Site Visit to Brookhaven National Laboratory (BNL).

Laboratory, B.N. Brookhaven Science: A Passion for Discovery. Available from: <http://www.bnl.gov/science/>.

Steffen-Fluhr, N., 2006. Advancing Women Faculty through Collaborative Research Networks. WEPAN—Women in Engineering Programs and Advocates Network Conference, Pittsburgh, PA.

Valian, V., 1998. Why So Slow? The Advancement of Women. The MIT Press, Cambridge, MA.

13

Moving FORWARD in Space: The Temple University Workshops

Jennifer L. Piatek[1] and Alexandra Davatzes[2]

[1]Department of Geological Sciences, Central Connecticut State University, New Britain, CT, USA [2]Department of Earth and Environmental Science, Temple University, Philadelphia, PA, USA

O U T L I N E

Introduction	211
Workshop Design and Implementation	213
Different Settings and Different Demographics	214
Participant Feedback	219
Workshop Follow-up	220
Conclusion	221
References	221

INTRODUCTION

Planetary science is a multidisciplinary field that draws researchers from a wide variety of backgrounds. There are only a small number of universities with extensive planetary science programs. More often, planetary scientists are hired by academic departments looking for expertise in their major field (such as geology or physics) with an "extraterrestrial" focus; and commonly, these departments do not have other faculty in the same field. These scientists may rely on support from local colleagues for terrestrial concerns (teaching physical geology, navigating the university grants office, etc.); however, their research interests leave them as "lone wolves," relying on outside contacts for advice and collaboration. In addition, there is a strongly biased male-to-female ratio of faculty members within planetary science. At large research institutions with full planetary programs, women account for less than 10% of the faculty. In contrast, the "lone wolf" faculty are disproportionately female. Within this community, there is, therefore, a strong need to develop a network of support and collaboration in order to ensure the successful tenure of early career faculty.

The Moving FORWARD in Space workshop takes its name from the project that funded the workshops (FORWARD to Professorship) and the discipline that most of the target audience belonged to (planetary science/astronomy). We were motivated to develop Moving FORWARD in Space after attending an unrelated workshop (the Early Career Workshop sponsored by Science Education Resource Center at Carleton College (SERC, 2010), which is geared toward earth scientists who are pre-tenure or in non-tenure-track academic positions). Five planetary scientists, including the authors, attended this meeting in a single year, an unusually high number for this workshop. After a few discussions, it became clear that we were all in very similar situations—and had similar needs. This informal group was comprised entirely of women in tenure-track positions who were the only planetary scientists at their institutions. While we all had colleagues in our departments whom we could look to for help with nonplanetary courses or resources (most of us teach earth science courses as well), there was no one with whom we could discuss issues within our specialties. Our discussions in this informal group touched on all aspects of the job (teaching, developing courses, funding and finishing research projects, etc.), and we came away from the workshop with an understanding of the importance of developing a network of colleagues to turn to with those important questions.

The underrepresentation of women in tenure-track and tenured academic positions is well documented: recent studies indicate that while the balance of male/female tenure-track or tenured faculty in all disciplines is slightly imbalanced [58% male/42% female (AAUP, 2014)], there is a distinct imbalance in science, engineering, and mathematics [67% male/33% female (NSF, 2013)]. The field of planetary science is no exception: a recent survey of 36 universities with faculty pursuing planetary science research (White et al., 2011) found that women made up only 13% of planetary science faculty but receive 39% of doctoral degrees awarded: some of the larger programs reported having no female tenured faculty at the time of the survey (e.g., Washington University, the California Institute of Technology, and Cornell University, with 5–10 faculty members in each department). The study also noted that many of these departments employed a number of non-tenure-track research scientists and postdoctoral scientists, of which 28% were women: although the gender imbalance was less striking in these positions, it still does not match the rate at which doctorates are awarded to women.

There are a number of associations that female planetary scientists can become involved with to help support networking (including Women in Astronomy, the Association of Women in Geosciences, and the Earth Science Women's Network). In particular, the Women in Planetary Sciences networking event held at the Lunar and Planetary Science conference has grown in size over the past few years from an informal breakfast meeting to an evening event with invited speakers that regularly draws over 100 attendees. These large events, however, do not lend themselves well to focused networking, especially as the large number of attendees has pushed the meeting format away from small-group discussions and more toward large question-and-answer sessions or presentations, followed by shorter small discussions. Although networking alone cannot fix the gender gap that is apparent in the demographic studies, it can foster a more positive environment that can encourage young scientists to pursue academic careers.

WORKSHOP DESIGN AND IMPLEMENTATION

The goal of the Moving FORWARD in Space workshops was to help develop that focused network for young faculty scientists. We developed a program of sessions that touched on both professional and personal issues with the goal of fostering connections between participants: we suggested that if the only thing they took away from the event was a stack of business cards of people they might contact for help in the future, that would be a small measure of success. We also wanted to provide a "safe space," where all agreed not to share specifics of discussions (such as names of people or their institutions) so we might encourage participants to share experiences that they would not want told to someone outside the workshop.

The event was structured around types of events that we had found successful at other workshops that we have attended: active discussions (whether in small breakouts or as a larger group), icebreakers designed to encourage participants to mingle, and more passive sessions to allow decompression and internalization.

The goal of active sessions was to promote the development of relationships: we encouraged attendees to interact with a variety of people, not only those they knew prior to the workshop or others with similar backgrounds. Mentors and speakers helped to facilitate this by not sitting in the same location for each part of the workshop. This was also accomplished directly by arranging groups prior to the event (using topics they identify as areas of interest before the workshop, for example) and, in other cases, by randomly assigning groups at the workshop (by having people count off from 1 to 6, and everyone with the same number forms a discussion group). In addition, the activities were intended to represent a variety of pedagogical techniques that could be of use to the participants: they ranged from simple discussions over a table to "gallery walks," where groups attempted to answer questions and write their thoughts on poster-sized paper (each group rotated through topics until everyone has had a chance to discuss different questions). It was important to make sure there was a large group "sum up" at the end so that the benefit of all discussions were shared, facilitating transition to the next item on the schedule.

Passive lectures were generally limited to less than a half hour, with ample time for questions. Both in-person and virtual (Skype) talks were given, with an overwhelming preference for in-person talks, as virtual talks provide little interaction with the speakers (who have difficulty seeing the people in the room they are talking to, especially when interacting with those who have questions at the end). In addition, both workshops included panel discussions, in which mentors and speakers were able to answer questions and give insight into a diversity of experiences (see Figure 13.1). These panels began with each individual providing the group with his or her career history, then fielding questions on topics such as work/life choices, the interview and negotiation process, or the tenure review process.

DIFFERENT SETTINGS AND DIFFERENT DEMOGRAPHICS

We organized two workshops, each with a different format: schedules for each workshop are shown in Tables 13.1 and 13.2. The initial workshop was a multiple-day event held in June 2012 at Temple University. Participants had the option to stay at a hotel within the university grounds or to stay elsewhere; travel stipends were available for those who did not have other sources to fund travel. The second workshop was a one-day event held the day before the Lunar and Planetary Science Conference in March 2013 at the conference hotel. Although this

FIGURE 13.1 Faculty mentors at the first workshop included Vicki Hansen (left), Tracy Gregg (middle), and Jennifer Anderson (right), here discussing their career choices.

workshop was shorter, holding it at the same venue as the conference would make it easier for attendees to find funds to support travel. Although neither format is necessarily "better," each has its benefits and drawbacks.

The majority of the participants in the first workshop were already in faculty positions, with a small number of postdoctoral scientists and "all but dissertation[1]" (ABD) graduate students. The second workshop had a higher proportion of postdoctoral researchers and ABD graduate students seeking faculty positions, with only a small number of pre-tenure faculty. This may be because it is a small community, and therefore many of the interested early career faculty had attended the meeting the first year, or it may have been because having the workshop attached to a conference made the workshop more attractive to graduate students and postdoctoral scientists (due either to scheduling or financial reasons).

The greatest benefit of the multiple-day workshop was that it allowed for more interaction between attendees; there was ample time for participants to mingle and get to know each other. The additional time also allowed attendees to follow up on questions and build some of the networks before the workshop ended. Some of this interaction continued outside the workshop, as participants who were staying near the workshop venue spent some time socializing after the workshop events were over for the day. In addition to this spontaneous social interaction, the workshop included a planned trip the Franklin Museum, as the transit of Venus (a rare event) happened to occur during the workshop. In

---

[1]ABD is a commonly used term to indicate graduate students who have fulfilled all the requirements for a PhD except the finalization of their dissertation.

TABLE 13.1   Workshop Schedule for Multiple Day Workshop Held at Temple University in June 2012

Moving FORWARD in Space Workshop
June 4-6, 2012
Temple University
Program

	Monday June 4, 2012	Tuesday June 5, 2012	Wednesday June 6, 2012
8:30am		Continental breakfast	Continental breakfast
9:00		Teaching Planetary Sciences in Physical Science Departments *Dr. Tracy Gregg, University at Buffalo*	Developing a lab/ syllabus with the mentors
10:00		Breakout Discussions: • Defining yourself • 5-year plan • Time management • Work/life balance	
11:00		Getting Funded *Dr. Sonia Esperança, NSF Program Director (via Skype)*	Snack. Summary and concluding statements
Noon	Registration	Lunch	Goodbyes and Workshop evaluations
1:00pm	Welcome from the University *Dr. Shohreh Amini, Associate Dean, Temple University* Welcome to the Workshop *Dr. Jen Piatek, CCSU and Dr. Alix Davatzes, Temple University* The FORWARD Program	Panel discussion *Dr. Vicki Hansen, UMD; Dr. Tracy Gregg; and Dr. Jennifer Anderson, Winona State University*	
2:00	*Dr. Paul Sabila, Gallaudet University* Snack break. Icebreakers: • Icebreaker Bingo • Gallery walk: Career Goals		
3:00	• "Where in the Solar System are you?"	Snack break	
4:00	Writing: Getting it done! *Dr. Dustin Kidd, Temple University*	Depart for the Franklin Institute *Speakers: Dr. Vicki Hansen; Dr. Tracy Gregg* Viewing of the Venus Transit Dinner afterwards	
	Hotel check-in Dinner afterwards		

TABLE 13.2 Workshop Schedule for Single Day Workshop Held in Conjunction with the Lunar and Planetary Science Conference in March, 2013

Moving FORWARD in Space Workshop
March 17th, 2013
Lunar and Planetary Science Conference, Houston, TX
Program

8:30am	Continental breakfast
9:00	Welcome and Icebreakers *Dr. Alexandra Davatzes and Dr. Jennifer Piatek* · Icebreaker Bingo · "Where in the Solar System are you?"
10:00	Teaching Planetary Sciences in Physical Science Departments *Dr. Tracy Gregg, University at Buffalo*
	Coffee
11:00	Morning breakouts · Dual-career/family balance · Teaching: involving undergrads and developing courses · Balance of research and teaching
Noon	Lunch
1:00	
	Panel discussion *Dr. Erin Kraal, Dr. Tracy Gregg, Dr. Jennifer Piatek, Dr. Alix Davatzes* Topics to include career paths, networking strategies, finding successful paths to funding, navigating the university promotion and tenure system.
2:00	
	Afternoon breakouts · Writing productively · Negotiating
3:00	
	Coffee and snack break
4:00	
	Summary and concluding statements
	Goodbyes and Workshop evaluations

addition to expanding the workshop to include this event (and dinner afterward), two of our workshop mentors (Tracy Gregg and Vicki Hansen) agreed to give presentations to the public about their Venus research as part of the activities at the Franklin Museum.

Another benefit of the multiple-day event was the increased amount of time in the schedule. This allowed for multiple speakers and break-outs covering a wider range of topics (noted here in the workshop schedules as appropriate). Participants were encouraged to choose breakout topics prior to the session, but they could switch groups if they felt the need to during the workshop. All groups were encouraged to share their conclusions at the end of the breakout so all attendees could benefit from the varied discussions.

Multiple-day on-site workshops, unfortunately, are more difficult and expensive to organize. We were fortunate to have an excellent venue available free from the university (a large, open room with kitchen access designed to accommodate multimedia presentations, normally used by the university president) that was also located near the hotel. This situation is unusual (normally, universities charge significant fees to use these rooms), and not all campuses have such convenient hotel accommodations. There were some minor logistics required to coordinate with attendees who chose to stay at off-campus locations to reduce their costs. It was also serendipitous that the transit of Venus fell during the workshop (this was not planned), which became the nucleus of the Franklin Museum trip. For attendees, traveling to the workshop required multiple days away from home and work, as well as securing travel funds: this in part may have been the reason why there were more early career faculty at the longer workshop, while graduate students and postdoctoral scientists dominated the second workshop.

The one-day conference workshop, by contrast, was significantly easier to organize. The Lunar and Planetary Science conference supports associated meetings by providing space at no additional cost (but with the requirement that participants cannot be charged a fee for the event). Catering was available through the hotel. Workshop participants would likely be planning to attend the meeting, so the cost to attend the workshop would only be for the additional hotel night (again, we had some funds available to help cover this expense, although not all participants requested these funds). Obviously, however, the shorter workshop time made it more difficult to address all the topics that participants might be interested in. An interesting result for the one-day workshop was that although a number of topics were suggested for the afternoon breakout, a majority of workshop attendees wished to discuss writing productively: three of the four breakout groups brainstormed on this topic (an outside speaker had covered this topic during the original multiple day workshop). There was also less time to mingle and get to know everyone over the course of a single day, and much less time to socialize outside the workshop framework. On the other hand, because the workshop preceded the meeting, there was an extended period for additional networking and sharing of feedback for those who stayed for most of the conference itself.

PARTICIPANT FEEDBACK

Both workshops were very well received: 100% of attendees commented (via follow-up surveys handed out at the end of the event) that they would attend another such event and would recommend it to friends. Some of the direct positive feedback included:

> I didn't think you'd have time to address everyone's questions, but you DID! It was very well planned.
> All I can say is that any expectations I had have been exceeded. It was incredible. Thanks.
> Learn. Be inspired. Be encouraged. Make new friends.
> I really enjoyed the out-of-the-box ideas on how to incorporate planetary ideas into geology classes.
> I also now feel that I have more female faculty that I can look to for mentoring and advice.
> I got so much out of this, information-wise and inspiration-wise. I feel much more confident after this workshop.

A number of participants specifically mentioned networking and socializing with other female planetary scientists as benefits of the workshop: they commented on seeing mentors as role models ("if she can do it, so can I") and also appreciated discussions with other attendees who were a bit more advanced in their careers. Some provided specific examples of who they hoped to keep in touch with after the workshop for various reasons: help with job applications or teaching specific courses, advice on negotiating, or as research colleagues. Some attendees noted that their career goals didn't include academia, but rather employment as research scientists (either in soft-money positions or as civil servants at NASA), but that the workshop topics still provided them with valuable information and networking opportunities. Many participants shared suggestions for improvement, including limiting workshops to specific themes (a workshop that focused on work/life balance issues, one for writing papers and proposals, etc.) A theme-specific event would make it easier to focus one-day workshops with limited time and to keep subsequent events from becoming repetitive or stale.

WORKSHOP FOLLOW-UP

Attendees at both workshops indicated the desire to continue contact through social media: a private (membership by invitation only) Facebook group was created following the original workshop and utilized for the second workshop to help maintain connections. A Google group was also created for those who did not wish to use Facebook. Classroom activities discussed during both workshops were also made available via a shared Google Drive. Several attendees also shared Twitter handles, although this was not a formal part of the workshop. In addition, a short workshop summary was posted to the Women in Planetary Science blog (Women in Planetary Science, 2014).

Unfortunately, maintaining this connection was somewhat less successful than the workshop portended. Although many attendees joined the Facebook and Google groups, there has been little post-workshop discussion. The Facebook group records minor activity—mostly infrequent posts of interesting links (e.g., relevant NASA programs) or requests for help or suggestions on job applications. However, connections made during the workshop have continued through more traditional channels: meet-ups at conferences, attendees using their "stack of business cards" to email a single person directly for assistance rather than relying on posts to the group as a whole via social media: a few attendees have contacted the workshop organizers at later conferences to ask for advice about negotiating, to share success with getting new faculty jobs, or to ask about sharing teaching resources. These are the interactions that the workshop was designed to foster, even if the whole group network remains somewhat silent.

Many of the workshop attendees expressed the need for these types of workshops: while there are a number of networking events associated with conferences (such as the Women in Planetary Science event held at the Lunar and Planetary Science Conference, as well as similar meetings at other planetary science conferences), there are few focused small-group workshops such as these. Unfortunately, follow-up workshops proved difficult to organize, partly due to the lack of available funding. There is no specific NASA grant program to support workshops such as these: the research programs will accept proposals to fund science-focused workshops, but not for career/networking workshops such as this. It might be possible to continue one-day workshops without funding when conferences provide meeting space and audiovisual (A/V) equipment to associated meetings, but this leaves no funding to cover travel costs or for catering. Hotel rules prevent meetings from bringing in outside food: a one-day workshop would have to include a longer lunch break at the expense of content.

Another area of concern for post-workshop follow-up and possible continuation of workshops is the level of recognition afforded the organizers. Although a significant amount of time is required to develop, schedule, promote, and ultimately deliver a successful workshop, this commitment is not universally recognized as valuable service, particularly in terms of promotion and tenure for those in university positions. Onsite workshops should provide immediate recognition by university administration (note that the multiple-day workshop schedule in Table 13.1 includes introductions from a university dean); but this type of recognition is typically short lived (as administrators leave positions) and not likely to come with written documentation to be included in tenure packets. In addition, professional service activities, as these workshops are likely to be qualified, are often not ranked with high priority in promotion and tenure decisions. This is discouraging, as pre-tenure faculty often have valuable insights for those looking for tenure-track employment: it is critical, therefore, to pursue recognition for organizing workshops through publications and funding so the organizers see a "return on investment" via recognition of effort in promotion and tenure discussions. However, as for the participants, this event does afford the organizers an opportunity to grow their network, which is critical for a successful career.

CONCLUSION

One challenge faced by women in academic science and engineering is the lack of women in the department with the same discipline focus. This is particularly true for women in planetary science where women are few and far between. FORWARD in Space sought to address this isolation through two workshop formats. While a multiple-day, free-standing workshop provides extensive time for networking and in-depth discussions, it is often difficult to get away for so long. An alternative is a workshop co-located with a national conference, which, while easing the travel dilemma, has less time to devote to content. Although neither format is optimal, each addresses a need for women in planetary science, and each format was deemed successful for the participants.

References

American Association of University Professors (AAUP), 2014. Distribution of Faculty, by Rank, Gender, Category, and Affiliation, 2013–2014 (Percent). Available from: <http://www.aaup.org/sites/default/files/files/2014%20salary%20report/table12.pdf> (accessed 29.09.14.).

National Science Foundation, National Center for Science and Engineering Statistics, 2013. Women, Minorities, and Persons with Disabilities in Science and Engineering: 2013. Special Report NSF 13-304. Arlington, VA. Available from: <http://www.nsf.gov/statistics/wmpd/> (accessed 29.09.14.).

Science Education Resource Center, 2010. Workshop for Early Career Geoscience Faculty, June 2010. Available from: <http://serc.carleton.edu/NAGTWorkshops/earlycareer2010/index.html> (accessed 11.11.14.).

White, S., Chu, R.Y., Ivie, R., 2011. 2011 Survey of the Planetary Science Workforce. Statistical Research Center/American Institute of Physics. Available from: <http://lasp.colorado.edu/mop/resources/links/PlanetaryScienceWorkForceSurvey2011/Report.pdf> (accessed 29.09.14.).

Women in Planetary Science, 2014. Available from: <http://womeninplanetaryscience.wordpress.com> (accessed 11.11.14.).

FORWARD Workshops: Strategies for Inclusion of the Deaf and Hard of Hearing

Paul S. Sabila, H. David Snyder and Charlene C. Sorensen

Chemistry and Physics Program, Department of Science, Technology, and Mathematics, Gallaudet University, Washington, DC, USA

OUTLINE

Gallaudet University	224
Deaf, Hard of Hearing, and the ADA Act	226
The Challenge of Bringing D/HoH into STEM	227
Origins of FORWARD at Gallaudet	228
FORWARD in SEM	229
The FORWARD to Professorship and Pay It FORWARD Projects	232
Evaluations: Participants' Views of the FORWARD Workshops at GU	233
Impact of FORWARD on D/HoH Participants and GU	234
Impact of D/HoH Participants and GU on FORWARD and on "Hearing" Participants	239
Strategies for Inclusion of D/HoH Participants and ASL Interpreters in Scientific Workshops	240
Acknowledgments	242
References	242

FIGURE 14.1   Gallaudet University.

GALLAUDET UNIVERSITY

The Focus on Reaching Women for Academics, Research, and Development (FORWARD) program was initiated to accelerate the advancement of women and underrepresented minorities in Science, Technology, Engineering and Mathematics (STEM) fields. While FORWARD has successfully engaged various demographic groups, this chapter will focus on activities at Gallaudet University (GU) and the incorporation of deaf and hard-of-hearing (D/HoH) participants in FORWARD projects (Figure 14.1).

GU was founded in 1864 by an act of Congress and is the world's only university with programs and services designed to accommodate D/HoH individuals, while also contributing knowledge likely to benefit the nation's D/HoH people, particularly in the areas of education and human services (Education of the Deaf Act, 1986). GU is considered a leader in research, service, and education to the deaf community. GU is a bilingual, diverse, and multicultural institution of higher learning that promotes the intellectual and professional advancement of D/HoH individuals and uses American Sign Language (ASL) and English for both instruction and communication. GU faculty members are required to demonstrate ASL proficiency before promotion or tenure. As of 2013, GU had approximately 220 faculty members with 51% of them classified as D/HoH. The percentage of women faculty in 2013 was 65% (GU, 2003–2013).

GU programs are open to D/HoH and hearing students and include more than 40 undergraduate programs leading to Bachelor of Arts or Bachelor of Science degrees. GU also offers several Master of Arts and Master of Science degrees, specialist degrees, and doctoral degrees involving professional services for D/HoH. GU offers educational programs on campus to D/HoH through the Kendall Demonstration

TABLE 14.1   The Integrated Post-secondary Data System (IPEDS) Survey of the
National Center for Education Statistics (NCES) Showing the Demographics of
Student Enrolled at GU from 2005 to 2013 (IPEDS-GU)

IPEDS year	2005	2006	2007	2008	2009	2010	2011	2012	2013
Unduplicated student head count	1985	1833	1746	1674	1530	1445	1522	1727	1707
% Non-Hispanic whites	61	62	64	66	67	68	63	64	62
% Non-Hispanic blacks	11	11	11	10	10	11	11	10	11
% Hispanic	6	8	8	7	7	8	8	8	12
% Asian	4	5	5	5	5	4	4	4	4
% American Indian or Alaska native	3	3	3	2	2	1	1	0	0
% Nonresident alien	11	9	8	7	7	6	6	6	7
% Unknown race/ ethnicity	3	3	2	3	3	2	2	3	3
% Women	–	60	59	62	62	61	61	61	62

Elementary School and the Model Secondary School for the Deaf. The
largest hearing and speech center in the Washington, DC area is located
at GU and provides services including assistive devices, audiological
evaluation, cochlear implants, hearing aids, speech reading classes, and
speech-language pathology. Each year, GU serves tens of thousands of
people on national and international levels through outreach programs,
and ASL classes that are open to the public (GU Fast Facts).

The number of D/HoH students attending GU and residential
schools for the deaf have steadily declined over the years. In his book,
titled Language Attitudes in the American Deaf Community (2012), Hill
notes that the percentage of deaf students attending residential schools
for the deaf declined from 80% in the 1960s to just about 24% in 2010
(Hill, 2012). The reason for this drop is that higher numbers of D/HoH
individuals are now attending mainstream educational institutions.
Data collected on the demographics of students enrolled at GU between
2005 and 2013 (Table 14.1 IPEDS 2005–2013) revealed a similar trend at
GU, where undergraduate student enrollment reached its lowest level
in 2010 and has only just begun to improve.

The 2013 GU annual report of achievements (GU, 2003–2013) reveals
that 95% of the GU undergraduate student population is classified as
D/HoH. The report shows that GU had an average of 1,064 undergraduates and a total of 1,812 students (including graduate students and
those in professional studies) in 2010 and 2013. Approximately 62% of

the student population was Caucasian, and approximately 37% were minorities (11% African-American and 9% Hispanic). The distribution of degree seeking undergraduates was 29% (freshmen), 20% (sophomores), 26% (juniors), 24% (seniors), and 1% (second degree). For graduate school, students enrolled in degree-awarding programs were 2% (certificate), 63% (Master's), 3% (specialists), and 33% (doctorate).

Apart from Linguistics, all the other STEM programs at GU (chemistry/physics, biology, and mathematics) only offer BA/BS degrees. Between 2010 and 2011, the percentage of GU students who had declared science majors/minors was as follows: chemistry/physics 0.9%, biology 2.4%, and mathematics 1.8%. This amounts to only about 5% of GU undergraduate students pursuing majors/minors in STEM.

DEAF, HARD OF HEARING, AND THE ADA ACT

The exact number of deaf people living in the United States cannot be easily determined due to the lack of a generally accepted definition of deafness. D/HoH individuals have varying degrees of hearing loss and sometimes provide varying responses during data collection depending on how the questions about hearing loss are phrased (Mitchell, 2006). A 1990 estimate by the National Center for Health Statistics (NCHS) of the U.S. Department of Health and Human services (Ries, 1994) reported 8.6% of the total US population as "having some degree of hearing difficulties." The percentage of people with hearing loss was found to increase with age, starting from 1.8% in the 3–17 year age range to 29.1% in the 65 years or older age range. Of these, 0.41% are considered to be deaf in both ears or not able to understand or hear any speech, while 0.49% can, at best, hear or understand words shouted into the better ear. A 2010 report on household economic studies for Americans with disabilities of ages 15 years and older (Brault, 2012), reported that 3.1% of Americans had hearing difficulties, with 0.5% of the population having severe hearing loss. On average, two to four out of every 1000 people in the United States are considered functionally deaf (Mitchell, 2006).

The enactment of the Americans with Disabilities Act (ADA) of 1990 and its later amendments of 2008 (ADA, 2008) have helped with the advancement of disabled individuals by making more facilities and services accessible to them. In addition to the ADA, the Individuals with Disability Act (IDEA) (IDEA, 2004) provides grants toward supporting research and demonstrations aimed at the advancement of disabled individuals. As a result of these acts, the enrollment of D/HoH individuals at mainstream education institutions in the United States climbed to more than 90% by 2006 (Marschark et al., 2006). In recent years, institutions, groups, and researchers have been inspired to work toward reducing barriers to the advancement of people with disabilities in various fields, giving rise to new programs. For example, a program was started at the University of Washington aimed at advancing D/HoH individuals in computing (Burgstahler and Ladner, 2006). In 2011, Dr Peggy Cebe, a Physics professor at Tufts University, received the Presidential Award for Excellence in Science, Mathematics, and Engineering Mentoring in recognition of her work mentoring D/HoH student interns since 2003 (Wang, 2011). However, people with disabilities (including D/HoH) continue to be underrepresented in STEM fields (Alston and Hampton, 2000; Hoette et al., 2011).

THE CHALLENGE OF BRINGING D/HOH INTO STEM

The low percentages reflect the fact that fewer D/HoH individuals advance through the leaky STEM pipeline, which eventually lead to the observed underrepresentation of D/HoH individuals in STEM (Hoette et al., 2011). An efficient pipeline has no leaks and unimpeded flow. For flow to occur at all, obstructions, leaks, barriers, and diversions everywhere along the pipeline have to be cleared or fixed. An effective plan for sustaining a STEM workforce must address needs from elementary school all the way to employment. Programs supported by the National Science Foundation (NSF) typically focused on logjams and leaks at critical stages in the educational pipeline.

At GU, informal discussions with students revealed some of the barriers facing students considering making a transition to graduate school. The hurdles seemed to be the graduate record examination (GRE) exam, attitudes of professors and administrators in the graduate schools toward students with disabilities, and the social and communication difficulties of being a lone D/HoH student in a competitive research group, especially when interpreting needs are not met. For example, Dr Snyder awarded fellowship funds from the District of Columbia Space Grant Consortium to a deaf student and had her ask that the fellowship money be directly provided to her department so they could more easily cover her sign language interpreting expenses. He thought that interpreting costs charged to an individual department would discourage many D/HoH students who worry that they are causing serious financial expenses and budget problems for their departments (In the end, the student's fellowship money could not be transferred to her department). Feedback from internships had indicated that some students were not properly prepared for the workplace, much less graduate school. D/HoH students typically spend more years in school due to various causes, making school "burnout" a real issue. Since many in the hearing community found it necessary to upgrade their skills and pursue further higher graduate education, we believed that solid work had to be done to explore the problems current D/HoH students were having in graduate school.

The early FORWARD program of the late 1990s focused specifically on the graduate school entrance stage of the pipeline. At this stage, interviews conducted within the FORWARD program revealed that D/HoH students expressed the following concerns about graduate school transitions:

1. The widespread geographic distribution of graduate schools and the diversity of programs made it hard to form and identify schools with a sizeable D/HoH community.
2. The GRE is a common requirement for graduate school admission and it is in a nonnative language for the D/HoH ASL signer.
3. The competitive and less structured research environment of graduate school could put D/HoH students at a disadvantage for communicating effectively and maintaining professional social relationships with colleagues and peers.

ORIGINS OF FORWARD AT GALLAUDET

The origin of the FORWARD program dates from 1995, when Dr Catherine Mavriplis was teaching an engineering heat transfer course at George Washington University (GWU) and encountered a deaf student from GU (since GU did not offer engineering curricula). In response to the student's special needs, and after discovering the difficulty for deaf scientists or engineers to communicate due to lack of technology and ASL scientific vocabulary, Dr Mavriplis contacted Dr Rachelle Heller from GWU, who, in turn, invited Dr Henry Snyder, a GU physics professor, to collaborate in an upcoming NSF proposal. At the time, Dr Snyder was involved in several collaboration efforts with other schools and teachers and wanted to make new connections and collaborate using the Internet. He was familiar with GWU because he had taken some graduate courses there and had also set up a dual-degree program with the engineering school at GWU. He was aware that most of the GU physics graduates went to good government jobs, but was concerned that few GU graduates were making a successful transition to graduate school. He saw this new collaboration as an opportunity to do substantial work removing barriers in the way of his students. Dr Snyder reached out to the newly hired Dr Charlene Sorensen of the chemistry department (since chemistry and physics had recently been combined into a single department). The proposed participation of

Dr Sorensen had the potential to greatly improve the effectiveness and impact of the program at GU by attracting women to STEM majors. This resulted in a partnership in which two GWU professors, Dr Heller and Dr Mavriplis, teamed up with two GU professors, Dr Snyder and Dr Sorensen, to submit a proposal to the NSF for starting a program of services called FORWARD. FORWARD's aim was to advance women and underrepresented minorities (including D/HoH) in STEM. The first proposal was collaboratively written and titled "FORWARD in SEM (Science, Engineering and Mathematics)." Though Dr Snyder and Dr Sorensen were both "hearing," FORWARD in SEM aimed at enlisting and recruiting D/HoH individuals to tell their story and participate in larger group discussions.

FORWARD IN SEM

GWU and GU received a grant from the NSF in 1997 for their FORWARD in SEM project (NSF Grant #9714729). Four other institutions included in the initial collaboration were Hood College, Hampton University, Smith College, and the National Technical Institute for the Deaf (NTID). It is worth noting that NTID is one of the nine colleges of Rochester Institute of Technology (RIT) and has more than 1,300 D/HoH students pursuing degrees in science and technical fields (RIT—National Technical Institute for the Deaf). NTID offers primarily Associates Degrees, so its partnership with RIT is an important arrangement for enabling a transition to higher degrees. However, back in the 1990s, not many NTID students successfully made the transition directly to RIT. One of the participating faculty members in FORWARD was Dr Harry Lang, who was a faculty member at NTID. He taught physics and mathematics at NTID and was a very successful grant writer and book author. Dr Lang's participation was important to the program because NTID is a center for Deaf science and technical education (The term Deaf with a capital D indicates those who associated with a Deaf culture). Dr Lang's background in science education and his involvement with Deaf education research made him valuable to the program as a faculty participant, an occasional adviser to help guide our efforts, and also as an internship adviser/mentor. We believed from the start that our effort had to include outreach to other institutions and had to be innovative in the use of technology and teaching style. It was becoming clear that significant populations of students were not being served well by current teaching methods and practices in STEM, and these populations would be open to new instruction techniques and schemes that would better address their needs. FORWARD at GU extended the reach of the FORWARD program to include D/HoH students of any gender and, by implication, any group underrepresented in technical and scientific fields. We intended to use FORWARD to cast light on the situation of D/HoH in graduate school, to both educate the larger public and help the next generation of D/HoH develop practical graduate school survival strategies.

While it was clear that many of the problems that we faced might not be solved any time soon, we felt it was time that the issues should be raised for the D/HoH community as well as the "hearing community." We felt our efforts would be of great interest to the NSF and their control of programs and their funding could have serious implications for setting future rules and guidelines. We were, of course, naïvely optimistic about how we could change the world. Our GWU collaborators were very understanding of our needs and they encouraged us to explore the widening dimensions of the problem. Their teaching, professional engineering, and administrative experience helped to broaden and deepen our discussions. We did face the difficulty/opportunity that many new STEM teaching tools, right practices, and techniques that we needed were just beginning to come to life in academic institutions: mentoring, student research opportunities, small or special interest online communities and groups, and classroom coaching and active learning as a new style of teaching and course management. These ideas were rather new and untested, so our discussions within the FORWARD group were very helpful for sorting out and forming effective strategies.

In order to foster collaboration skills for both hearing and D/HoH students, an interdisciplinary science and engineering seminar course was offered concurrently at GWU and at GU (Mavriplis et al., 2000). For the GU community, the course was offered through distance education. Advertising for D/HoH participants was done with flyers, face to face recruitment, through the GU College of Continuing Education website, and by sending mail to 1,000 D/HoH employees in the DC area. This course was intended to serve as an introduction to collaboration between scientists of different disciplines, while enabling us to explore modes of education that were not mainstream, but were obviously practiced by scientists in their work. One has to keep in mind that there were few reliable tools available in the late 1990s for online group collaboration, but it was an exciting idea that many wanted to attempt. For example, many hours were spent trying to experiment with ways to use the CU-SeeMe Internet videoconferencing system to transmit sign language. The course assignments were arranged in such a way as to encourage collaboration and participation between the engineering students from GWU and the liberal arts science students at GU.

FORWARD encouraged the establishment of mentoring networks by connecting participants to accomplished D/HoH and hearing women.

A recruitment packet prepared for mentors included an explanatory letter, advertising flyer, and a response postcard. Respondents were sent a questionnaire to assist in matching students and mentors. At the time, we had a booklet that listed scientists with disabilities; we used this as one primary source of prospective mentors to contact. There was a high response rate from the scientists with disabilities, showing their willingness to cooperate.

Summer research opportunities were provided through the FORWARD in SEM research competition where female first-year graduate students applied for research positions listed by FORWARD principal investigators and faculty from participating institutions. An application form was developed, and a competition for the funds was advertised via e-mail, departmental announcements, and flyer postings. The main criteria for the scholarship award were academic excellence and potential for continued success in graduate school. All the awardees were women, in keeping with the main focus of FORWARD. At the same time, GU students chosen on the basis of their task-relevant skills and experience within the D/HoH community were hired to work on all phases of materials development, workshop and seminar participant recruitment, the FORWARD website updates, library and web research of graduate school special services information, and assessment of learning and teaching strategies. FORWARD also provided partial tuition waiver awards to the GU students involved.

Within the previously mentioned FORWARD seminar course, various deaf communication and integration strategies were explored using electronic communication models. The FORWARD website was made deaf-friendly by adding more visual content. Postings were made for D/HoH students to share their experiences on various topics including discussions on how to interview, find assistance, pick a supportive graduate school, etc. The website also had resources for employers or graduate school faculty to learn some basic ASL or arrange for more formal training. Sample graduate schools that would be of greatest interest to students with disabilities were selected and their links included on the FORWARD website. We also provided opportunities for GWU engineers and GU science majors to collaborate using videoconferencing systems like CU-SeeMe.

FORWARD sponsored a technical interpreting workshop highlighting the needs and challenges facing interpreters serving in technical and scientific. It took place at GU in the Kellogg Conference Hotel. Resources were prepared to provide interpreters basic, common, and technical vocabulary used in science. The idea was to select common vocabulary related to major topics to help the interpreter gradually learn the important technical terms. Our impression was that the interpreter would transmit information more clearly once he/she had a rudimentary understanding of the vocabulary being used. A website was created to provide easy access to a simplified glossary of course-specific engineering vocabulary. In retrospect, we should have perhaps targeted a single course and done an in-depth research study to determine a most effective scheme for assisting interpreters.

Following the first FORWARD to Graduate School (F2GS) workshop held at GWU in 1998, the spring workshops were moved to GU. Participants were provided with information for how to apply to graduate school, prepare for the GRE, and how to find the right graduate school. In one of the F2GS workshops, the welcoming address was given by the GU Dean of the College of Arts and Sciences, Dr Jane Dillehay (a deaf female professor with a PhD in Molecular Biology), where she encouraged the participants to "learn more about the process of getting into graduate school" and to learn the "basic communication skills to prepare for professional careers."

FORWARD at GU then started offering Saturday GRE classes to help D/HoH students adequately prepare for GRE tests. It was believed that most commercial GRE prep courses were not capable of adapting to the wide range of needs of GU students. In addition, we, as teachers, wanted to better understand the linguistic barriers that some students encountered on the test and develop coping strategies. A website was created to specifically help students with common vocabulary that showed up on GRE tests.

THE FORWARD TO PROFESSORSHIP AND PAY IT FORWARD PROJECTS

As the FORWARD in SEM project drew to a close, the FORWARD to Professorship project was developed in 2001 (see Chapter 2 and Mavriplis et al., 2010) to address the "leaky pipeline" at the graduate school-to-professorship junction, with the goal of advancing women and minorities into faculty positions in STEM. Several studies (e.g., Nelson, 2004) had shown the discrepancy between the growing percentage of women and minorities graduating with PhDs in STEM and those obtaining faculty positions. The situation was further exacerbated by even lower numbers advancing into associate professorship and eventually to full professorship positions in STEM. National FORWARD to Professorship workshops to advance women to tenure-track assistant professorship were arranged at GU as outlined in Chapter 2; by design, these events had a lower participation of D/HoH undergraduates as the projects and activities were specifically targeted to participants who were senior PhD students, postdoctoral researchers, and junior faculty.

However, we felt it necessary to also provide participants advancing into faculty positions with training on interpreter etiquette, deaf culture, and exposure to D/HoH needs to help them become more sensitive to the needs of D/HoH and other individuals with disabilities in their classrooms or research laboratories. As a result, GU administrators, faculty, and interpreters were intrinsically involved in the FORWARD to Professorship workshops and activities.

As a follow-up to FORWARD to Professorship, the Pay It FORWARD project was started in 2009 to create a cadre of trainers able to provide structured mentoring workshops targeted toward specific regions, groups and disciplines (see Chapter 2). Ten teams were awarded grants to adapt the FORWARD to Professorship model and develop workshops to meet the needs of their targeted audiences. The selected teams developed workshops in various STEM disciplines (computer and mathematical, planetary and physical sciences, etc.), societal groups (e.g., African-American, Pacific Islander, and Latina women), institutions, and geographical regions (e.g., the US Southwest, US Midwest, New York City). The workshop developers were brought to GU in Washington, DC, for training, while, at the same time, observing one of our national FORWARD to Professorship workshops. More in-depth information on the FORWARD to Professorship, Pay It FORWARD, and trainer workshops are provided in the other chapters in this book.

EVALUATIONS: PARTICIPANTS' VIEWS OF THE FORWARD WORKSHOPS AT GU

Participants at the F2GS workshops were asked to evaluate the workshop experience, speakers, activities, and topics. The information gleaned from these evaluations gave us insights into the participants' expectations and the impact of the workshop on them, and was then used to improve the subsequent workshops. The participants have generally found the workshops beneficial and provided positive ratings on the workshop, speakers, venue, and activities. For example, the spring 1999 F2GS Weekend Workshop at GU had 25 participants. Seventeen participants rated the workshop as "excellent," 20 described it as "well organized," while 19 indicated that the speakers were beneficial. When asked to name the kind of FORWARD activities that they would like to participate in, 10 indicated interest in a seminar course, 17 in a mentoring program, 14 in a summer research competition for first year graduate students, while some hearing participants expressed interest in deaf access activities. At the same time, 14 indicated that the workshop "surpassed their expectations," while 22 participants would "definitely recommend the workshop" to their friends. Similar results were observed in the subsequent FORWARD workshops.

We do not know which respondents to the written evaluations were D/HoH, therefore, we cannot isolate their comments. General participant feedback from the workshops is given in Chapters 2, 15, and 18, while comments pertaining to GU are discussed here. Many participants appreciated the uniqueness of the venue and the chance to meet D/HoH participants and introduction into the deaf culture; "...It also gave me exposure to the deaf community." Participants thought that GU and the Kellogg Hotel and Conference center accommodations were "flawless and excellent" and that the whole workshop helped broaden their views. Though a few people thought that too much time was spent on disabilities, the majority described these presentations as "very inspiring." They indicated that they learned a great deal on "how to include people with disabilities," learned "useful lessons on teaching people with disabilities," got a "good introduction to common concerns of women and underrepresented minorities in science," and appreciated the "interesting perspectives on disabilities." One of the participants indicated that this was "the best talk on disabilities" she had ever attended.

IMPACT OF FORWARD ON D/HOH PARTICIPANTS AND GU

From the very start, the FORWARD projects planned and delivered workshops that brought a group of women together aimed at addressing the challenges to the progress of women and men of underrepresented groups in STEM. The FORWARD project at GU saw the participation of D/HoH individuals, including 10 PhD scientists and more than 35 undergraduates. In the early days of the program, we had sought to challenge ourselves by engaging in new types of activities that would enrich and broaden our experiences while giving us a firm basis for responsively making future program course corrections.

Did our efforts succeed? To some extent, our efforts did succeed and brought problems to light, while providing a new way of tending to the leaky pipeline in STEM with respect to women and minorities, especially D/HoH.

The FORWARD projects were instrumental in enhancing collaborations and cultural awareness among hearing and D/HoH participants. The interactions during the workshops, seminar classes, and other activities provided D/HoH students with opportunities to work on skills that are essential when transitioning into STEM careers in a hearing environment. As a result, participants developed sets of communication strategies, which in turn enhanced their confidence and ability to work or collaborate with others in both hearing and D/HoH environments. The exchange and seminar courses offered by GU and GWU faculty enabled cross-discipline collaborations between science students and faculty in a predominantly D/HoH liberal arts college (GU) and engineering students and faculty at a hearing Research 1 (R1) (Carnegie Classifications) Institution (GWU), at a time when such collaboration did not exist and electronic tools were few. Recent advances in technology have made it easier for hearing and D/HoH individuals to collaborate without heavily relying on ASL interpreters.

The F2GS workshop provided the D/HoH participants with the information and skills for applying for graduate study in STEM. In addition, a summer research competition enabled students to help sharpen their research skills in preparation for higher-level research at graduate schools. As a result, more students began taking interest in summer internships in STEM, applying to graduate school, and pursuing careers in STEM and related fields.

One of the students who participated in the early F2GS was Susan Chin. Susan has been deaf since she was an infant. In a video interview (translated by an ASL interpreter) (Miller, 2001), she said that she was not sure what she wanted to pursue as a major. FORWARD provided Susan with a safe environment to seek guidance and work with a support group. She says that F2GS provided her with a lot of help to the extent that she started considering graduate school. Susan also participated in the summer research competition. This research competition allowed women in their first year of graduate study to write proposals and work with mentors from various institutions including GWU, GU, Hood College, University of Maryland, and NIST. This provided students with opportunities to work independently, providing them with confidence required to succeed in STEM.

Susan says that she was "excited about writing [a] research proposal" for competition and that this was the first time she "wrote something from scratch." She wrote a proposal focused on analyzing water from the nearby Anacostia River. Susan ends the video by saying that the research provided her with a "taste of what the research at graduate school will be like." Susan says she gained "incredible experience" by participating in F2GS. It is interesting to note that Susan Chin went on to receive a Master of Science degree in Civil Engineering from the University of Maryland. She acknowledges Dr Snyder in her Master's thesis for his "wisdom and guidance" that made it possible for her to complete the Master's degree.

At a video interview during the F2GS, Dr Sorensen said that many D/HoH students had difficulties with communication and had bad experiences with interpreters. She says that FORWARD was a "perfect fit" as it "provided answers to all these concerns." She says that the initial workshop had indicated that many students were struggling with "what to include in their graduate school application and where to apply." She also noted that many students "didn't understand the financial aid situation they were going to get into in graduate school." Throughout the 4 years of the F2GS project, we found that the student capabilities were improving due to growing confidence in their ability to write and express themselves, to take tests, and to develop new content.

The FORWARD program inspired GU faculty to collaborate more broadly and open up more opportunities to GU students. Dr Sorensen had started a collaboration with Dr Martha Absher from Duke University building on Dr Absher's work with K-12 students at local public schools. As a result, Dr Absher gave presentations at GU and at FORWARD related programs, while Dr Sorensen recommended many students for Dr Absher's REU (Research Experience for Undergraduates) program at Duke. It is important to note that this internship collaboration has continued through the years with an average of one to two GU students participating in Duke's REU program under Dr Absher. In a recent (Fall 2014) e-mail exchange with Dr Absher, she described her interactions with Dr Sorensen, GU, and FORWARD as very productive. She reported that many GU students that participated in these internships have gone on to great successes including Dr Daniel Lundberg and Dr Raymond Merritt, who are now faculty members in the Department of Science, Technology, and Mathematics (DSTM) at GU. At the same time, she mentioned that "Dr Sorensen's interactions have been of great benefit in building and strengthening my ties with the deaf and hard of hearing community, and she has facilitated the involvement of many deaf students in my programs here at Duke. Incorporating these students in my programs has enriched them, providing great diversity, and introducing many other students and faculty here to the potential and value of including students with disabilities in our research and educational efforts." Dr Absher also added that these interactions have helped her learn valuable lessons on the accommodation of D/HoH students including "doing preparation beforehand, understanding the particular student's issues and needs, and careful education and instruction of the hearing community with whom the student is working, so that everyone feels comfortable and can focus on the science and research being done." She added that she works closely with interpreters to make sure that they are aware beforehand of the technical vocabulary used frequently and tries to use the same interpreters at "repetitive events such as presentation classes, to provide the interpreters with the opportunity to familiarize [themselves] with the highly technical vocabulary of cutting-edge research."

The FORWARD projects linked participating D/HoH students with professional scientists, some of them classified as minorities or people with disabilities. This enabled participants to meet with potential mentors in one place, while giving them fresh perspectives to help set reasonable expectations and reprioritize their objectives. Mentorships initiated in this way help cover for the lack of critical mass in STEM fields for D/HoH and other underrepresented groups by providing a wide range of examples of minority players who have adapted and succeeded in different ways. As a result, new realms of possibilities were provided to mentees encouraging them to advance to graduate school and careers in STEM.

However, change and transformations required to aid with the advancement of D/HoH happen slowly because more time is needed to change perceptions ingrained in both the hearing and D/HoH communities. The number of STEM majors at GU is significantly smaller compared to other programs. After an initial increase, the number of D/HoH students declaring majors in STEM at GU has continued to be a challenge, generally fluctuating over the years in tandem with the number of students matriculating at GU. It is difficult to effectively track the overall impact of FORWARD on D/HoH, as we are always dealing with very small numbers of individuals with diverse needs who become widely dispersed after graduation. On a positive note, some of our efforts laid a foundation for future progress in the advancement of D/HoH in STEM. More STEM majors are now taking summer research internship positions, both within and outside GU, and are presenting at both local and regional science conferences.

GU faculty have participated in several workshop activities and provided interesting insights in such discussions as work/life balance from D/HoH perspective. FORWARD has also had a positive impact on the lives of several GU students hired to work on various activities. Several Deaf undergraduates served as logistics assistants for the workshops and benefited from the presentations and the networking with speakers. Dr Yell Inverso graduated with a doctorate in Audiology (AuD) and a PhD in Audiology while managing the logistics of the FORWARD workshops for several years. She recently shared that the information she had helped distribute is now helping her own advancement in professorship and concluded by writing "I feel the impact of FORWARD every day. Even though I started not as participant but as a graduate assistant, learning from these amazing women and being a part of this program created a pull for me and I now find myself in professorship."

The FORWARD projects at GU have also contributed to the personal career development and advancement of several GU faculty and staff. While Dr Snyder was a full professor at the inception of FORWARD, Dr Sorensen joined the program while she was an associate professor and advanced all the way to full professor while still working on FORWARD programs. Dr Sabila joined FORWARD while still an assistant professor and is now a tenured associate professor. Another faculty member who participated and also presented at some FORWARD workshops is now a tenured associate professor at GU. In addition, FORWARD has helped the GU principal investigators to hone their collaboration and grant-writing skills. This has helped them participate in various collaborations and receive several awards.

Dr Snyder credits FORWARD with providing him an early practical experience in using electronic media for education and greater understanding of hurdles that GU and other underrepresented students face in preparing for and entering graduate school. He has received NSF grants for (i) bringing the first Internet connection to the GU campus, (ii) fully outfitting laboratories for new technical degree programs and curricula that he established, and (iii) conducting experiments and training activities in collaboration with teachers and students at Deaf institutions around the country. He obtained and managed grants from the Keck Foundation, and MCI provided funding for supplying videoconferencing systems and implementing distance education courses for high school teachers at Deaf institutions. He has been active as GU's NASA Space Grant associate director for 18 years. He works on remote sensing imagery at the NASA Goddard Space Flight Center in the Biospheric Sciences Laboratory.

Dr Sorensen received a $2.7 million grant from the U.S. Department of Health and Human Services for Health Resources and Services Health Careers Opportunity Program (HCOP). HCOP activities at GU (2000–2003) included summer enrichment academies to provide classes to students interested in the allied health fields. Dr Sabila has collaborated on other grants supported by the NSF including a major instrumental grant (NSF #1040094), Partnerships in Reduced Dimensional Materials (with Dr Sorensen as GU Co-PI, NSF #1205608), and a science and technology center (NSF #1231319). These grants have enabled Dr Sabila to provide research internships, training, and mentorship in nanotechnology and organic synthesis to more than 16 GU students. Dr Sabila is also a Co-PI on a Science-STEM program (NSF #1259237) that provides scholarships to GU students intending to major in mathematics, biology, or chemistry.

Dr Daniel Lundberg, a chemistry and physics faculty member at GU, was one of the participants in the FORWARD to Professorship workshop. He also presented at the work/life balance session of the 2011 workshop where he shared his career pathway. He noted a variety of challenges, including having to interact with both the hearing and the D/HoH worlds. He graduated with a Bachelor of Science at GU (D/HoH) then proceeded to complete a PhD in the hearing world, getting a job in the hearing world, and navigating geographic challenges and the two-body problem.

FIGURE 14.2   Dr Daniel Lundberg, Gallaudet faculty member, presenting at one of the FORWARD workshop panels.

Dr Lundberg is now a tenured associate professor at GU and is actively involved in teaching, research, and mentoring GU students to prepare them for STEM internships and careers in the hearing world (Figure 14.2).

Ms. Sharron Cargo assisted in the preparations for FORWARD workshops and activities while she served as a laboratory assistant within the chemistry and physics department at GU. She also attended various sessions of FORWARD workshops and interacted with workshop participants and presenters. Ms. Cargo credits FORWARD, Dr Sorensen, and Dr Snyder as having played a role in motivating her to pursue further education. She recently completed an online Master of Science Degree from Eastern Kentucky University's College of Justice and Safety in safety, security, and emergency management. She currently serves as the overall campus chemical hygiene and safety specialist.

IMPACT OF D/HOH PARTICIPANTS AND GU ON FORWARD AND ON "HEARING" PARTICIPANTS

The FORWARD project has enabled STEM faculty members from GWU and GU to collaborate for the advancement of women and minority faculty members. The participation of GU deans, department chairs, provosts, administrators, faculty, ASL interpreters, and students has provided workshop hearing participants with cultural enrichment opportunities, enabling them to broaden their views on working with people with disabilities, especially D/HoH individuals.

Hosting the FORWARD workshops at GU has helped broaden the perspectives of hearing participants and made them more informed on D/HoH people and culture. The workshop activities and one-on-one interactions provided the hearing participants with first-hand experience working with D/HoH people and interpreters. They also learned a few ASL signs. The exposure will make them better prepared when planning for activities in the future that will be more sensitive to the needs of participants who might be D/HoH, people with disabilities, or from other underrepresented groups. In fact, many participants have indicated that they will always treasure the experience gained through the workshop and from interactions with D/HoH participants. In the words of one participant, "I enjoyed new information on deaf access (I am a hearing person)."

The FORWARD workshops provided diverse groups with multiple levels of opportunities to network and collaborate. They provided a safe environment for hearing and D/HoH students to learn more about each group and to appreciate the cultural diversities and sensitivities. The workshop organizers had an opportunity to collaborate to ensure that adequate accommodations were provided to all workshop participants, regardless of their hearing condition. The projects and activities enabled workshop organizers, facilitators, and participants to work towards a common goal. New tools like email list-servs, Internet, and, in later years, social media and texting, which were just starting to gain popularity, were employed toward this end.

STRATEGIES FOR INCLUSION OF D/HOH PARTICIPANTS AND ASL INTERPRETERS IN SCIENTIFIC WORKSHOPS

Our chapter would not be complete without providing some practical information to help workshop organizers prepare for D/HoH participants (attendees and speakers). While these suggestions are directed at including D/HoH individuals, the practices support a good workshop environment for all participants. To begin, the organizers should communicate with D/HoH participants to determine their preferred mode of communication. Various communication strategies can be used in workshops including ASL, Signed English, Sign Language Interpreter, video relay service, and captioning services (CART). In addition, hand

and facial signals and gestures, lip-reading, typing, and writing can be used for one-on-one interactions. Organizers should arrange to meet D/HoH participants and interpreters in advance to review common vocabularies, communication preferences, workshop topics, and seating arrangements.

Organizers should request the presentation notes and slide presentations from the speakers in advance and then forward them to the interpreters and D/HoH participants prior to the meeting. Alternatively, an online "workshop folder" can be created, which could then be shared with all the workshop participants and interpreters. This practice will enable the interpreters to review the material and vocabulary to be signed and, if necessary, ask for clarification prior to the event.

Workshop venues should provide clear lines of sight and avoid sources of glare. Venues should have adequate voice amplification for both the speaker(s) and questioners from the audience, so that the interpreter or CART can hear clearly. Sufficient lighting should be provided to help the D/HoH participants see the interpreter if the room lights are turned off for a video or projected presentation.

The organizers also have to think through the kind of workshop activities if they plan to use interpreters. For example, one person should be allowed to speak at a time in round-table discussion formats to allow for interpreters to relay the speaker's information and also reverse interpret for D/HoH participants. To cover for the inherent time lag caused by using interpreters, breaks and pauses should be provided in discussion settings to provide D/HoH participant opportunities to join in the discussion. The breaks will also benefit hearing participants who process information more slowly.

The other workshop participants should be made aware of the presence of D/HoH participants. The workshop should start with some kind of ice-breaker activities. This reduces stress associated with communication barriers between hearing and D/HoH participants and interpreters. This will also be a good place to introduce some etiquette on communicating with D/HoH participants, with or without an interpreter.

Organizers can always check with the office of people with disabilities or office of disabilities services in their institutions for locally available resources, including ASL interpreters and other modes of accommodation. The GU Career Center has prepared a Supervisor's Manual handbook (Career Center—GU) to help employers planning to hire D/HoH students. The handbook provides an overview of the role of an ASL interpreter as a facilitator for two-way communication, common mistakes, and assumptions made while using interpreters, and the best place to position the ASL interpreter. Other helpful information on working with the D/HoH and interpreters can be found at the NTID website (RIT—NTID—NCE, 2014), GU Career Center (Career Center—

GU), GU captioning services (Captioning Services (CART-GU)), and GU Interpreting Services (GIS) (Gallaudet Interpreting Service (GIS)). Offsite ASL interpreters are also provided by Sorenson Video Relay Services (Sorenson VRS®).

Acknowledgments

We thank the National Science Foundation (NSF #s 9714729, 0123582, 0540016 and 0930112) for supporting all the FORWARD projects. We also thank Ms. Karen Cook from the GU Career Center for helpful discussions and also for providing us with copies of the Supervisor's Manual handbook. We thank Dr Martha Absher from Duke University for her contribution to the involvement of D/HoH students at Duke REU programs. Lastly, we thank Dr Yell Inverso and Dr Jane Dillehay for their contributions and insights on workshop accommodations and on working with ASL interpreters.

References

Alston, R.J., Hampton, J.L., 2000. Science and engineering as viable career choices for students with disabilities a survey of parents and teachers. Rehabil. Couns. Bull. 43, 158–164.

Americans with Disabilities Act, (ADA), 2008. Available from: <http://www.ada.gov/pubs/adastatute08.pdf> (accessed 14.11.14.).

Brault, M.W., 2012. Americans with Disabilities: 2010, Current Population Reports [P70–131]. Washington, DC: US Census Bureau.

Burgstahler, S., Ladner, R., 2006. An alliance to increase the participation of individuals with disabilities in computing careers. ACM SIGACCESS Accessibility Comput. 3–9.

Captioning Services (CART-GU). Available from: <http://www.gallaudet.edu/academic_catalog/services_and_activities/academic_services/captioning_services.html> (accessed 28.06.14.).

Career Center—GU. Available from: <http://www.gallaudet.edu/career_center.html> (accessed 06.28.14.).

Carnegie Classifications. Available from: <http://carnegieclassifications.iu.edu/> (accessed 08.15.15.).

Education of the Deaf Act, 1986. Available from: <http://www.gallaudet.edu/clerc_center/clerc_center_priorities/guiding_legislation/education_of_the_deaf_act.html> (accessed 14.11.14.).

Gallaudet Interpreting Service (GIS). Available from: <http://www.gallaudet.edu/gis.html> (accessed 30.06.14.).

GU Fast Facts. Available from: <http://www.gallaudet.edu/about_gallaudet/fast_facts.html> (accessed 14.11.14.).

Gallaudet University, 2003–2013. Annual Reports of Achievements, 2003–2013. Available from: <http://www.gallaudet.edu/academic_affairs/resources/annual_reports_of_achievements.html> (accessed 15.05.14.).

Hill, J.C., 2012. Language Attitudes in the American Deaf Community. Gallaudet University Press, Washington, DC.

Hoette, V.L., Rebull, L.M., McCarron, K., Johnson, C.H., Gartner, C., VanDerMolen, J., et al., 2011. Multi-sensory approach to search for young stellar objects in CG4. Bull. Am. Astron. Soc., p. 24813.

Individuals with Disability Education Act (IDEA), 2004. Available from: <http://www.gpo.gov/fdsys/pkg/PLAW-108publ446/html/PLAW-108publ446.htm> (accessed 15.05.14.).

IPEDS—GU. Available from: <http://www.gallaudet.edu/office_of_academic_quality/institutional_research/ipeds.html> (accessed 30.06.14.).

Marschark, M., Leigh, G., Sapere, P., Burnham, D., Convertino, C., Stinson, M., et al., 2006. Benefits of sign language interpreting and text alternatives for deaf students' classroom learning. J. Deaf Stud. Deaf Educ. 11, 421–437.

Mavriplis, C., Beil, C., Dam, K., Heller, R., Sorensen, C., 2010. An analysis of the FORWARD to professorship workshop—what works to entice and prepare women for professorship? In: Godfroy-Genin, A.S. (Ed.), Women in Engineering and Technology Research: The PROMETEA Conference Proceedings. LIT Verlag, Berlin, pp. 443–460.

Mavriplis, C., Heller, R.S., Snyder, H.D., Sorensen, C.C., 2000. A walk on the moon: an interdisciplinary inquiry-based course. In: Proceedings of the WEPAN 2000 National Conference.

Miller, C., 2001. FORWARD in SEM, 20 mn video, GW Television, Washington, DC.

Mitchell, R.E., 2006. How many deaf people are there in the United States? Estimates from the survey of income and program participation. J. Deaf Stud. Deaf Educ. 11, 112–119.

Nelson, D.J., 2004. Nelson Diversity Surveys, Diversity in Science Association: Norman, OK. Available from: <http://faculty-staff.ou.edu/N/Donna.J.Nelson-1/diversity/top50.html> (accessed 02.11.14.).

Ries, P.W., 1994. Prevalence and characteristics of persons with hearing trouble: United States, 1990–1991. National Center for Health Statistics. Vital Health Stat. 10 (188).

RIT—National Technical Institute for the Deaf. Available from: <http://www.ntid.rit.edu/> (accessed 30.06.14.).

RIT-NTID-NCE. Tips for Communicating with Deaf and Hard-of-Hearing Employees, 2014. Available from: <http://www.ntid.rit.edu/nce/employers/tips-comm-deaf-hoh-employees> (accessed 28.06.14.).

Sorenson VRS®. Available from: <http://www.sorensonvrs.com/> (accessed 28.06.14.).

Wang, M. 2011. Tufts professors receive Presidential Award for mentoring achievement. The Tufts Daily. Available from: <http://tuftsdaily.com/news/2011/11/21/tufts-professors-receive-presidential-award-for-mentoring-achievement/> (accessed 06.10.14.).

15

The Participant Experience

Elizabeth Freeland

School of the Art Institute of Chicago, Chicago, IL, USA

OUTLINE	
Introduction	245
Why are Workshops for Women Needed?	246
Pre-conference: Participant Expectations	248
During the Conference: Participant Activities	248
Post-conference: Overall Impressions	251
The Future	252
References	253

INTRODUCTION

A small group of women were discussing if and when to have children, given our career choice of being scientists. I already had two small children, another woman was trying to figure out the best time to get pregnant, and a third woman had decided not to have children. At some point, one of us complimented another, "Hey, I really like your shoes." Suddenly, I was blown away. Here we were talking about children and clothing, and *no one thought less of another as a scientist because of it!*

A group of intelligent, highly educated women were having a discussion about their personal lives and work, and no one subtracted points from their IQ or concluded they weren't "serious about science"!

This was a novel and incredibly freeing experience.

It was the spring of 2003, and I was attending the first FORWARD to Professorship conference. I was between jobs, married to a physicist, and looking for information. I had a 5-year goal of obtaining a tenure-track position. I wanted advice on job hunting and getting grants. I wanted suggestions for navigating the "two-body problem" (the marriage of two scientists). I wanted to know how to improve my resume, and what to expect on the tenure track. I was also hoping to network and find a support system to help me achieve my goals.

I realize I had a challenging task for the workshop organizers. Amazingly, the conference delivered everything I was looking for and addressed issues I had not even thought of. It took me 8 years to achieve my 5-year goal, and there is no doubt in my mind that the advice and networking that I gained from the workshop were a major component of my success. Ultimately, I attended several FORWARD to Professorship workshops, the first as a participant, and later as a speaker on career breaks. At each workshop, I absorbed a great deal by listening to the other speakers and participants.

In this chapter, I describe the experience of being a participant in these workshops. I first address why women-focused workshops are useful and even necessary to improve diversity. Then I discuss participants' expectations before attending the workshop and their reactions during the workshop. Finally, I comment on what the future of such conferences may be. This is not a quantitative picture of the workshops, that can be found in Chapter 18; rather, it is based on long-form responses to questionnaires and personal interactions with other participants, and framed by my own experience. Not all workshops were identical, but they had the same general features. I focus here on the positive aspects, of which there were many. I hope people see the utility of this type of workshop and that they are encouraged to host one of their own!

WHY ARE WORKSHOPS FOR WOMEN NEEDED?

Why should there be career workshops for women or other under-represented groups? I have many male friends and colleagues who would benefit from much of what I have learned at these workshops, and workshops open to everyone would be a great way to demystify the academic and research path for most beginning scientists. There are, though, specific benefits for women who attend women-in-science workshops. A very important one is that they provided an environment for discussing issues that are generally much more of a concern to women than men. Some obvious examples are pregnancy, dealing with the two-body problem (which affects more women than men (Rosser, 2004; Blondin et al., 1990), and sexual harassment. A less obvious example is what type of clothing works when you have to wear a clip-on mic! In some of these cases, the experience of women is different from that of men physically (i.e., women dress differently; women, unlike men, may get pregnant) and sometimes culturally (i.e., women are still seen as primary caregivers). While men, because of their greater numbers in the field, have many opportunities for informal mentoring or sharing knowledge, the relatively small amount of women scientists often preclude such same-gender networking.

Another benefit of these workshops is the experience of being in a room filled with other scientists "like you." Until the FORWARD workshop, I had *never* been at a scientific conference or seminar where the audience was overwhelmingly female. I have sometimes thought it would be nice to invite a few men and say, "This is what it's like for us—all the time!"[1] For me, simply being around so many smart, scientific women at once was very uplifting. Other participants felt the same, writing: "It was good to meet so many women who have the same issues. The feeling of isolation has been broken," and "We are not alone!"

Finally, workshops that focus on underrepresented groups can focus on the differences, bad or good, between the way majority and minority groups traverse the same career path and give insights for success to the minority group. Time can also be spent honing skills that may be weaker in the minority group due to cultural influences. For example, I learned that many men will say "yes" to a task and figure out how to accomplish it later, while women, including myself at the time, often feel the need to acquire a skill or knowledge before agreeing to use it. Growing up, I picked up the habits of not "asking for too much" and considering what I perceived others needed, sometimes to the detriment of my own needs. Negotiation workshops and practice have taught me how to figure out what I am worth and ask for it, even after an offer has been made. I learned to ask, ask, ask. As a direct result, I've obtained travel funds from deans and significant increases in salary during contract negotiations.

---

[1]The Grace Hopper Celebration for Women in Computing has become a well-known and important conference in the computer science world. For an informal take on what it is like to be a guy and in the minority at such a conference, read Jamie Talbot's description in "Is this what it's like for women at every conference?" at <https://medium.com/@majelbstoat> (accessed 24.08.15.).

PRE-CONFERENCE: PARTICIPANT EXPECTATIONS

As I applied to the workshop and later began making arrangements for the trip, my mind was on what practical information I would learn for improving my job application, preparing for interviews, negotiating a contract, applying for grants, and navigating the early years of tenure. These topics were main concerns of most women attending the workshops, in addition to getting "advice and feedback on effective teaching methods," information on "balancing teaching and research," and "learn (ing) about the tenure process." In this respect, there was no "female" agenda of the participants.

Participants were clearly aware that the workshop would be a unique opportunity to talk with other women scientists, though. They wanted to "hear from women leaders in science regarding their academic experiences," "meet women faculty," have "a chance to interact with people with similar issues and concerns ... obtain information regarding the specific issues facing women in academia," and "hear from women in various stages of life/career." Some also hoped to get information on work/life balance. A few hoped for information that would help them decide "whether to pursue an academic career and, if so, at what type of institution."

DURING THE CONFERENCE: PARTICIPANT ACTIVITIES

The evening of the 2003 conference opened with a dinner and keynote speaker: Maria Klawe, then dean of engineering at Princeton. Dr Klawe's candor about her career ups and downs was remarkable. It wasn't all smooth sailing, she didn't always have the answers, and she once went into her office and cried. For me, and many others, that honesty was eye-opening and encouraging. One woman commented, "It was great to see such a *human* dean." Another wrote, "I learned more about being a professional woman, in academics or elsewhere, from Maria than from all the other talks, articles, conversations, etc., I've ever digested." This style of openness and willingness to share was a trait of many later keynote speakers as well. Audience members appreciated the style and found the speeches useful and "inspirational." We learned that academics and researchers were not perfect and even people we looked up to had struggles. We also learned how they dealt with those struggles and came through them. It made the entire prospect of an academic career seem much more possible.

Keynote speakers were not the only ones who opened up their lives to us. Each workshop included a speaker, or panel of speakers, discussing work/life balance and many of these people told personal stories. They shared their dilemmas, setbacks, and achievements. They shared conversations with spouses, department chairs, and colleagues. They were very willing to answer questions, and most were around for a day or more of the workshop and available for individual conversations. Overall, the audience valued hearing about the "diversity of experiences and diversity of solutions," found speakers to be "inspiring and encouraging," and were happy to "to learn there are other people out there with the same problems." It is worth noting that not everyone's family issues revolve around how to deal with the two-body problem or when to have children. As the workshops have evolved, work/family balance has become work/life balance, and the title referred to a more inclusive interpretation of family: children, parents, significant others, and an inclusion of personal time outside of scholarly endeavors. Speakers who could discuss being single or broader life issues were included, and participants responded positively to them.

Learning about the diversity of institutions was valuable to many participants. Graduate studies are overwhelmingly focused on research and often done at Research I (R1) institutions. Round-table discussions with chairs and deans from a variety of institutions allowed us to get a picture of life elsewhere. I, and others, found it was, "good to hear their (dean/chair) point of view," and ask "all the questions I'd never ask my own chair/dean." As a result, we were better able to target the right schools when applying for tenure-track jobs.

Beyond these round-table discussions of institutions, the open, discussion-friendly atmosphere of the workshop brought questions and comments like "This is how I have heard it was done here," or "Do you do it that way at R1 institutions?" to almost every session, no matter the topic. These conversations helped participants understand the range of possibilities in academia, what an institution might do, or what one could ask about. This information can clearly help at the individual level, but I have found it useful beyond that. There have been many times when I have discussed policy with someone and been able to say, "but other places do it this way." That ability can be powerful.

Talks about life in academia by keynote speakers, chairs, deans, and others were surrounded by a *workshop*—time to hear about, learn, practice, and discuss the nitty-gritty of how to manage and do research, teaching, service, and balance it all with "life." This is a type of training that is absent at the home institution of most graduate students and postdocs, but which is an integral part of an academic career. Participants are aware of this and many praised the hands-on nature of the workshop. Many of the sessions included worksheets, discussion questions, or activities. Significant time was spent on activities. It's one thing to have someone lay out a "personal career plan" and another to work on one yourself, discuss it, and get feedback from others.

I found it incredibly useful to be walked through the intricacies of a National Science Foundation (NSF) grant proposal. I learned that it is OK to contact a program director if you have questions about a grant offering, and was even encouraged to do so. Who knew! I attended a very useful discussion group with a woman who helped professors write grants at her institution. She went over the do's and don'ts, told us about public and private funding sources, and was specific in her examples and suggestions. I can say without doubt that my success in getting grants was directly influenced by grant-writing information and resources I gathered at the FORWARD workshop.

Negotiation skills also had a direct payoff for me. Since I was lucky enough to attend more that one workshop, I heard several negotiation sessions. An amazing one was led by a woman who gave clear examples of successful negotiation in her own life and gave us insight and tips about negotiations that were easy to implement. At the end, she had us practice negotiation in pairs on cleverly designed scenarios that emphasized knowing and asking for what you need. She showed us that negotiation does not have to be a win-lose proposal. Through other speakers and discussions, we learned what we could negotiate for—lab location, parking spots, childcare, teaching load and courses, and basically anything else. When I negotiated the contract for a tenure-track position, I used what I had learned and ended up with a contract that suited my needs.

I have used funding and negotiation as examples of the type of detailed information we were given. It often felt like insider information, although it is not. Many other topics were covered as well: how to say "no" to too many service requests, how to choose and manage service responsibilities, pedagogy, and classroom management tips.

There was also time to relax and just chat with the other women, but even then we were given ideas to think about. At several workshops, we were assigned a book to read beforehand, for example, Brenda Maddox's *Rosalind Franklin: The Dark Lady of DNA* or Barbara Goldsmith's *Obsessive Genius: The Inner World of Marie Curie*. We then discussed the book during a lunch. Did we relate to these women or not? How are circumstances now the same or different? Each workshop also included a dinner where we heard a special speaker or attended a relevant performance. Two that stand out in my mind are the one-woman theater show (Website for Manya) about the life of Marie Curie by Susan Marie Frontczak (Figure 15.1), and a performance of "The Faculty Meeting" by the University of Michigan's CRLT Players [Website for the Center for Research on Learning and Teaching (CRLT)]. The latter is an interactive theater experience that addresses the biases, politics, and hierarchies that can come into play in academia.

FIGURE 15.1 Backstage photo of Marie Curie (played by Susan Marie Frontczak, left) in discussion with FORWARD to Professorship participants, including Elizabeth Freeland (right).

POST-CONFERENCE: OVERALL IMPRESSIONS

The workshop held different value for different people, but many voiced similar thoughts:

> "It was great discussing issues and approaches with people who have lots of experience in the field and have been in the academic environment for years." The workshop was a "source of a great deal of useful information that is not easily available/navigable on your own."
> It was "a jolt to get me thinking about my future goals and how I can achieve them," and a "unique opportunity to discuss women's issues."
> "This is the most friendly and encouraging conference/workshop I've ever attended."

One comment seen often is, "We *definitely* need more time." Participants wanted more time to discuss, ask questions, or to practice skills, which suggested that the material was engaging and useful to them.

I view the FORWARD workshop fondly in part because of the contacts I made, many of which I still maintain ten years later, and in part because of the gratitude I feel for someone taking the time to pass along so much concrete advice that has had such a positive effect on my career. Although ten years have passed since FORWARD began, I still have to agree with this 2005 participant that, especially for graduate students and postdocs, "You cannot get this info, advice, support anywhere else."

In the years after I attended my first FORWARD workshop, I received two grants, had job interviews, and finally received a tenure-track offer. Of course, I put in a great deal of effort to achieve these successes, but I also know that the insights, materials, and relationships that came out of the workshop had a very positive effect. I felt more confident, asked for more, was encouraged by women I met and given support and feedback from them over the years. I put into practice writing, planning, and negotiation skills. For all my efforts, I am not sure I would have obtained a tenure-track job without the edge given to me by the knowledge and support gained from the workshops.

THE FUTURE

The Internet has dramatically changed our options for communicating information and connecting with others, and institutional policies and programs have improved with respect to efforts to retain women. Nevertheless, the experience of being in a large, all-women group of scientists is as relevant now as it was before. The style of senior scientists sharing real-life personal experiences is not the sort of interaction that can easily take place in an online forum. The interactive nature of the sessions is also most easily done in person. These properties—all women, real-life sharing, and interaction—are the hallmarks of an in-person workshop like FORWARD.

Still, the rise of the Internet does suggest some changes and help. Training on effective use of social media for both outreach and career promotion would be very useful. Although younger scientists may have grown up in a world with the Internet, professional protocol and best practices are evolving. It may not be long before a short video describing your research becomes de rigueur, and being able to give an "elevator speech" to your institution's media person becomes a worthwhile skill.

A way to increase the impact of a workshop beyond the meeting itself is by maintaining contact among participants. After the first workshop, I not only had a mentor, but also several contacts that I maintained for many years. These people have been motivational and acted as a sounding board for job applications, negotiations, and other career decisions. I have benefited greatly from their friendship. Contact with other women scientists can also help with isolation. Participants have said, "I know that I'm not alone now." How can that connectedness be maintained?

Existing social network sites such as Facebook and Google+ have done some of the work already. These networks allow participants to meet again at scientific meetings. Professional networks such as LinkedIn provide a more formal, online connection between people that may be more appropriate in some situations and more comfortable for some people. Networking sites or emails can provide opportunities for workshop organizers to have neutral check-ins with participants, such as asking "Are you reaching your goal(s)?" Questions like this can help people stay on track and remember to use skills learned in the workshop.

As for post-workshop discussions, clearly one has to be careful about what one writes online. For that reason, phone-in groups, or internet-based versions, like Skype or Google Hangouts, may make more sense. These could allow for long-term mentoring or peer support. Group conversations can become casual very quickly and feel much like a workshop discussion.

Finally, national and local workshops provide different opportunities to participants. National workshops allow for broader networking and discussions covering a broader variety of institutions. Local workshops can promote local networking and in-person connections and mentoring.

Workshops for underrepresented groups, like women in science, are valuable places to find community, network, and address concerns of the group. The FORWARD to Professorship workshops allowed all of this, conveyed much crucial information about navigating academia, and allowed the development of related skills, like negotiation. Participants had great expectations for the workshops and left feeling that many of their workshop needs had been met. The success of this program, in all its variations, makes it a good template for future workshops.

References

Blondin, P.H., Benedict, A., Chu, R., 1990. American Physical Society Membership Survey. American Institute of Physics, New York.

Rosser, S.V., 2004. The Science Glass Ceiling. Routledge, New York.

Website for Manya—The Living History of Marie Curie by Susan Marie Frontczak. Available from: <http://www.storysmith.org/manya/index.html> (accessed 14.01.15.).

Website for the Center for Research on Learning and Teaching (CRLT), University of Michigan. Available from: <http://www.crlt.umich.edu/crltplayers> (accessed 11.19.14.).

16

Speakers Find Value in Workshop Participation

Lynnette D. Madsen[1] and Catherine Mavriplis[2]

[1]National Science Foundation, Arlington, VA [2]University of Ottawa, Ottawa, Canada

OUTLINE

Introduction	255
Eager Speakers	258
Unanticipated Impact on Presenters	261
Conclusion	264
Acknowledgments	265
References	265

INTRODUCTION

In 1998, the FORWARD team ran its first workshop on a Friday night and Saturday morning: FORWARD to Graduate School was our first foray into event planning around structured mentoring for women and minorities, including the deaf and hard of hearing, in science, technology, engineering, and mathematics (STEM). As a group of discipline-diverse, principal investigators on a shoestring budget, the FORWARD team delivered the material and activities to the participants. As speakers we certainly did not have all the answers, but we were able to offer very pertinent advice or refer to our colleagues across the nation through our extended network. We gained much experience and appreciated the positive feedback and gratitude shown by our participants.

In a second (1999) and third round (2000) of the FORWARD to Graduate School workshops, the team invited master's students who had participated in the FORWARD Summer Research Competition to present their research. We had calculated that their presence at the workshop as near peers: that is, students only slightly ahead of our participants (say 1 or 2 years ahead), would have a positive effect on our participants, as they might provide more up to date "on the ground" advice that students tend to communicate with each other, under the radar of their professors. For example, students are better able to discuss the work/life conditions of graduate school and how they found their advisors and research funding in order to pursue their graduate degrees. This certainly ended up being beneficial to the participants, and we watched as our initial hunches not only became reality, but also surpassed our expectations. The power of near peer speakers cannot be overemphasized. The graduate speakers themselves felt empowered by the opportunity. One participant from Hood College even changed her concentration from chiropractic school to chemistry as a result of the workshop (Miller, 2001).

As the FORWARD team evolved their offerings into the FORWARD to Professorship workshop, the project took on a bigger scope. First, we would have to provide advice on how to secure research funding. As frequent reviewers for the funding agencies and being located in Washington, DC, all four of the team members had direct contacts to invite for a session on research funding. Furthermore, program directors at the funding agencies have a mandate to speak to potential grantees, to find new blood, to encourage young researchers, and to recruit for diversity. At the time of the planning of the FORWARD to Professorship workshop, Catherine Mavriplis had worked as a program director in Mathematics at the National Science Foundation (NSF). There she met Lynnette Madsen, program director in the Division of Materials Science who volunteered to speak many times at subsequent workshops. Though now funding agencies have less funds to let program directors travel to specific events across the country, as noted in some of the previous chapters, their mandate remains the same. All the program directors we invited to our workshops (from NSF, the Office of Naval Research (ONR), the Air Force Office of Scientific Research (AFOSR), the US Army Research Office (ARO), and the National Institutes of Health (NIH)) were delighted to participate in our workshops. They enthusiastically presented their programs, agency's structure, websites and, most importantly, explained the review and re-application process. As noted in our outcomes, some participants and organizers (see Chapter 17) directly benefited from these interactions, obtaining research grants that were built upon these initial interactions at our workshops. For the program directors, the workshops also represented a good opportunity to recruit reviewers, for either mail or panel review. The diversity of a review panel is an important criterion at the funding agencies, one that is hard to fulfill given the low percentage of women and minorities in STEM. These program directors returned to our workshops to speak year after year and became avid supporters of the program.

As our thinking evolved we wondered, if we could get experts in a specific area such as research funding, why not get experts in other fields? First off, we would need a fantastic keynote speaker to set the tone for the event. Our first keynote speaker in 2003, Maria Klawe, then-dean of engineering at Princeton University, enthusiastically accepted our invitation and gave the kind of heart-to-heart talk that spellbinds a room. After our opening evening event where she spoke, Maria stayed up late in the foyer of the conference center talking to participants and creating mentoring bonds that went years beyond that first night. Clearly, we were on to something. Other speakers were invited to address topics including new teaching techniques, active learning, communication, negotiation, stress management, and writing. For work/life balance panels, we strived to find a variety of speakers with different life situations, and often near peer speakers worked best in this category. Finally, our career planning send-off session included deans and department chairs from a variety of institutions, mostly in the Washington, DC, area, again, to save costs. Many of these speakers enthusiastically returned every year as they felt they were able to make a difference in someone's life, showing them the ins and outs of obtaining and navigating a tenure track position. Some of the male speakers were even surprised at their ability to give advice to women, after being reticent to participate in the first place.

Over the years of offering the workshop, we shifted more of the presentation opportunities from ourselves as organizers to the invited speakers. Having given the earlier incarnations of the presentations and knowing the typical reactions of our participants, we were able to select our speakers with more accuracy to obtain the kind of talks and the specific information that would best serve the purpose of the workshop. Some of our advisors from the Experts in Leadership Development (ELDers) group (see Chapter 2) go so far as to "micromanage," as they say, their speakers' slides. We did not find it necessary to do so, although, at times, we were surprised by the outcomes. For example, one researcher who presented her strategies for obtaining research funding for us several years in a row, came back one year to present a very personal story of her career development instead. Apparently, the presentations of the other sessions had inspired her.

Unexpected moments like these often enhanced the quality and authenticity of the interactions.

Overall, we have had a tremendous array of motivating speakers who were able to connect with our participants on a deep level. We are extremely indebted to them for their enthusiasm, time, and commitment.

EAGER SPEAKERS

Many workshop presenters, even keynote speakers, participated in these workshops at no charge and often without reimbursement for travel and their associated costs—why? We perceive that the reasons were many and varied and they certainly enabled the overall workshop costs to be much lower. These presenters fall into several categories: helping others, helping themselves, and having "fun." It could often be the case that it was a combination of these reasons.

In some cases, the speakers were interested in helping others, particularly those underrepresented in STEM fields—they felt that this was something that they could easily give that would have a huge impact in a much needed area. Ellen Kandell, president of Alternative Resolutions, noted: "I learned that negotiation is a topic that postdocs thirst for. There are few places in graduate school where students get this knowledge. The Q and A was full of very practical, strategy oriented questions."

Dr Daniel Lundberg has been a Professor of Chemistry at Gallaudet University (GU) since 2008. He spoke during the work/life balance "Having It All" panel: "I accepted the offer to speak, because I wanted to share my experience with others. During the panel and after it, I learned how common the issue is for junior faculty and how difficult it is, amid an uncertain economy and rising student to faculty ratio."

Dr Jean Chin of the NIH spoke in the session that dealt with competing for research support from federal agencies and private foundations. The first time she was asked, she answered positively: "I was curious about the group and am supportive of mentoring new faculty and hopeful applicants. As a program director at NIH, I talk with lots of faculty of all levels and from all kinds of institutions; see their missteps in grant applications as well as in career moves." Dr Chin was invited back several times to speak at various locations and she accepted because she enjoys talking with the graduate students, postdoctoral associates, and new faculty. Her presentations grew more and more detailed and her enthusiasm seemed to grow with each session.

Dr Gail Simmons, currently provost and vice president for academic affairs at Manhattanville College, relayed the following comments: "It has been a number of years since I spoke at the FORWARD workshops, but the experience stands out as a highlight of my career. The primary reason I accepted the offer was that it was an opportunity to speak more intimately with young women in science about some of the realities of life as a scientist, and to talk about some of the life-changing things that happen to you. I was particularly happy to be able to talk about the choices one makes in one's personal relationships—not just whether to get married, but the sort of person you'll marry and how that will affect your ability to have your career as well as family—and how those choices can lead to some very difficult decisions. Things you read in the literature on 'work/life balance' often sanitize the discussion—being able to talk openly about the messy realities of childbirth, breastfeeding, divorce, housework, etc., seemed very important. The session I spoke at, which got great comments and conversation afterward, felt very honest, and was cathartic for me in a number of ways. I was also able to communicate to a group of women mostly focusing on research how their teaching experiences could change their lives as scientists—somehow teaching often seems like an afterthought in grad school, and may be nonexistent during a post-doc."

Drs. Keri Kornelson and Noel Brady, both faculty members in the Department of Mathematics at the University of Oklahoma, spoke in a panel on work/life balance on three different occasions. They discussed the "two-body problem"; that is, a dual career, academic couple trying to find positions at the same university or at least in the same geographic location. Dr Kornelson said: "It took us a long time to have jobs in the same location, and looking back we didn't always make the best decisions along the way. We wanted to talk about that—about how, even though every situation and every couple is different, there are some lessons we learned that we wanted to pass along. I also think it is encouraging to just open up a discussion about this issue with people who are getting ready to face it." Her partner, Dr Brady, added: "I was intrigued by the idea of the conference; it appeared to address many issues that I was thinking about (graduate student recruiting, quality of life issues, professional development) as graduate director at the University of Oklahoma. The invitation gave me the opportunity to attend the conference and to learn new ideas."

Dr Samantha Sutton, a life coach who now runs her own firm, attended the MIT FORWARD workshop as a graduate student participant in 2005, and returned in 2011 to speak at the panel on work/life balance at GU. She was excited to give back to a program that had been so beneficial to herself and her friends. She cited the following reason for her participation: "I have found that often, it is easy for would-be-academics to focus on the reasons why a professorship position will be difficult to attain or be good at. We talk about all of the challenges, the poor funding climate, the difficulties in 'squeezing in' enough family time, etc., and as a result we leave the discussion feeling even MORE convinced that an academic position is unattainable. I wanted to provide a different viewpoint: that if we spend our mental resources looking for solutions instead of focusing on the problems, we will likely find them. I challenged my audience to think of what they wanted to prove was possible in their careers, and then get busy problem-solving."

Some speakers may have agreed simply to help the organizers since they appreciate that the organizers have a long and difficult task ahead of them. Some speakers felt that it was simply their turn to repay favors given to them in the past, or a way of acknowledging the benefits they currently receive from others (perhaps at higher levels). Dr Maria Klawe, now president of Harvey Mudd College, who gave keynote addresses at two FORWARD workshops, one held at GU and the other held at the MIT, said: "I agreed to participate because I'm very passionate about getting more women into STEM faculty positions and give many talks at various workshops and conferences on this topic." It has been noted that it is critical for the retention of many women in STEM fields to have female role models (Drury et al., 2011).

Dr Elizabeth Freeland, a high-energy physicist, now at the School of the Art Institute of Chicago, spoke in the work/life balance panels. She said, "I had been to the first workshop and knew it was worthwhile. I also knew that there was little information about career-breaks out there and yet people had questions about it. I was happy to be able to pass along information about family, science, and career-breaks that I knew people had questions about (I knew because I had had all these questions myself!)."

While most speakers' travel costs were covered, many did not accept the support or the honoraria. This is particularly true of speakers working for government agencies. Some speakers may have accepted the invitation because of who asked them—one of the workshop organizers or someone senior to them in their organization that they did not want to say "no" to. In keeping with this idea—some may have agreed to help with a workshop because of the recognition they anticipated from more senior officials at their workplace or to fulfill a service requirement.

Finally, in the "fun" category—the workshop may have been in keeping with their personal and/or career goals and therefore made giving a presentation enjoyable. For some, they liked the challenge of giving a great, and in many cases, an unusual and highly personal presentation. Or, they simply like giving presentations, travel, visibility, the feelings of being a leader or guide, etc.

Not all speakers provided content during sessions; some welcomed the participants to the workshop as well as to GU and some provided interpretation. Despite their short roles, the GU welcomers, Deans Jane Dillehay, Karen Kimmel, and Isaac Agboola, always provided heartfelt

FIGURE 16.1   Dean Isaac Agboola of Gallaudet University inspired participants and organizers alike with his heartfelt welcome comments delivered in American Sign Language.

encouragement to our participants and to us organizers in our pursuits to advance underrepresented groups in STEM (Figure 16.1). Our American Sign Language interpreters were also enthusiastic about their work and the content of the workshops, returning to work with us year after year.

UNANTICIPATED IMPACT ON PRESENTERS

Although people agreed to speak for a variety of reasons, I do not think they really could anticipate the many wonderful benefits of participating in these workshops, says Lynnette Madsen.

The initial workshops were held at GU—simply put GU is the world leader in liberal education and career development for deaf and hard of hearing students. The university has an international reputation for this reason and because of the quality of the research it conducts on the history, language, culture, and other topics related to deaf people. The experience of being immersed in deaf culture in an academic environment is life-changing. The environment of the entire workshop is transformative. The energy of the participants is powerful, you feel their confidence grow alongside their hopefulness for their futures, and one starts to understand fully the need that the workshop fulfills. Some of the speakers saw a need in young women, but didn't know how to address it—the workshops showed the path to address this need and became their "ah-ha" experience.

Small, symbolic, thoughtful gifts were given to each speaker—these were never anticipated and provided for lasting memories. They embodied the overall welcoming and accepting environment that encourages differences, individuality, etc. It is a new experience for some—and in turn this may lead to a greater acceptance of changes on campus, altering procedures to recreate a similar environment, and an appreciation that things can be different than they have been and still be okay (or even better).

For Ellen Kandell, who teaches negotiation and focuses her business on conflict resolution, giving the FORWARD seminars turned out to be good business sense: "As a result of the sessions I was invited to give a similar presentation at Purdue University and at Woods Hole Oceanographic Institute, where I did a longer workshop. I also did a workshop for the Society of Toxicology's conference." She also found it to be personally rewarding because, as she said: "I loved interacting with the students," and "One of the participants in the first George Washington—Gallaudet University FORWARD to Professorship Workshop told me that she specifically used the material and role play lessons that she learned and negotiated a better deal for herself in her first college teaching position. That was very gratifying to hear—that as a result of my workshop she was able to be a better self-advocate and negotiator."

Inevitably, many speakers would arrive early or leave late after giving their talk. In doing so, one caught at least a little bit of the other lectures and surprisingly, this was often a beneficial learning experience. For example, Lynette Madsen says: "My spot in the program always followed the talk about negotiating. I learned some new 'trick' each time and was fortunate in a second way, although I was returning year-after-year, that the organizers kept changing the speaker for the negotiation session, so I got to hear someone different each time." Dr Brady had a similar experience: "I learned lots from the negotiation strategies session. I remember that they had a former dean speak about negotiation strategies. It was an eye-opener for me, and brought home how woefully underprepared I was when I was negotiating terms of my tenure track position." There was also the possibility of exposure to entirely new topics, areas of scholarship, etc., that the speakers might not otherwise explore.

Dr Elizabeth Freeland also said, "I stayed every time. I always learned something new because there were new speakers. I learned about negotiation, grant writing, and work/family balance. Also, I had questions about my own career and those changed with time, so being at the workshop allowed me to ask new questions. As time passed, I sometimes learned about changes, for the better, in culture and policy."

Dr Kornelson recalls: "Each year that I attended FORWARD to Professorship workshop, I learned something new. One year it was tips for successful negotiations, and a chance to practice the skill. Another year, I took copious notes about the different ways men and women are judged in terms of power, confidence, and likability. It was delightful to finally have these instincts so clearly articulated. I'm certain FORWARD was the first place I heard the term 'Imposter Syndrome,' and I knew the definition immediately. I found each conference also a terrific source for new reading material. Every year, I left with a long list of books to read about networking, implicit bias, gender roles, and negotiation. The list also invariably included great memoirs and biographies of women in science and business as well. Some of the standard books in the field of women in STEM were first suggested to me at this workshop. The greatest delight for me, though, was the opportunity to meet and hang out with so many bright energetic early-career academics. I enjoyed finding out about their research, their goals, their current jobs and the jobs they hoped to have soon. They knew about bad job markets and the challenges of the tenure track, but they loved what they were doing enough to go for it anyway. I would come home from FORWARD workshops newly appreciative of my job and extra-willing to help out the early career professionals back home."

Dr Sutton agreed that the participants themselves were a significant benefit of attending: "I met many bright, passionate, and inquisitive scientists in FORWARD, and still keep in touch with several to this day. They are the type of people who are up to big things in their lives, and those are the people who I want to know."

In addition to learning skills, speakers often learned more about themselves from other speakers and participants. Dr Maria Klawe met two young women who were struggling in their careers. She recalls that "for the next two years we did mentoring phone calls about once a week. [One] completed her PhD and is now a faculty member [and the other] is active in research again. Mentoring [these two women] was my first experience in mentoring people outside computer science and mathematics and it made me realize that it's possible to help people outside my own disciplines." Similarly, another keynote speaker reported being shocked that she could give a non-scientific talk that would be of any use. Her speech was riveting, bringing attention to her personal struggles with career path, self-confidence and health issues, despite her stellar career.

Dr Jean Chin found the sessions to be useful in improving her communications with the research community: "I like and need to get a pulse for what people are concerned about. Their questions indicate what they are confused by/worried about or what they don't know so I try to respond directly then and to improve my next presentation to clarify things for the workshop participants." She also found the other parts of the workshop that she attended to be beneficial: "I have stayed for other sessions and have heard about honing skills in bargaining/negotiating, developing career plans, and writing skills. It is quite a comprehensive and useful workshop for all levels and career goals."

In discussing their joint sessions, Dr Kornelson said: "The first year we spoke, we made a conscious decision not to gloss over the details. To me, there's nothing more annoying than someone telling you how they navigated a difficult problem, but in the process making it seem smooth and simple. Our path wasn't smooth, and we talked about the bumps in the road. Surprisingly, many participants liked that. They asked questions during the session and also came up to us afterward to say they appreciated hearing our story. Being on this panel, I learned something about the power of authenticity. We could have spun the story to make it seem like we were clever or exceptionally organized and forward-thinking, but it turned out the truth of things resonated much more." Her partner, Dr Brady concurred: "I recall that we weren't sure how our story would go over with the audience, but were very pleasantly surprised by the audience reactions."

Many speakers told very personal stories—that perhaps they had told in this way before —and they found it to be a moving experience. Overall there were unanticipated feelings of camaraderie, friendship, acceptance, well-being, and relaxation—including during question-and-answer period, even more so at breaks and meals. The overall ambience was not aggressive or competitive. This climate is consistent with the atmosphere many women and minorities would welcome in their academic world (Moyer et al., 2009).

CONCLUSION

In conclusion, we can say that finding speakers for such skills-building and mentoring workshops can be surprisingly easy. Colleagues who have tread the difficult path in STEM seem eager to "give back" or "pay it forward," which is what inspired us to name our follow-up project "Pay It FORWARD." Although, at first, we did not offer any funds for these tasks due to a shoestring budget, we evolved towards a policy of always paying at least a token honorarium to our eligible speakers (government employees cannot receive payment). Convincing the funding agency that such work is valuable in the development of STEM academia, and that, in particular, mentoring and sharing, often associated with the term "women's work," have been traditionally undervalued and underpaid if paid at all, was key. It is important to build these expenses into your budget to plan such events. Our speakers were eager to participate and often reported to us that they were surprised at the outcomes and their own reflections on the experience. For some, these opportunities led to direct outcomes in their work, while for most the satisfaction of having helped someone and connected with young people was paramount.

Acknowledgments

Our gratitude is extended to all the wonderful motivational speakers at the FORWARD workshops who shared often very private parts of their lives with our participants. We especially thank those who provided comments for this chapter and for allowing us to identify them and reproduce their image. Part of this chapter was written by Lynnette Madsen while working at NSF with the support of an Independent Research/ Development (IR/D) program. Any opinion, finding, and conclusions or recommendations expressed in this material are those of the authors and do not necessarily reflect the views of NSF.

References

Drury, B.J., Siy, J.O., Cheryan, S., 2011. When do female role models benefit women? The importance of differentiating recruitment from retention in STEM. Psychol. Inq. 22, 265–269.

Miller, C., 2001. FORWARD in SEM, 20 mn video, GW Television, Washington, DC.

Moyer, A., Salovey, P., Casey-Cannon, S., 2009. Challenges facing female doctoral students and recent graduates. Psychol. Women Q. 23 (3), 607–630.

Possible Benefits for Workshop Organizers

Catherine Mavriplis[1] and Lynnette D. Madsen[2]

[1]University of Ottawa, Ottawa, Canada [2]National Science Foundation, Arlington, VA, USA

OUTLINE

Introduction	268
Motivations	269
Social Entrepreneurship and Advocacy for One's Underrepresented Group	270
Enlarging One's Personal Network	271
Training High-Quality Personnel	272
Mentoring	272
Skills Building and Learning	272
Benefits to Organizers	273
Learning	273
Networking and Collaboration	274
Gratitude and Satisfaction	275
Visibility	275
Leadership and Organizational Skills Development	276
Empowerment	277
Improved Climate	278
Springboard to Other Events and Roles	279
Intellectual Outcomes	280
Drawbacks and Difficulties Encountered	281
Time Requirements	281
Possible Negative Perception by Others	281

267

Sustainability	*282*
Some Difficulties and Concerns	*282*
Conclusion	283
Acknowledgments	284
References	284
Examples of Intellectual Outcomes	285

INTRODUCTION

The original FORWARD workshop organizers developed the workshop out of a need to fill a void: very little information on how to apply for a faculty position existed at the time in the late 1990s, other than from informal mentoring of a PhD advisor, if one were lucky enough to receive it. Many women and men (though far more women percentagewise) we knew as colleagues felt that such information was only selectively released, often to the "golden boy" of the group. As noted in Chapter 1, faculty development programs were few and far between; moreover, they were less prominent in science, technology, engineering, and mathematics (STEM) fields. Certainly there were none available at institutions at the graduate student and postdoctoral stage in STEM, at least to our knowledge. Faculty development was usually reserved for faculty members already employed by an institution.

As we came to understand our own motivation, drive, commitment and empowerment, through several years of workshop development and refinement, we began to see the value in propagating our model and recruiting new organizers. The PAY IT FORWARD project that we proposed to the National Science Foundation (NSF) aimed to provide training and a model that new organizers could adopt, adapt, or build upon to deliver tailored career development workshops, either by regional, ethnic group, or discipline focus. The call for proposals for these new groups was issued and, unsurprisingly, several leaders emerged with viable projects across the United States. While the previous chapters describe these successful efforts, in this chapter, we outline the motivations, benefits, and drawbacks of taking on this task of workshop organization.

The literature on "workshop organizers" is slim to nonexistent to our knowledge. However, many established volunteer and grassroots organizations seem to recognize the motivations and benefits of their actions, as they list them prominently on their websites (e.g., Willis,

2013; 350.org). In recruiting organizers, they [in this case, Willis (2013)] speak of the primary benefits being the chance to engage members of your group with information that directly affects their employment and profession, the ability to innovate and shape your profession, and the chance to "make a real difference" in the lives of these people, as well as those they serve. For professors who are geared toward serving students as well as research and education, especially women professors, this message resonates well with their personal motivations. Some even recognize the particular motivation and drive of women, notably mothers: "*Motivated* women make the best *organizers* and activists" [author's emphasis], says Britell (2010) of environmental activism. Certainly, volunteerism and grassroots action have been shown to provide empowerment to organizations and individuals, while weighing the costs (e.g., Prestby et al., 1990 and the references therein). Unsurprisingly, research finds that those who get more involved in these efforts draw more empowerment, especially as their involvement takes on a prolonged commitment. On a personal level, participation in organizing relates to higher competencies, higher confidence, and lower sense of helplessness.

The desire to offer information to younger colleagues in similar fields certainly resonates with the role of mentor. The mentoring literature is concentrated mostly on the effects of mentoring on protégés and their careers, but some studies address the motivations of mentors and the effects of acting as a mentor on their own careers. The authority on mentoring, Kram (1985), notes that mentors have an interest in helping to develop others' careers out of both "instrumental and psychological needs": the desire to build a competent workforce and improve their specific organization on the instrumental side, and a sense of personal satisfaction in helping others and to connect with them personally on the psychological side. The FORWARD workshop organizers displayed many of these characteristics and reported them after their experience, sometimes to their surprise, as noted next.

MOTIVATIONS

It is interesting to note that, as the original organizers, our motivations were not always self-evident. Many of us had a drive to do this work without fully recognizing why. The empowerment of running such an event brought the motivations to the surface upon reflection and attainment of satisfaction. We list here several of the motivations that workshop leaders report as they organize a grassroots faculty development workshop.

Social Entrepreneurship and Advocacy for One's Underrepresented Group

Organizing a FORWARD workshop is an opportunity to fill a void that one might recognize in the development of faculty members in one's field. For example, Alexandra Davatzes and Jennifer Piatek recognized the "Lone Wolf" sociology of women in planetary sciences and took action to develop FORWARD in Space (see Chapter 13). Similarly, the City Tech group felt that City University of New York (CUNY) mathematics and computer science researchers were so disconnected because they were distributed over 24 campuses that they could benefit from linking together and creating a community to develop resources (see Chapter 11). The University of Guam FORWARD workshop sought to address the ethnic dimension of Western Pacific women's sociology in advancing women to the professoriate (see Chapter 5). In each case, the organizers who emerged from the scientific community felt strongly that they recognized a need and that they could offer some constructive steps to improve the situation.

As mentioned previously, according to Kram (1985), mentors seek to improve the workplace culture and contribute to workforce development. They may even be seen as playing a "vital role" in their organization (Allen, 2003). The FORWARD workshops, by design, were geographically diverse, and, as such, they do not seem to fit into the "organization" structure that many mentoring articles refer to: the workshops covered several, if not many, institutions, as well as disciplines and regions. For this reason, we see the efforts of these workshop organizers as grassroots actions and leadership in the move to change the culture of STEM academia. Their actions represent concrete steps toward advocacy for their underrepresented groups—actions that can be categorized as social entrepreneurship. Truly, these are entrepreneurs in the sense defined by the dictionary: "a person who organizes and manages any enterprise, especially a business, usually with considerable initiative and risk" (Dictionary. com retrieved October 29, 2014). Short et al. (2009) add to this concept the refusal "to accept limitations in available resources." The initiative needed to form a new group of organizers, to secure funding and other resources, and to deliver a tailored product can come only from a group of passionate leaders. The risks, ever present in the research field, are (i) the schedule requirements, taking time away from disciplinary research, and (ii) unfavorable perception by others, mainly men, the wielders of power in STEM academia. Despite these risks, organizers seem ready to take on the task to contribute to a better culture for women and other underrepresented groups in STEM.

Enlarging One's Personal Network

The opportunity to organize a workshop and invite keynote speakers of considerable stature, as well as experts in various domains, presents an immediate networking opportunity. Communicating goals for the workshop and faculty development for women and minorities in STEM to potential speakers provides grounds for immediate rapport. Overwhelmingly, the speakers we contacted were able to immediately connect with us on the goals, as they were as passionate as we were about the prospect of supporting young faculty members starting out (see Chapter 16). Many of the keynote speakers invited were leaders in academia, either deans of faculties (e.g., Leah Jamieson, dean of engineering at Purdue University) or higher up in university administration (e.g., Janie Fouke, senior advisor to the president for international affairs at the University of Florida), or else they were prominent leaders of professional societies. Access to such decision makers can open doors for your career, just as mentoring from a senior colleague has been known to do for men (Riskin et al., 2005; Straus et al., 2013; Davis, 2001). For organizers, the connection made with these keynoters lasts for several years after the event and even continues today.

Connections with funding agency program managers invited to the research panels also build a network for future funding. Often, these speakers would return year after year and suggest alternates when they could not attend. The breadth of the speakers invited for different topics (such as writing, teaching, negotiating and work/life balance) also fills out one's network in areas in which one might not have many contacts. At the organizers' institution, the network is also expanded through seeking support from the administration and academic leaders, as well as through working with support staff and Fellow faculty members, often from across the university. For STEM women, who often find themselves isolated in their departments due to lack of critical mass of women professors, working in a predominantly, if not exclusively, female interdisciplinary team is an unfamiliar yet attractive possibility. Organizing the workshop with colleagues from neighboring or collaborating institutions provides an opportunity to enlarge one's local circle, as the University of Virginia team did with Virginia Commonwealth University and Norfolk State University (see Chapter 7), or discipline, as the Central Connecticut University and Temple University organizers did with their Temple workshop and the Lunar and Planetary Science Conference (see Chapter 13) network. Finally, connecting with the participants themselves is a significant network builder. These are the future leaders of the academic world. Indeed, Mullen and Noe (1999) note that mentors often seek information from their protégés and derive benefit from it.

Training High-Quality Personnel

As professors, our natural role and inclination are to train students and develop their scientific and technical careers. Training and mentoring often go beyond the classroom and the opportunity to encourage students to develop their potential and push their limits comes in small but constant doses. Apart from the handful of graduate students and postdoctoral researchers that we actively supervise and mentor every day, we often wait for students (especially undergraduates) to seek us out as mentors. The workshop, however, allows one to have a major impact on a large number of people in a very concentrated timeline. It also provides an opportunity to mentor and train future academicians from a wide range of disciplines that one might not usually have access to. In so doing, organizers contribute to the shaping of the future academic world, for example, to create a more interdisciplinary and career development-aware faculty body, as noted in the goals for social entrepreneurship.

While training comes naturally to professors, it also appears as a natural stage in midcareer professional life: Dalton et al. (1977) describe the four stages of professional careers as learning, producing, training, and directing. Many of the FORWARD organizers were in the midcareer stage, one in which, Dalton and colleagues note, people "play the critical role in helping others through Stage I." Furthermore, a call for organizing training of future faculty (Austin, 2002 and the references therein), in particular women faculty, and women faculty in STEM (NSF ADVANCE) motivates the training aspect of career development workshop initiatives.

Mentoring

As mentioned previously, mentoring comes naturally to many professors in the setting of research groups and departmental programs. However, the desire to mentor often comes from a passion to support someone (perhaps a person like ourselves) to steer him or her clear of the struggles we have experienced, or at least to be a guide as the protegée faces difficulties. Mentoring provides a satisfying deeper connection with one or several individuals at crossroads in their career or life development (Kram, 1985). Mentoring requires commitment and time dedication, which can be effectively delivered in the focused format of the workshop. Certainly the mentoring relationship can continue beyond the workshop, but the 1- to 3-day format provides for a focused and meaningful contact in an otherwise very busy life.

Skills Building and Learning

The opportunity to develop and run a workshop builds organizational and leadership skills. Most STEM professors are never trained in anything but their scientific research, so they learn on the job how to run a research program, manage a team, and teach a class (Austin, 2002). As PhDs, we rarely return to the classroom to learn new skills. Learning by doing, then, is the modus operandi. Organizing a workshop forces one to learn to work in a multidisciplinary team; communicate training and interpersonal goals; contact a large number of speakers and secure funding (involving sales and negotiation skills); deal with logistics such as registration, room rental, and catering; and generally run an event with large numbers of people. de Ridder et al. (2014) discuss the importance of developing these "soft skills" in organizing graduate student events in computational biology; that is, in the context of a scientific career development stage where time and energy are "scarce commodities." These skills can translate into managerial skills for larger event organizing or leadership positions.

The workshop itself provides opportunities for learning through the various presentations. As a workshop organizer, you have control over the content, and the material to be presented can be shaped by your preferences. For example, we were motivated to invite the authors of *Women Don't Ask*, Linda Babcock and Sara Laschever, to speak at the first workshop at the Massachusetts Institute of Technology (MIT) in 2005. In so doing, we were able to get direct access to a large body of knowledge on women's negotiation styles and possible solutions for successful actions for women in male-dominated fields.

BENEFITS TO ORGANIZERS

Learning

One of the main and most immediate benefits of running the workshops is learning: learning facts, strategies, and ways of thinking from the speakers and the ensuing discussions. Learning how to secure funding and tap into resources both from the program managers speaking on the research panel and from contact with them individually furthered the work of several organizers. For the original FORWARD organizers, National Institutes of Health (NIH) program managers steered us to applying for and eventually winning a R13 grant to enhance the workshop for health sciences participants. For the City Tech group, one of the organizers was successful in obtaining an Office of Naval Research grant after discussions with one of their program managers for applied mathematics. Both of the grants are discussed in the section entitled "Intellectual Outcomes," later in this chapter.

Creating a new workshop format can encourage the learning of new techniques, as it did for the University of Virginia, Virginia Commonwealth University, and Norfolk State University team: Dr Gertrude Fraser reported benefits from the "lessons learned about the dialogue method's success with STEM academics: [...] We learned how to collaborate cross-institutionally in organizing a conference. Individuals on the planning team learned more about one another and have subsequently worked on other projects. Facilitators developed expertise in a structured dialogue process."

The organizers also learned from the participants. Professor Shiping Deng of Oklahoma State University agreed: "We discover some of the things we encounter are not unique to us. Sharing experiences on dealing with difficult situations would empower us with options that are tailored to each of us. I suppose that many of these issues are discussed over a beer among our male colleagues; we need to go to a workshop to open up."

And, finally, graduate student organizers, such as Virginia Rich at MIT, get a head start on their careers, as she explains: "Today, I am a postdoctoral researcher at the University of Arizona. When my husband was offered a job here, the insights from FORWARD helped guide our negotiations for a second position, resulting in a unique postdoctoral position with my own salary and research money. Just a few months ago the DOE [Department of Energy] funded a large international grant that I developed and am co-PI [Principal Investigator] on."

Networking and Collaboration

Going through the entire organization process provides enhanced networking opportunities, both in the research and campus communities, and for the target group (young people transitioning between graduate student or postdoctoral scholar and their first faculty position). For example, the Arizona State University (ASU) team pointed out: "Organizers of the program have the added opportunity to network with STEM professionals as they recruit speakers and interact with other organizers across the country." Dr Jeanmarie Verchot of Oklahoma State University shared the following thoughts: "For me, this helped me to expand my network on campus. I felt more involved in the university. I wanted to expand my own professional tool box. Organizing the workshop helped me to know more about the university infrastructure and network with other faculty and administrators on campus." The University of Toledo (UT) group noted: "We received excellent local support from [the] administration and faculty at UT."

In terms of collaboration, the UT team formed long-term connections: "The workshop planning and implementation resulted in the strengthening of community for the workshop organizers. While the team was originally assembled as an organizing team for 'When and Where I Enter,' the group remains in close contact and have continued to collaborate on other initiatives in the area of the advancement of women of color in STEM in academia. The diversity of the group is one of its greatest strengths." The ASU team started with a strong community connection: "We partnered with the local chapter of the Association for Women in Science (AWIS) to host the workshop. This partnership has helped both the national AWIS organization as well as the university by working closely with the attendees to find out what their needs were and where the university system should concentrate to improve the chances for advancement of women in STEM."

Gratitude and Satisfaction

The organizers received very positive evaluations from attendees and were gratified by active discussions and engagement during the workshop. For almost every team, satisfaction of the participants was high: "Almost all of the participants (95%) said they would recommend this workshop to a friend or colleague" reported the Oklahoma State team. According to Professor Deng, "The main benefit to workshop organizers is to feel good that we did something to help Fellow female colleagues on the road to tenure."

As the UT team noted, part of the benefits they obtained was in the form of the satisfaction that the participants had with the outcome: "A personalized plan was started for each participant." One faculty member who participated in a workshop stated: "I have attempted a plan in the past. Then, I got to about 5 months ahead and stopped. After this workshop, I'm more motivated to complete a 5-year plan and make sure that everything I do is strategic." A rather new faculty member remarked: "Speaking with department chairs did help me to understand what is required to move through the ranks of academia. I have not written a plan. The strategies for measuring productivity, the family-work balance, and mentoring were helpful." Similarly, the ASU team told us, "Many of our attendees were able to obtain successful careers following this training and have credited much of this success to the workshop."

Visibility

The visibility of talented women of STEM faculty at their own institution and in the region was raised through their participation in the workshop organizing. Inevitably, the organizers become role models for the participants. For example, Lynnette Madsen said, "I recall one workshop when Professor Catherine Mavriplis was clearly very pregnant—I am guessing about seven months along. She came across as calm and collected throughout the workshop and acted like being in this state was perfectly normal. I am confident that she set an impression with everyone in the room."

Without a doubt, these workshops presented an opportunity to show off one's campus and facilities. Professor Rachelle Heller, now associate provost at the Mount Vernon Campus of the George Washington University (GWU), often hosted the FORWARD workshop dinner at the elegant and historic Post Hall, with its chandelier lighting, a lovely terrace, and a portrait of the "ever cheerful" Elizabeth J. Somers. University of Virginia organizers also noted that "participants said they learned about the University of Virginia in a much more positive way than previously."

As Professor Deng of the Oklahoma State University team noted: "I am sure that we are recognized, not for direct contribution to our specific scientific discipline (and we should not expect this), but for contributing to build a more diverse and positive academic working environment, especially for women and minority in STEM. Additionally, we could expect to be recognized as being generous in offering our time, effort, and experience to help colleagues and younger generations to be successful on the road to tenure and to have a fulfilling career life in general. Moreover, these contributions demonstrated our willingness to serve. Adding the strengthened leadership skills through organizing the workshop, we should be more competitive for leadership roles when opportunity arises."

There is also a kind of spotlight effect from organizing anything big and noticeable on campus or at a conference. Some of these effects may be welcome—others, not so much. For example, it could overshadow your accomplishments in other areas (Park, 1996), or people may not think that you are dedicated to science and engineering research. Either of these effects could add to your pressure. You could become the go-to person for career development, women's issues, and related subjects, which can be positive, but these issues may also be considered less important areas to be known for and can distract others from seeing your science/engineering research accomplishments. There is no doubt that your name recognition will increase, and there will be added visibility and exposure. Of course, when you sit back after running a successful workshop (or workshop series), your success will be evident to others; that, in turn, may open other doors for you.

Leadership and Organizational Skills Development

As noted in the motivations described up to this point, organizational skills development and the desire to take on a leadership role in one's professional community are definite benefits of organizing a career development workshop. Many organizers found their strengths while working with a diverse team of like-minded colleagues. Isabel Escobar (see the section entitled "Springboard to Other Events and Roles," later in this chapter) discovered that hers was fundraising, which then empowered her to chair a larger professional meeting. The interdisciplinary (and, at times, intergenerational and ethnically diverse) teams functioned well due to their aligned goals of effecting change for women and underrepresented minorities in STEM. As an outcome of the Women in Engineering Leadership Institute program that developed around the same time as FORWARD, Zoli et al. (2008) make the case for the need for women to become agents of change in the STEM academic environment. In particular, they note that women's styles of leadership, which are transformational and collaborative, are critical to climate transformation in these fields. FORWARD workshop organization provides a testing ground for the development of these leadership skills.

Within the teams themselves, clear leaders often emerged. At times, these were more junior members (e.g., graduate students), with a specific drive and talent for leadership, such as those on the Oregon State team. The MIT team (see Chapter 3) specifically employed graduate students in the delivery of each Path of Professorship offering, with the intention of developing the students' organizational and leadership skills. The student organizers appreciated the opportunity to hone these skills in the context of a very demanding graduate program of almost exclusively scientific research.

Empowerment

Organizing a FORWARD workshop can produce a boost in confidence from accomplishment and empowerment. As Isabel Escobar noted, this sometimes was an unexpected development to organizers: "It was surprising to experience the level of personal connections developed with total strangers during the workshop. We had a session to share experiences, during which organizers and participants had an open forum to share their feelings in a safe environment. This led to connections and empowerment of all."

When asked what was the most surprising outcome of organizing a workshop, Amanda Bryant-Friedrich, of the UT College of Pharmacy and Pharmaceutical Sciences, said: "The effect the experience had on my career. When I decided to participate, I did not perceive this to be something that would advance my career. However, through the preparation and delivery of the workshop content, I gained insight into life planning that I had not considered. After applying these concepts to my own life, I have found more success in many of my adventures."

It is likely that women involved in organizing these activities will believe that they can have a greater voice in departmental matters, and in turn, this is likely to increase job satisfaction (Settles et al., 2007).

Improved Climate

A possible and highly likely outcome is that the climate on campus, within your community, or both will improve. However, as Professor Deng notes, these changes are "slow and gradual." She comments, "Awareness is one of the main accomplishments of the effort. The effect of the workshop itself is limited. In combination with the ADVANCE program, some visible changes are shown. Funds for ADVANCE are substantially larger, which benefited many men and women faculty members on campus. As a result, there are some changes in attitude toward hiring female and minority faculty and/or administrators. However, changing culture is a long-term devoted effort, which is not possible to be accomplished by one workshop or one ADVANCE program." The Oklahoma State University team also noted, "The junior faculty who attended expressed benefits for their career development." Namely, this is due to two effects: running the workshop naturally draws attention to the issues and facilitates changes, and in addition, there are ripple effects from educating others and the visibility that the workshop brings. Ultimately, it is important that the workshops are part of a larger strategy to address the problem of women's underrepresentation among science and engineering faculty, and that the gendered structures and normative practices at the academic institution be modified or replaced (Bird, 2011).

The University of Virginia and Virginia Commonwealth University took the next steps toward further improvement. Dr Fraser conveys what happened: "In listening to the dialogue during the 2010 'Engaging Across Difference' conference, we noted that participants frequently referenced senior colleagues and advisors at their home institutions as key players in facilitating or inhibiting their career progress and as having more or less capability to see and leverage difference on behalf of early career STEM women. This suggested that a workshop for administrative and departmental leaders would be an important next step and well aligned with the FORWARD to Professorship goals. Working with colleagues at Virginia Commonwealth University, we brought together a diverse group of about 16 senior faculty and department chairs to engage in facilitated small group discussions modeled on our 'Engaging Across Difference' conference. STEM departments are complex, dynamic domains. The focus in this effort was to structure facilitated dialogues about diversity and heterogeneity and how participants, as STEM leaders, can encourage high-level involvement of departmental colleagues and other stakeholders in efforts to learn about difference, appreciate and engage with the perspective of diverse others, and identify common goals and shared commitments that can improve the departmental climate for STEM women faculty, graduate students and post-docs."

When the organizers are working with conferences and professional societies, their workshops can trigger other related workshops and outreach sessions; this may also hold true on a university campus. It brings the community together (both physically and intellectually), and therefore, it can help form interest groups or new award mechanisms within the professional society or community. For the ASU team, "Experience gained by the organizers is being transferred to other professional societies by assisting these groups in the development of their conference programs. Successful training/educational seminars are included into the conference program which extends the reach to a broader audience as well as enriches their conferences."

In many cases, it was common that the workshops brought a heightened awareness of the issues concerning academic advancement to people in power positions. This included powerful professors (frequently men) and senior officials or administrators on campus or in professional societies. It is apparent that many efforts can trigger larger changes and that without these events, the timeline to equity is quite long (Madsen, 2000).

Springboard to Other Events and Roles

The organizer role is a possible stepping stone to more complex or higher-level efforts. As Professor Deng notes: "If one is interested in going into an administration position, this is a great opportunity to learn and practice some of the [necessary] skills." Dr Jeanmarie Verchot of Oklahoma State University spoke of specific skills acquired through the experience: "ADVANCE has given me some credentials as a trained mentor and an understanding of human resource development. I also think that the reflection on my career path through ADVANCE has helped me gain some political skills." For Isabel Escobar of the UT, "The biggest benefit of organizing the workshop was working with my co-organizers. In dividing the work and assigning tasks, I learned my strengths and weaknesses; for instance, I learned that fundraising was truly my strength. Knowing my strength is in fundraising helped me to successfully chair a professional conference in 2012 and to develop/sustain K–12 outreach programs. Friendships developed during organizing the workshop have also been very beneficial to my personal life and professional career."

Graduate student organizers were empowered to self-organize other events, such as Virginia Rich at MIT: "Under the encouragement of Dr Mavriplis, several of us ran a 'women in science' lecture and discussion group for the remainder of the year, bringing in speakers on particular topics of interest and strengthening the connections we had made."

Certainly the University of Virginia, Virginia Commonwealth University, and Norfolk State University team found long-term benefits. As Dr Gertrude Fraser reported, they included "lessons learned about the dialogue method's success with STEM academics. These contributed to the success of our ADVANCE-IT submission. [...] We learned how to collaborate cross-institutionally in organizing a conference. Individuals on the planning team learned more about one another and have subsequently worked on other projects. Facilitators developed expertise in a structured dialogue process." Indeed, Dr Fraser built on the structured dialogue experience of the University of Virginia workshop to build a larger proposal to the NSF ADVANCE Institutional Transformation program, winning a $3 million grant in 2012 (see the section entitled "Intellectual Outcomes," later in this chapter).

For the original FORWARD organizers, several important initiatives have been developed. Professor Charlene Sorensen at Gallaudet University (GU) competed for and won a $2.6 million grant from the US Department of Health and Human Services for Health Resources and Services Health Careers Opportunity Program for Deafness. Professor Rachelle Heller heads the Elizabeth J. Somers Leadership Program at the Mount Vernon Campus of GWU: a selective, year-long, living and learning program for freshmen women to explore and develop their leadership skills. For Professor Catherine Mavriplis, her experience running the workshops parlayed nicely into a chaired professorship in Canada: the Natural Sciences and Engineering Research Council of Canada/Pratt & Whitney Canada Chair for Women in Sciences and Engineering, a $1.5 million 5-year program to advance women in science and engineering, despite a career break taken for family reasons.

Intellectual Outcomes

The workshop organizations provide additional benefits in the realm of scholarship value and academic products. For example, it is important to publish accounts of the events and, if possible, to develop analysis publications in scholarly journals. Indeed, it may be difficult to identify possible "homes" for these investigations and findings. Connections with others on campus (or elsewhere) that have a mandate for research in these areas can be greatly beneficial. A co-author who knows how to construct a survey and how to present the findings in the best way, and who can and has the time to write and knows which journals to target, is a great asset. Not only that, but many of the organizers have contributed chapters to this book. Professor Deng notes, "Regardless whether we will get credit for the publication (since it is not in our scientific field), it feels good that we have scholarly outcome from the effort." For some, as noted previously, major grants were obtained with the experience gained from their efforts. For the original organizers, this experience led to the development of substantial leadership programs: the Elizabeth J. Somers Leadership program at GWU and the NSERC/Pratt & Whitney Canada Chair for Women in Science and Engineering in Canada. Examples of intellectual outcomes that were produced as a result of running these workshops are listed at the end of this chapter.

DRAWBACKS AND DIFFICULTIES ENCOUNTERED

Time Requirements

Is it worth the time and effort to hold these workshops? That is hard to say—the largest drawback is that organizing these workshops is a huge time sink, often calling for much more time than originally anticipated and also being intensely demanding at certain times. It may be detrimental to advancement to carry too great of a service load (such as a workshop) before being appointed as a full professor (Link et al., 2008). The UT team noted: "We received no funding for administrative help and spent countless hours on administrative duties." The ASU team elaborated on the time issue: "One of the biggest challenges is to create a good workshop team that will equally divide the workload. Many times, there will be only a few that take on the majority of the work. It is also difficult to have the same volunteers continue to help in the following years." The key seems to be to form a productive team that functions well together. This can only be done with time invested in the relationships in the team, as several teams reported. For some teams, the time investment was a deterrent to offering a second workshop, along with the lack of financial resources. But for most, the time invested was deemed well worth it for the personal satisfaction and other benefits mentioned in this chapter. As Cyndee Gruden of the UT team mentioned, she was surprised at "the willingness of many others to donate time and resources to help us during the event."

Possible Negative Perception by Others

There is little doubt that these types of activities include outreach as well as scholarship, training, and leadership. Will these efforts count as service? They may, but they may not. They can be viewed as optional service, an activity that was neither required nor essential, as many of our male colleagues have commented. However, as a motivated agent of change for our underrepresented group and the general STEM workforce, one might deem them as quite the opposite—that is, necessary—this is particularly the case if you, the organizer, identified the need. It may also be discounted as "women's work," although most changes are known to benefit both men and women and highly appreciated by the younger faculty (DeAro and Madsen, 2009). As Professor Deng cautions, "To gain support from administration and colleagues, it is critical that we communicate the needs and potential positive impact to the academic working environment."

Sustainability

As the original FORWARD organizers, we were pleased to be able to sustain the workshop through the Pay It FORWARD project of training the 10 teams included in this book, as well as through MIT's institutionalization of the workshop. However, running the workshop once was not enough for some teams. Indeed, when asked what their biggest disappointment was, Professor Cyndee Gruden of the UT team said: "The fact that it was not sustainable. The cost and effort associated with this workshop was significant. We were unable to find support at NSF (through subsequent submissions to ADVANCE) or elsewhere to repeat this with the needed finances, infrastructure, and support. We were able to find many people who thought what we were doing was significant but no *real* additional support." The ASU organizer, Dr Page Baluch, said: "One of my biggest concerns is if the workshops/symposia will continue once the originating organizers move on with their careers." It is interesting to note that continuity was considered from the beginning and presented a challenge to the team. However, getting the people is only part of the problem, says Page: "Another concern is obtaining ongoing financial support for the workshops. Many groups will start their program through grant funding, but this will only sustain the program for the first couple of years. One of the biggest challenges is to establish ongoing support to continue the program."

Some Difficulties and Concerns

Running these workshops is indeed a lot of work, and there are many hurdles to jump along the way. For all the organizers, it took considerable effort to identify speakers who were available on the workshop dates. As for the UT group, the members also had difficulty in identifying participants: "Locating women of color in STEM in the Midwest was challenging (24 applicants, 20 accepted, 18 attended with an expanded geographical region)." Furthermore, they found that "[t]he need to dissect the term Women of Color and how we fit or do not fit into this group was lacking during the workshop." Tracking and obtaining long-term data from surveys can be difficult, as the UT team discovered: "Feedback from the surveys has been extremely positive, indicating a long-term impact on attendees. However, response rate to surveys has been very low."

Many teams were concerned with time allocation for each activity. Striking the right balance for the participant group is tricky and is best determined from feedback from the participants and running the workshop two or more times. The UT team reported, "We needed to allocate more time for certain program elements (such as the Personal Plan development)." It was sometimes difficult to gauge in advance what would be appreciated the most; "It became clear during the course of the workshop that mainstream topics were appreciated by the participants but topics such as work/life satisfaction, personal planning and exchanging experiences were key in creating the overall feel of the workshop experience."

Evaluation of these workshops was desirable. However, some teams felt that "[w]e were inexperienced at preparing/quantifying/interpreting program assessments." The most unfortunate aspect for some, such as the UT group, was that "[a]lthough there has been much work with respect to storytelling, we have not found a way to leverage these stories into policy changes on our campus or in our STEM disciplines as a whole."

CONCLUSION

Organizers of faculty development workshops such as FORWARD to Professorship find many motivations to take on the task, and they derive multiple benefits from it. The drive to mentor younger colleagues and to build a better STEM academic workforce is strong and provides the impetus to chart new ground, be it for securing resources, innovating content, or taking risks in creating "safe" spaces for emotional discussion. In so doing, the organizers sharpened their organizational and leadership skills and derived personal satisfaction from connecting in a meaningful way with younger colleagues. The main drawback identified by some of the organizers was the intense time commitment, couched in the context of concern for their own career reputation in a research-intensive environment that ignores career development and underrepresented group concerns. Overwhelmingly, though, the FORWARD organizers reported a transformative experience.

Acknowledgments

Thanks are extended to the organizers of the workshops, who provided comments and reflections. This article was written in part by Lynnette Madsen while working at NSF, with the support of an Independent Research/Development (IR/D) program. Any opinion, finding, and conclusions or recommendations expressed in this material are those of the authors and do not necessarily reflect the views of NSF.

References

Allen, T.D, 2003. Mentoring others: a dispositional and motivational approach. J. Vocat. Behav. 62 (1), 134–154.

Austin, A.E., 2002. Preparing the next generation of faculty: graduate school as socialization to the academic career. J. Higher Educ. 73 (1), 94–122.

Bird, S.R., 2011. Unsettling universities' incongruous, gendered bureaucratic structures: a case-study approach. Gend. Work Organ. 18 (2), 202–230.

Britell, J., 2010. Organize to Win—A Grassroots Activist's Handbook—A Guide to Help People Organize Community Campaigns. Available from: <http://www.britell.com/text/OrganizeToWin.pdf> (accessed 30.10.14.).

Dalton, G.W., Thompson, P.H., Price, R.L., 1977. The four stages of professional careers—a new look at performance by professionals. Organ. Dyn. 6 (1), 19–42.

Davis, K., 2001. "Peripheral and subversive": women making connections and challenging the boundaries of the science community. Sci. Educ. 85 (4), 368–409.

DeAro, J., Madsen, L.D., 2009. Transforming universities and colleges in the United States with federal government support. Proceedings of the 6th European Conference on Gender Equality in Higher Education. Stockholm, Sweden.

de Ridder, J, Meysman, P, Oluwagbemi, O, Abeel, T, 2014. Soft skills: an important asset acquired from organizing regional student group activities. Public Libr. Sci. Comput. Biol. 10 (7), e1003708. Available from: < http://dx.doi.org/10.1371/journal.pcbi.1003708 >.

Kram, K.E., 1985. Mentoring at Work: Developmental Relationships in Organizational Life. Scott Foresman, Glenview, IL.

Link, A.N., Swann, C.A., Bozeman, B., 2008. A time allocation study of university faculty. Econ. Educ. Rev. 27 (4), 363–374.

Madsen, L.D., 2000. University Science and Engineering: promotions, programs and progress in Sweden, Canada and the USA. Proceedings of the Canadian Coalition for Women in Engineering, Science, and Technology (CCWEST): New Frontiers and New Traditions Conference, St John's, Canada.

Mullen, E.J., Noe, R.A., 1999. The mentoring information exchange: when do mentors seek information from their protégés? J. Organ. Behav. 20 (2), 233–242.

National Science Foundation (NSF), ADVANCE at a Glance. Available from: <http://www.nsf.gov/crssprgm/advance/> (accessed 30.10.14.).

Park, S.M., 1996. Research, teaching, and service: why shouldn't women's work count? J. Higher Educ. 67 (1), 46–84.

Prestby, J.E., Wandersman, A., Florin, P., Rich, R., Chavis, D., 1990. Benefits, costs, incentive management and participation in voluntary organizations: a means to understanding and promoting empowerment. Am. J. Community Psychol. 18 (1), 117–149.

Riskin, E., Ostendorf, M., Cosman, P., Effors, M., Li, J., Hemami, S., et al., 2005. Mentoring for academic careers in engineering. Proceedings of the PAESMEM/Stanford School of Engineering Workshop. Grayphics Publishing, Santa Barbara.

Settles, I.H., Cortina, L.M., Stewart, A.J., Malley, J., 2007. Voice matters: buffering the impact of a negative climate for women in science. Psychol. Women Q. 31 (3), 270–281.

Short, J.C., Moss, T.W., Lumpkin, G.T., 2009. Research in social entrepreneurship: past contributions and future opportunities. Strateg. Entrepreneurship J. 3 (2), 161–194.

Straus, S.E., Johnson, M.O., Marquez, C., Feldman, M.D., 2013. Characteristics of successful and failed mentoring relationships: a qualitative study across two academic health centers. Acad. Med. 88 (1), 82–89.

Willis, B., 2013. What Are the Benefits of Grassroots Advocacy. Available from: <http://www.votility.com/blog/bid/262023/What-Are-The-Benefits-Of-Grassroots-Advocacy> (accessed 30.10.14.).

Zoli, C., Bhatia, S., Davidson, V., Rusch, K., 2008. Engineering: Women in Leadership. Morgan & Claypool, San Rafael, CA.

350.org, Why Organize? Available from: <http://workshops.350.org/toolkit/organize/> (accessed 30.10.14.).

Examples of Intellectual Outcomes

Social Media

- Facebook, Linked In and earlier email list-serv groups were started and maintained by organizers and participants.

Videos and Movies

- Dr Vivian Pinn's 2011 keynote speech, "Women's Health in the USA" recorded and broadcast by PBS. Available from: < http://www.wgte.org/wgte/item.asp?item_-id = 10035 > (accessed 30.10.14.).
- The UT group recorded the grant writing panel for their College of Engineering.
- Miller, C., 2001. FORWARD in SEM, 20 mn video, GW Television, Washington, DC.

Lectures and Invited Presentations

- Escobar, I., Grant, C., Nave, F., 2013. More than a Data Point: Engaging Voices of Women of Color from Within the STEM Academy, presented a session at the Keeping Our Faculty of Color Symposium, hosted by the University of Minnesota, Minneapolis.
- Gruden, C., Shaffer, A., 2013. To Tenure and Beyond: Building an Intentional Academic Career, presented interactive session at American Council on Education (ACE) Women's Network, Ohio.
- Heller, R.S. and Washington, G., 2004. Men and Women Faculty: Do They Work Differently?, SIGCSE 2004 Conference, Norfolk, VA.
- Heller, R.S., 2005. How Women Lead: Libyan Women's Empowerment Workshop: For Women by Women, Tripoli, Libya.
- Heller, R.S., 2007. FORWARD to Professorship: A Workshop for Pre-tenured Women and Under-Represented Minorities in Science, Technology, Engineering and Math, Spring Symposium, Mathematics Initiative Steering Committee, George Washington University.
- Heller, R.S. and Mavriplis, C., 2007. Clues to Avoiding the Pitfalls on the Road to Tenure. SACNAS Conference, Kansas City, Missouri.
- Heller, R.S., 2012. Women in STEM, Women in Computing, Michigan Technical University.
- Heller, R.S., 2013. Status of Women in STEM, Pregel Lecture, National Institute of Chemistry, Ljubljana, Slovenia.
- Heller, R.S., 2013. Publishing in Peer Reviewed Journals, Plant and Animal Genome Asia, Singapore.

- Heller, R.S., 2013. The Status of Women in Science in Slovenia, Women in Science, Maribor, Slovenia.
- Heller, R.S., 2014. Mind The Gap, Supercharging Re-entry to STEM, Office of Science and Technology Policy workshop, US White House.
- Heller, R.S, 2014. FORWARD to Professorship, Indo-US Roundtable on ADVANCing Women Faculty in STEM, New Delhi, India.
- Catherine Mavriplis: 27 invited presentations in the period 2007–2014 including Princeton University Alumni Association, Women in Astronomy and Space Science Meeting, Massachusetts Institute of Technology and the Royal Institute of Technology, Sweden.

Poster Presentations

- Fraser, G., Hobson Hargraves, R., Black, S., Harden, M., 2011. Engaging Difference: Diverse Women in STEM Building Careers, Creating Alliances, Professional and Organizational Network Developers in Higher Education and the Historically Black Colleges and Universities Faculty Development Network Joint Conference, Atlanta.
- Baluch, D.P., Traynor, K., Cease, A., Coulombe, M., Stout, V., Sweazea, K., 2012. Jumpstarting STEM Careers, American Society for Cell Biology, San Francisco, CA.
- Cease, A., Traynor, K., Coulombe, M., Stout, V., and Sweazea, K., Baluch, D.P., 2013. Jumpstarting STEM Careers, Society for Integrative and Comparative Biology, San Francisco, CA.
- Sweazea, K., Baluch, D.P. Traynor, K., Cease, A., Coulombe, M., Stout, V., 2013. Jumpstarting STEM Careers, Experimental Biology, Boston, MA.
- Baluch, D.P., Kavuma, S., Harris, L., Gonzales, A., 2013. Career Training for Aspiring Neuroscientists, Society for Neuroscience, San Diego, CA.

Magazines, Newsletters, and Newspapers

- Baluch, D.P., 2010. Looking for a few good women. AWIS Magazine 41(3), 10–12.
- Baluch, D.P., 2012. Moving forward with AWIS-Central Arizona. AWIS Magazine Chapter News 43(3).
- Baluch, D.P., 2013. AWIS-Central Arizona heats up. AWIS Magazine Chapter News 44(2).
- Leander, S., 2013. Jumpstarting STEM Careers supports women and minority students. Available from: <https://sols.asu.edu/news-events/news/jumpstarting-stem-careers-supports-women-and-minority-students> (accessed 30.10.14.).
- Grobmeier, D., 2012. STEM Workshop geared toward women. The State Press. Available from: <http://www.statepress.com/2012/01/16/stem-workshop-geared-toward-women/> (accessed 30.10.14.).
- Coulombe, M., 2011. Jumpstarting STEM Careers workshop provides training, support. ASU News. Available from: <https://asunews.asu.edu/20111114_jumpstartSTEM> (accessed 30.10.14.).
- Leander, S., 2013. Jumpstarting STEM Careers symposium supports women, minority students. High Beam Research. Available from: <http://www.highbeam.com/doc/1G1-316422671.html> (accessed 30.10.14.).
- Jumpstarting STEM Careers Workshop, 2011. High Beam Research, NewsRX Health and Science. Available from: <http://www.highbeam.com/doc/1G1-275091340.html> (accessed 30.10.14.).
- Halber, D., 2005. Workshop offers guidance to help future female academics succeed. Tech Talk (MIT newspaper), Oct 5, 2005.
- Thomas, C., 2006. Industry corridors or ivy-covered walls. SWE Magazine 52(4), 44–50.

- Mavriplis, C., Heller, R., Sorensen, C., 2009. A new identity for science. International Innovation, 32.
- Sorensen, C., Mavriplis, C., Heller, R., 2005. Lessons in professorship. Nature 438, 392.

Book Chapters and Conference Proceedings

- Boersma, K.S., Kavanaugh, M.T., Ganio, L.M., Hooven, L.A., Close, S.L., Lachenbruch, B., 2012. Advancing toward professorship in biology, ecology, and earth systems sciences: Perceptions of confidence in early career scientists. Ecological Society of America Annual Meeting, Portland, OR. Available from: <http://eco.confex.com/eco/2012/webprogram/Paper39715.html> (accessed 06.09.14.).
- Bujaki, M., Lennox Terrion, J., Mavriplis, C. and Moreau-Johnson, F., Group mentoring programme for mid-career women associate professors. In: Clutterbuck, D., Poulsen, K. M. (Eds.), The Diversity Mentoring Case Book, McGraw Hill.
- Mavriplis, C., Beil, C., Dam, K., Heller, R. and Sorensen, C., 2010. An analysis of the FORWARD to Professorship workshop—what works to entice and prepare women for professorship. In: Godfroy-Genin, A.S. (Ed.), 2010, Women in Engineering and Technology Research: The PROMETEA Conference Proceedings, 443–460.
- Mavriplis, C., Heller, R. and Sorensen, C., 2011. FORWARD to professorship: mentoring for success in academia. In: Clutterbuck, D., Poulsen, K.M. (Eds.), The Diversity Mentoring Case Book, McGraw Hill.
- Mavriplis, C. and Moreau-Johnson, F., 2010. Women engineers moving up in Ontario. Proceedings of the 2010 CCWESTT Conference.
- Mavriplis, C., 2010. Growing women's leadership in Canadian aerospace. Proceedings of the 2010 Canadian Aeronautics and Space Institute ASTRO Conference.

Peer-Reviewed Journal Articles

- Heller. R.S. Yassinskaya, N., Dam, K., Shaw, M., Beil, C. Mavriplis, C., Sorensen, C., 2010. Mind the gap: women in STEM career breaks. J. Technol. Manage. Innov. 5, 140–151.

Grants and Programs

- FORWARD to Professorship: Workshop for Pre-Tenured Women and Under-represented Minorities, National Institute of General Medical Sciences Grant # 1R13GM080942-01, Rachelle S. Heller (PI), $15,000 (2007).
- The Elizabeth J. Somers Leadership Program. Available from: <http://wlp.gwu.edu/about-us> (accessed 30.10.14.).
- University of Virginia NSF ADVANCE Institutional Transformation grant: Structured Conversations and Re-imagined Spaces: Effecting Systemic Change for Women in STEM at UVA, Gertrude Fraser (PI), $3M (2011). Available from: http://advance.virginia.edu/images/ADVANCE%20Proposal.pdf (accessed 30.10.14.).
- New Approaches to Information Security Based on Group Theory, Office of Naval Research Grant 2012–2015, Delaram Kahrobaei (PI), $448,962.
- The NSERC/Pratt & Whitney Canada Chair for Women in Science and Engineering 2011–2016, $1.5M, Catherine Mavriplis, Chairholder.

CHAPTER

18

Evaluation of the
Pay It FORWARD Program

Patricia K. Freitag[1] and Catherine Mavriplis[2]

[1]Education Consulting, Potomac, MD, USA [2]Department of Mechanical
Engineering, University of Ottawa, Ottawa, Canada

OUTLINE

Introduction	290
Workshop Leadership Team Training	292
The FORWARD Workshop Model	296
Adaptations of the National Model Workshop	298
Format and Schedule	298
Recruitment	299
Evaluation Methods	300
Pay it FORWARD Results and Follow-up Questionnaire Responses	300
Formative Feedback	300
Brief Check-In Interviews	301
Participant Experiences	303
Workshop Leader Efficacy	304
Results from the Follow-up Questionnaire	307
Snapshot of the Participant Group: STEM Women at Critical Academic Career Junctures	313
Lessons Learned Through the Evaluation Process	317
Conclusion	318
References	318

INTRODUCTION

Pay It FORWARD is a project for the dissemination of successful practices in career mentoring and career advancement workshops based on a "train the trainers" model. Building on the positive outcomes and many years of experience in developing a model for advancement workshops (namely, the FORWARD to Professorship workshop) to help women and minority scholars navigate critical transition points in their science, technology, engineering, and mathematics (STEM) academic careers (see Chapter 2), the Pay It FORWARD project revised the model and offered two national workshops in the first 2 years of the project to provide a context for the professional development, training, and mentoring of new FORWARD workshop leadership teams, hereafter referred to as the FWDers (enunciated as "FORWARDers"). These FWDers would, in turn, expand the capacity of the FORWARD to Professorship workshops, career advancement mentoring, and professional networks to have broader impact in the community of STEM women and minority scholars by developing and delivering their own workshops (termed second-tier workshops in this chapter). The workshop and mentoring models are able to meet the needs of more individuals, provide access to workshops throughout the regions of the United States (and its territories), and focus on issues for special populations, disciplines, or regions.

The Pay It FORWARD logic model (Figure 18.1) shows the major inputs, activities, and intended outcomes from the 4-year project. Key to this model are the inputs of extensive experience among the leadership team members in developing and conducting career advancement workshops, their willingness to seek input from an expert group of experts in leadership development (known as ELDers) that served to advise the team in the workshop model revisions, and consistent extramural support that enabled the various stages of STEM academic careers for women and minority scholars to be better understood through mentoring and workshop interactions. From the evaluation perspective, the logic model provides a critical starting point in designing a mixed-methods evaluation approach (Clewell and Campbell, 2008). The recruitment of new workshop leadership teams and their training included a multifaceted, two-tiered approach to evaluation. First, the quality of the materials and workshop model to be disseminated were evaluated, along with the effectiveness of the new leadership team training through mixed quantitative data elements and session ratings and more qualitative information gathered from pre-workshop application materials, participant interviews, and participant observer interactions during the national workshop events. Second, the second-tier FORWARD

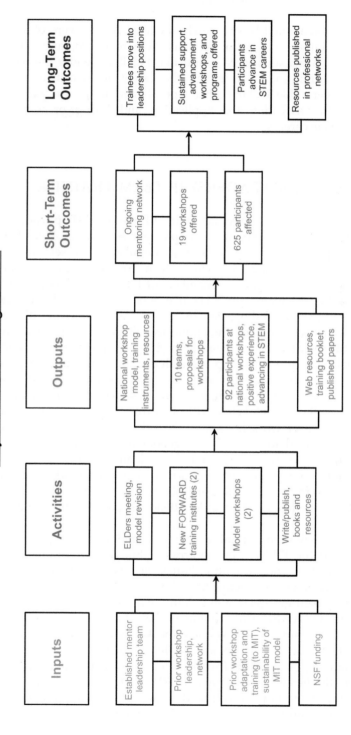

FIGURE 18.1 The Pay It FORWARD logic model.

workshops implemented by the newly trained FWDers were observed, agendas and impact ratings of sessions were reviewed, and selected interviews of participants were conducted. Finally, a wider participant survey was administered to gauge the extent to which workshop participants were able to take advantage of mentoring, use workshop information in navigating the application and hiring process, and advance in their careers.

WORKSHOP LEADERSHIP TEAM TRAINING

As a direct output of project activities, 10 new workshop leadership teams (FWDers) were prepared to implement second-tier FORWARD workshops specific to a region, special population, or set of STEM disciplines. The collaborative mentor team provided pre-workshop training institutes for up to two members of the selected FWDers (four teams in 2010, six teams in 2011) that were coordinated with two model FORWARD workshops for 45 and 47 participant (in 2010 and 2011, respectively) women and minority STEM doctoral students, postdoctoral researchers, academics, and government and industry professionals. The pre-workshop leadership training institutes engaged the trainee teams in thoughtful reflection and planning for their own workshops. The training institutes were designed to (i) provide a description of the model FORWARD to Professorship workshop and report the effects of workshops over the prior 7 to 10 years, (ii) alert trainees of the need to diversify the gender and cultural diversity of those entering and continuing STEM academic careers, (iii) clarify the expectations for minigrant support of their own workshops, and (iv) prepare them to be participant observers in the model national FORWARD workshops they would attend as part of the leadership training.

Various presentations, training activities, and mentoring conversations prepared the FWDers in the areas of budgeting, administration, workshop logistics, and evaluation issues for adapting the FORWARD workshop model and implementing the second-tier workshops with specific participant groups in mind. Additional mentoring conversations with Pay It FORWARD team members served to respond to specific questions, link teams to appropriate speaker and facilitator contacts, coach the teams on teamwork, and facilitate greater understanding of the roles and responsibilities of workshop leaders. This enabled trainees to "get into the heads" of the Pay It FORWARD project team members and to begin to see how choices and decisions were made that influenced the design and development of the model workshop.

Each team identified their own target audience for participation in their specific workshops. While all of the teams emphasized women in STEM as a focus for recruiting participants, three teams chose to conduct disciplinary-focused workshops for planetary scientists (Temple—Chapter 13), mathematics and computer scientists (City Tech—Chapter 11), and environmental scientists (Oregon State—Chapter 10). Several teams specifically sought minority women STEM scholars (Guam—Chapter 5, Toledo—Chapter 6, Virginia—Chapter 7). The remaining teams designed regional activities. While the model workshop was open to men, many second-tier workshops limited participation to women.

On-site observations were conducted throughout each of the two national model workshops held in Washington, DC, in 2010 and 2011. In addition, a workshop evaluation session was included in the leadership team training institute held prior to the workshops. In this session, FWDer team members were introduced to evaluation tools that would facilitate their roles as participant observers of the model workshop and enhance their capacity to evaluate their own workshops. They were provided with an informal interview protocol that would enable them to investigate the motivations and expectations of participants attending the workshop. They were also asked to observe, in depth, one of the workshop sessions and share their observations with the other teams during the post-workshop debriefing. All the FWDer teams were encouraged to use or adapt the session-by-session feedback forms in their own workshops as well.

All 10 of the FWDer teams trained in 2010 and 2011 successfully implemented second-tier FORWARD workshops based on the national workshop model. Each team was able to plan and implement their workshop in the year following their initial training. Table 18.1 provides a comparison of the agenda elements of the various workshops in terms of the national model framework. There is an extensive integrity of the core components of the model mentoring process and workshop in the adapted second-tier workshops. In addition, two of the four FWDer teams trained in the first cohort (2010) and four out of six in the second cohort (2011) revised and offered six additional workshops. Two FWDer teams applied for additional funds to conduct a third workshop and have been successful in garnering other funds to support and sustain their work. Two other teams have sustained the work begun in their workshops by institutionalizing program elements through alignment with professional associations and disciplinary annual meetings or through providing additional workshops with fees to cover the costs. Overall, the two national workshops and 19 FWDer workshops included more than 625 women and minority participants over the 4-year award period. Overall, six of the trainee leadership teams (or some members

TABLE 18.1 FORWARD to Professorship Workshop Session Topics: Adopted and Adapted Sessions Offered by MIT and the Second-Tier FWDer Trainee Teams

National Model Workshop Session Topics	MIT	Arizona State	University of Guam	University of Toledo	University of Virginia	Case Western Reserve University	Oklahoma State	Oregon State	City Tech	Brookhaven and Stony Brook	Temple University
Communication techniques	✓	✓	✓	✓	✓	✓			✓		
Keynote speaker		✓	✓	✓			✓	✓	✓		✓
Negotiation strategies and skills	✓	✓		✓	✓			✓			
Personal and professional career plan		✓	✓	✓		✓					✓
Research and grant resources		✓	✓	✓		✓			✓	✓	✓
Service—balancing commitments			✓	✓			✓				
Teaching practices and tips		✓	✓	✓			✓		✓		✓
Tenure overview	✓			✓		✓	✓	✓		✓	
Work/life balance	✓	✓		✓		✓	✓	✓	✓	✓	✓
Writing—application materials and proposals			✓	✓					✓	✓	✓

Topics added by second-tier workshops								
Careers								✓
Career challenges						✓		
Collaborations	✓		✓	✓				
Field work								
Interview process	✓							
Lab management			✓					✓
Leadership panel					✓	✓		
Management skills				✓			✓	
Mentorship/network	✓			✓				
Open discussions				✓				
Research poster session	✓					✓		
Time management							✓	
Values							✓	

of those teams) are continuing this work to expand the number of and support the advancement of women and minority scholars in academic STEM careers.

Pay It FORWARD has had a direct impact on the 10 trainee FWDer teams. A total of 23 women directly participated in the leadership training institute at Gallaudet University, and an additional 20–30 members participated on the local FWDer teams for planning and implementing the new FORWARD workshops at their respective sites. There were also 92 model workshop participants served directly by the Pay It FORWARD mentors, session speakers, and facilitators. This direct impact includes the ELDers group that contributed advice used for revising and refining the model prior to the first model workshop. Secondary impacts of the Pay It FORWARD project expand greatly as the trainee leaders met with expanded workshop planning and implementation teams for their second-tier workshops. There were more than 50 academic faculty, staff, and administrators directly involved as FWDer team members for the second-tier workshops (both cohorts), and many additional participants if the presenters and facilitators of the second and third-tier workshop sessions are taken into account. Nearly all of the FORWARD workshops connected the host campus administrators, faculty deans, and department chairs in welcoming, supporting, and attending the workshops.

THE FORWARD WORKSHOP MODEL

Selected from over 200 applicants, the 92 national workshop participants of 2010 and 2011 were actively engaged in a mentoring and career development process that helped to build professional and collegial networks, addressed key issues in STEM careers, and brought them face to face with nationally recognized female and minority leaders from an array of STEM fields. The participants in each of the two national model workshops (as well as the participant observer trainee leaders) provided overwhelmingly positive responses to every session and to the workshop overall, as evidenced by these typical comments on evaluation forms collected at the workshops:

> This is so much more than we get in our institution! There should be a course or something, maybe that's not the best way, but everyone should be able to access this information.
> I am already thinking of ways I can share this information with the others [at my institution, implied] that didn't apply or come! They really need this...this would be great for them. I will definitely recommend this to other students that I know.

The groups of participants seemed to "gel" and value deeply the expertise and experiences shared by the presenters and facilitators. In fact, in the national workshops, between the number of invited speakers, trainee FWDers, and the project leaders, the ratio of STEM leaders and near-peer mentors to participants was approximately 1:2. This meant that nearly every participant was able to identify a peer group, as well as a specific role model or mentor during the workshop, and have time to interact with those individuals in a meaningful way.

The model workshop included many different and participatory session formats that were noted by the participants as important to sustaining their engagement with the content. Pre-conference reflective prompts and writing samples were very effective in bringing issues and questions to the forefront. Participants were ready to engage in dialogue with others and benefited from opportunities to share their own experiences. Similarly, the model workshops created a "safe" place for everyone to share their personal and professional experiences openly with one another. This was key to the success of the workshops. Participants noted over and over again the impact of having so many women scientists in one place and at one time, with the opportunity to address serious issues of career development, perceived barriers, and effective strategies for advancement.

It is important to note that the range of session formats offered in the national model workshops included significant time for participants to interact with one another and with the presenter or facilitator as part of the session. The sessions ranged from presentations from keynote speakers who shared important and personal aspects of their own career path to panels of three to five experts, followed by extended time for interaction with the audience through question-and-answer periods and group discussions. Additional interactive panel sessions with participant questions peppered throughout, role-playing exercises, small table-facilitated discussions, and personal reflection and writing activities ensured that participants were actively engaged in problem solving, sharing, and peer mentoring. Many of the participants rated the substance and format of these sessions as very high (4–5 out of a possible 5 points) and wrote in qualitative comments about how engaging the workshop was and how effectively it captured and held their attention. The impact of having so many female scientists in one place and the fact that the workshop was a "safe" environment that encouraged interaction and mutual engagement was echoed over and over again in the qualitative comment sections of the evaluations. For example:

> I really enjoyed talking in groups, learning through real examples. It was useful to also have everyone to talk a little in the large group, created a safe and welcome environment.

ADAPTATIONS OF THE NATIONAL MODEL WORKSHOP

Format and Schedule

Despite participating in a two-and-a-half day experience of the national model workshop, most of the FWDer teams shortened their own workshops to less than two days. Unfortunately, few of the teams chose to reduce the content structure of the workshop to correspond with the shortened time frame. The model emphases on research, teaching, and service were kept, as well as sessions on writing, communication, and work/life balance. Several innovations were offered at some of the second-tier workshops, including "Starting and Managing a Laboratory," "Comparing University and Community/Liberal Arts College Careers," and "Engaging Dialogue Across Difference" (see the second page of Table 18.1); and in one case, specific discussion was fostered among minority participants to facilitate candid and open dialogue.

The shorter duration of the second-tier workshops was noted by participants at these workshops in their evaluations. Quite a few participants felt that a longer time frame or multiple meetings would be beneficial. Another unintended consequence of the abbreviated schedules was that the interactive nature of several of the sessions reverted to a more directed lecture or panel presentation format, leaving little time for participant questions. Since the participants had less opportunity to interact with one another, the strength and continuity of the professional networking resulting from these workshops may also have been affected.

In fact, the evaluation summary reports of the second-tier workshops indicated that the participants would have appreciated a somewhat longer duration or a less full agenda of topics to allow for more networking and interactivity among the participants:

> Yes, absolutely, I would recommend. So many terrific sessions, all I could recommend would be more time.
> We ran out of time to discuss our plans so I didn't get the chance to discuss mine.
> These panel members represented a wide range which was very helpful, but also left many open questions. Perhaps a longer discussion would be valuable. And also having groups collect by table to discuss specific challenges within each represented category (married/two-career couple, quick advancement, mother, single).

This was supported in several of the evaluation responses of the national model workshops as well. Informed by the first training cycle, the Pay It FORWARD project team placed increased emphasis on "active learning" strategies in the subsequent training institute.

One successful and potentially sustainable alternative implemented by one of the leadership teams includes "piggybacking" on the national meeting for the discipline as a pre-session of the conference. This strategy reduces the overall expenses for travel, lodging, and meals, while reaping the benefits of a wider audience and potentially expanded participation. However, most of the FWDer teams chose to offer workshops at various times throughout the academic year rather than in the late spring/early summer period of the national workshops. One consequence of these choices was that the planning time for adapting the workshops was significantly shortened. In some cases, it was a struggle to recruit participants and have them actually attend the full workshop. Since many of the second-tier workshops were held on home campuses, there were often participants who came in and out of the workshop due to competing priorities for their time on campus. Time stresses and leadership team dynamics may also have been exacerbated by choosing to conduct the workshops during the academic year.

Recruitment

The most effective recruitment strategies for participants varied somewhat by career stage. First and foremost, the funding to provide travel support, lodging, meals, and a "free" workshop to participants was by far the most significant factor in gaining participation at all levels, as indicated by this comment:

> WOW, it is hard now to assess after the workshop. The application process was surprisingly easy, almost too easy, I was like asking if this is for real. But the information sounded relevant, and it was funded. Oh yeah, the fact that it was funded for me was significant. I probably would have never even considered it, if it wasn't funded.

After that, graduate students were predominantly recruited by faculty mentors or other students who recommended the workshop to them specifically. This highlights the importance of faculty mentors who are engaged with the wider STEM community, aware of development opportunities, and seeking to link their own students with resources of the wider STEM community. Pre-tenure faculty were also encouraged by faculty colleagues to participate but were also more likely to have initially heard of the opportunity through professional association listservs and announcements, or by actively seeking professional development opportunities. Thinking broadly in terms of professional associations, special-interest groups, and divisions of major STEM associations can be key to reaching early career and pre-tenure faculty. Finally, the postdoctoral participants had the widest range of interests, expectations, and means of finding out about the workshops. The postdoctoral researchers took a great deal of personal initiative in finding the workshops, applying, and participating.

EVALUATION METHODS

The framework for the evaluation of the Pay It FORWARD project stems from the logic model and incorporates several key data elements. Qualitative approaches of participant observation in the national workshops and training institutes, along with interviews of trainees and participants, provided rich anecdotes and insights that were useful in the further development of the career mentoring model and adapting the model workshop to new audiences in new settings.

Short session-feedback forms were used and adapted by the trainee FWDer teams for use in their own workshops. Participants were generous with their comments and responded to the various sessions with overwhelmingly positive ratings (4–5 out of a possible 5). Examples of the questions on these forms can be found in the appendices of this text.

Individual participants were interviewed briefly toward the end of the national workshops and at the trainee workshops observed by the evaluator. Making contact with individual participants in this way enlivened the understanding of some of the session feedback and follow-up questionnaire data. Trainee FWDer teams were also debriefed and wrote brief workshop reports of their work, which were helpful in identifying issues and innovations to the career mentoring model.

Finally, a follow-up questionnaire was developed to evaluate the impact of the workshops and their career mentoring components, as well as to explore climate issues for women in STEM. In 2013, the questionnaire was sent to national workshop participants, a larger contact list of prior workshop attendees, and to the FWDer trainee leaders to disseminate to their respective second-tier workshop participants. Although the response rates varied widely among the second-tier workshop participants, overall the close to 200 respondents paint a picture of the positive impact of the Pay It FORWARD project.

PAY IT FORWARD RESULTS AND FOLLOW-UP QUESTIONNAIRE RESPONSES

Formative Feedback

Participants responded in daily evaluation forms to questions appropriate to the program of the day regarding the application process, pre-workshop communications, the quality of the facilities, and the content and quality of presentation of the sessions that day. The responses were qualitative statements written directly on the forms provided in their packets and left on the tables at the end of each day. Generally, participants were generous with their comments after the first half-day and into the first full day. However, by the second day and closer to the end of the workshop, the comments were more concise or at times not given at all. Overwhelmingly, the responses speak to the positive value of the workshop, the well-organized flow, the "amazing" and "awesome" qualities of the presenters, and the intensity and relevance of the experience to the participant's career stage. At every stage, the participants expressed amazement—perhaps even relief—at being in a workshop with so many women scholars in STEM. For most participants, presenters, and facilitators, it was indeed a unique experience. Comments like the following express their enthusiasm:

> It is so amazing to realize I am not alone!
> Excellent speaker! I learned so much and was truly engaged!
> Getting some feedback on effective teaching methods was one of my expectations coming to this workshop, and I really enjoyed the presentation...
> This will stick with me, probably forever.
> Awesome! Very helpful, really appreciated the personal comments on my materials. So many good tips!

While there were some less positive comments scattered among the responses to each session, they seemed to focus on a mismatch between the career stage of the individual and the most relevant career stage for the content. In a sense, the participant did not see the material as relevant because they were not in the particular situation or dealing with the specific issue. To wit, compare the following responses:

> This was too field-specific, I found it boring.

versus

> It was pretty general and most info available on websites. The small group Q & A was very useful and more tailored to participant needs. I would allow more time for Q & A and use handouts to cover the basics.

versus

> Yes, I got very good ideas about proposal writing. I also like having the opportunity to discuss with the invited speakers.

All three of the previous quotes were speaking of the government research panel.

Brief Check-In Interviews

In addition to the daily feedback forms, the external evaluator conducted short interviews with six randomly selected participants from each national workshop. The participants were asked explicitly the following questions:

- "How did you hear about the workshop, to apply?"
- "Where are you in your career? Why were you interested in attending?"
- "Are there any critical events in your career that bring you to this point?"
- "Which aspect of the workshop has had an impact on you?"

Nearly everyone interviewed started by enthusiastically stating how wonderful it was to be in a workshop with so many accomplished women, women in STEM, and women who had so many "similar" experiences (apparently in "male-dominated" fields). For example, "Thank you for giving me the opportunity to speak with you, this has been great so far. Ask me anything."

Of the 12 interviews conducted, two participants were alerted to the opportunity for the workshop after the deadline to apply had closed. They submitted applications anyway and were invited. Six of the interviewees were sent an email by an advisor or faculty member at their institution and encouraged to apply. Two participants indicated that they had been looking for a professional development opportunity and this one (i) met during the summer, (ii) was nearly free or local for them, and (iii) addressed something they needed. One participant was invited to apply by a friend in the same discipline, but at a different institution, who wanted this respondent to take part as well. The final interviewee had had several career changes and difficulties and wanted to participate specifically in a STEM career workshop. These insights highlight the importance of personal and professional networks in identifying and getting the word out about professional opportunities. Most participants indicated that they first heard of the workshop through a professional list-serv email or news blast or were directly referred by a friend.

Each of the interviewees expressed being at a key decision point in their careers and needing information to help them through the decision making and transition. Several faced personal relationship decisions that could affect their job prospects or whether they would commit to an academic position given their relationship work/life balance issue. Three others had just started in a new position and found it most helpful to be at a workshop with other women who were at different stages in their careers, "even though they are from so many different fields." The rest were postdoctoral researchers. Surprisingly, the postdoctoral researchers by and large did not see themselves as academics, even the ones at research universities (Carnegie classification). They seemed to be the most varied in terms of their career paths. Some indicated that they were "seriously considering" whether or not to enter academia. Another individual put herself on an expected time line of 5 years and was eager to seek a tenure-track position somewhere (implying anywhere that she would like to live, e.g., large coastal city) whenever she could over the next year or two, before her postdoctoral appointment ran out.

The participants interviewed were asked to identify a session that had a particular impact on them. Interestingly, they selected different sessions:

Teaching! I really struggle with that one, with so many students. —*First year assistant professor*

Negotiation, for sure. I just had an interview before I came here and am really hopeful about that opportunity. If I AM offered that opportunity, I will know what to ask for…. I don't expect I'll get much, but before I wouldn't even have asked. —*Postdoctoral researcher, applying for tenure-track positions*

Communications. She was a terrific presenter. I never really thought about it that way. I am not always confident in communicating. I will think about my dress more when I am teaching too. —*Doctoral candidate/teaching assistant*

Subsequent interviews at the second-tier workshops were very similar and showed similar diversity of responses to the workshop sessions. Again, the overall impression of the responses revealed how unique it was to have so many women in science in the same place and at the same time to discuss the similarity of their experiences. They valued the experience and were very positive about the workshops. In the initial interviews, participants did not seem reticent to share their personal stories but may have not had time to process any "quick" critique of the workshop they were attending. They were on the whole enthusiastic and somewhat overwhelmed from the experience:

Meeting women from all STEM fields in various levels was super useful!

Participant Experiences

The evaluation responses reflected a diversity of participant experiences regarding expectations and key takeaway messages from the workshops. Students (finishing doctoral candidates) had rather general expectations across the broad array of agenda items, eager to take it all in without having very focused personal needs (i.e., predominantly a skill-building interest). Postdoctoral responses and expectations showed the greatest variety, ranging from rather general-interest topics to specifically considering how to maintain their research and affiliation with research universities, and whether a tenure-track position would be the "right" move for them as a next step. Several postdoctoral researcher responses to the question asking to identify key takeaways from the workshop experience are provided here:

> Transitioning from completing your PhD to a faculty or research position can be extremely difficult. However, the workshop leaders (May 2011) were all extremely inspiring and supportive and have demonstrated that it can be done. So my biggest "take-away" from this workshop is that there is hope and that it is possible to succeed as a woman in science, as demonstrated by the workshop leaders. I came away from the workshop being very inspired. The workshop leaders were great role models and examples that we can learn from and follow.
> I felt empowered, but in the end my job search did not lead to a permanent position. My biggest takeaway is that there's a lot of room for shaping the type of experience you want from the academic world (salary, starting package, work/life balance, etc), but you have to negotiate, network, and articulate those plans properly to be successful. Decide what you want and ask for it, otherwise you probably won't get it. Colleagues

New faculty and pre-tenure faculty responses reflected greater interests in teaching and research productivity and work/life balance. Associate professor responses were fairly evenly spread across the workshop sessions in their responses. While senior faculty benefited from attending the workshop, they were also pleased to offer their assistance to others in hopes of making a difference. They were reminded of the importance of mentoring and role models in their own careers (personal communication, 2011) and contributing intentionally to supporting others, as reflected in several of their comments:

> A reminder of how important and useful it is for those of us who have "made it" to offer a shoulder and a hand up to younger academics. It is tremendously gratifying to be involved in this type of initiative.
> I was a speaker on a panel about work/family balance. I found that many women in the room were in a similar boat to me. It was important to share different pathways with participants.
> Energy of participants. Renew faith in the community, that there are people out there who are concerned about diversity, hiring of women and URM [Under-Represented Minorities] etc in the community. Learning perspectives of deans, chairs, etc. Learning perspectives from faculty in other departments and at other institutions than my own.

Workshop Leader Efficacy

The preliminary trainee efficacy questionnaire data showed that the members of both trainee FWDer cohorts started out as confident in their facilitation skills, self-identified as comfortable working in teams and calling on colleagues and administrators to serve as presenters, and were good communicators. The lowest scores in the efficacy instrument were in the areas of adequate resources: their own time allocated to the effort, additional student or assistant help that might be needed, and/or specific materials to use in delivering the workshop. Individuals rated themselves very highly in the aspects of teamwork, change agency, and setting direction.

However, one-on-one informal interactions with FWDer team members at the second-tier workshops observed revealed that teams "got the job done" using a variety of different strategies. One team clearly delineated the role of each member and met infrequently, relying on each individual to do the assigned job. Several members of this team expressed some dissatisfaction with the process. They indicated a willingness and desire to be involved with a more collaborative effort where the interactions among the team members may have stimulated new ideas and alternative approaches to the workshop. They indicated that when this was "allowed" to happen, early in the planning stages, the meetings "took a lot more time than expected," but they felt they were more engaging and very worthwhile. However, as time pressure mounted and the workshop date approached, several team members indicated that other team members took a more directive and authoritative stance rather than continuing the initially more collaborative approach. Perhaps this is what they felt was needed to create a good workshop. In the end, the workshop went very well, and the evaluations from participants were largely positive. During the course of the workshop, the participants were listened to and a closed-door session of only the minority women participants and leaders was added. This was deemed reasonable, but it did exclude several of the six team members, the evaluator, and some of the participants as well.

A different team of four persons, with two members at one institution, let those team members who were co-located take the lead. They prepared most of the recruitment materials, dealt with the site logistics, and were able to garner the most institutional support. This may have been due in part to their administrative leadership positions at the institution and being outside traditional faculty roles. One consequence of this management strategy was that recruitment materials were distributed from the lead institution, and recruitment was less successful at the other schools. The initial recruitment efforts did not produce a large enough pool of applicants. A decision was made to reach beyond the region and expand the workshop focus to be more issue-oriented and less about establishing and sustaining a regional network of women in STEM among the collaborating campuses. Other differences stemmed directly from the limited experience with, and partial understanding of, the facilitation model (personal communication, 2012). A second consequence of this approach was that the team only met to be trained in the facilitation process to be used to conduct the workshop immediately preceding the workshop. Then, during the workshop, various team members interpreted and implemented their training somewhat differently when facilitating their small groups. Some of the differences seemed to be due to individual personalities, perhaps different underlying institutional cultures, or individual communication styles. Still, this second-tier workshop stood out for the depth and quality of the interpersonal interactions, shared stories, and personal/professional support for the participants. The facilitation process of the workshop overall produced an uncommon depth and candor in the table conversations and working sessions.

One other workshop benefited from a staff member who took the time to lead the effort, convene meetings as needed, and enlist her students' assistance in handling logistics. This workshop also chose to capitalize on an existing college (within the university) seminar series and professional association activity. These brought added resources to the effort, enabling this second-tier workshop to use the FORWARD minigrant resources to enhance the level of the outreach efforts and presentations. Consequently, there is strong institutional support to sustain the workshop into the third tier; the workshop is now the "baby" of that staff member and reliant on her continued student support; the leadership team has collapsed to solely her network of contacts. She reports that she readily calls on the original team members to identify resource people and presenters, but most likely, the workshops will continue to be given every other year so that incoming students may be included as core participants. Future third-tier efforts may lead to insights regarding a "desirable" leadership team configuration that would make ongoing workshop planning and implementation cost effective and sustainable.

Overall, there has been remarkably high implementation fidelity to the model FORWARD workshop. Participants in the second-tier workshops are having positive experiences, developing an understanding of mentor/mentee relationships, and establishing peer networks across disciplines. Follow-up interviews and the large-scale survey of participants help to understand the longitudinal impacts of these experiences.

The Pay It FORWARD team has reached its goal of successfully training and supporting 10 FORWARD workshop leadership teams (FWDers), who, in turn, have offered 16 of the 10−20 anticipated second-tier workshops. In addition, several sites intend to complete or have completed (for an overall total of 19) the third-tier workshops with supporting funds and then sustain and institutionalize their workshops at their respective institutions. Toward this goal, nearly all of the second-tier workshops invited and succeeded in having institutional administrators attend and support their workshops.

Results from the Follow-up Questionnaire

All together, 197 participants from the national FORWARD workshops (2003–2011) and the second-tier workshops (2011–2013) filled out the online questionnaire; and 166 of these divulged their gender: 95% female, 5% male.

In the Pay It FORWARD project, "diversity" came to be measured in many different ways. First, of course, is the racial and ethnic diversity of the participants. Table 18.2 shows the percentage participation of those who responded to the questionnaire: overall, for the two national workshops of 2010 and 2011, and for the second-tier workshops. The proportion of each ethnicity within the minority respondents group is indicated in the last column. While all the workshops were overwhelmingly successful in recruiting female participants, the second-tier workshops showed higher participation rates among several minority groups than at the national workshop. The more focused recruitment by these somewhat smaller workshops proved effective in combination with their regional location proximate to particular ethnic minority groups. Several of the trainee-led workshops had approximately 50% minority

TABLE 18.2   Percentage of Representation of Ethnic Diversity in Pay It FORWARD Participant Follow-up Questionnaire Respondents (Willing to Disclose)

Ethnicity	All responses 2003–2012 ($n = 160$)	National workshops 2010, 2011 ($n = 54$)	Second-tier workshops 2011, 2012 ($n = 52$)	Distribution among minorities ($n = 55$)
African American	8%	19%	4%	22%
American Indian	0%	0%	0%	0%
Asian	16%	14%	14%	45%
Black (other than African American)	3%	7%	4%	9%
Hispanic/ Latina/Latino	8%	0%	18%	24%
White	65%	60%	60%	N/A

The last column gives the distribution of the minority respondents into the different ethnic groups (excluding white).

TABLE 18.3   Variation in Major Disciplines of Pay It FORWARD Participant Follow-up Questionnaire Respondents (Total n = 177)

Engineering and computer science (n = 66)	Physical and mathematical sciences (n = 39)	Life and medical sciences (n = 43)	Earth and planetary sciences (n = 22)	Social sciences or other (n = 7)
Aerospace	Biochemistry	Anatomy	Astronomy	Counseling
Biomedical	Biophysics	Biology	Atmospheric	Geography
Chemical	Biotechnology	Ecology	Science	Global Health
Civil	Chemistry	Epidemiology	Earth Science	Law
Computer	Environmental	Medical	Environmental	Life Coaching
Cognitive	Chemistry	Sciences	Sciences	Policy
Education	Mathematics	Neuroscience	Geoinformatics	Philosophy
Electrical	Physics	Nutrition	Geology	Psychology
Environmental	Statistics	Pathology	Geophysics	
Industrial		Pharmacology	Geosciences	
Materials		Physiology	Hydrology	
Mechanical		Plant	Marine Science	
Naval Systems		Virology	Oceanography	
		Speech		
		Pathology		

participation, but only a few respondents chose to submit to the follow-up questionnaire sample. For the Toledo workshop "When and Where We Enter" (2011), the leadership team found it very challenging to recruit and engage African American women STEM academics in the Midwest. They expanded their recruitment region, sent out second and third announcements to participants, and extended application deadlines to attract enough participants to fill the workshop.

Second, diversity in terms of STEM disciplines was broader among the participants at the national workshop than at the second-tier workshops. Overall, more than 50 separate disciplines were identified by the participants, with the largest representation across all fields of engineering (n = 66) and in the life sciences (n = 43). Responses from physical and mathematical sciences (n = 39), and earth and planetary sciences (n = 22), may reflect the disciplinary emphasis of several of the second-tier workshops. Table 18.3 provides the distribution of major field and subdisciplines identified.

Finally, the career stage demographic for each of the workshops was similar, with the highest proportion of participants in the doctoral candidate stage and fewer tenured faculty participants than expected (see Table 18.4). Notably, minority respondents were predominantly doctoral candidates. This is significant, as it shows the potential to retain and advance women and minority candidates by intervening with career mentoring opportunities early on in their careers. Note also that since

TABLE 18.4   Percentage of Participation by Career Stage at Workshop for Pay It FORWARD Follow-up Questionnaire Respondents

Career stage at workshop	All responses 2003–2012 ($n = 197$)	National workshops 2010, 2011 ($n = 155$)	Second-tier workshops 2011, 2012 ($n = 48$)	Distribution among minorities ($n = 55$)
Doctoral candidate	43%	41%	33%	44%
Postdoctoral researcher	25%	24%	21%	27%
Part-time, non-tenure-track	4%	6%	8%	2%
Assistant professor	15%	17%	8%	18%
Associate professor	5%	4%	13%	7%
Professor	4%	4%	10%	0%
Government/ industry	4%	4%	6%	0%

Some respondents attended several workshops. The last column gives the distribution of the minority respondents into the different career stage groups.

some second-tier workshops focused on minorities, these more recent participants were still in graduate school at the time of the survey. The second-tier workshops had a higher proportion of senior faculty participating (or at least responding to the questionnaire), which may help advance the mentoring model on a regional basis. Since the second-tier workshops admitted more advanced career stage participants than the national workshops, the broad spectrum of career stages is an expected outcome. Similar results are clear in the age demographic comparison as well (see Table 18.5).

Participants have moved ahead in their careers since the workshop. Figure 18.2 illustrates the shift from earlier career stages of graduate student and postdoctoral researcher (68% at the time of their workshop attendance) to assistant and associate (and even some full professor) positions (54% at the time of the questionnaire) over the course of the existence of the FORWARD workshops. A total of 66% of the follow-up questionnaire respondents have applied to new positions since attending the workshop, and more than 50% have accepted new positions or advanced their careers since the workshop. The number of interviews ranged from 0 to 12, averaging 3.3 per person. While at the time they

TABLE 18.5   Age Bracket Demographic in Percentage of Pay It FORWARD Follow-up Questionnaire Respondents

Age bracket	All responses 2003–2012 (*n* = 167)	National workshops 2010, 2011 (*n* = 144)	Second-tier workshops 2011, 2012 (*n* = 40)	Distribution among minorities (*n* = 55)
21–30	15%	10%	28%	20%
31–40	58%	57%	42%	57%
41–50	19%	24%	18%	15%
>50	8%	8%	12%	8%

The age reported is at the time of the response. For some respondents, the workshop attended had been as early as 9 years prior, for some others as recently as in the prior year. The last column gives the distribution of the minority respondents into the different age brackets.

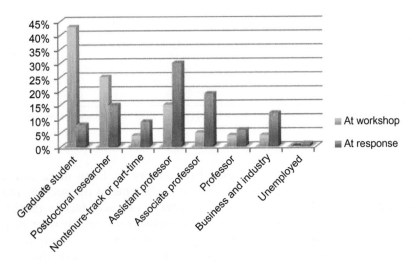

FIGURE 18.2   Career progression over the course of the existence of the FORWARD workshops: Career stage at the time of workshop attendance (2003–2012) and at the time of response to the questionnaire (2013) for Pay It FORWARD follow-up.

attended a workshop, only 8% of the participants were tenured, at the time of the survey, more than 21% reported being tenured. An interesting statistic—which is worth investigating as to why these choices were made—is that the number who reported being professional scientists but not being in academia rose from 4% to 11.5%. Non-academic jobs include such titles as research associate and project manager.

For minorities, the numbers are similar. The 72% graduate student and postdoctoral group at the time of the workshop changed to 54% assistant, associate, and full professor at the time of the questionnaire.

For Blacks, African Americans, and Hispanics, many of whom were in the later, second-tier workshops and hence are less advanced in their careers, the numbers are somewhat lower, consistent with the time frame. This was also correlated by their age group. The 75% graduate student and postdoctoral group at the time of the workshop changed to 39% assistant, associate, and full professor at the time of the questionnaire.

Negotiation skills training stood out as an important aspect of the national workshops. The training included role-playing exercises that have been found to be very useful in helping participants to internalize and change their own behaviors. The overall ratings for the national workshop respondents and those from the minority participants showed that both groups responded very positively (rating 3–5 out of a possible 5) in terms of the impact of these session activities on the hiring process, as shown in Table 18.6.

Each of the respondents was asked to rate their frequency of use of the workshop components after the workshop, with a rating of 1 being the lowest and 5 the highest. Table 18.7 presents the percentage by career stage at the time of the questionnaire for the two highest ratings (4 and 5) for each of the response groups. These data show that the following sessions had the greatest impact on participants: (i) work/life balance, (ii) developing a personal and professional career plan, (iii) negotiation strategies and skills, (iv) teaching practices and tips, and (v) balancing service commitments. These varied somewhat by career stage, however. The graduate students rated the personal and

TABLE 18.6 Importance of Negotiating Skills on the Hiring Process for National Workshop and Minority Groups Reported in the Percentage of Sample of Pay It FORWARD Follow-up Questionnaire Respondents Rating 3–5 of a Possible 5 Points

Negotiating skills	National workshop ($n = 109$)	Minority responses ($n = 36$)
Overall hiring process	83%	80%
Negotiating release for research	67%	68%
Negotiating for startup funds	70%	62%
Negotiating for staff/students	64%	60%
Confidence in meeting faculty	82%	81%
Confidence in interactions with search committee	80%	75%
Partner/spouse employment negotiation	71%	59%
Success in obtaining position	75%	78%

Percentages calculated on those responding anything other than "Not Applicable."

TABLE 18.7 Workshop Component Rating Percentage by Position for Ratings 4 and 5 out of 5 with Regard to Frequent Use by Pay It FORWARD Follow-up Questionnaire Respondents

Component	Doctoral candidate (n = 14)	Postdoctoral (n = 23)	PT/non-TT[a] (n = 14)	Assistant professor (n = 48)	Associate professor (n = 34)	Full professor (n = 9)	Industry government (n = 17)
Peer network	33%	52%	27%	32%	31%	20%	29%
Mentoring resources	36%	23%	27%	22%	41%	33%	0%
Negotiation strategies and skills	27%	36%	50%	56%	39%	43%	25%
Navigating dual careers	17%	31%	0%	34%	26%	14%	31%
Personal and professional career plan	50%	39%	43%	51%	38%	29%	25%
Work/life balance	36%	48%	21%	56%	48%	25%	47%
Online resources	17%	19%	17%	18%	5%	0%	8%
Research and grant resources	25%	38%	43%	38%	15%	29%	22%
Teaching practices and tips	23%	61%	21%	39%	46%	14%	10%
Balancing service commitments	21%	60%	25%	56%	48%	17%	23%

[a] Part-time, non-tenure-track.

Percentages calculated on those responding anything other than "Not Applicable."

professional career plan highest (50%). Many of the postdoctoral researchers rated the peer-networking aspect of the workshops highly (52%), and this was echoed in their interviews and observed interactions throughout the workshops. They also found the sessions on teaching (61%) and service (60%) especially useful. Work/life balance seemed to consume this segment of the participants as well (48%), as they were struggling with temporary positions that demand mobility at a time in their lives when they are starting to plan for stability. Assistant professors were most affected by the negotiation skills component (56%), with also strong impact from the work/life balance (56%), service (56%), and personal and professional career plan (51%) sessions. Associate professors also appreciated the work/life balance sessions (48%). Surprisingly, they continued to hold an interest in the teaching session (46%), or perhaps they found the tips useful in attaining their positions. Finally, those in industry or government had reduced levels of interest in all areas except work/life balance (47%). Predictably, the part-time and non-tenure-track professors did not find the teaching sessions particularly useful (21%), as they probably spend much of their time teaching, but they rated the negotiation sessions highly (50%), as well as the research grants and resources session (43%). This probably points to their desire to obtain a tenure-track or funded position. While most activities were highly rated, the online resource library seemed to be of little interest or usefulness to participants.

Overall, the use of the project-gathered Web resources is disappointing. There may be many reasons for this, including lack of clear communication regarding the Web address and the fact that the second-tier workshops frequently established their own "go-to" sites for their own participants. Establishing a central repository requires not only gathering materials and getting permissions for postings, but also cultivating an audience to use and expand the usefulness of these resources. Networking through the different levels of dissemination projects is challenging work, as is evaluating how these networks are established, develop, and persist.

Snapshot of the Participant Group: STEM Women at Critical Academic Career Junctures

The follow-up questionnaire offered a unique opportunity to study a population of STEM women at critical junctures of the academic pipeline. 197 respondents to the questionnaire, who had attended FORWARD workshops in the 10-year period of 2003–2013, answered questions on their career progression, their work habits related to tenure-track professorship, their mentoring, and their perception of the climate in STEM. The respondent group is predominantly female, and 95% of those 166 willing to divulge their gender were female.

As indicated by Figure 18.2, the progress of these cohorts of doctoral STEM women through the ranks is encouraging. A total of 113 respondents replied to the questions on new positions attained since attendance at the workshop; 79% of these had received an offer, 77% had accepted an offer, 62% found the workshop had prepared them to negotiate salary, and 56% to negotiate startup funds. Overall, 55% felt the workshop had adequately prepared them for negotiation. These numbers were higher for the national workshop respondents, as negotiation played a more prominent part in those workshops than in most second-tier workshops: 86%, 84%, 64%, 56%, and 57% respectively.

The FORWARD workshop participants seem to be fully engaging in the activities of tenure-track professor roles. As a group, these participants are highly productive. More than 39% report becoming a principal investigator on a research grant since the workshop and 51% have extramural funding. In the 3 years prior to the questionnaire response, 78% had submitted research grant proposals, ranging from 0 to 30, averaging out to 4 per person for the 3-year period. Since 23% of the respondents were still graduate students or postdoctoral researchers, this number is consistent with career stage. 88% had submitted journal papers ranging from 0 to 20, averaging out to 5 per person for the 3-year period. On average, 7 conference papers had been submitted in this same period.

Asked to report time spent on grant-funded research, respondents reported values ranging from 0–100%, or even "90% of waking hours." Assistant professors ranged from 0–100%, with an average of 35% of their time. Associate professors also ranged from 0–100%, with an average of 35% of their time. Full professors ranged from 15%–80%, with an average of 38% of their time. As expected, doctoral students and postdoctoral researchers spend more time on grant-funded research: 74% and 61% respectively.

Mentoring was seen as a common practice. A total of 36% of respondents report that mentoring is available in their department; 55% have established informal mentoring relationships within the university, and 36% outside; 43% are active in a professional society related to their discipline; 54% feel the FORWARD workshop helped them see the need for mentoring; and 69% serve as informal mentors themselves.

At the national workshops, 29% of respondents indicated that they had taken a leave from work or reduction in time worked due to family reasons, with minority responses showing 35.5% having taken leave. For the second-tier workshop participants, the percent reporting was significantly higher, at 50%. Concerning the work-time adjustment for these leaves, of those reporting, approximately 15% said they experienced lack of support and resistance from within their departments, while 68% found their departments supportive and 17% found them helpful. Over half (54%) marked this question "Not Applicable."

Further to this climate issue, participants were directly asked about their perceptions of the climate for a number of categories, as shown in Table 18.8. Doctoral students have a positive or very positive view (69% combined) of the climate for women. This drops significantly at the postdoctoral level (38%) and the part-time or non-tenure-track level (33%), before rising for assistant professor positions (72%). At the associate and full professor levels, the positive view experiences another significant drop, to 45% and 44%, respectively. Respondents in industry have a better impression of the climate for women (78%). While many respondents indicated "Not Applicable," and the remaining ones were mostly neutral to the question of climate for faculty of color, the impression is certainly that the climate is worse for faculty of color than for women, except in the postdoctoral and industry and government groups. The climate is generally viewed positively for collaboration, research, graduate students, and disposition toward students, although postdoctoral researchers were less positive for students. Postdoctoral researchers also thought teaching was not valued (15%). The climate for mentoring was not seen as particularly positive by any group, especially not postdoctoral researchers (27%). The climate for collegiality was viewed as positive in some groups: graduate students (72%), assistant professors (78%), and industry (73%), but not very positive by postdoctoral researchers (29%) and part-time and non-tenure-track professors (30%). On the whole, the full professor group seems more negative in their views, except for climate for collaboration and whether teaching is valued as an activity.

While no direct comparison exists between this follow-up survey and others, many academic STEM climate studies provide insight into how these data points compare with responses from individuals who may not have attended any development workshops or training. Doctoral students at the University of Michigan (2006) indicate a high intention of pursuing an academic career consistent with our data, but they indicate that they have had very few or no training experiences in teaching, negotiation, or grant proposal writing. Exact comparable information for faculty data does not exist, but some studies report similar findings. For example, in the 2012 climate survey report at the University of Michigan (2013), which was based on a larger population and including male and female faculty, there was no difference in perception of climate for women across all levels of faculty, while our data show a "glass ceiling" effect on climate for associate and full professors. Moreover, our data present less positive feelings about the climate in terms of race and sexual orientation from the advanced ranks. Consistent with the trend in the Michigan study, our responders saw positive department climate on research and collaboration.

TABLE 18.8 Pay It FORWARD Questionnaire Respondents' Views of Department or Workplace Climate by Career Stage at the Time of the Questionnaire

% of those who answered positive or very positive to:	Doctoral candidate (n = 14)	Postdoctoral researcher (n = 24)	Part-time professor (n = 14)	Assistant professor (n = 47)	Associate professor (n = 33)	Professor (n = 9)	Industry/ Govt (n = 15)	Overall (n = 164)[a]
Graduate Overall, the climate in my department or workplace is	85%	41%	50%	66%	51%	55%	85%	60%
The climate for women is	69%	38%	58%	72%	45%	44%	75%	59%
The climate for faculty of color[b] is	37%	53%	33%	59%	39%	11%	78%	44%
The climate for lesbian, gay, transgendered persons is	78%	47%	44%	54%	46%	17%	43%	49%
The climate for collaboration is	62%	67%	50%	52%	67%	78%	67%	62%
The climate for research is	86%	84%	57%	54%	67%	62%	33%	62%
The climate for mentoring is	50%	27%	46%	53%	39%	33%	50%	43%
The level of collegiality is	72%	29%	39%	78%	45%	55%	73%	56%
The respect for teaching as a valued activity is	57%	15%	46%	72%	59%	77%	50%[c]	56%
The disposition toward students is	72%	47%	71%	78%	69%	66%	100%[c]	70%
The climate for graduate students is	72%	37%	67%	60%	68%	50%	100%[c]	62%

[a] Numbers do not add up exactly due to some respondents skipping certain questions.
[b] Most of the remaining respondents were neutral and many noted N/A.
[c] Few respondents (n = 6)—data reliability doubtful.
Percentages calculated relative to the number responding anything other than "Not Applicable (N/A)."

LESSONS LEARNED THROUGH THE EVALUATION PROCESS

The evaluation of the Pay It FORWARD project through direct observation, interviews, and survey questionnaires and the analysis of the results gathered by these instruments produced several conclusions:

- Wider dissemination of career advancement training can be effectively accomplished by preparing new leaders to adapt and implement workshops relevant to specific target groups of interest while still drawing on well-researched and established best practices.
- Distributed leadership allows for adaptations and innovations that persist and that can be readily shared and replicated within the wider network of established sites.
- Training that includes direct observation, action research, and firsthand experience is highly effective for maintaining implementation fidelity and facilitating successful implementation into subsequent program offerings, adaptations, and innovations.
- A clear plan for follow-up, or to follow along with trainees and participants, must be established from the outset so that expectations for data, communications, and the use of Web site resources can be realized. Increased use of social media, networking groups, and professional associations can help to sustain and strengthen the peer networks started at the initial career mentoring workshops.
- In terms of the evaluation process itself, in hindsight, the database and source group data streaming protocols should have been established prior to the first workshop to increase the questionnaire return rate from the multitiered project sites, to the extent possible. Ensuring that all the relevant institutional and participant data records are set up within a larger data framework and accessible by permissions at the various levels of the project may have been helpful to trainee FWDer teams, as well as the larger project leadership. This would serve to facilitate formative feedback, standardize instruments across sites, provide data to be used in project decision making, and expand the data-mining potential of large data sets. While administering surveys through an external vendor makes the data collection easier, the analysis packages vary greatly among survey providers and permission levels. Similarly, session ratings and daily participant evaluation forms quickly get disaggregated from their respective demographic frames of reference, making breakout analyses difficult for the summative reporting.

CONCLUSION

Building on the strengths of the network of trainee (FWDer) leaders, and extending to their workshop participants, there may be opportunities for further research on STEM career pathways and effective retention strategies for women and minorities in STEM. Clearly, providing additional opportunities for more women and minorities in STEM to experience and benefit from career mentoring workshops is one effective approach to inspiring and motivating women to persist in STEM academic careers.

References

Clewell, B.C., Campbell, P.B., 2008. Building Evaluation Capacity: Guide I Designing a Cross Project Evaluation. The Urban Institute, Washington, DC. Available from: <http://www.urban.org/UploadedPDF/411651_guide1.pdf> (accessed 22.01.15.).

University of Michigan, 2006. Assessing the Climate for Doctoral Students at the University of Michigan. Available from: <http://www.advance.rackham.umich.edu/PhD_Report.pdf> (accessed 25.02.15.).

University of Michigan Advance Program, 2013. Assessing the Academic Work Environment for Science and Engineering Tenured/Tenure Track Faculty at the University of Michigan in 2001, 2006, and 2012: Gender & Race in Department- and University-Related Climate Factors. Available from: <http://sitemaker.umich.edu/advance/files/advance-report-1-2012.pdf> (accessed 25.02.15.).

19

Fortifying the Pipeline to Leadership: The International Center for Executive Leadership in Academics at Drexel

Diane Magrane[1] and Page S. Morahan[2]

[1]Professor of Obstetrics and Gynecology, Drexel University College of Medicine, Philadelphia, PA, USA [2]Emerita Professor of Microbiology, Drexel University College of Medicine, Philadelphia, PA, USA

OUTLINE

Program Design: Strategies for Developing a Community of Leaders   320
Why Build Programs for Academic Women Leaders?   320
Evolution of the ICELA Program Design   321
Experiential Program Design Builds Both Individual and Organizational Capacity   323

Translating the ICELA Model for National Leaders in Engineering and Science: Conception, Birth, and Nurturing   326
Testing the ICELA Model with Leaders in Engineering and Technology   326
Interviews   326
Pilot with Engineering Women Faculty   327
Building Interest and Recruiting for ELATE: Facilitator Partners, Coaches, Consultant Teachers, and a National Advisory Board   327
Expanding Awareness About ELATE: Marketing Challenges, Awards, and Recognition   328

Lessons from the First Class   329

Multiple Mirrors to Evaluate Outcomes and Guide Improvement
of Leadership Development Programs   330
  Within Class Assessment: Reflections on Process and Products   330
  Program Review and Process Improvement   331
  Evaluation of Outcomes   331

Looking to the Future: Diversity, Collaboration Across Programs,
and Sustaining Alumnae in Leadership Roles   332

References   333

PROGRAM DESIGN: STRATEGIES FOR DEVELOPING A COMMUNITY OF LEADERS

Why Build Programs for Academic Women Leaders?

Much has been written about the "pipeline" of women in science, technology, engineering, mathematics, and medicine (STEMM), most of it indicating the need to increase the number of talented young women with an interest in science and technology, and to retain those who choose academic careers (NAS, 2006; Bickel et al., 2002; Carr, 2013). The pipeline model works well to describe the need to recruit and advance women under circumstances in which the flow is relatively unimpeded and equally available to men and women. It does appear to be working at entry levels of graduate students and, to a large degree, for medical students (NSF, 2013; AAMC, 2012). It also is useful to describe departures from academic careers as leaks in the pipeline. In medicine, departures are high for both men and women; in science and engineering, although attrition is of more concern prior to tenure, it is a continuing concern even among accomplished faculty (Alexander and Lang, 2008; Liu and Alexander, 2011; NAS, 2006; Xu, 2009).

Two specific problems arise with applying a pipeline metaphor to women's leadership career development. First, few women role models sit at the end of this pipeline to attract others. Second, women who emerge from the pipeline of academic advancement expecting to step into leadership roles may find that the academic ladder has been insufficient in preparing them. While both men and women leaders benefit from leadership preparation, men are more often promoted on their potential, while women must already have proven competence (Barsh and Yee, 2012). While mentorship is important for everyone, men are more likely to be sponsored into roles that advance them in their organizations (Foust-Cummings and

Dinolfo, 2011). At the leadership end of the pipeline, institutions of higher education are operating in what is being described as "permanent white water" (Vail, 1996) and men are assisting each other in mastering the turbulence. Like salmon swimming upstream, women in academic STEMM find themselves looking for the "fish ladder"—that is, the system of support that helps them leap visible and hidden hurdles in advancing to and being sustained in institutional leadership roles.

The phenomenon is well known in medicine, where numbers of women have been increasing slowly for several decades. In the late 1960s, medical schools expanded in size and number. This opened an occupational pipeline to white women who had received quality science education in high schools and colleges. Over the next 40 years, the proportion of women applicants increased from 20% in 1975 to just over 51% in 2003; however, since then, the proportion has steadily decreased, reaching 47% of all applicants in 2012 (Roskovensky et al., 2012). In medicine, women are turning away from a pipeline that appeared only a few years ago to be self-perpetuating. While the reasons for the decrease are not clear, the data show that gains in gender equity are fragile. Women continue to fill entry positions but are vastly underrepresented at top leadership levels. We celebrate each new woman dean and CEO, although they comprise percentages of only 10–15% in the United States (AAMC, 2012; ASEE, 2012). Clearly, the pipeline model, which relies upon recruiting academic professionals without appropriate support and attractors along the full career pathway, is an inadequate model for leadership development. Models that address the complexities of opportunity and environment are better suited to describe professional career development (Magrane et al., 2012; Eagley and Carli, 2007; Ely and Meyerson, 2000).

Our research has demonstrated that a leadership development program can contribute to the promotion of women to leadership roles in academic medicine (Dannels et al., 2008; Morahan et al., 2010). We have recently extended this research based upon a model that acknowledges the complexity of organizational, societal, and personal influences on academic career development (Magrane et al., 2012, Figure 19.1), and is designed to explore both quantitative and qualitative factors. The results demonstrate that participation in national career development programs is advantageous to women in academic medicine in retention, academic promotion, and administrative leadership appointments, as compared to men and nonparticipant women of the same rank and institution (Chang et al., 2013).

Evolution of the ICELA Program Design

The Executive Leadership in Academic Technology and Engineering program at Drexel University (ELATE at Drexel®), a national program

Systems of influence on professional development of academic women in medicine

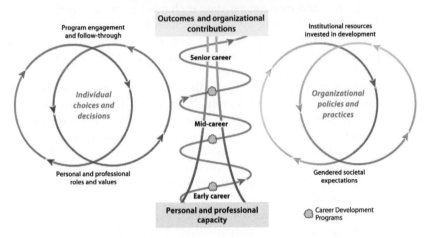

FIGURE 19.1 Systems of influence on professional development of academic women in medicine. The Systems of Career Influences Model presents three dynamic systems of career development: a central cyclic trajectory of career advancement; a system of organizational influences, some of which promote and some of which inhibit career advancement; and a system of individual decisions about career and personal life, which may either promote or inhibit career advancement. The potential for formal career development activities to enrich faculty potential and advancement is represented by expansions along the career trajectory (Magrane et al., 2012).

for women in STEM fields, is modeled after the Hedwig Van Ameringen Executive Leadership in Academic Medicine program (ELAM®) (Morahan et al., 2010). Program infrastructure is provided by the International Center for Executive Leadership in Academics (ICELA at Drexel®), part of the Institute for Women's Health and Leadership, which is accorded department status within the Drexel University College of Medicine. Both programs address the original purpose established at the founding of ELAM in 1995—to increase women in academic institutional leadership roles and to lay a foundation for longer-term influence within sponsoring institutions and national leadership (Morahan et al., 2010). Both programs are intensive, part-time, year-long fellowships for women who have been successful in academic promotion and have demonstrated high potential for institutional leadership. They are designed around the development of competencies in four essential areas: personal and professional leadership effectiveness, strategic resource management, organizational dynamics, and community building (ELAM, 2014). Three week-long sessions over the course of the year's fellowship take a developmental approach to enhancing institutional leadership prowess, moving from an intensive focus on organizational and interpersonal fundamentals to a mid-fellowship session that expands strategic thinking, planning, and execution. The program concludes with capstone and transition events to bridge into the larger alumnae community.

Three elements are central to ICELA programs: (i) competitive selection with institutional support and recognition, (ii) intense career and skill development through workshops and coaching, and (iii) networking with peers and role models. Fellows are nominated by a senior official in their institution (usually the dean, vice president, or provost). This immediately gives the nominees visibility as leaders in their institutions, thus increasing their potential for formal executive positions and informal leadership roles. The nominator and two recommenders are asked in the semistructured nomination to validate the academic and management achievements of the candidate, suggest likely leadership roles, and describe an organizational mentoring plan. The second program element, intense career and skill development, occurs through a combination of background readings and reflections to prepare for on-site sessions, experiential workshops, simulations that expand competency, assignments that apply the new skills to daily work, and processes to expand that learning through reflection on the outcomes of the new practices. The third element focuses on building communities of leadership practice (Wenger and Snyder, 2000), which are intentionally developed through a variety of small-group activities within the class. Communities of trust develop through the support of learning circles that share confidence and accountability for each other's success (Baldwin and Linnea, 2010). The networks of class and learning communities expand to the full alumnae community through post-fellowship activities and referrals.

Experiential Program Design Builds Both Individual and Organizational Capacity

The design of the fellowship leverages the experience and skills of diverse and accomplished women faculty who have demonstrated potential for institutional leadership. Program activities contribute to the development of individuals' organizational savvy and self-efficacy (Sloma-Williams et al., 2009). Assignments link these activities with advancing an agenda of the nominating organizations. Creating an active learning environment at the home institution is an effective way to apply skills and demonstrate talent to senior officials. Being tasked with new change initiatives is both useful to the institution and gives a platform for exercising leadership. However, even as this visibility

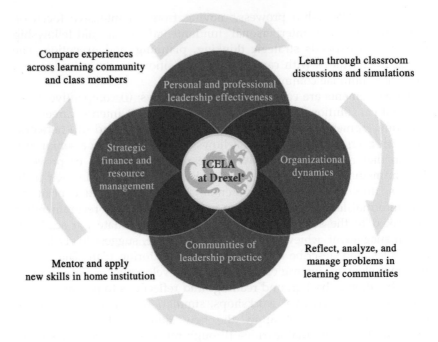

FIGURE 19.2   ICELA at Drexel Leadership Learning Cycle. This cycle organizes professional learning activities around four essential competencies and acknowledges the experience that each participant brings to a professional development experience and the risk in applying new skills in the spotlight of executing organizational change. Learning activities build trust and confidence as they advance from didactic and simulation to small-group discussions with peers. Skills are then applied to each participant's work at home, and results are analyzed and compared by trusted peers.

increases opportunity for new roles, it also places the Fellow in a very vulnerable position of trying new skills in the very environment in which she is being judged for her effectiveness (Catalyst, 2007).

The ICELA Leadership Learning Cycle (Figure 19.2) acknowledges the diversity, breadth, and depth of experience, organizational knowledge, and personal effectiveness of each participant. Entry lessons introduce participants to literature about the challenges of gender in leading and to interacting with each other virtually. Knowledge expansion is facilitated by readings in social and organizational science, lectures and workshops from experts in finance and organizational change, simulations such as Barry Oshry's Organization Workshop (The Organization Workshop, 2014), group problem solving using a variety of Liberating Structures (Liberating Structures, 2014), case studies, role modeling, peer coaching while practicing, and analysis of observations and data collection across institutions.

Learning rapidly moves to application for the Fellows' own personal and organizational experience, through group discussion and reflective analysis. Considerable attention is given to developing a safe learning environment that encourages the risk taking required for behavior change. Planning and reflecting on outcomes of actions occurs in a small learning community (LC) of six Fellows from different institutions who establish personal trust and mutual accountability. These LCs also analyze differences in institutional characteristics and policies, thus broadening each Fellow's perspective. Support of LC members mitigates the real and perceived risk of taking on new responsibilities and trying out new approaches in the course of leadership work in the home institution.

Three specific assignments that support executive level learning include senior leadership interviews, individual development plans, and institutional action projects. They integrate classroom lessons with institutional experience, while advancing work that is important both to the Fellow and her institutional mentors.

Senior leadership interviews explore the pathway through organizational hierarchy and the narratives that lead others to executive positions. The process of introduction, or of being introduced and then scheduling an appointment with the president, chancellor, and their senior management staff, gives insight into the institutional culture of accessibility and formality. The interview itself is an open-ended query of the executives' leadership paths. While narratives are held in confidence, Fellows compare themes to reveal the many leadership paths available, as well as the complex balance of preparedness, networking, opportunity, and personal choice involved in each person's journey.

Individual development plans are designed with initial executive coaching consultation on the results of organizational 360-degree anonymous assessment of leadership effectiveness and inventories of leadership styles, reflective conversations with key personal and professional stakeholders about interpersonal challenges, and personal experience. Fellows implement plans for small progressive changes throughout the fellowship and complete a self-assessment at the end.

Institutional Action Projects (IAPs) integrate fellowship lessons, organizational change resources, and community support into a visible leadership contribution to the Fellow's institution (Mennin et al., 2013). Although most IAPs are not fully completed until months (or often years) after the fellowship, the IAP process expands the network of stakeholders, showcases the Fellow's talents, integrates lessons on collaboration and strategy execution, and advances institutional initiatives. Initiatives may be in investigative, planning, implementation, or evaluation stages; they are selected through discussion and negotiation between each Fellow and her institutional leaders/mentors. Projects range from new organizational structures for department units, to new methods for teaching and research, to new cross-disciplinary approaches to research and governance. Each Fellow presents the intentions and lessons of her IAP during a capstone Leaders Forum attended by institutional leaders from the Fellows' universities. Presentations are given in three media—oral presentations and posters at the forum and subsequent publication of those posters and abstracts on the ELAM and ELATE websites (International Center for Executive Leadership in Academics, 2014).

TRANSLATING THE ICELA MODEL FOR NATIONAL LEADERS IN ENGINEERING AND SCIENCE: CONCEPTION, BIRTH, AND NURTURING

Testing the ICELA Model with Leaders in Engineering and Technology

Just as the ELAM program began with a focus on faculty in medicine and then later expanded to include dentistry and public health, ELATE began with a focus on engineering and technology disciplines. There was a great national need and Drexel University leaders were interested in making a difference. However, questions remained about how receptive the national audience would be and what content would be adaptable to faculty outside health professions. We explored this in two ways: (i) interviewing leaders in the fields of engineering and science and (ii) offering ELAM participation to Drexel University women faculty leaders in engineering. The results confirmed both interest in and the approach of the program.

Interviews

We interviewed more than 30 leaders in engineering and science, including deans and university presidents, leaders in gender diversity, and executives of national associations and corporations, with special efforts to identify women leaders. Each of these key informants described his or her path to leadership, current challenges of leaders, perceived challenges of women leaders, and listed the skills and experiences that they viewed as important to the development of academic leaders in their field. Each interview concluded with a query about interest in further involvement. Although most informants expressed some skepticism that a program modeled after one designed for women in academic medicine would be a good fit for their field, once the key program elements were described there was general agreement that the curriculum ideas were on target. Most interviews concluded with a request to provide the informants with updates and a statement of willingness to become engaged in the program in some fashion.

Pilot with Engineering Women Faculty

To prepare for ELATE, we followed an approach that had proven successful with diversifying ELAM disciplines and in expanding capacity of an international health professions leadership development program (Burdick et al., 2010). Beginning in 2010, one female faculty member from the College of Engineering at Drexel University participated in the ELAM program for each of the sessions over 3 years. Each completed an IAP in collaboration with the dean of engineering and the provost, interviewed university officers, and advanced an individual development plan that supported her leadership within the university. Each also verified the value of the program, but expressed a desire to build a network within her own field rather than within the health sciences. It was clear that professional affiliation was important to developing the most beneficial community of practice. Each of the three participants continues to play an integral role in the delivery of the program and recruitment of applicants.

The results of the ELAM experiences and key informant interviews confirmed that the experiential learning model and key activities were appropriate for a national program for academic engineers and scientists. However, adaptations would be required to focus on the university culture and operations rather than on the medical and clinical environments. Some skepticism was also expressed about the openness of technical faculty to methods that included creative imagery and self-reflection, which were seen as potentially being counter-culture to the field and yet important in expanded leadership roles.

Building Interest and Recruiting for ELATE: Facilitator Partners, Coaches, Consultant Teachers, and a National Advisory Board

The work of contacting, interviewing, and following up with key informants clarified methods and content for ELATE, and revealed a strong pool of potential consultants and faculty. Eight prominent leaders became members of a national advisory board that would guide the design, monitor outcomes, and assist with recruitment of teachers and applicants (ELATE Advisory Board, 2014). Almost every member has participated in an instructional or advising role or sponsored a Fellow. Other leaders were invited to participate as career consultants and facilitators of conversations about the challenges of leadership; all who were available agreed and have spent at least 1 day onsite with Fellows. Each has been an ambassador for the program within his or her institution, professional societies, and professional network. This deep engagement in program development has provided candid reviews, increasing interest and national awareness in the value of the ELATE Fellowship for women faculty in engineering, which is now extending to a variety of science fields.

Expanding Awareness About ELATE: Marketing Challenges, Awards, and Recognition

At the time that ELATE was being planned, ELAM was well established for its value and international name recognition—but largely within the health sciences (Morahan et al., 2010). The idea of a national program that benefitted both participants and their institutions through their leadership development was novel, even to the universities that had profited from ELAM graduates taking positions as graduate school deans, provosts, and presidents.

We realized that marketing would require a multipronged approach of advertising for awareness and opportunity, establishing credibility in relevant fields, and building a network to sustain participation through personal testimonial. Infrastructure for effective marketing required trademark registration of the name "International Center for Executive Leadership in Academics (ICELA at Drexel)," and separate websites for ELAM and ELATE.

The primary target audiences for ELATE were engineering and computer science professionals; this worked well for marketing because both have established networks of leaders and women's career development within professional societies. Electronic and hard copy letters signed by the Drexel dean of engineering were distributed to deans and faculty affairs officers of colleges of engineering and computer science who had participated in the National Science Foundation (NSF) ADVANCE activities, and those with medical schools with ELAM alumnae (NSF ADVANCE, 2014). Board members distributed the information to their own networks and began speaking to qualified faculty in their own institutions. Advertisements were placed in list-servs and newsletters of organizations such as the Women in Engineering Programs and Advocates Network (WEPAN), the Anita Borg Institute, and the American Society for Engineering Education. ELAM alumnae and deans were contacted through email, presentations at conferences, and the ELAM Forum, encouraging them to invite their Fellow deans to nominate faculty. The campaign fell short of its intended 30 applicants for

20 positions slated for the inaugural program. However, 11 strong applicants were accepted into the inaugural program in 2012.

We established credibility by leveraging affiliation with the renowned ELAM program, testimonial of respected national leaders, and recognition by noted foundations, which funded program development and evaluation systems. Within its first 18 months of development, ELATE was awarded funds from the NSF, the Henry Luce Foundation, and the Alfred P. Sloan Foundation. Each award moved the program forward in meeting its goals; press releases acknowledged the importance of the effort in furthering leadership in engineering and the sciences. The national spotlight was shining on the first ELATE Fellows and their faculty.

Lessons from the First Class

While developers and consultants believed that the learning model and activities would apply to faculty in engineering and the sciences, we recognized the need for adaptations of key content. Lessons needed to address the organizational structure and function of colleges and universities rather than academic medical centers. Consultants would need to have credibility in this arena in order to provide inspiration and useful information about leadership pathways. And finally, the methods used in classroom activities needed to be scaled to a class of 11, in contrast to ELAM classes of 54 Fellows.

We designed lessons to meet the goals of the four key leadership competencies and tailored content by changing the focus of some key lessons for ELATE. For example, the case study of opening week, strategic allocation of resources presented as a collaborative activity of teams of six to eight Fellows, addressed university governance and resources. ELATE's "Incredible University" simulation presents the challenge of an ambitious endowment request and its impact on the other missions of a small college. This contrasts with ELAM's "Ann Preston School of Medicine" simulation (Magrane, 2011), which requires decisions to reduce and integrate resources of a medical school facing decreasing clinical incomes and over expenditures on infrastructure.

Another curriculum adaptation involved the initial senior leadership interviews. While ELAM focused on school executives and chief financial officer (CFO) positions, ELATE began with the college dean and CFO positions, but also included the provost. Additional interview requirements for ELATE extend to other deans and university officers, including the university president. A third curriculum adaptation involved inviting career consultants from engineering and science disciplines to meet and consult with Fellows in both classroom and individual discussions. For ELAM, the alumnae community is now abundant with accomplished leaders from which to draw consultants. For ELATE, as initially with ELAM, the program takes advantage of accomplished leaders from relevant fields of engineering and the sciences, many of whom have ascended to positions of dean, provost, and president.

Thus, the lessons for both programs are comparable for leadership development and unique in the audience of participants and consultants. Materials and methods are adapted to fit the size and small-group configurations possible in each program. The size of the initial ELATE cohorts allows classroom discussions that engage everyone; ELAM, with 54 Fellows per class, is open to a variety of permutations of more intimate small groups that deepen network building and understanding of each Fellow's contributions. As ELATE's reputation is established, we expect class size to increase, and teaching and learning methods will evolve accordingly, as they did with ELAM over time.

MULTIPLE MIRRORS TO EVALUATE OUTCOMES AND GUIDE IMPROVEMENT OF LEADERSHIP DEVELOPMENT PROGRAMS

Measures of program effectiveness involve both process and outcome evaluation, including analysis of in-class products, anonymous online feedback, staff and faculty observations, periodic focus groups during sessions, and tracking of outcomes through longitudinal surveys, career advancement, and project outcomes. All this data is used to improve the program and to deepen understanding of how leadership programs affect career development.

Within Class Assessment: Reflections on Process and Products

Although instructors work independently within their areas of expertise, communications between instructors and program directors aid the integration of lessons. Most lessons result in display of individual or group products (e.g., presentations of analysis on flip charts or Microsoft PowerPoint presentations). This allows teachers to immediately see the learning and address Fellows' questions. Since many of the lessons span more than 1 day or more than one session, teachers have an opportunity to revise lessons to enhance Fellows' understanding and offer additional reflection and practice. These conversations continue after each session during telephone debriefings between staff and consultant teachers based upon participant feedback.

The in-class and after-class analysis was particularly important in the inaugural year of ELATE. While adaptation to participants' feedback was continuous during the first year, substantive changes were made in the second year. For example, as a result of in-class observations, initial lessons in resource management were decompressed, allowing more time to focus on basic economic indicators of organizational finances. Time was also reallocated to allow additional time for integration of the finance and strategy lessons; the structure of the simulation was reorganized to allow for more preparation for Fellows prior to arrival, and teachers offered more structured assistance during the time of case study development. As a result, presentations were improved in both content and process the second year.

Program Review and Process Improvement

Program staff members compile their own observations of program process, informal feedback from participants with results of daily anonymous feedback surveys. We use this information to improve both subsequent sessions in the same class year as well as for the next year. Summaries of the anonymous feedback and program director's notes are shared with the national advisory board, allowing reflection and inquiry from stakeholders. These lively discussions result in both priority setting of changes and praise for effective outcomes.

Other important improvements have occurred in response to review of class products. For example, opening round table discussions of the challenges women face in exercising their leadership are presented in flip charts of responses and in polarity mapping of their academic environments (Magrane, 2012). Opening activities for the winter session include posting of challenges, achievements, and learning goals. Fellows also submit confidential reports of leadership development plans and progress with institutional action projects; the content is used to gain insight into Fellows' experiences and the degree to which program goals are being addressed through individual and institutional work. Finally, public presentations of action projects demonstrate skill in communication, strategy, and project management. All of these activities reflect ongoing learning, gap analysis and alignment with the curriculum competencies, and goal achievement in evaluating program success.

Evaluation of Outcomes

The proof of effectiveness, of course, is in how well the ICELA programs meet the stated goals of advancing women in academic leadership in both numbers and effectiveness. Previous surveys of ELAM graduates have shown increases in self-efficacy and a variety of leadership skills, as well as expanded definitions of leadership (Dannels et al.,

2008; Morahan et al., 2010). The deans of medical and dental schools in the United States and Canada have reported positive impacts of the ELAM program on their schools (Dannels et al., 2009a,b). Research funded by the National Institutes of Health (NIH) is providing additional data to compare the retention, academic promotion, and leadership appointment trajectories of ELAM women with similar female and male faculty in academic medicine, as well as survey and qualitative interview data from participants (Chang et al., 2013; Helitzer et al., 2014). Current research funded by a grant from the Alfred P. Sloan Foundation tracks ELATE alumnae progress to advanced leadership roles, compares ELAM and ELATE graduates in self-perception of leadership competencies, and analyzes the outcomes of institutional action projects in terms of both individual impact and institutional implementation. Fellows are invited to participate in surveys that assess individual confidence and sense of importance of program competencies to their work. These 15- to 20-min online surveys are administered immediately prior to the first program session, 6–8 weeks following graduation, and 2 years after fellowship completion (ICELA, 2014).

The long-term effectiveness of the programs requires advancement of graduates into leadership positions in which they can effect change. At the time of application, faculty academic rank and leadership roles are entered into a master program database. Alumnae communications that support the network also contribute to maintaining current titles and thus can be used to track progress of graduates over time. The database is used to produce regular reports of graduates' leadership positions (ELAM Fast Facts 2014; ELATE in Brief, 2015), and recently has been used to conduct research on geographic mobility and administrative advancement of ELAM Fellows (McLean et al., 2013). The relationships between program participation, alumnae community support, and evaluation are interdependent and reflective of a vibrant community of academic women leaders.

LOOKING TO THE FUTURE: DIVERSITY, COLLABORATION ACROSS PROGRAMS, AND SUSTAINING ALUMNAE IN LEADERSHIP ROLES

The ultimate purpose of the ELAM and ELATE fellowships is to increase organizational capacity in higher education by increasing the number and effectiveness of women in leadership roles. Our 20 years of experience in this field has shown us that the strength and diversity of the alumnae community as a global community of practice is essential to achieving this purpose. The programs themselves embody inclusive, strategic, collaborative practices through explicit learning activities and through discussions within and across learning communities with diverse membership. Over ELAM's 20 years, it has expanded from a program largely composed of MD faculty to include dental and public health faculty participants and has increased the numbers of Fellows with PhDs. Admissions criteria were broadened from preferring traditional scientific investigators to seeking candidates with scholarship in community-based research and educational innovation. This diversity of scholarship and practice has enriched discussions in the classroom and learning communities. We expect similar enhancements with the expansion of ELATE beyond engineering and technology to include a wide range of sciences. Both programs will benefit from global participation and from an integration of alumnae activities.

Leadership is a continuous process of learning from success, from failure, from individual reflection and from discussion with colleagues. Effective leadership plays out over a continuum of preparation, transition, execution, and often, transition into new leadership roles (Morahan et al., 2011). Thus, a vibrant alumnae community is key to sustaining the leadership of ICELA program graduates. ELAM and ELATE contribute to this through encouragement of continuing interactions among members of the learning communities established during the fellowship year, through informal gatherings at professional society meetings, through workshops conducted on campuses, and during professional meetings of graduates. ICELA issues an electronic newsletter with announcements of alumnae achievements, job postings, and links to readings of potential interest. The program has a presence on social media and maintains class list-servs.

In addition, alumnae are invited to participate in the fellowship program as peer consultants for IAP development and discussions of how to sustain leadership energies and connections "after ELATE" and "after ELAM." The cross-campus and cross-institutional collaborations that are needed to navigate the white waters of change in higher education are now in the hands of more than 800 ELAM alumnae and a growing number of ELATE alumnae. The future looks promising for these women and their institutions, and through them, for higher education.

References

Alexander, H., Lang, J., 2008. The long term retention and attrition of U.S. medical faculty. AAMC Anal. Brief. 8 (4), 1–2.

ASEE, 2012. Personal Communication, Dwight Wardell, Director, Membership, American Society for Engineering Education, July 16.

Association of American Medical Colleges, 2012. Women in U.S. Academic Medicine and Science: Statistics and Benchmarking Report, 2011–2012. AAMC. Available from: <https://members.aamc.org/eweb/upload/Women%20in%20U%20S%20%20Academic%20Medicine%20Statistics%20and%20Benchmarking%20Report%202011-20123.pdf> (accessed 22.07.14.).

Baldwin, C., Linnea, A., 2010. The Circle Way: A Leader in Every Chair. Berrett–Koehler, San Francisco, CA.

Barsh, J., Yee, L., 2012. Unlocking the Full Potential of Women at Work. McKinsey & Company. Available from: <http://www.mckinsey.com/careers/women/ ~ /media/ Reports/Women/2012%20WSJ%20Women%20in%20the%20Economy%20white% 20paper%20FINAL.ashx> (accessed 07.22.14.).

Bickel, J., Wara, D., Atkinson, B.F., Cohen, L.S., Dunn, M., Hostler, S., 2002. Increasing women's leadership in academic medicine. Report of the AAMC project implementation committee. Acad. Med. 77, 1043–1061.

Burdick, W.P., Diserens, D., Friedman, S.R., Morahan, P.S., Kalishman, S., Eklund, M.A., et al., 2010. Measuring the effects of an international health professions faculty development fellowship: the FAIMER Institute. Med. Teach. 32 (5), 414–421.

Carr, R., 2013. Women in the Academic Pipeline for Science, Technology, Engineering and Math: Nationally and at AAUDE Institutions. Association of American Universities Data Exchange (AAUDE). Available from: <http://aaude.org/system/files/documents/public/reports/report-2013-pipeline.pdf> (accessed 07.22.14.).

Catalyst, 2007. The Double Bind Dilemma for Women in Leadership: Damned if You Do, Doomed if You Don't. Available from: <http://www.catalyst.org/knowledge/doublebind-dilemma-women-leadership-damned-if-you-do-doomed-if-you-dont-0> (accessed 07.22.14.).

Chang, S., Helitzer, D.L., Magrane, D., Morahan, P.S., Newbill, S.L., 2013. Retaining talent in academic medicine: the impact of professional development programs for women faculty. "Abstract" Presented at AAMC Annual Meeting November 2013. Available from: <https://www.aamc.org/members/gwims/362372/2013gwimsposters.html> (accessed 02.09.14.). (manuscript in preparation).

Dannels, S.A., Yamagata, H., McDade, S.A., Chuang, Y., Gleason, K.A., McLaughlin, J.A., et al., 2008. Evaluating a leadership program: a comparative, longitudinal study to assess the impact of the Executive Leadership in Academic Medicine (ELAM) Program for women. Acad. Med. 83 (5), 488–495.

Dannels, S.A., McLaughlin, J.M., Gleason, K.A., Dolan, T.A., McDade, S.A., Richman, R.C., 2009a. Dental school deans' perceptions of the organizational culture and impact of the ELAM program on the culture and advancement of women faculty. J. Dental Educ. 73 (6), 676–688.

Dannels, S.A., McLaughlin, J.M., Gleason, K.A., McDade, S.A., Richman, R., Morahan, P.S., 2009b. Medical school deans' perceptions of organizational climate: useful indicators for advancement of women faculty and program evaluation of a leadership program's impact. Acad. Med. 84, 67–74.

Eagley, A.H., Carli, L.L., 2007. Women and the labyrinth of leadership. Harvard Bus. Rev. 85, 63–71.

ELAM Curriculum. 2014. Available from: <http://www.drexelmed.edu/Home/ OtherPrograms/ExecutiveLeadershipinAcademicMedicine/AboutELAM/Curriculum. aspx> (accessed 02.09.14.).

ELAM Fast Facts. 2014. Available from: <http://www.drexelmed.edu/Home/ OtherPrograms/ExecutiveLeadershipinAcademicMedicine/AboutELAM/FastFacts.aspx> (accessed 02.10.14.).

ELATE Advisory Board, 2014. Available from: <http://www.drexel.edu/engineering/ programs/special_opp/ELATE/AdvisoryBoard/> (accessed 02.09.14.).

ELATE in Brief, 2015, Available from: <http://www.drexel.edu/engineering/programs/ special-programs/ELATE/> (accessed 08.11.15.).

Ely, R.J., Meyerson, D.E., 2000. Theories of gender in organizations: a new approach to organizational analysis and change. Report No. 8. Center for Gender in Organizations. Simmons School of Management, Boston, MA.

Foust-Cummings, H., Dinolfo, S., 2011. Sponsoring women to success. Catalyst. Available from: <http://www.catalyst.org/knowledge/sponsoring-women-success> (accessed 07.22.14.).

Helitzer, D.L., Newbill, S.L., Morahan, P.S., Magrane, D., Cardinali, G., Wu, C., et al., 2014. Perceptions of skill development of participants in three national career development programs for women faculty in academic medicine. Acad. Med. 87 (6), 896–903.

ICELA at Drexel®, Leadership Learning and Career Development Survey, 2014. Available from: <http://www.drexel.edu/icela/programevaluation/survey/> (accessed 02.09.14.).

International Center for Executive Leadership in Academics at Drexel University, ELAM Leaders Forum, 2014. Available from: <https://www.drexelmed.edu/Home/OtherPrograms/ExecutiveLeadershipinAcademicMedicine/Forum.aspx> and ELATE Leaders Forum available from <http://www.drexel.edu/engineering/programs/special_opp/ELATE/Leaders%20Forum/> (accessed 02.09.14.).

Liberating Structures, Including and Unleashing Everyone. 2014. Available from: <http://www.liberatingstructures.com/> (accessed 02.09.14.).

Liu, C.Q., Alexander, H., 2011. The changing demographics of full-time U.S. medical school faculty, 1966–2009. AAMC Anal. Brief. 11 (8), 1–2.

Magrane, D., 2011. Living the Ann Preston School of Medicine (APSOM) Simulation— Strategic Finance in our Daily Lives. Message from the Director available from <http://www.drexelmed.edu/drexel-pdf/program-elam/ELAM_Directors-Message-April-2011.pdf> (accessed 02.09.14.).

Magrane, D., 2012. Women's Ways of Leading: Polarity Management in Academic Health Centers and Universities. Available from: <http://www.drexelmed.edu/Home/OtherPrograms/ExecutiveLeadershipinAcademicMedicine/DirectorsMessage/DirectorsMessageDecember2012.aspx> (accessed 02.09.14.).

Magrane, D., Helitzer, D., Morahan, P., Chang, S., Gleason, K., Cardinali, G., et al., 2012. Systems of career influences: a conceptual model for evaluating the professional development of women in academic medicine. J. Women's Health. 21 (12), 1–8.

McLean, M., Morahan, P.S., Dannels, S.A., McDade, S.A., 2013. Geographic mobility advances careers: study of the Executive Leadership in Academic Medicine (ELAM) Program for women. Acad. Med. 88 (11), 1700–1706.

Mennin, S., Kalishman, S., Eckert, M., Diserens, D., Friedman, S.R., Morahan, P.S., et al., 2013. Project-based faculty development by international health professions educators: lessons learned. Med. Teach. 35 (2), e971–e977, Epub 2012 Oct 26.

Morahan, P.S., Gleason, K.A., Richman, R.C., Dannels, S.A., McDade, S.A., 2010. Advancing women faculty to senior leadership in U.S. academic health centers: fifteen years of history in the making. J. Women Higher Ed. 3 (1), 137–162.

Morahan, P.S., Rosen, S.E., Richman, R.C., Gleason, K.A., 2011. The leadership continuum: a framework for organizational and individual assessment relative to the advancement of women physicians and scientists. J. Women's Health. 20 (3), 387–396.

National Academy of Sciences, 2006. Beyond Bias and Barriers: Fulfilling the Potential of Women in Academic Science and Engineering, NAS. Available from: <http://www.nap.edu/catalog.php?record_id = 11741> (accessed 07.22.14.).

National Science Foundation, 2013. Women, Minorities, and Persons with Disabilities in Science and Engineering. Available from: <http://www.nsf.gov/statistics/wmpd/2013/pdf/nsf13304_full.pdf> (accessed 07.22.14.).

National Science Foundation, 2014. ADVANCE: Increasing the Participation and Advancement of Women in Academic Science and Engineering Careers (ADVANCE). Available from: <http://www.nsf.gov/funding/pgm_summ.jsp?pims_id = 5383> (accessed 07.21.14.).

Roskovensky, L.B., Grbic, D., Matthew, D., 2012. The changing gender composition of U.S. medical school applicants and matriculants. AAMC Anal. Brief. 12 (1), 1–2.

Sloma-Williams, L., McDade, S.A., Richman, R.C., Morahan, P.S., 2009. The role of self-efficacy in developing women leaders: a case of women leaders in academic medicine and dentistry. In: Dean, D.R., Bracken, S.J., Allen, J.K. (Eds.), Women in Academic Leadership: Professional Strategies, Personal Choices. Stylus, Sterling, VA, pp. 50–73.

The Organization Workshop, 2014. Available from: <http://www.powerandsystems.com/workshops-with-impact/organization-workshop.html> (accessed 02.09.14.).

Vail, P., 1996. Learning as a Way of Being: Strategies for Survival in a World of Permanent White Water. John Wiley & Sons, San Francisco, CA.

Wenger, E.C., Snyder, W.M., 2000. Communities of practice: the organizational frontier. Harvard Bus. Rev. January–February, 139–145.

Xu, Y.J., 2009. Gender disparity in STEM disciplines: a study of faculty attrition and turnover intentions. Res. High. Educ. 49, 607–624.

Synthesis

Rachelle S. Heller[1] and Catherine Mavriplis[2]

[1]Department of Computer Science, George Washington University, Washington, DC, USA [2]Department of Mechanical Engineering, University of Ottawa, Ottawa, Canada

OUTLINE

Faculty Development—How Are Existing Models Faring?   337

How Are Faculty Development Models Evolving?   345

Some New Faculty Development Models Are Evolving to an Online Presence   347

What Is the Future of Faculty Development?   348

References   351

FACULTY DEVELOPMENT—HOW ARE EXISTING MODELS FARING?

The journey toward programs for faculty career development began in earnest in the early 1970s. Models have changed and the focus of these models has evolved (see Chapter 1). The program structures described in this book report the successes and challenges in designing and delivering the FORWARD faculty development program. However, questions remain: How are these and other models described faring? Are they being repeated? Adapted? Expanded? Abandoned?

Of all the models that are an outgrowth of Pay It FORWARD, only one, at the Massachusetts Institute of Technology (MIT; see Chapter 3), has been institutionalized "as is" and is still regularly offered (yearly since 2005). Another, at the Arizona State University (ASU; see Chapter 4), is offered from time to time based on the goodness and energy of one leader. However, even the continuation of the model is not without stress and adaptation. The leadership at ASU reports: "We still continue the FORWARD to Professorship/Jumpstarting STEM Careers event (AWIS Central Arizona, 2014). It has been shortened to a half-day symposium with three speakers and an occasional panel of additional guests, typically local experts in the topic field. We must find sponsors each year to run the event from various sources, the largest amount coming from the Graduate Student Government organization at ASU. Others include AWIS (Association for Women in Science), FWA (Faculty Women's Association), the ASU School of Life Sciences, Biodesign, Fisher Scientific, Thermofisher, etc. This year all three speakers were from the East Coast, so travel was the biggest cost, but usually the biggest cost is catering" (D. P. Baluch, 2015, personal communication).

Case Western Reserve University (CWRU; see Chapter 8) institutionalized their offering in the Office of Faculty Development as "To Tenure and Beyond: Building an Intentional Career at CWRU" (TT&B, for short). The program is now open to all second-year, ladder-rank faculty nominated by their dean and consists of four half-day workshops spread over an academic year. Many of the components inaugurated in the FORWARD-funded project remain, such as a focus on career trajectory that includes tenure as a single milestone, executive coaching sessions for each participant, and panel discussions with senior faculty. TT&B is funded by the school deans, who contribute a portion of the overall cost for each faculty member who participates from their school. The program is not required and is sometimes declined or delayed by faculty for reasons such as parental leave or duties that cannot be reassigned or shifted. To compensate for the abbreviated nature of the curriculum in its institutionalized form, an additional series of "Lunch & Learn" sessions are scheduled in months without a workshop. The "Lunch & Learn" sessions may cover skill-building topics such as "Conflict Management," "Negotiating in the Academy," or "Research Grants: from Request for Proposals to Final Report" (A. Shaffer, 2015, personal communication).

The group from the University of Virginia (see Chapter 7) took their workshop in a slightly different direction. They chose to offer a follow-up workshop for institutional leaders (department chairs, diversity administrators, faculty developers) and change agents (faculty members) from the University of Virginia and Virginia Commonwealth University. The follow-up expanded the number of campus leaders who could support or help adopt enriched faculty development (G. Fraser, 2015, personal communication).

City Tech (see Chapter 11) did not receive additional funding to institutionalize the workshops, but the organizers have continued to host a spring luncheon to keep the concept alive. All women Science, Technology, Engineering, and Mathematics (STEM) faculty are invited, and they have in-house associate and full professors speak on work/life balance, strategies for tenure and promotion, and developing leadership skills. And, based on the outcomes of their Collaborative on Academic Careers in Higher Education (COACHE; Harvard, 2015) survey responses, they intend to craft future professional activities.

Not all former Pay It FORWARD workshop leaders were able to continue offering workshops. One of the hurdles was knowing about funding support in the discipline specific to their workshop area. While the leadership from Moving FORWARD in Space (see Chapter 13) found it difficult to find external funding—their "go-to" source for funding, the National Aeronautics and Space Administration (NASA), did not seem to have a track that they could follow to make a proposal—their major challenge was that they "have [sic had] very little institutional support for workshop organization: time spent organizing workshops was not considered desirable for tenure (similarly to time spent attempting to find funding, although a funded grant might certainly have looked better)" (A. Davatzes, 2015, personal communication). An additional challenge was sustaining the original workshop leadership group. In one case—namely, Advancing Toward Professorship in Biology, Ecology, and Earth System Sciences (ATPinBEESS; see Chapter 10)—where many of the leaders were graduate students and postdoctoral scientists (which brought great value to them as student leaders), the challenge to continue was to find sustained leadership above sustained funding.

Other groups sought new venues for faculty development opportunities, especially conferences. The "Moving FORWARD in Space" team (see Chapter 13) took this approach on their second offering of their workshop.

For many years, COACh has been offering their career-building workshops in conjunction with such associations as the American Chemical Society (ACS). COACh (University of Oregon, 2015) was an early example of tailored career development programs, starting in chemistry, that has been in existence for 18 years and has benefited over 12,000 scientists and engineers (men and women). COACh was developed by Geraldine Richmond of the University of Oregon, with the support of the National Science Foundation (NSF). She was elected president of the American Association for the Advancement of Science (AAAS) in 2014.

Making workshops available at major meetings provides easier access, reduces travel costs, and expands individual networks. However, these workshops are often pre-selected and may not meet the individual's specific needs. For example, at the spring meeting of the ACS, COACh offered a half-day workshop called "The Power of Persuasion," the goal of which is "honing communication skills so that one can be more effective in interpersonal relationships in the workplace, in teaching situations and in scientific research presentations. The session includes self-assessment, role playing, and practicing the techniques learned. Topics include effective communication styles for women, projecting confidence and credibility through voice, image, and body language, dealing with difficult conversations and questions, using powerful rather than weak words, methods for effective cyber-communication, and effective scientific presentations" (ACS, 2015). This workshop audience is noted as ranging from students to graduate students to faculty to researchers.

Does the fact that only a few FORWARD workshops have reached sustainability mean that there is no success beyond the first two models mentioned? And, of equal importance, what are the hurdles to institutionalization for the other programs that have to be met?

If we measure success in terms of the Pay It FORWARD project's ability to expand faculty development offerings, we see the project was successful on that measure. The 11 adaptations of the original FORWARD project described in this book (see Chapters 3–13) are proof of that. Expansion has been achieved on a numerical scale (Figure 20.1), a geographical scale (Figure 20.2), and on scales of diversity of disciplines and diversity of ethnic groups.

Figure 20.1 illustrates the growth in the number of people impacted by FORWARD over the timeline of the project. The Pay IT FORWARD phase (2011–2013) drastically increased participation through the sponsored trainee workshops. Overall, more than 1300 doctoral women were touched by the FORWARD program over a 10-year period. These efforts continue today with the institutionalized programs mentioned here, as well as through a number of other avenues. Take, for example, the ATP in BEESS workshop sponsored by Oregon State University (see Chapter 10): while they did not continue to offer a workshop on campus, "the workshop mission was continued at other venues, including socials at Earth Science Association (ESA) meetings and social media discussions" (M. Kavanaugh, 2015, personal communication).

Geographically, the Pay It FORWARD program was also significantly expanded. Figure 20.2 shows the first-tier FORWARD workshops as dots in red, the second tier (trainees and MIT; see Chapter 3) workshops in blue, and the third tier (information sessions and dissemination efforts) in green. Shaded states and provinces are those from which we had participation. The circles are sized by categories of numbers of participants as indicated in the legend. Most notable, geographically in the case of Guam (see Chapter 5), is the reach to cultures, Pacific Islander women

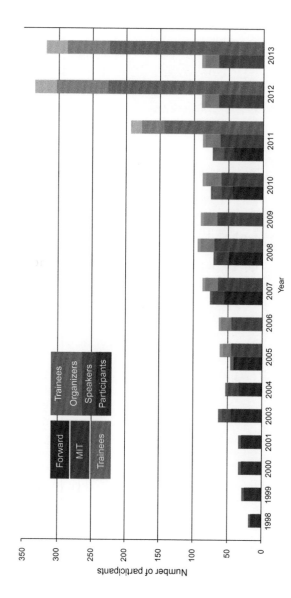

FIGURE 20.1 Numbers of people affected by the FORWARD program, 1998–2013. People participating are indicated in red for FORWARD activities, blue for MIT activities, and gray for trainee (Pay It FORWARD) workshops according to their roles: from darkest to lightest shade: participants, speakers, organizers, and trainees. This graph includes the FORWARD to Graduate School activities during the period 1998–2001.

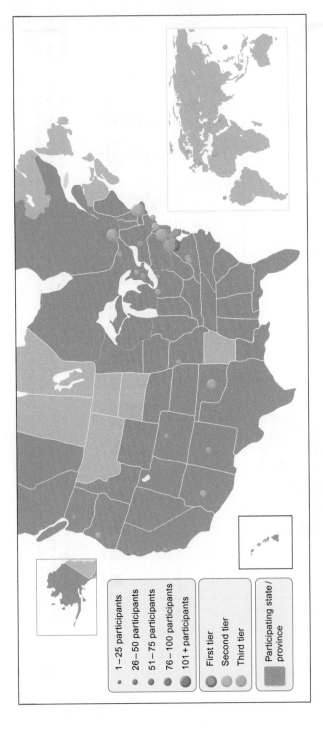

FIGURE 20.2   Geographical impact of the FORWARD program.

there, that we could not cover in a national workshop in Washington, DC, nor for which we could ever be credible, given our ignorance of the nuances of those different cultures. Other cultures best addressed by our trained leaders, were "women of color in the Midwest" at Toledo (see Chapter 6), Hispanic and Native American women in the Southwest (Arizona—see Chapter 4, and Oklahoma—see Chapter 9), and racial diversity in Virginia (see Chapter 7). Discipline cultures were addressed by City Tech (math and computer science—see Chapter 11), Brookhaven National Laboratory (physics—see Chapter 12), Temple (planetary sciences—see Chapter 13), and Oregon State (scientific disciplines with field studies—see Chapter 10). Regional culture was addressed by CWRU (northern Ohio area—see Chapter 8), Oklahoma State (Oklahoma, including small institutions and a tribal college—see Chapter 9), Arizona State (Southwest—see Chapter 4), and City Tech (New York City distributed campuses—see Chapter 11). In our own national workshops, we had approximately 35% minorities, with a handful of deaf PhD scientists.

If the success measure pertains to whether the trainees (FWDers) in the FORWARD model workshops became leaders in recruiting and retaining academic women in STEM, then the project is deemed successful. The leadership roles taken by the trainees are evident in many of the ongoing activities, such as those who institutionalized a program (e.g., Debra Baluch at ASU). The leadership of the University of Toledo project (see Chapter 6) interpreted their success in this way: "We have not organized another workshop, but the lessons learned from our work with this program are definitely evident in our efforts to recruit and retain women and women of color in the STEM disciplines. Many of us are involved with initiatives from the Association of Women in Science, both at the local and national level, to advocate for mentoring, resources, and ultimately equity in STEM education and career success." Project leader Charlene Gilbert was recently named dean and director of The Ohio State University at Lima.

The hurdles for sustainability are both quantitative and qualitative. Funding is paramount to providing continuity of faculty development plans such as workshops. Even programs that are part and parcel of a specific university face the challenge of sustained funding. While an academic teaching or research center itself might see a reliable budget stream, when the center develops a new program, it is not often clear that the specific program will be funded for years. Without commitment from the university leadership, a primary component of sustainability is lost. Obtaining this commitment requires a process of educating and re-educating individuals and administrations (i.e., not a one-time event), especially as campuses have gone through, and continue to experience, great change.

Challenges for faculty development remain: namely, how best to (i) institutionalize individual-level faculty development programs to support, and reduce hurdles to, faculty members' career and personal development and, at the same time, (ii) initiate new work aimed at structural and cultural change focused at departmental school or institutional levels. The two are interrelated, but the latter draws on a change model that suggests that systemic, long-term transformation depends on building infrastructure, normative routines, and procedures and policies that incorporate professional and career development as a part of institutional culture, as well as a positive, proactive orientation to equity and inclusion. Other challenges include the perception that faculty development programs are additive rather than foundational, which means that faculty may find it hard to incorporate participation into their already fully committed schedules or may view these as icing on the cake compared to research or disciplinary-based activities and responsibilities; also challenging is the perception that faculty development is for those who are failing or in need of extra "help" or support. Convincing faculty members that programs such as these are an honor or measure of achievement or professional requirement may resolve these challenges.

To lend support to our arguments presented here, we queried a few directors of faculty development programs across the country. Rania Sanford is the assistant vice provost for faculty development and diversity at Stanford University (Stanford University, 2015). Dr Sanford identified three challenges for faculty development programs. The first is the challenge that faculty face of the changing demands on their time and productivity and how a faculty development center can address this. The second challenge is rooted in faculty autonomy. Faculty members are rarely *required* to do something outside the classroom, and so often attendance at faculty development sessions is predicated on a sort of deficit model—that is, the faculty is lacking something they need. The challenge is to turn faculty development into a value-added model. Finally, the challenge that perhaps time will eliminate is the generational difference among faculty: many of the older faculty managed to sink or swim in their position, learning by fire as it were; the younger faculty are concerned with issues of the workplace, seek more clarity on expectations, and want benchmarks (R. Sanford, 2015, personal communication).

R. Eugene Rice supports this notion, saying: "Some of our best new faculty are being attracted to a new set of priorities focused on the essential missions of our institutions. On the other hand, the old priorities—the assumptive world of the academic professional—remain intact. To the old, the new has been added, and faculty who will be in place at the opening of the new century will have little sense of coherence and direction in their professional lives, particularly when tenure and promotion decisions are being considered" (Rice, 1996, p. 10).

HOW ARE FACULTY DEVELOPMENT MODELS EVOLVING?

Many institutions have established teaching and learning centers, which provide what they call "faculty development." With the increased focus on STEM at every stage in the K−16 pipeline, concomitant focus in faculty development is targeted to preparing faculty to teach within their STEM field. The goal is student-improved learning, not the direct advancement of faculty in their careers. In a report on the role of scientific societies in faculty development, Robert Hilborn noted: "Simply stated, the goals of all of the STEM faculty programs discussed here are to develop expert competence in teaching, to enhance faculty views of teaching as a scholarly activity, and to promote the use of evidence in evaluating the effectiveness of teaching practices. Underlying these goals is the broader goal of enhancing student learning in STEM fields and improving student attitudes about the importance of STEM in our society and in the attractiveness of STEM careers. All of the initiatives focus on the goals directly related to faculty professional development and there is reasonable evidence, to be described below, that indicates that they are successful in increasing faculty members' knowledge about effective pedagogy and encouraging them to adopt those pedagogical methods in their classes. On the other hand, evidence also indicates that the programs may not be as successful as one would like in having faculty continue to use effective pedagogical techniques" (Hilborn, 2012, p. 6).

While most models of faculty development only include programs introducing new teaching techniques and faculty collaboratives [e.g., the George Washington University's University Teaching and Learning Center (GWU, 2015) and many others], a few have chosen a more comprehensive model. Most faculties of medicine provide such training. The University of Kansas Medical Center, for example, hosts a Career Development Center. Their goal is to successfully guide new faculty through the complex path to their first promotion: "To ensure a successful career as defined by both personal and professional success, we provide each faculty member with the mentoring and resources to become an excellent teacher, clinician, and scholar, as well as a good citizen of the division, department, university, and to local, regional, and national professional communities" (The University of Kansas Medical Center, 2015).

There is no clear-cut impetus for changing the faculty development model from pedagogy support to a more comprehensive career development model. The program at San Jose State University did make that change, based on center leadership. Amy Strage, assistant vice president for faculty development and director of the Center for Faculty Development, reported: "Our center began many years ago as a 'teaching and learning' center focused on supporting faculty in their teaching role, through the services of a director/assistant director, an instructional designer and a small number of faculty in residence. When the opportunity to apply for the position of center director arose, I applied, sharing my vision of a more comprehensive center. The person to whom the center then reported (the Associate Vice President for Graduate Studies and Research) was very supportive of that vision, so I was provided with the latitude and resources to develop the Research/Career Planning/Service/Collegial Conversation collaborations and programmatic aspects of our work. Timing, as they say, is everything, as the campus has embraced the breadth of what we do, on our own and in collaboration with other units and offices on campus. The faculty role at institutions like ours—masters comprehensive—with a student population that is so immensely diverse in background, in preparation, and in aspirations and with increasing pressures to bring in external funds—is complex and evolving. In my opinion, it is no longer sufficient to simply help people hone their teaching skills. Faculty need to be able to teach a demanding course load and engage in research, scholarship and creative activity, whether this means figuring out how to recalibrate after being graduate students or post-docs at an R1 institution, or how to re-invigorate their research careers. Work/life balance and juggling the teaching, research, and service aspects of one's career are important topics. Providing opportunities for faculty to plan their careers very intentionally and to collaborate with colleagues is key to their success" (A. Strage, 2015, personal communication).

Other centers echoed the same leadership impact. The director of the Center for Teaching and Faculty Development at the University of Massachusetts, Amherst, also said: "The breadth of programs in our Center is largely the result of the vision of our previous Director, who has engaged in scholarship on the subject of faculty development for many years" (G. Weaver, 2015, personal communication). Gabriela Weaver is also vice provost for faculty development. We can only assume that she is referring to Mary Deane Sorcinelli.

Rania Sanford, assistant vice provost for faculty development and diversity at Stanford University, noted that there seems to be a trend to offer more than pedagogy as part of faculty development. She pointed to the University of Montana Faculty Development Office (University of Montana, 2015), under the direction of Amy Knich, and the Michigan State University Office of Faculty and Organizational Development (Michigan State University, 2015), under the direction of Deb De Zure, as two models from which she took direction. The Office of Faculty Development at Stanford (as opposed to the Center for Teaching and Learning) is a relatively new office, less than 3 years old. It was developed by the provost to look at the status of women on the faculty at Stanford. Originally, the tasks were often legalistic in nature—how to work on faculty searches, for example.

As with other centers, leadership played a role. With the center staff change, the focus became broader. Dr Sanford came to the post from serving as an assistant dean in charge of postdoctoral researchers, of which there were more than 2000 at Stanford. She realized that much of her time was spent resolving conflicts and management issues that had roots in the lack of training and experience on the part of the faculty beyond classroom pedagogy. She felt that helping faculty beyond their typical role would eliminate the issues between postdoctoral researchers and faculty members. Her model is to develop programs for what faculty members need to know beyond teaching. Hence, she began with development programs for junior faculty. Then mid-career faculty, those who had just received tenure, entered into conversations on how the university could best support them, what was expected of them for future advancement, and even identity development given the many different trajectories now open to them. The center partnered with the Center for Teaching and Learning to develop programming. Now, even emeriti faculty are interested in faculty development at their stage of career, she says. The faculty development programs, funded by the university, rely on faculty members and staff as presenters and are short in nature so as not to take a lot of faculty members' time. Programs are designed to an audience of their peers, and the material is presented "in their voice and mindset." Faculty members attend because they see the topic as representing a real problem, and the material is relevant to where they are in academia (R. Sanford, 2015, personal communication).

SOME NEW FACULTY DEVELOPMENT MODELS ARE EVOLVING TO AN ONLINE PRESENCE

While faculty members report being overscheduled and too busy to take time to invest in their careers, some faculty development models have gone to an asynchronous model, providing material and development activities online.

Individual faculty development workshops have posted videos of their sessions as a dissemination effort to further their investments. See, for example, Harvard University's New Faculty Institute 2014 (Harvard, 2014). While the face-to-face interaction is missing, the candidness of the speakers and the tone in the room can still be felt through the video presentations.

As universities embrace more and more online course delivery, and, hence, online teaching, the faculty development for such new modes of teaching has been, understandably, online as well: practice what you preach. Faculty development in these forums revolves around the teaching aspects of online teaching, often on the technical requirements of the online learning software platforms, as well as the challenges of engaging the students and assessing their learning through the online platform (Infande, 2013; Penn State, 2015; MERLOT, 2015). These follow the traditional model of faculty development, focusing on teaching only.

Other, broader, faculty development efforts have gone online simply to offer material and resources to a wider audience. The National Center for Faculty Development and Diversity (2015) has grown by leaps and bounds, according to William Haupricht, vice president for institutional relations: "We have been in existence for 5 years, over which time we have gone from 0 to 77,000 members. People are increasingly comfortable with online education." President and CEO Kerry Ann Rockquemore started the center as a result of an increasing demand for her faculty development material that focused at first on writing in the academy, then time management and support for achieving tenure (K. A. Rockquemore, 2015, personal communication). The most popular topics at the center reflect this; the following workshops are the most in demand: (i) "Every Semester Needs a Plan," (ii) "How To Develop, Write, and Submit Your Article in Nine Weeks," (iii) "How to Overcome Shame, Impostor Feelings, and Become a Prolific Scholar," and (iv) "How to Write Proposals That Get Funded and Papers That Get Cited." With the availability of multiple resources online, faculty members are shifting from a single mentor model of faculty development to a network model of mentoring, as advocated by Rockquemore (2013). Rockquemore notes, however, that she started the center as an independent entity in particular to create a "safe space for faculty to get help without feeling vulnerable to power dynamics" (K. A. Rockquemore, 2015, personal communication), much as we had in designing FORWARD to Professorship as an independent workshop, held at Gallaudet University [i.e., fairly unconnected to other universities (due to its specialization)].

WHAT IS THE FUTURE OF FACULTY DEVELOPMENT?

We queried our trained Pay It FORWARD leaders and directors of faculty development programs at select universities to ask them for their "crystal ball" vision of the future of faculty development programs. Here are their verbatim responses.

Amanda Bryant-Friedrich of the University of Toledo (see Chapter 6) said: "I believe that mentoring will become even more defined in coming years than it is today. Mentoring, advocacy, and championing will move into the academy and take a major role in training of all individuals, but most importantly, women and those from underrepresented groups. Mentoring will become more intrusive as individuals become more informed of the cultural and societal barrier experienced by those not found in the mainstream of STEM disciplines. This training will allow mentors to understand their roles, limits, and relationships in a new and enlightened way. Social media will definitely play a role in this new wave as the information will be more available and the world will become smaller, making it easier for all of us to understand each others' needs and desires" (A. Bryant-Friedrich, 2015, personal communication).

Jennifer Piatek of Central Connecticut State University (see Chapter 13) said: "As for the future of faculty development, I think we're seeing a change in the job market—as tenure-track jobs are getting harder and harder to find, we might focus more on workshops for those planning faculty careers rather than for early career faculty. I think we're also going to see a trend towards virtual workshops (video-conferencing), and focusing on using the Internet for faculty develop-ment, including strategies for online teaching (hybrid and online only courses) and use of social media (etiquette, promotion/networking via Twitter/Facebook/etc.)" (J. Piatek, 2015, personal communication).

Maria Kavanaugh of Woods Hole Oceanographic Institute (WHOI; see Chapter 10) said: "One thing I wonder about is how NSF ADVANCE can ameliorate institutional inertia, much like the recent Sloan Foundation initiative on work/life balance. For example, close to our [chapter's] heart, in late 2013, the Office of Management and Budget released a new rule that stated that some child and family care costs during professional travel could be legitimate expenditures to federal grants. In my mind, this is huge for professional development and advancement in that it may facilitate travel to meetings, networking, and remote field sites. The agencies appear to leave it up to each institu-tion to develop oversight programs. Until the program is in place, the rule cannot be enacted in practice. I don't know what/if a program is in place at Oregon State University, but WHOI has been working on guidelines for over a year. This is just one example where the feds have been progressive on policies related to STEM faculty, but the institu-tions may need more support enacting these policies" (M. Kavanaugh, 2015, personal communication).

Sarah Close of the National Ocean and Atmospheric Administration (NOAA; see Chapter 10) responded to her colleague, Maria Kavanaugh: "I think Maria brought up a good point about the potential for a discon-nect between agency and OMB [Office of Management and Budget] policies and institutional support and guidelines and the institutional inertia therein. I have thought about these types of issues a lot, especially since transitioning from graduate school to a policy fellowship and now job in an agency that funds research (NOAA). The OMB rule that Maria mentioned is fantastic, but as Maria notes, institutions vary in their responses to new rules and policies, and for the most part the implementation of these directives is at the hands of those institutions (as far as I understand it, anyway). So, while national policies do help elevate issues and provide the rules to allow progressive institutional policies to evolve, they are not sufficient and institutions will need to step up to ensure that their faculty are being allowed the full benefit of what these rules provide. That in itself is hard enough, but to do that without then penalizing them (implicitly or explicitly) for taking advantage of these benefits requires, I imagine, an added layer of attention to these issues. Fully leveraging and learning from previous efforts to show how this can be accomplished is a great first step for that—Maria mentioned the Sloan initiative on work/life balance, the ADVANCE program is another, as well as the FORWARD to Professorship program (and this book will be a great contribution to that)."

But more than that, I think (hope?) the future of faculty development is in having leadership at institutions who will affirm the value of *people* (happy, productive people, ideally) to their institution, not just the research funding and students and papers they crank out. And that these leaders then work to ensure that academic institutions are actually responding to some of the issues their faculty face, whether it's learning from past efforts, developing (and enforcing) more progressive policies, fostering innovative approaches to support healthy and productive workplaces, etc." (S. Close, 2015, personal communication).

Amanda Shaffer at CWRU (see Chapter 8) said: "The future of faculty development at Case Western Reserve University, as it is at most research intensive universities, is evolving as faculty needs shift and change. Our office strives to remain nimble and responsive to requests for new or ad hoc programs (e.g., an LGBTQ Research Group, an NSF CAREER Award writing group) while maintaining core programming like To Tenure and Beyond. And while career development for faculty of all ranks is the primary charge, the office has three additional priorities: information dissemination, community building, and partner hiring assistance, which support and engage the faculty member as a whole person" (A. Shaffer, 2015, personal communication).

Gertrude Fraser of the University of Virginia (see Chapter 7) said: "The future of faculty development may lie in customized programs delivered to individuals as they need it via online modules/interactions with a menu of options and perhaps a systematic means of self-diagnosing when additional or more personalized support is needed (i.e., a mentor, or career recharge; leadership development; or help with grant writing or so on). Or a system in which faculty have a certain amount of resources specifically geared towards faculty development that they can spend, as needed. Future challenges are funding for faculty development in state institutions with scarce resources" (G. Fraser, 2015, personal communication).

And finally, Gabriela Weaver, vice provost for faculty development and director of the Center for Teaching and Faculty at the University of Massachusetts, Amherst, said: "My crystal ball is not working at the moment. But I can tell you that my hope is that programs like ours will be able to take greater advantage of technologies that allow multiple modes of providing support and training to our stakeholders, and which allow us to multiply our access to information through networks of institutions who can share instructional resources" (G. Weaver, 2015, personal communication).

As general and tailored offerings in faculty development increase via a number of avenues (including those described here), and more material is available to faculty members online via a growing online community, it is clear that face-to-face, one-on-one, and group support are critical to the success and growth of faculty members, especially for underrepresented groups. Due to their lack of critical mass and hence isolation in their institutions, these groups benefit greatly from coming together periodically in a task-oriented forum such as the workshops described in this book, where the nuts and bolts of developing a successful career can be discussed, while providing a psychosocial support system that can be continued or replicated beyond the event.

So long as faculty development continues to evolve as a mechanism responsive to the needs of the individual in concert with the needs of the academy, both will be well served.

References

American Chemical Society (ACS), 2015. 249th ACS National Meeting & Exposition. Available from: <http://www.acs.org/content/acs/en/meetings/spring-2015.html> (accessed 15.05.15.).

Association for Women in Science (AWIS) Central Arizona, 2014. JumpStarting STEM Careers. Available from: <https://www.awis-caz.org/jsc.html> (accessed 15.05.15.).

George Washington University (GWU), 2015. University Teaching and Learning Center. Available from: <http://tlc.provost.gwu.edu/> (accessed 15.05.15.).

Harvard Graduate School of Education, 2015. Collaborative on Academic Careers in Higher Education (COACHE). Available from: <http://sites.gse.harvard.edu/coache> (accessed 15.05.15.).

Harvard University, 2014. New Faculty Institute 2014. Available from: <http://www.faculty.harvard.edu/Faculty%20Development/New%20Ladder%20Faculty%20Resources/New%20Faculty%20Institute%202014> (accessed 07.05.15.).

Hilborn, R.C., 2012. The Role of Scientific Societies in STEM Faculty Workshops. A Report of the May 3, 2012 Meeting Council of Scientific Society Presidents. American Chemical Society, Washington.

Infande, A., 2013. The Five Components of a Successful Online Faculty Development Program, Faculty Focus, August 16, 2013. Available from: <http://www.facultyfocus.com/articles/distance-learning/the-five-components-of-a-successful-online-faculty-development-program/> (accessed 07.05.15.).

MERLOT, 2015. MERLOT Faculty Development. Available from: <http://facultydevelopment.merlot.org/> (accessed 07.05.15.).

Michigan State University, 2015. Office of Faculty and Organizational Development. Available from: <http://fod.msu.edu/> (accessed 15.05.15.).

National Center for Faculty Development and Diversity, 2015. Available from: <http://www.facultydiversity.org/> (accessed 15.05.15.).

Penn State, 2015. Faculty Development—Outreach and Online Education. Available from: <http://wcfd.psu.edu/> (accessed 07.05.15.).

Rice, R.E., 1996. Making a Place for the New American Scholar. AAHE Working Paper Series, Inquiry #1.

Rockquemore, K.A., 2013. A New Model of Mentoring, Inside Higher Ed, July 22, 2013. Available from: <https://www.insidehighered.com/advice/2013/07/22/essay-calling-senior-faculty-embrace-new-style-mentoring> (accessed 07.05.15.).

Stanford University, 2015. Professional Development Programs. Available from: <https://facultydevelopment.stanford.edu/professional-development> (accessed 15.05.15.).

The University of Kansas Medical Center, 2015. Faculty Development and Mentoring Overview. Available from: <http://www.kumc.edu/school-of-medicine/internal-medicine/faculty-development-and-mentoring.html> (accessed 15.05.15.).

University of Montana, 2015. Faculty Development Office. Available from: <http://www.umt.edu/provost/faculty/faculty-development-office/> (accessed 15.05.15.).

University of Oregon, 2015. COACh. Available from: <http://coach.uoregon.edu/domestic-workshops/> (accessed 15.05.15.).

Lessons Learned

Rachelle S. Heller[1] and Catherine Mavriplis[2]

[1]Department of Computer Science, George Washington University,
Washington DC, USA [2]Department of Mechanical Engineering, University
of Ottawa, Ottawa, Canada

OUTLINE

Introduction	353
The Whole Is Bigger than the Sum of the Parts	354
So You Want to Host a Workshop...	355
The Devil Is in the Details	356
Creating a Buzz	358
Watching Your Creation Mature	359
References	362

INTRODUCTION

When we started planning FORWARD to Professorship in 2001, our major focus was on participant impact and their outcomes. Now, after more than 14 years of implementing this program, it is clear that the project provided guidance and tools for faculty development workshops, team building, and sustainability. Outcomes that we never expected materialized, and others that we expected never happened. What follows is our analysis of our journey in this project, as well as the journeys of our colleagues as they, too, endeavor to provide FORWARD motion to Professorship.

THE WHOLE IS BIGGER THAN
THE SUM OF THE PARTS

A well-run development workshop is a team effort, and not everyone on the team has the same capabilities. Further, not everyone is in the same place or space, sees the same value in the project, nor has the same time to commit to the effort. Cohen and Bailey (1997, p. 241) describe a team as "a collection of individuals who are interdependent in their tasks, who share responsibility for outcomes, who see themselves and who are seen by others as an intact social entity embedded in one or more larger social systems (for example, a business unit or the corporation), and who manage their relationships across organizational boundaries." Keeping these characteristics in mind when forming the team is important. Team diversity is an important value. Building a team with individuals who come from different disciplines, social groups, and even geographic areas expands the abilities of the team. Team members have different individual networks that serve as resources. They have different strengths that lead to different leadership skills so that one member takes on the accounting details, for example, while another member may perform most of the communication tasks.

Serving on a team directly affects the team members, often for the good but sometimes not. Serving on a team brings new professionalism, especially in today's world of collaboration. Team members learn to work together, acknowledge the strengths in others, find new contacts as well as mentors (and mentees), and learn to see the field of Science, Technology, Engineering, and Mathematics (STEM) through different eyes. New skills are acquired, and latent ones are expanded. Team discussions often bring out the creative abilities of the participants through collective decision making and brainstorming. Simple tasks like making posters are learned by watching each other; social abilities, such as how to approach potential speakers and how to network, are just a few of the skills learned. Being on the team that presents a workshop brings the members new visibility, both within their home institutions and with the participants and presenters at the workshop. That said, workshop projects and teamwork take a lot of time, and the outcomes are not always valued as scholarship. There can be a lack of acknowledgment of effort and value that the team provided to the attendees.

But team diversity also brings challenges and distractions. Each discipline has its own vocabulary and value system. Conversations among faculty and staff or faculty from different types of colleges and universities, or across universities and research institutes, can be misinterpreted. While publications are key to one group, service may be key to another. These cross-purposes can hold the team back and are best discussed from the start of the project. Keeping open lines of communication helps! And leaving a bit of ego at the door is another good idea. Come together often and work on lingering problems. Team spirit will grow through shared goals, collaboration, and attention to and resolution of these issues.

Beyond keeping the group together, the challenge is to be sure that the work gets done, milestones are met, and materials are shared. Take time to think about how best to do that and communicate it well, so everyone is on the same page. Some teams use Dropbox or Google drives to share materials, and others use email attachments. Some assign a "librarian" as a keeper of the materials. While each member of the team may begin with an agreed-upon timeline and agenda, teams are forgiving and often lose sight of deadlines. A "timekeeper" or "team-nag" is a lonely job, but an important one to keep the project moving forward (no pun intended!).

If your project is intended to last multiple years, giving careful thought to team succession is important. Good team planning would include a succession plan. Phasing in new team members, so that there are always members who have worked on the team before and have some "collective" memory of how various aspects were accomplished, is useful. A note of caution, though—team members also have to be open to new ideas and not be wedded to the concept that "we didn't do it that way before." As one can imagine, bringing in an entirely new team every time is tricky at best, but sometimes it is unavoidable. Having kept clear and accurate notes on the various aspects of the workshop will serve as a reminder of how to proceed and will prove invaluable for the new team members.

SO YOU WANT TO HOST A WORKSHOP...

As we have described in this book, we believe that a workshop is a valid and valuable model for disseminating information and skill practice in faculty development. But workshops do not just appear, like Athena leaping out of the head of Zeus.

Once a team is in place—even a skeleton team—the first step is to position the workshop so that it meets a need for the target community and meets a goal or has a target outcome. A needs assessment, formally done with your office of institutional research or based on materials gathered by this office on such metrics as faculty retention, mentorship programs, faculty climate, and university policy information, can also serve as a departure point. There are many stakeholders for these types of workshops—and it behooves the team to consider the various needs of these groups: (i) within the institutions, the faculty, the administration, and other supporters, and (ii) beyond the institutions, funders, the larger academic and science communities, policy makers, and society at large. Hosting a few focus groups with stakeholders is a good process for establishing the needs for the workshop. Projected outcomes should be in line with the needs assessment. Base your goals on data—analyze your environment in the context of broad research on women in STEM, but understand your individual situation. Having clear goals is the key to creating a successful workshop.

There are different theories on faculty development (some outlined in Chapter 1) that can also serve as a basis for the workshop. Develop your rationale for how you will achieve the stated goals. Choose an approach for how you will deliver the content and what the content will be. The aphorism is that people generally remember 5–15% verbal (lecture) material, 10–20% visual material, 40–50% when presentations include both visual and verbal information, 60–70% of materials generated during discussion, and a whopping 90% of what is experienced, typically through active learning (Dale, 1969). We strongly recommend fewer "talking heads" and a mix of active sessions. The amount of content that you want to offer may be overwhelming to try to fit into a limited time schedule. Choose wisely so that your workshop can have maximum impact and uniqueness. Future workshops can build on your initial content. Check what else is available and retain essential elements while positioning your workshop for your intended audience.

One of the most important actions that you can take when goal setting is to plan assessment, evaluation, and follow-up with your participants. Evaluate for continuous workshop improvement. Having evaluation data will also help in the future with requests for sustainability of your workshop. Consider positioning your workshop as a model that can become the basis of a sustained project. Projects that integrate these plans from the start find that the entire process is more worthwhile and that the assessment report can elevate the project to the level of scholarship. Having an outside evaluator or a team member whose role is to guide the assessment is an example of best practice.

THE DEVIL IS IN THE DETAILS

Once the goals are set, or they are in the process of being set, it is time to think about the details. The more attention paid to detail, the more rewarding (and less frustrating) the experience will be for the team members and for the participants. The appendices (see page 363) of this book have many materials to help you get started, such as examples of workshop programs, budget sheets, and sample flyers. We will leave those to you to review and focus on workshop time.

Time is key when planning a workshop, and even more important to presenting it. To be blunt, there is never enough time. Participants want, and need, time to process the information provided. Presenters want lots of time to present their valuable materials. Everyone wants time to take a break, network, and connect with others. How much time is provided for each topic or session and how the session is structured has a big impact on the outcome. Remember that reflection is part of learning: structure the time so that participants can think about what they just experienced. And, of course, networking time is vital: for the team to engage with the participants, for the attendees to meet each other to establish new connections, for the presenters to resolve individual concerns and questions, and for potential mentorships to form. Do not underestimate the value of mini-exercise breaks or social events to provide some networking time. Also, be sure to factor in break time after sessions for bathroom runs and caffeine and food refills.

Another challenge in providing networking and establishing contacts is getting the conversation going. Even though we are all highly educated and used to speaking in public, the perfect opening line is hard to come by. Have your team members be distributed among the tables or sitting with the participants, as opposed to team members being clustered together, to get the conversation rolling. This serves a few purposes: the discussions move along, the team members get to know many of the attendees, and the team members can take the pulse of the workshop and get a sense of how it's going. This last item is especially important, in that it raises the team's awareness of unique population needs and challenges and how they are being met. Sitting among the participants provides insight into such issues as how well the visuals project, whether the microphone is working well, and are food choices provided to accommodate allergies and preferences? This allows for midcourse corrections if necessary.

Finally, collecting daily data on the progress of the workshop as part of your assessment provides invaluable information for formative revisions to both context and presentation.

It is tempting to start with thinking about presenters from the very first day that the idea of a workshop comes to mind, but that's putting the cart before the horse. Now that you have a team in place and a structure, the time is right to do this. Speakers set the tone for your workshop, especially the first one. Be sure that you have heard the speaker give a formal presentation, no matter how well you know him or her in other settings. No matter whom you invite to speak, remember that you want to outline what you expect from the presentation—the topic, the length, the handouts, etc.—and understand the expectations that the speaker might have from you. Our experience has proved that a combination of presentation styles works well for a workshop with lots of opportunity for interaction. As you select presenters remember to think about a variety of presentation styles and mix them up during the workshop.

Recruiting speakers is an effort that combines all your networking skills, memories of individuals whose presentation captured you, a concern for a balance among the various speakers and, of course, your budget. Sometimes the best place to find presenters is in your own institution. First, you know them and have easy access to them to explain your needs; and they probably know the audience. Second, while you may want to offer an honorarium, you will not have to compensate for travel. Why not forgo the honorarium? This has to do with the professionalization of women's careers. We know that "women don't ask" (Babcock and Laschever, 2003), and therefore are often not compensated for their time. In a recent email discussion on the Systers network (systers.org), the question was posed of whether speakers to a local conference should be offered an honorarium. The FORWARD group advocates paying speakers, though when the workshops first began, because of our shoestring budget we could only afford to cover travel expenses. What made us change our minds? (That is, what made us advocate to the funding agency for honoraria funds in our budget and to offer them to speakers?) We thought about the difference between volunteering and consulting. While both offer the participating individuals the same intrinsic benefits concerning self-satisfaction, consulting carries more respect and is more likely to be listed on a resume, and more often, our male colleagues choose to consult rather than volunteer. With an honorarium comes respect, a notion that this is an important, valued contribution, and that the speaker is a leader in the field. For advice on the amount to offer for speaker fees, check the recommendations by Lukas (2014).

However, remember that your circle of contacts is wider than your campus or institute. Seek out the individuals who were involved with your research grants: funding officers, evaluators, and budget analysts. If they are not well suited to speak at your event, seek their advice. Cast your net widely.

CREATING A BUZZ

No workshop will succeed if it is a secret. Workshops rely on advertising, recruitment, internal and external support, and evaluation. Once you have settled on the elements of the workshop, it is time to recruit participants. This is often the most difficult step—remember that your audience is made up of very busy people who have many demands on their time. In your promotions about the workshop, be sure to explain the value-add of attending the workshop. You can use quotes from previous workshops (or general quotes from the open literature, if this is your first attempt and you do not have a track record) to indicate what attendees can hope to gain from participation. Advertise where the audience is, by using appropriate list-servs and mailings; consider adding information to the calendars of Web sites of appropriate organizations; be creative. Add information about the workshops on research posters you are presenting, or have a flyer nearby. Even without a big budget, you can create a viral advertisement by including a link to the information about the workshop on your own email signature and that of everyone on your team. Remember, though, to be sure that the website you link to is working and interesting, and consider adding information regularly to make it worthwhile to revisit your site. Think about the use of other social media to attract participants. If you are not a user of such sites as Facebook or Twitter, get help from your institution's media office. The bottom line: look everywhere for potential participants.

Attracting participants is closely allied to positioning the workshop, both in time and in space. Consider the general activity cycle for your participants. If they are university faculty members, the first weeks of a new term are generally not the best time. And, if the summer sounds perfect, remember that faculty often plan on using their summers to make intense strides on research and may not be as available as they first thought. Considering the place to hold the workshop requires similar thinking about the potential audience. While your home institution might seem perfect, realize that attendees may be drawn away by classes, students, and other commitments, and you might lose the flow of the event as a result. For example, combining the criteria for time and place might lead you to develop a series of small workshops on your own campus, meeting every month or so at lunchtime.

WATCHING YOUR CREATION MATURE

As you plan the workshop over a long period of time (say several months to a year), it's exhilarating to see the first participants arrive. The first session is often a bit tense for organizers, as you watch to see if there is an audience for what you had planned to present. The tone needs to be set early, and participants may not necessarily react the way you expected. It is critical to observe and reflect once the day is done and the whole workshop is done. Solicit feedback from speakers and colleague observers, as well as the participants. A carefully planned evaluation will also guide you to gauge the reaction of participants.

It is not uncommon to feel exhilarated and yet deflated after a workshop ends, as you read the attendees' criticisms amid your relief that it's over and you are recovering from the fatigue from running a full-on event for a few days. Advice for the wise: don't read the evaluations on the final day of the workshop. Wait a few days. With a few days' perspective and some rest, you can digest the comments more objectively. Discuss them with your fellow organizers. Jot some notes down, since memory fades and details are hard to recall months later.

On the other hand, you will receive email or social media messages from participants thanking you for the "wonderful experience." Keep those as well. Maintaining the conversation online is time consuming but useful in spreading the word and fomenting enthusiasm. Often, throughout the workshop, several participants emerge from the audience who take on leadership roles in continuing the conversation online. Several times, we had participants organize a LinkedIn group or organize a writing group once they return to their institution.

Word of mouth was definitely the best way we found to enhance recruitment. Delivering a good product—the workshop experience—will allow your creation to grow by leaps and bounds as participants return to their institutions and colleagues with news of their transformative experience and recommend the program to them. For us, we heard in the following years (either informally from new participants or formally through messages from these past participants) that the newcomers had been encouraged to explore our opportunity based on this feedback.

With each rendition of the workshop, new ideas are sparked, by your own observations of the event, by the evaluation comments, by suggestions from speakers and participants, and by your own reflections over time. Further, as you relate the results of the workshop to administrators or through formal conference presentations and written articles, the impetus to be concise and distill the overall impact of the workshop experience allows your vision to gel and leads to new or more focused requirements, goals, and priorities. After the first rendition of your workshop, it is not uncommon to realize that "less is more": the first program tends to be packed with information and "talking head" sessions, while subsequent versions might focus more on active participation and time for networking. The participants, being highly motivated and self-efficacious doctoral scientists, provide plenty of direction for less structured, open-ended sessions.

Finally, as your creation matures, you will see offshoots grow in what your participants, speakers, and fellow organizers choose to do with their time to build on the experience you furnished them. First, it's rewarding to witness many participants going off to successful tenure-track positions and exciting postdoctoral appointments. From time to time, they have written to inform us of their professional progress and successes, give some happy personal news such as marriage or a baby, or ask for further advice. As mentioned previously, several participant leaders take inspiration from the workshop to create new support groups or activities at their institution or in their discipline. Otherwise, you can formally drive the new offshoots by seeking new opportunities and resources to further develop your program, recruit, and groom new leaders, as we did with Pay It FORWARD. Identifying the gaps in your offerings and the areas for which you may need more expertise, you can target new directions for others to develop. For example, as we could not be experts about certain disciplines or ethnic groups, we recruited people who were and provided the structure and funding for them to develop more targeted programs. The result, described in this book, is a rich set of faculty development activities that could not have existed without the sum of our experiences and the longitudinal aspect of the program. In the end, serving more than 1300 doctoral women in a wide range of fields and institutions was the most rewarding aspect of these past 15 years.

As we close this chapter, we offer this final succinct list of recommendations for new workshop organizers:

Suggestions for New Organizers

- Create a strong team with complementary skills: accept that conflict is OK (it yields a better product), divide tasks, and monitor emotions.
- Secure funding.
- Get administrative buy-in on campus or elsewhere.
- Look for allies (e.g., administrators or professional societies—which can result in additional funding).
- Make a timeline and stay organized and on task without sucking up too much time—use the concept of "good enough."
- Use what's out there—don't reinvent the wheel at first, because that can be left to a subsequent iteration.
- Recruit by all methods possible: the Web, social media, networking, direct contact at events, allies, word of mouth, asking participants to spread the word or recommend, and invoke administrators to formally invite or sponsor.
- Invite men (especially as speakers), as they can become allies if they are transformed by the experience.
- Look for diversity (ethnic, geographic, discipline, type of institution, career stage).
- Stay calm.
- Show your enthusiasm, it's contagious.
- Pick speakers who show their enthusiasm and have professional stature to give legitimacy to your event.

- Get feedback, evaluate, and improve.
- Publish! Report your outcomes in print, but also verbally to administrators and decision makers.
- Use your experience and outcomes to influence policy change.
- Build coalitions.
- Keep up the network—reach out to others and pay it FORWARD.
- Enjoy the experience.

References

Babcock, L., Laschever, S., 2003. Women Don't Ask: Negotiation and the Gender Divide. Princeton University Press, Princeton, NJ, USA.

Cohen, S., Bailey, D., 1997. What makes teams work: group effectiveness research from the shop floor to the executive suite. J. Manage. 23 (3), 239−290.

Dale, E., 1969. Audiovisual Methods in Teaching. Dryden Press, New York, NY.

Lukas, J., 2014. A formula for speaking fees. Available from: <http://www.thenerdary.net/post/84544230452/a-formula-for-speaking-fees> (accessed 14.04.15.).

Appendices

TABLE OF CONTENTS

	Page	Description
Overview of FORWARD workshops and sample schedules	364	Appendix A: FORWARD workshops, host institution, workshop title, target audience, and chapter in this book
	366	Appendix B: FORWARD workshop details, duration of each workshop in days, average number of participants per workshop, number of workshops held, and contact person
	367	Appendix C: Sample of a 2.5-day workshop schedule—national model workshop
	369	Appendix D: Sample of a 2-day workshop schedule—Brookhaven National Laboratory and Stony Brook University: CARE 2012
Workshop management resources	371	Appendix E: An example of a poster—Brookhaven National Laboratory and Stony Brook University: CARE 2013
	372	Appendix F: Generic budget—Temple University and Central Connecticut University
	373	Appendix G: Example of Participant Application/Registration Form—Temple University and Central Connecticut University
	374	Appendix H: Sample photography release form—national model workshop
Workshop planning, recruitment, outreach, and follow-up strategies	374	Appendix I: Outreach, recruitment, follow-up strategies, interactive activities, mentoring, and resources used at FORWARD workshops
	376	Appendix J: Workshop planning, handout resources, and workshop sessions
	377	Appendix K: Workshop panel and active session ideas and sustainability strategies
	379	Appendix L: FORWARD ELDers: Experts in Leadership Development for women in STEM academia—Recommendations
	382	Appendix M: Pay It FORWARD Trainees Observation Form

(Continued)

(Continued)

	Page	Description
	383	Appendix N: FORWARD to Professorship participant interviews for future workshop leaders
Workshop resources: Sample icebreaker activities, evaluation forms, and resource list	385	Appendix O: Icebreaker example "M&M"—national model workshop
	386	Appendix P: Icebreaker example "BINGO"—national model workshop
	386	Appendix Q: Workshop evaluation questions
	388	Appendix R: Resource list provided at the FORWARD to Professorship Web site
Reference list for FORWARD	393	Appendix S: Reference list provided to Pay It FORWARD trainees
Work/life integration dialogue	397	Appendix T: A Dialogue on Work/Life Integration

APPENDIX A: FORWARD WORKSHOPS, HOST INSTITUTION, WORKSHOP TITLE, TARGET AUDIENCE, AND CHAPTER IN THIS BOOK

Institutions	Workshop title	Target audience	Chapters
GWU and GU National Workshop	FORWARD to Graduate School	Undergraduate women in STEM	1, 2, 14
GWU and GU National Workshop	FORWARD to Professorship	Women in all STEM fields: doctoral, postdoctoral, and pre-tenure faculty	1, 2, 14, 18
MIT	Path of Professorship	Women in STEM at MIT: doctoral and postdoctoral	3
Arizona State Univ. (ASU)	Jumpstarting STEM Careers	Women and minority faculty and postdocs in the Life Sciences at ASU, Central Arizona AWIS, community college faculty, Hispanics, and Native Americans	4
Univ. of Guam	Advancing Female STEM Faculty in the Western Pacific region	Female STEM faculty at 2- and 4-year institutions within their first 3 years of employment in the Western Pacific region	5

(Continued)

(Continued)

Institutions	Workshop title	Target audience	Chapters
Univ. of Toledo	When and Where I Enter... Women of Color in STEMM	Women of Color in the Midwest: doctoral, postdoctoral, and pre-tenure faculty	6
Univ. of Virginia	Engaging Across Difference	Mid-Atlantic region, HBCU: doctoral, postdoctoral, and pre-tenure faculty	7
Case Western Reserve Univ.	To Tenure and Beyond: Building an Intentional Career in STEM	Full-year longitudinal program in northern Ohio, regional, professional development	8
Oklahoma State Univ. (OSU)	FORWARD OSU	Women and minority faculty at Oklahoma colleges and universities: doctoral, postdoctoral, and pre-tenure faculty	9
Oregon State Univ.	Advancing Toward Professorship in Biology, Ecology, and Earth System Sciences (ATP-BEESS)	Women in Biology, Ecology, and Earth Sciences: doctoral, postdoctoral, and pre-tenure faculty	10
New York City College of Technology (City Tech)	FORWARD to Professorship	Women in Math and Computer Science: doctoral, postdoctoral, and pre-tenure faculty	11
Brookhaven National Lab (BNL) and Stony Brook Univ. (SBU)	Career Advancement in a Research Environment (CARE)	Early career faculty and research staff at SBU and BNL in physics-oriented fields particularly women and minorities, transitions from government to faculty positions	12
Temple Univ. and Central Conn. Univ.	Moving FORWARD in Space	"Lone Wolf" women in planetary sciences: doctoral, postdoctoral, and pre-tenure faculty	13

GWU: George Washington University; GU: Gallaudet University; AWIS: Association for Women in Science; HBCU: Historically Black Colleges and Universities; STEMM includes medicine.

APPENDIX B: FORWARD WORKSHOP DETAILS, DURATION OF THE WORKSHOP IN DAYS, AVERAGE NUMBER OF PARTICIPANTS PER WORKSHOP, NUMBER OF WORKSHOPS HELD, AND CONTACT PERSON

Workshop	Days[a]	Part.[b]	No. of wrks.[c]	Team leaders and contact person*
GWU and GU National FORWARD to Graduate School Workshop	1.5	21	4[d]	Rachelle Heller*, Catherine Mavriplis*, H. David Snyder, Charlene Sorensen*
GWU and GU National FORWARD to Professorship Workshop	2.5	45	7[e]	Rachelle Heller*, Catherine Mavriplis*, H. David Snyder, Charlene Sorensen, Paul Sabila*
MIT Path of Professorship	1.5	60	Yearly[f]	Blanche Staton*, Shannon Morey
Arizona State Univ.	0.5–2[g]	70[g]	5[g]	D. Page Baluch*
Univ. of Guam	3	26	1	Helen Thompson*, Grazyna Badowski, Roseann Jones
Univ. of Toledo	2	33	1	Lesley Berhan, Amanda Bryant-Friedrich*, Nancy Collins, Isabel Escobar*, Charlene Gilbert, Cyndee Gruden*
Univ. of Virginia	0.5–1.5[h]	18	7[h]	Gertrude Fraser*, Margaret Harden*
Case Western Reserve Univ.	1[i]	11	12[i]	Amanda Shaffer*, Susan Freimark*
Oklahoma State Univ.	9	20	1	Jean Van Delinder*, Shiping Deng*, Jeanmarie Verchot*
Oregon State Univ.	2.5	30	1	Kate Boersma*, Sarah Close, Lisa Ganio, Louisa Hooven, Maria Kavanaugh*, Barbara Lachenbruch
City Tech	1	60	5	Pamela Brown, Delaram Kahrobaei*, Nadia Benakli

(Continued)

(Continued)

Workshop	Days[a]	Part.[b]	No. of wrks.[c]	Team leaders and contact person*
Brookhaven National Lab and Stony Brook Univ.	1–2[j]	43[j]	3[j]	Simerjeet Gill*, Triveni Rao*, Kristine Horvat*
Temple Univ. and Central Conn. Univ.	1–2[k]	24	2	Alexandra Davatzes*, Jennifer Piatek*

[a] Duration of the workshop in days.
[b] Average number of participants per workshop (excluding speakers and organizers).
[c] Number of workshops held.
[d] Additional smaller workshops, meetings and/or other activities were held.
[e] Additional activities and smaller scale workshops are not included in this count.
[f] First FORWARD to Professorship workshop in 2005. This model was adopted by MIT and has been used to run yearly workshops since 2006.
[g] A total of five events (most recent in January 2015) but the first two were multiday workshops with an average attendance of 40. The last three events were in the new format of half-day symposia focused on one topic, with three speakers and an average attendance of 90.
[h] A total of seven events. The first was a 1.5-day workshop, while the other six were adapted-format 0.5-day workshops. The first two events were supported by grants from FORWARD that helped develop a model that was used for the subsequent five events supported by a National Science Foundation (NSF) ADVANCE-IT grant.
[i] A longitudinal program of 4 1-day workshops per academic year, giving a total of 12 workshops over three years. Each workshop had an average of 11 participants.
[j] Two 2-day workshop and one 1-day workshop. Planning for the fourth workshop (March 2015) is underway.
[k] Two workshops were conducted: a 1-day workshop and a 2-day workshop.

APPENDIX C: SAMPLE OF A 2.5-DAY WORKSHOP SCHEDULE—NATIONAL MODEL WORKSHOP

Day	Time	Topic
Day 1	11:00 a.m. to 1:00 p.m.	Registration
	1:30 p.m. to 3:30 p.m.	Overview and Welcome: Asking the Tough Questions. The FORWARD Team. How to advance to tenure and promotion by addressing the three legs of teaching, research and service while standing on the fourth leg of home life
	3:30 p.m. to 3:45 p.m.	Break
	3:45 p.m. to 5:15 p.m.	Getting the Most Out of Teaching, Susan McCahan, Univ. of Toronto. Classroom management, using effective teaching and administration methods to minimize disruptions and create a successful learning environment
	6:30 p.m. to 7:30 p.m.	Dinner
	7:30 p.m. to 8:30 p.m.	Keynote Address: Janie Fouke, Senior advisor to the president for international affairs at the Univ. of Florida

(Continued)

(Continued)

Day	Time	Topic
Day 2	8:15 a.m.	Continental Breakfast
	9:00 a.m. to 10:30 a.m.	Planning and Funding Research: Panel and Breakout Sessions. Sonia Esperança, NSF; Jean Chin, NIH; Mary Ann Stepp, Amy Butler, George Washington Univ.; Stephen Lee, U.S. Army Research Office. Finding funding opportunities, planning your approach, writing proposals, resolving reviews, and getting started in your project
	10:30 a.m. to 10:45 a.m.	Break
	10:45 a.m. to 12:45 p.m.	Writing in the Profession: Linda Heller, Writer; Carol Hayes, George Washington Univ. Writing cover letters, teaching philosophy, research plan, and skills descriptions for job applications or promotion. Proposal writing
	12:45 p.m. to 2:00 p.m.	Lunch
	2:00 p.m. to 4:00 p.m.	Communicating in a Male-Dominated Field, Jenepher Lennox Terrion, Univ. of Ottawa
	4:00 p.m. to 4:15 p.m.	Break
	4:15 p.m. to 5:00 p.m.	Service without Overcommitment, Paul Sabila, Gallaudet Univ.
	7:00 p.m.	Museum Visit (light meal)
Day 3	8:00 a.m.	Breakfast
	8:45 a.m. to 10:45 a.m.	Negotiation: Getting What You Want and When To Say No! Ellen F. Kandell, Esq., President, Alternative Resolutions LLC. Strategies for professional negotiation and collegiality as a member of underrepresented groups in academic environments
	10:45 a.m. to 11:00 a.m.	Break
	11:00 a.m. to 12:30 p.m.	Having It All! Panel: Kelly Mack, U. Maryland Eastern Shore, Keri Kornelson and Noel Brady, U. of Oklahoma, Theresa Jefferson, Virginia Tech, Carla Romney, Boston U., Daniel Lundberg, Gallaudet U.
	12:30 p.m. to 2:00 p.m.	Lunch
	2:00 p.m. to 4:00 p.m.	A Personalized Plan, Philip Clifford, Medical College of Wisconsin. Meet with Deans and Chairs to review your plan
		James H. Johnson Jr., Howard Univ.; Ann Powell, Gallaudet Univ.; Carla Romney, Boston Univ.; and others
	4:00 p.m. to 4:30 p.m.	Evaluations and Wrap-Up

APPENDIX D: SAMPLE 2-DAY WORKSHOP SCHEDULE—BROOKHAVEN NATIONAL LABORATORY AND STONY BROOK UNIVERSITY: CARE 2012

Day	Time	Topic
SESSION 1: TENURE, CHAIRS: TRIVENI RAO AND CARRIE-ANN MILLER		
Day 1 morning	9:00–9:30 a.m.	Opening Remarks; Sam Aronson, Director, BNL; Peter Paul, Vice President, Office of Brookhaven Affairs, SBU
	9:30–10:45 a.m.	Presentations: Overview of Tenure. Doon Gibbs, Deputy Director of Science and Technology, BNL; Vitaly Citovsky, College of Arts and Sciences, SBU; Alan Tucker, College of Engineering and Applied Sciences, PTC Chair
	10:45–11:00 a.m.	Coffee Break
	11:00–12:30 p.m.	Panel Discussion. Joanna Fowler, Doon Gibbs, Rita Goldstein, BNL; Vitaly Citovsky, Wendy Tang, Alan Tucker, Lori Scarlatos, SBU
	12:30–1:30 p.m.	Lunch
SESSION 2: RESEARCH GRANT WRITING. CHAIRS: SIMERJEET GILL AND BERNADETTE UZZI		
Day 1 afternoon	1:30–1:50 p.m.	Group Photo
	1:50–3:30 p.m.	Program Manager Presentations: Guebre Tessema, NSF; Jennifer Becker, ARL; Ann Satsangi, FES-DOE; James Davenport, BES-DOE; Sarah Dunsmore, NIH
	3:30–4:30 p.m.	Coffee Break and Interaction with Program Managers (Roundtable Discussions)
	4:30–5:30 p.m.	Critique of Sample Abstracts by Program Managers
	6:00 p.m.	Dinner—Three Village Inn, Stony Brook, NY
SESSION 3: MENTORSHIP. CHAIRS: VINITA GHOSH AND VIVIAN STOJANOFF		
Day 2 morning	9:00–9:45 a.m.	Reshmi Mukherjee, Barnard College, Columbia Univ.
	9:45–10:30 a.m.	Carol Rudman, Rudman Associates
	10:30–10:45 a.m.	Coffee Break
	10:45–11:30 a.m.	Discuss requirements/recommendations for a mentorship program. Discussion leaders: Maricedes Acosta-Martinez, SBU; Peter Daum, Elaine Dimasi, Carol Kessler, BNL; Reshmi Mukherjee, Barnard College; Carol Rudman, Rudman Associates, LLC
	11:30–12:30 p.m.	Panel Discussion and Recommendation Summary
	12:30–1:30 p.m.	Lunch

(Continued)

(Continued)

Day	Time	Topic
SESSION 4: WORK/LIFE BALANCE. CHAIRS: LYNNE ECKER AND LINDA BOWERMAN		
Day 2 afternoon	1:30–1:50 p.m.	Donna Buehler, Director of EAP, SBU—"Work/Life Balance Policies at Stony Brook University"
	1:50–2:10 p.m.	Shirley Kendall, Manager Diversity and International Services Office—"World Class Companies Welcome Work/Life Balance Programs"
	2:30–2:45 p.m.	Coffee Break
	2:45–4:00 p.m.	Panel Discussion: Donna Buehler, SBU; Kathleen Flint Ehm, National Postdoctoral Association; Lauren Hale, SBU; Shirley Kendall, BNL; Marci Lobel, SBU; Bonita London, SBU; An Sickles, BNL
	4:00–4:30 p.m.	Closing Remarks

APPENDIX E: AN EXAMPLE OF A POSTER—BROOKHAVEN NATIONAL LABORATORY AND STONY BROOK UNIVERSITY: CARE 2013

CARE Workshop | 2013

Career Advancement in Research Environment | **March 25-26**

Berkner Hall, Brookhaven National Laboratory | http://www.bnl.gov/care2013/

CARE 2013 for early career

scientists and professionals

in STEM fields will address

skills and strategies needed

to write an effective

research proposal.

Key Dates

Registration deadline: **March 8, 2013**
Acceptance: **March 15, 2013**
Proposal abstract submission:
March 8, 2013

Topics

Opening Remarks:
Dr. Doon Gibbs, BNL
Dr. Peter Paul, SBU

Proposal Submission and Review

Focus Workshops:
Detectors and Instrumentation
Theory and Computation in Basic Science
Nuclear Engineering and Materials
Teaching and Learning tools in STEM fields
Life, Structural Biology and Environmental Sciences
Engineering and Engineering Applications

Writing Grants and Proposals:
Dr. Lester Hoffman

Organizers

BNL

Simerjeet K Gill
Triveni Rao
Vivian Stojanoff

SBU

Carrie-Ann Miller
Kristine Horvat

Contacts

Gretchen Cisco (cisco@bnl.gov)
Mercy Baez (baez@bnl.gov)

APPENDIX F: GENERIC BUDGET—TEMPLE UNIVERSITY AND CENTRAL CONNECTICUT UNIVERSITY

Moving FORWARD in SPACE 2012 Budget

Item	Amount	Amount
Hotel accommodations		
Hotel	$3492.48	
Participant checks	($660.00)	
Subtotal	*$2832.48*	$2832.48
Food + housekeeping	*$1866.96*	$1866.96
Supplies		
Supplies	$600.28	
Mugs/folders/bookstore	$71.52	
Subtotal	*$671.80*	$671.80
Honoraria (4 speakers)		
Speaker 1	$100.00	
Speaker 2	$500.00	
Speaker 3	$500.00	
Speaker 4	$500.00	
Subtotal	*$1600.00*	$1600.00
Travel reimbursements (participants and speakers)		
Person 1	$609.35	
Person 2	$78.00	
Person 3	$239.00	
Person 4	$464.38	
Person 5	$356.60	
Person 6	$309.20	
Person 7	$70.00	
Person 8	$215.20	
Organizer	$273.05	
Subtotal	*$2614.78*	$2614.78
Total		**$9586.02**

APPENDIX G: EXAMPLE OF PARTICIPANT APPLICATION/REGISTRATION FORM—TEMPLE UNIVERSITY AND CENTRAL CONNECTICUT UNIVERSITY

Moving FORWARD in SPACE Application

Contact Information

Name:............................. Institution:.........................

E-mail:............................. Mailing Address:...................

Participant Profile:

The following information is not required but is appreciated in order to help us tailor our program and to complete our reporting to NSF. The information will not be attributed to names [with the exception of your field of expertise unless you indicate that you DO NOT want the field divulged]. Submission of the information is voluntary.

1. Highest degree completed:
2. If you have finished your PhD, how many years ago was it completed?
3. Field of study/research:
4. Current institution/employer:
5. Job title:
6. Primary job function:
7. Desired position 5 years from now:
8. Summarize your professional experience:
9. Your needs:
10. Your career constraints and barriers:
11. Your reason(s) for attending the workshop:
12. Your special workshop requests/needs (disability services, food, transportation, lodging).
13. Your gender (we will be asking participants to share rooms in order to keep costs down):
14. Your ethnicity (for NSF reporting only):

APPENDIX H: SAMPLE PHOTOGRAPHY RELEASE FORM—NATIONAL MODEL WORKSHOP

Pay It FORWARD 2011

Photo Release Form for Training the Trainers

I grant to the FORWARD to Professorship Workshop training 2011 the right to use and incorporate in whole or in part photographs, video, or footage taken of me as a result of my participation of this conference, in any and all media, whether now known or hereafter existing. (Typically, this means publications on the Web site or as part of a professional journal article.)

This agreement shall not obligate the FORWARD to Professorship Workshop training 2011 to use the photographs or to use any of the rights granted hereunder, or to prepare, produce, exhibit, distribute or exploit the photographs.

I will make no monetary or other claim against the FORWARD to Professorship Workshop 2011 for the use of the photographs or footage.

• You may use my photograph with my name attached.
• You may use my photograph only (without my name attached).

AGREED TO AND ACCEPTED this _____ day of _____ 20_____
Participant's Signature:_____
Printed Name of Participant: _____
Telephone/TTY number: _____
E-mail Address: _____

APPENDIX I: OUTREACH, RECRUITMENT, FOLLOW-UP STRATEGIES, INTERACTIVE ACTIVITIES, AND RESOURCES USED AT FORWARD WORKSHOPS

1. **Outreach and Recruitment Strategies**: Participants can be recruited via contact with department chairs, deans, and other senior administrative personnel at target institutions. Also, via contacts within the Science, Technology, Engineering, and Mathematics (STEM) community, e-mails to professional organizations, list-servs, and previous participants. Other common methods used include personal contacts, flyers and posters, Web sites, newsletters, and articles in institution newsletters. Organizers should be open to new ideas; for example, one workshop even provided a 1-year complimentary membership to the Association of Women in Science (AWIS).

2. **Follow-up Strategies**: Several methods have been used by FORWARD workshops to engage participants after the workshops. They include e-mails, post-workshop surveys, and periodic announcements and updates. Other strategies used include follow-up workshops, short meetings, discussion groups, mentoring and buddy systems, phone and video conferences, e-mail list-servs, social media connections (including online discussion forums), LinkedIn groups, Facebook pages, Twitter, and blogs. Care must be taken not to overuse some of these strategies to avoid people opting out of the system. Also, workshop participants can be encouraged to start collaborations among themselves and online networking via www.academia.edu. Other traditional approaches include providing workshop participants with resources on thumb drives, articles, and books after the workshop. Some motivated participants can also be invited to help organize for the next workshop.

3. **Interactive activities**: Several interactive activities have been used at FORWARD workshops. Icebreaker activities are best when done during the first day of the workshop—usually during the first workshop session. They help create a friendly, nonthreatening atmosphere that invites everyone to be engaged during the workshop. Other interactive activities include follow-up discussions on issues arising from previous sessions, working on personalized plans, question-and-answer panels, breakout and group discussion sessions, a networking dinner, a trip to a museum or facility related to STEM, a theater performance related to STEM, a book discussion related to STEM, a movie night, sightseeing, etc.

4. **Mentoring**: The goal in mentoring is to link the workshop trainee teams or participants with mentors who can provide helpful information and advice. The mentors are required to have the necessary experience like successfully running career development workshops, navigating the tenure and promotion process, applying for external grants, and running a research laboratory. Other achievements or experiences are also helpful, including having served as dean or department chair and experience reviewing grant proposals and publications. Mentors can also include minorities or people with disabilities who have overcome barriers to obtain an advanced degree or attain a major career achievement. Pay It FORWARD mentors provided advice to teams developing new workshops for the advancement of women and underrepresented minorities in STEM academia. The mentors offered the benefits of their experience and expertise in organizing workshops for content, logistics, evaluation, and lasting outcomes. The exchanges between trainees and mentors may be done by phone, electronically, in person, or any combination. We also had specialized mentors who were accomplished women, minorities, and people with disabilities who were willing to provide guidance to deaf and hard-of-hearing participants.

5. **Resources**: Various types of materials are provided to workshop participants. Some workshop materials can be distributed to participants electronically or via printed matter. Examples include speaker Microsoft PowerPoint presentations, biographies for speakers and organizers, a contact list of workshop attendees, and a library of relevant reading materials to be borrowed and then returned at the end of the workshop. In addition, participants are usually provided with a bibliography of full-text articles, Web sites, and videos relating to women in STEM or the theme of the workshop.

APPENDIX J: WORKSHOP PLANNING, HANDOUTS, RESOURCES, AND WORKSHOP SESSIONS

Workshop Planning:

- Determine the best dates for the workshop—that is, not during final exams or other busy times.
- Prepare a list of topics and speakers 9–12 months in advance. Consult the "suggestions" provided by pre-workshop surveys or evaluations from previous workshops. The topics should address the needs of the intended workshop participants.
- Start contacting speakers and reserving workshop venues.
- Prepare a resource list of helpful books and Web sites.
- Create the workshop's Web site with program, logistics, and application information and e-mail contacts.
- Accessibility—Determine if any of the participants will need special accommodation (i.e., wheelchair access, sign language interpreter, food allergies, etc.).
- Prior to workshop date: Ask speakers for handouts and presentations to be included in the workshop booklet or to be distributed electronically.
- Provide maps and directions to help those who may not be familiar with the workshop venue or those attending from out-of-town.

Handouts and Resources to Prepare:

Prepare the "check-in" packages, which may include any of all of the following:

- Handouts of full workshop schedule
- Name tags for all workshop attendees, speakers, and organizers
- List of all workshop participants, including their contact information (e-mail)

- Biographies and contact information of the organizers, speakers, and panelists
- Evaluation forms, travel reimbursement forms, and photography release forms (remember to take group photos)
- Icebreaker and other interactive activity worksheets
- Speaker's notes, handouts, and PowerPoints
- Articles of interest (after obtaining permission from publisher or author)
- Maps, directions, and information on meeting venues, restrooms, bus stops, restaurants, etc.

Workshop sessions: Typical workshop sessions

- Welcome and keynote speaker addresses
- Panels and group discussions
- Interactive sessions
- Presentations on teaching, service, research, grants and grant writing, tenure process, etc.
- Optional sessions on starting a research laboratory, managing graduate students and postdoctoral scientists, developing a personal career plan, and other topics pertinent to your target group
- Soft skills sessions: communication skills especially for women or minority groups within the STEM environment, negotiation (which can touch on salary, laboratory startup costs, dual career, stopping the tenure clock, etc.)
- Sessions on work/life integration and time or stress management
- Integrate time into your program for networking, relaxing and discussion

APPENDIX K: WORKSHOP PANEL AND ACTIVE SESSION IDEAS AND SUSTAINABILITY STRATEGIES

Panels and Active Sessions

- Consider panelists with diverse experience or backgrounds. Inclusion of university administrators (i.e., department chairs, deans, provosts, or president) adds important perspectives to issues like salary negotiations, stopping the tenure clock, work/life integration, starting a research laboratory, promotion, and tenure. Panels can also be set up to address issues of interest to the workshop attendees, or issues or topics raised during the previous workshops or pre-workshop evaluations.
- Assemble a writing panel to assess written examples of abstracts, research statements, teaching statements, and grant proposals.

- Provide examples and critique of cover letters, research statements, teaching statements, and other written pieces such as grant proposals or private foundation requests.
- A promotion and tenure panel can feature faculty who have recently received tenure or served in promotion and tenure committees.
- Grant writing skills need to be addressed by knowledgeable agents: a discussion on funding opportunities featuring program officers, faculty, or both with strong funding records brings participants in contact with tangible resources.
- Work/life integration panel—This session is enriched by having panelists with diverse lifestyle backgrounds and experience.
- Negotiation skills can be taught and practiced within the context of the workshop once many of the issues have been raised.
- Role-playing: Participants can practice scenarios that they are likely to find themselves in, such as salary negotiations, conflict resolution, laboratory startup negotiation, work/life integration issues, discussions on expectations for tenure and promotion or merit increases, and how and when to say "No."
- Question-and-answer sessions to address issues of interest to participants.

Sustainability Strategies:

For workshops to be sustainable, several issues must be taken into consideration, including sources of funding and optimum use of resources already available.

- **Monetary:** Workshops can be supported by (i) funding from within the institution, department or grants—e.g., MIT Path of Professorship; (ii) funding from external organizations—e.g., Arizona State University's partnership with the Association of Women in Science (AWIS) or a funding agency such as NSF or NIH or a private foundation; (iii) participant fees; or (iv) a combination of these elements.
- **Leadership:** Workshops can be sustained by actively recruiting and mentoring new leadership teams, who bring an influx of creativity and ideas. Having more people engaged generates a sense of ownership and buy-in while distributing the workload more evenly. Involving or reporting successes and achievements to a senior administrator or stakeholders can lead to sustainability.
- Suggestions for lowering workshop costs:
    - *Minimize fees:* Institutional and regional conferences can keep their registration fees low by using locally available speakers and having participants commute from their homes rather than staying in a hotel.
    - *Meeting location:* Some institutions provided meeting space free of charge or at a subsidized rate—e.g., Arizona State University (ASU) and Brookhaven National Laboratory (BNL).

- *Conference-pooling:* Moving FORWARD in Space (Temple University and Central Connecticut University) blended their second workshop with their discipline's annual national conference which provided the meeting venue free of charge. This also saves time and money for the participants as it makes it possible for them to attend both events at the same place.
- *Speakers:* Advancement in technology has made it possible for speakers to attend or present via videoconferencing (e.g., Skype, Google Hangouts). This is less demanding on the speakers and also cuts down on the travel and accommodation costs, making it easier to invite high-profile speakers who have a tight schedule or live very far from the conference location. Some speakers who cancel their travel at the last minute could still be able to give their presentations virtually.
- *Recycle:* Recycle materials and handouts from the previous meetings. Only update the portions that require updating.

APPENDIX L: FORWARD ELDERS: EXPERTS IN LEADERSHIP DEVELOPMENT FOR WOMEN IN STEM ACADEMIA—RECOMMENDATIONS

Role of the Leadership Development Caucus

Leadership development workshops are few and far between, especially those focusing on women in scientific fields. However, several new programs have emerged over the years, while some more established ones have been increasing and tailoring their offerings. The training of new workshop developers should benefit not only from the FORWARD workshop experience, but also from the collected wisdom of other leadership development programs for women in STEM. As part of our training program, we solicited input from other workshop providers, specifically from some who have devoted their energies to advancing women in science-related disciplines. These ELDers, or "Experts in Leadership Development," helped to guide our efforts in training a new generation of workshop developers.

The ELDer participants were:

- Telle Whitney, president and CEO of the Anita Borg Institute and cofounder (with Anita Borg) of the Grace Hopper Celebration of Women in Computing, first held in 1994. Today, Grace Hopper attracts over 8000 participants.
- Eve Riskin, professor of electrical engineering and director of the ADVANCE Center for Institutional Change at the University of Washington.

- Page Morahan, founding director of the Executive Leadership in Academic Medicine (ELAM) program at Drexel University.
- Jeanne Narum, founding director of Project Kaleidoscope (PKAL), an initiative funded by the National Science Foundation (NSF) to catalyze the transformation of undergraduate STEM learning environments.
- Judy Dilts, professor of biology and associate dean for the College of Science and Mathematics at James Madison University. Judy acted as codirector of the PKAL Leadership Institutes for the Faculty for the Twenty-First Century and the PKAL Leadership Initiative.
- Katie Flint Ehm, project manager at the National Postdoctoral Association (NPA) and organizer of NPA's annual meetings.
- Ted Hodapp, director of education and diversity at the American Physical Society (APS), which offers professional skills development workshops for women in physics.
- Michele Montgomery, of the American Astronomical Society Committee on the Status of Women.
- Anke Lipinsky, scientific associate at the Center of Excellence Women and Science (CEWS), Department of GESIS—Leibniz Institute for the Social Sciences in Bonn, Germany.

ELDers' Recommendations:

A caucus of these program developers was held in 2010, and their recommendations were included in the model developed for trainees. Some of the ELDers' recommendations are presented below. We thank them for their contributions.

1. Team
- A reliable and balanced leadership team is essential for creativity, smooth facilitation, and efficient running of background logistics.
- The team should be able to store all the essential information, listen to everyone, and integrate their ideas to make key decisions.
- The team should be able to seek advice and know how to reconcile conflicting information.
- The roles of all coordinators (everyone in the leadership team) should be clearly defined.

2. Time Management
- Ask your department chair for course release to focus on the workshop preparation.
- Make a timeline backing out dates from the workshop date.
- Recruit other people to handle e-mails and data analysis.
- Set up a planning and communication schedule. Ask presenters *way* in advance so that they have time to prepare and include the event in their schedules.

3. **Preparation**
   - Expect to spend more time than anticipated in preparation—talking to participants, speakers, and facilitators.
   - Study adult learning principles.
   - Meeting time should be efficiently managed to ensure maximum productivity (suggestion—1 slide per speaker!—depending on the context).
   - Do a good literature search and develop a personal resource portfolio.
   - Tell everyone about the program.

4. **Workshop Design**
   - Develop an exercise to get buy-in and lead with it.
   - Design to appeal to every learning type (see, e.g., Myers-Briggs Type Indicator).
   - Use the Kolb Learning Cycle emphasis. Make the workshop as interactive as possible.
   - Consider cultural differences if the audience is diverse.
   - Career advice: Align yourself to your school/department's needs—don't expect them to change for you.

5. **The Agenda**
   - Don't overpack the agenda; leave time for networking; be up front about "less is better."

6. **Attendees and Speakers**
   - Cherry-pick some of the attendees.
   - Invite someone in a position that you wish to have (who may be leaving!).

7. **Running the Workshop**
   - Pick a good venue that will also help set the tone of the meeting (open minds to self-awareness).
   - Build ground rules that help develop trust and confidentiality, while paying attention to facilitation to make the workshop active.
   - Put participants into small groups and foster peer support to counter isolation.
   - Use process observers and take time each day to check on how it's going.
   - Be prepared at the drop of a hat to make midcourse corrections if things are not going well or if they are going in a direction that is better.
   - Know everything about the culture and environment where the meeting will take place—helpers, traffic patterns, food...
   - Pay attention to detail—so attendees have a good experience—no glitches with food, information technology (IT), etc.
   - Have an upbeat activity at the end—e.g., your "aha" moment or peak moment—and make it fun!

APPENDIX M: PAY IT FORWARD TRAINEE OBSERVATION FORM

Pay It FORWARD: FORWARD to Professorship Trainee Workshop
June 2010

Team:_____Participant(s) Observation/Interview:_____

In order to help you understand how the workshop appears to the participant, it may be useful to follow a single participant or small group of participants throughout the workshop. Getting their qualitative impressions of the workshop experience in relation to their own needs may help in the design of your future workshop. For this purpose, we suggest you use this sheet and "interview"[1] the person before the workshop and after the workshop, as well as every day of the workshop. Typically, we see an opening up of awareness that is key to the workshop experience and career development beyond the workshop. A longitudinal interview may help you understand this process.

Please use this form—either in paper or on your laptop— as you make your observations. Topic headings are included to help you generate questions[1] for the face-to-face or e-mail interview.

Pre-workshop	Day 1	Day 2	Day 3	Post-workshop
Expectations	Expectations—met? Changing?	Usefulness of content	Expectations—met?	Reflections
Needs	Take-home messages	Networking	Take-home messages	Follow-up activities?
Awareness	Lingering questions	Usefulness of resources	Outcomes	Outcomes
Mood	Awareness	Awareness	Overall impression	Overall impression
			Awareness	
Pre-workshop experience	Mood	Mood	Mood	

[1]Guiding questions for these interviews are provided in Appendix N.

APPENDIX N: FORWARD TO PROFESSORSHIP PARTICIPANT INTERVIEWS FOR FUTURE WORKSHOP LEADERS

Guiding Questions

You must introduce yourself and assure the participant that these interviews are being conducted for your training and development as a future workshop leader—any insights/quotes selected to be shared will be done so anonymously and shared only in the context of the debriefing session and workshop evaluation reports. Please ask for permission to talk with the participant you select and be clear about how long it will take (10–15 min, tops)—since the main aim during the workshop is for the participants to get to know one another and start to build a network of human and material resources that will provide support for their next steps in their own career trajectory.

Once you have permission to begin, choose 2–3 questions to ask. Listen to the responses and jot a few notes if possible. Afterward, take time to reflect and write down more details of how the participant responded and what she or he said. Be self-reflective as well—if you ad-lib questions, record them, and if you interjected your own comment or story, make a note of it. If you choose to quote an individual, please check back with that person to ensure that the quote is accurate.

Some questions to choose from:

Pre-workshop:

1. Is there a critical event or particular reason you chose to apply and attend this workshop?
2. How did the application process and pre-workshop writing activities influence your expectations for this workshop?
3. What are you looking for in this workshop?
4. Have you participated in other professional development, leadership, or career development activities? (List, describe, how often, how useful, and where—at the home institution, professional meetings, other location?)
5. Are you ready to be here? How are you feeling?
6. Did you run into any obstacles to attending this workshop?
7. What are your first impressions of the agenda?

Workshop Day 1:

1. What were the take-home messages from today for you?
2. In thinking about your "teaching statement," what might change for you?

3. Do you have a lingering thought or question that you would like to ask one of the presenters or workshop leaders?
4. Have your expectations for the workshop changed?

Workshop Day 2:

1. Did you feel that the approach to the sessions fit the content of the session well? How so? Why or why not?
2. What emotions did you face throughout the day today?
3. Are the workshop material resources useful? Is there something that stands out for you?
4. What is your impression of the participants in the workshop?
5. How does the diversity of the workshop participants enhance or diminish your experience of the workshop?
6. What sort of academic service activities interest you most? Are they the same ones that you feel would be best for your career?

Workshop Day 3:

1. How did the workshop compare with your initial expectations?
2. Everyone is a bit tired and full today—but is there something from the workshop that stands out for you?
3. Is there something you wanted more of?
4. Is there something you already knew or would leave out of the workshop?
5. In what ways might you stay in contact or work with the other participants in the workshop or workshop leaders? Do you use Facebook, blogs, Twitter, e-mail, professional meetings, publications, other?
6. What has changed most for you in these 3 days?

Post-workshop: (3 days—3 months later)

1. Reflecting on your experience at the FORWARD to Professorship workshop, what stands out for you?
2. Have you followed up with any additional work on your personal plan started at the workshop?
3. How have you used the resource materials from FORWARD? Print materials? Universal serial bus (USB) drive, forms and

articles, Web links, other participants, the FORWARD leaders, or the Web site?
4. Has anything changed for you since the workshop? (New position, marriage, divorce, baby, negotiated new terms, taken on a leadership role, service, innovated teaching?)
5. Would you recommend this experience to others?

APPENDIX O: ICEBREAKER EXAMPLE: "M&M"—NATIONAL MODEL WORKSHOP

M&M Icebreaker for Introductions

1. **Materials**: M&Ms, small candies, or small tokens such as paper clips.
2. **Instructions**:
   a. Place a large bowl of material in the center of the table or in another place that is easily reachable by participants.
   b. Ask each participant to take as many of the items as they wish and place them in front of themselves.
   c. **Option 1**: Once everyone has taken their share, the rules are announced. For each item you take, you should tell the table or small group a fact about yourself. For example, if you took 10 M&Ms, you would have to make 10 statements about yourself.
   d. **Option 2**: After the rules are announced, everyone is required to find a partner and then share facts about themselves depending on the number of M&Ms taken. At the end, everyone reports back to the whole group one interesting fact that they discovered about their partner.
3. **Comments**: Usually the first person or two will try this task, and after that, the laughs happen, and participants start sneaking back to the bowl to eat!
4. **Outcome**: Most participants do introduce more than two or three facts about themselves.

APPENDIX P: ICEBREAKER EXAMPLE: "BINGO"—NATIONAL MODEL WORKSHOP

- Find someone who fits the criteria in one of the boxes below and **write their first name** in that box.
- The aim is to fill in as many names as possible, preferably completing a line of boxes in a **horizontal, vertical,** or **diagonal** direction. Then yell out **"BINGO!"** when you do.

B	I	N	G	O
DOESN'T OWN A CELL PHONE	HAS GROWN UP ON A FARM	HAS WORKED IN ANOTHER COUNTRY	SPEAKS MORE THAN 3 LANGUAGES	HAS BEEN OR WILL GO TO THE OLYMPICS
HAS BEEN TO ASIA IN THE LAST YEAR	DOESN'T MIND GOING FOR A MAMMOGRAM	HAS RECENTLY READ A GREAT BIOGRAPHY OF A WOMAN	HOLDS A PATENT	IS A GRANDMOTHER
HAS BEEN TO A LIVE COMEDY SHOW LATELY	HAS A DEGREE IN FINE ARTS	LOVES CALCULUS	HAS HAD A BRUSH WITH FAME	IS FROM SCANDINAVIA
FAVORITE COLOR IS PURPLE	DOES A GOOD JOB OF PROMOTING HERSELF	HAS TAKEN A LINGUISTICS COURSE	OWNS MORE THAN ONE DOG	WAS/IS THE MIDDLE CHILD IN HER FAMILY
HAS HAD A STRAIGHTFORWARD CAREER PATH	HAS SHAKEN PRESIDENT OBAMA'S HAND	SEES HERSELF AS BEING DIPLOMATIC AT WORK	CAME FROM OUTSIDE THE COUNTRY TO BE HERE TODAY	HAS WRITTEN A BOOK

APPENDIX Q: WORKSHOP EVALUATION QUESTIONS

Evaluations: In order to assess the participants' expectations and overall workshop experience, evaluation questionnaires (including pre-workshop and pos-tworkshop evaluations) were provided. Specific workshop sessions are evaluated by providing the relevant evaluation questionnaires after the session, when the information is still fresh in participants' minds. Evaluation questions help gauge participants' expectations pre-workshop and what they learned post-workshop. The responses also help organizers to determine which portions of the work-shop were well received and which ones were not, while providing suggestions on what to improve or new topics to include in the next workshop. Included below are some evaluation questions asked at a typical FORWARD workshop. Bear in mind that each workshop will also include evaluation questions that are specific to their audience, region, and session being evaluated.

1. How would you rate the *"insert session name here"*?
   Excellent   *Good*   *Average*   *Fair*   *Poor*
   Comments: _____

For each session, you can ask the same question and add subquestions that are specific to the topic to prompt open-ended comments, such as:

   a. *For the Negotiation session:* Did you have to negotiate for your position? What tip would you offer that the negotiation speaker did not include? What strategy did she or he suggest that might work for you?

   b. *For the Personalized Plan session:* Have you ever written a plan? What strategies that were offered helped you the most? Did the presence of the department chairs and deans enhance this session?

   c. Should we include this topic again next year?

   d. Did this presentation provide you with direction? New ideas for your presentation? New inspiration? New appreciation of the "minefields"?

2. How would you rate the selection of speakers for this workshop?
   Excellent   *Good*   *Average*   *Fair*   *Poor*
   Comments: _____

---

3. How would you rate the activities in terms of their meeting your needs and expectations?
   Excellent   *Good*   *Average*   *Fair*   *Poor*
   Comments: _____

---

4. Overall, how would you rate the *"insert workshop name"* experience?
   Excellent   *Good*   *Average*   *Fair*   *Poor*
   Comments: _____

---

5. How did you find out about this workshop?
6. What other topics would you suggest?
7. Which speaker(s) would you suggest for future workshops?
8. Would you recommend this workshop to your friends?
9. Do you have any other comments or suggestions?

APPENDIX R: RESOURCE LIST PROVIDED AT THE FORWARD TO PROFESSORSHIP WEB SITE

General Guides

1. Caplan, P., 1994. Lifting a Ton of Feathers: A Woman's Guide to Surviving in the Academic World. Univ. of Toronto Press, Toronto.
2. Williams, F.M., Emerson, C.J., 2008. Becoming Leaders: A Practical Handbook for Women in Engineering, Science, and Technology. American Society of Civil Engineers, Reston.
3. Sorcinelli, M.D., Austin, A.E., 1992. Developing New and Junior Faculty. Jossey-Bass, San Francisco, CA.
4. Reis, R. Tomorrow's Professor. Available from: <http://cis.stanford.edu/structure/tomorrowprof.html> (accessed 26.02.15.).

General First-Person Accounts

1. An author to read: A.P. Bucak
2. Gaugler, J.E., 2004. On The Tenure Track in Gerontology—I Wish I Had Known Then What I Know Now. Educational Gerontology, 30, 517−536. Available from: <http://www.tandfonline.com/doi/abs/10.1080/03601270490445122#.VOxSfy51zEc> (accessed 26.02.15.).

Getting the Job

1. Golde, C.M., 1999. After the Offer, Before the Deal: Negotiating a First Academic Job, Academe. AAUP Bull. 85, 44−49. Available from: <http://www.jstor.org/discover/10.2307/40251718?sid=21105464177251&uid=3739256&uid=3739704&uid = 2&uid=4> (accessed 26.02.15.).
2. CRA Workshop on Careers for Women. Available from: <http://www.cs.ucsd.edu/gradedu/resources/applyingforjobs/industryjobapp.html> (accessed 26.02.15.).
3. Ernst, M. Getting an Academic Job. Available from: <http://pag.lcs.mit.edu/~mernst/advice/academic-job.html> (accessed 26.02.15.).
4. Carter, R.G., Scott, J.M., 1998. Navigating the Academic Job Market Minefield. Political Science & Politics, 31, 615−622. Available from: <http://journals.cambridge.org/action/displayAbstract?fromPage=online&aid=8812253> (accessed 26.02.15.).
5. Job Hunting. Available from: <http://www.job-hunt.org/> (accessed 26.02.15.).

6. Negotiating a Job Offer for an Academic Position. Available from: <http://www.brown.edu/about/administration/sheridan-center/ consultations/academic-job-market-resources/negotiating> (accessed 26.02.15.).
7. Northern California Higher Education Recruitment Consortium. Available from: <http://www.hercjobs.org/northern_california/> (accessed 26.02.15.).
8. Online Job Guides and Web site Resources
   a. Academic Careers for Engineering. Available from: <http:// engineering.academickeys.com/> (accessed 26.02.15.).
   b. Graduate Schools. Available from: <http://www.phds.org/> (accessed 26.02.15.).
   c. Physics and Astronomy. Available from: <http://cosmology. berkeley.edu/jobs/jobover.html> (accessed 26.02.15.).
9. Southern California Higher Education Recruitment Consortium. Available from: <http://www.hercjobs.org/southern_california/> (accessed 26.02.15.).
10. Advice Column: Career Talk—Practical Guidance for Academic Job Seekers from Professional Career Counselors. Chron. High. Educ. Available from: <http://chronicle.com/section/Advice-Columns/ 144?cid=megamenu> (accessed 26.02.15.).
11. The Gap that Won't Go Away, 2003. Chron. High. Educ., A12-A16. Available from: <http://chronicle.com/article/The-Gap-That-Won- t-Go-Away/12613> (accessed 26.02.15.).

Having It All

1. Balancing Your Career and Family Life. Available from: <http:// serc.carleton.edu/NAGTWorkshops/earlycareer/balance/family. html> (accessed 26.02.15.).
2. Mason, M.A., Goulden, M., 2004. Do Babies Matter? The Effect of Family Formation on the Lifelong Careers of Academic Men and Women. Available from: <http://www.aas.org/cswa/status/2004/ JANUARY2004/DoBabiesMatter.html> (accessed 26.02.15.).
3. Elizabeth Freeland's article on her career break, plus several articles on the dual career opportunity from the Gazette, a newsletter of the Committee on the Status of Women in Physics of the American Physical Society:
   a. Freeland, E., 2004. Getting back into research: some thoughts and advice on career breaks in physics. CWSP Gazette 23(1), Spring 2004, 4—7.
   b. Freeland, E., 2006. My career break. CWSP Gazette 25(2), Fall 2006, p. 1 and 8.

c. Snyder, K., 2006. Breaking for families—Women physicists find taking a leave is often hazardous to their career. Symmetry, March 2006.

4. Elizabeth Freeland's Career Breaks Webpage. Available from: <http://home.earthlink.net/~papagena/CareerBreaks.html> (accessed 26.02.15.).

5. Ostrow, E., 2003. How to Cope on the Market as an Academic Couple. Available from: <http://chronicle.com/article/How-to-Cope-on-the-Market-as/45351> (accessed 26.02.15.).

6. Beckman, M., 1997. How to Succeed in Science Without Being Single. Available from: <http://www.chroniclecareers.com/article/How-to-Succeed-in-Science/46115/> (accessed 26.02.15.).

7. Marshall, K., 1997. Job Sharing. Perspectives, 6–10.

8. Schneider, A., 2000. Job-Sharing Rises as Professors Seek Flexible Schedules. Chron. High. Educ. Available from: <http://chroniclecareers.com/article/Job-Sharing-Rises-as/32530/> (accessed 26.02.15.).

9. Williams, J., 2004. Singing the Grad-School Baby Blues. Available from: <http://chronicle.com/article/Singing-the-Grad-School-Baby/44567> (accessed 26.02.15.).

10. The A–Z of Dual Career Couples, 2011. Available from: <http://chronicle.com/article/The-A-to-Z-of-Dual-Career/128096/?sid=oh&utm_source=oh&utm_medium=en> (accessed 26.02.15.).

11. McNeil, L., Sher, M., 1999. The Dual-Career-Couple Problem. Report. Available from: <http://www.physics.wm.edu/~sher/survey.html> (accessed 26.02.15.).

12. Wagner, R.B., 2001. The Plight of the Trailing Partner. Available from: <http://m.chronicle.com/article/The-Plight-of-the-Trailing/45389> (accessed 26.02.15.).

13. Williams, J.C., 2003. The subtle side of discrimination. Chron. High. Educ. 49(32) (April 18, 2003), p. C5.

14. Elizabeth, P., Lewis, P., 2000. Two Academic Careers and One Fulfilling Job. Chron. High. Educ. Available from: <http://chronicle.com/free/v46/i28/28b00701.htm> (accessed 26.02.15.).

15. Wilson, R., 1998. When Officemates Are Also Roommates. Chron. High. Educ. Available from: <http://m.chronicle.com/article/When-Officemates-Are-Also-R/101466> (accessed 26.02.15.).

Planning and Funding Research

1. A summary of federal young investigator programs, UC Berkeley. Available from: <http://www.spo.berkeley.edu/fund/newfaculty.html> (accessed 26.02.15.).

2. Army Research Office: Broad Agency Announcement. Available from: <http://www.aro.army.mil/research/arlbaa00/finalarlbaa1.htm> (accessed 26.02.15.).

3. Army Research Office: Young Investigator Program. Available from: <http://www.arl.army.mil/www/default.cfm?page = 8> (accessed 26.02.15.).

4. NASA Headquarters Research Announcements. Available from: <http://www.nasa.gov/about/research/#.VO8TEC51zEc> (accessed 26.02.15.).

5. National Institutes of Health: Award Data. Available from: <http://report.nih.gov/nih_funding.aspx> (accessed 26.02.15.).

6. National Institutes of Health: Career Development Awards. Available from: <http://grants.nih.gov/training/careerdevelopmentawards.htm> (accessed 26.02.15.).

7. National Science Foundation: ADVANCE Program Solicitation. Available from: <http://www.nsf.gov/pubs/2002/nsf02121/nsf02121.htm> (accessed 26.02.15.).

8. National Science Foundation: Award Data. Available from: <http://www.nsf.gov/awards/about.jsp> (accessed 26.02.15.).

9. National Science Foundation: CAREER Program Solicitation. Available from: <http://www.nsf.gov/pubs/2002/nsf02111/nsf02111.htm> (accessed 26.02.15.).

10. National Science Foundation: General Grant Conditions. Available from: <http://www.nsf.gov/funding/pgm_summ.jsp?pims_id=503214> (accessed 26.02.15.).

11. National Science Foundation: Grant Proposal Guide. Available from: <http://www.nsf.gov/pubsys/ods/getpub.cfm?gpg> (accessed 26.02.15.).

12. Office of Naval Research Young Investigator Program. Available from: <http://www.onr.navy.mil/science-technology/directorates/office-research-discovery-invention/sponsored-research/yip.aspx> (accessed 26.02.15.).

13. Matkin, R.E., Riggar, T.F., 1991. Persist and Publish: Helpful Hints for Academic Writing and Publishing. University Press of Colorado, Niwot, CO.

Getting the Most Out of Teaching

1. Learning Styles
   a. Overview. Available from: <http://www.ldpride.net/learningstyles.MI.htm> (accessed 26.02.15.).
   b. Felder Styles. Available from: <http://www.ncsu.edu/felder-public/Papers/LS-1988.pdf> (accessed 26.02.15.).
   c. Felder Index. Available from: <http://www.ncsu.edu/felder-public/ILSpage.html> (accessed 26.02.15.).

d. Identifying your style. Available from: <http://www.inspiration.
com/blog/2012/02/what-learning-style-type-best-fits-you/>
(accessed 26.02.15.).

2. Teaching Tips. Available from: <http://www.honolulu.hawaii.edu/
facdev/guidebk/teachtip/teachtip.htm> (accessed 26.02.15.).

3. University of Wisconsin, Women in Science and engineering
Leadership Institute. Available from: <http://wiseli.engr.wisc.edu/>
(accessed 26.02.15.).

Negotiation: Getting What You Want and When to Say No!

1. Babcock, L., Laschever, S., 2003. Women Don't Ask: Negotiation and
the Gender Divide. Princeton University Press, Princeton, NJ.

2. List of web resources on salary negotiation. Available from: <http://
jobstar.org/tools/salary/negostrt.php> (accessed 26.02.15.).

3. Tillman, L.D. The Power of Saying No. Available from: <http://
www.selfgrowth.com/articles/tillman6.html> (accessed 26.02.15).

Service Without Overcommitment

1. Baez, B., 1999. Faculty of Color and Traditional Notions of Service.
The NEA High. Educ. J. 15(2), 131–138.

2. On Collegiality as a Criterion for Faculty Evaluation, 1999. AAUP.
Available from: <http://www.aaup.org/report/collegiality-
criterion-faculty-evaluation> (accessed 26.02.15.).

Beyond Academia

1. Wagner, R. Consulting Careers Beyond the Big Companies. Available
from: <http://www.chroniclecareers.com/article/Consulting-
Careers-Beyond-the/45441/> (accessed 26.02.15.).

2. Newhouse, M., 1999. Deprogramming From the Academic Cult.
Available from: <http://chronicle.com/article/Deprogramming-
From-the-Acad/45598/> (accessed 26.02.15.).

3. Wagner, R., 2001. Informational Interviewing 101. Available from:
<http://chronicle.com/article/Informational-Interviewing-101/
45380/> (accessed 26.02.15.).

4. Bradley, G., 2001. Negotiating Salary in the Nonacademic World.
Available from: <http://chronicle.com/article/Negotiating-Salary-
in-the/45407/> (accessed 26.02.15.).

5. Advice Column: Beyond the Ivory Tower—What you should know
about nonacademic careers for PhDs, Chron. High. Educ. Available
from: <http://chronicle.com/section/Advice-Columns/144/>
(accessed 26.02.15.).

6. Johnson, M.D., 2002. What You Don't Know About Cover Letters. Available from: <http://chronicle.com/article/What-You-Dont-Know-About-C/46129/> (accessed 26.02.15.).
7. Zientara, M., 1987. Women, Technology and Power—Ten Stars and the History They Made. Amacom, New York, NY.

APPENDIX S: REFERENCE LIST PROVIDED TO PAY IT FORWARD TRAINEES

1. American Association of Colleges of Pharmacy, 2007. Academic Pharmacy's Vital Statistics. Available from: <http://www.aacp.org/about/pages/vitalstats.aspx> (accessed 26.02.15.).
2. American Veterinary Medical Association, 2007. 2007 is DVM Year of the Woman. Journal of the American Veterinary Medical Association News. Available from: <https://www.avma.org/News/JAVMANews/Pages/070615d.aspx> (accessed 26.02.15.).
3. Babcock, L., Laschever, S. (2003). Women Don't Ask: Negotiation and the Gender Divide. Princeton Univ. Press, Princeton, NJ.
4. Bell, A.E., Spencer, S.J., Iserman, E., Logel, C.E.R., 2003. Stereotype Threat and Women's Performance in Engineering. J. Eng. Education. Available from: <http://onlinelibrary.wiley.com/doi/10.1002/J.2168-9830.2003.tb00774.x/abstract> (accessed 26.02.15.).
5. Castellanos, J., Jones, L., 2003. The Majority in the Minority: Expanding the Representation of Latina/O Faculty, Administrators and Students in Higher Education. Stylus.
6. COACh, 2007. Committee on the Advancement of Women Chemists (COACh), Professional Skills Development Workshops. Available from: <http://coach.uoregon.edu/coach/> (accessed 26.02.15.).
7. Cole, S., Barber, E., 2003. Increasing Faculty Diversity: The Occupational Choices of High-Achieving Minority Students. Harvard University Press, Cambridge, MA.
8. Cuny, J., Aspray, W., 2002. Recruitment retention of women graduate students in computer science and Engineering: results of a workshop organized by the Computing Research Association. SIGCSE Bull. 34(2), 168–174.
9. Early Career Geoscience Faculty. Available from: <http://serc.carleton.edu/NAGTWorkshops/earlycareer/index.html> (accessed 26.02.15.).
10. Etzkowitz, H., Kemelgor, C., Uzzi, B., 2000. Athena Unbound: The Advancement of Women in Science and Technology. Cambridge University Press.

11. Gindl, M., Zauchner, S., Bammer, D., 2007. ADVANCED Training for Women in Scientific Research—Reviews on an Innovative Concept. Women in Engineering and Technology Research, PROMETEA International Conference. Available from: <http://www.donau-uni.ac.at/imperia/md/content/department/imb/forschung/publikationen/gindl_zauchner_bammer_advance_2008_preprint.pdf> (accessed 26.02.15.).

12. Ginther, D., Kahn, S., 2006. Does Science Promote Women? Evidence from Academia 1973–2001, National Bureau of Economic Research conference paper. Available from: <http://www.nber.org/~sewp/Ginther_Kahn_revised8-06.pdf> (accessed 26.02.15.).

13. Gustin, T.J., Semler, J.E., Holcomb, M.W., Gmeiner, J.L., Brumberg, A.E., Martin, P.A., et al., 1998. A clinical advancement program: creating an environment for professional growth. J. Nurs. Adm. 8, 33–39. Available from: <http://www.ncbi.nlm.nih.gov/pubmed/9787678> (accessed 26.02.15.).

14. Halber, D., 2005. Workshop offers guidance to help future female academics succeed, MIT Tech Talk. Available from: <http://newsoffice.mit.edu/2005/workshop-1005> (accessed 26.02.15.).

15. Ivie, R., Ray, K.N., 2005. Women in Physics and Astronomy 2005. Am. J. Phys. R-432.02. Available from: <http://www.aip.org/statistics/reports/women-physics-and-astronomy-2005> (accessed 26.02.15.).

16. Johns, M., Schmader, T., Martens, A., 2005. Knowing Is Half the Battle: Teaching Stereotype Threat as a Means of Improving Women's Math Performance. Psychol. Sci. 16, 175–179. Available from: <http://pss.sagepub.com/content/16/3/175.abstract> (accessed 26.02.15.).

17. Jones, L., ed., 2001. Retaining African Americans in Higher Education: Challenging Paradigms for Retaining Students, Faculty and Administrators. Stylus, 2001.

18. Laroche, L., Rutherford, D., 2007. Recruiting, Retaining and Promoting Culturally Different Employees. Elsevier.

19. Long, J.S., ed., 2001. From Scarcity to Visibility: Gender Differences in the Careers of Doctoral Scientists and Engineers. National Academy Press, Washington.

20. Mason, M.A., Goulden, M., 2002. Do Babies Matter? The Effect of Family Formation on the Lifelong Careers of Academic Men and Women. Academe 88, 21–27.

21. Mavriplis, C., Beil, C., Dam, K., Heller, R., Sorensen, C., 2007. An Analysis of the FORWARD to Professorship Workshop—What Works to Entice and Prepare Women for Professorship? Women in Engineering and Technology Research, PROMETEA International Conference.

22. Mavriplis, C., Heller, R., Sorensen, C., Snyder, H.D., 2005. The 'FORWARD to Professorship' Workshop. Proceedings of the 2005 American Society for Engineering Education Annual Conference and Exposition.
23. MIT, 1999. A Study on the Status of Women Faculty in Science at MIT. The MIT Faculty Newsletter. XI. Available from: <http://web.mit.edu/fnl/women/women.html> (accessed 26.02.15.).
24. MIT Graduate Students Office, 2008. Path of Professorship workshop. Available from: <http://odge.mit.edu/development/pop/> (accessed 26.02.15.).
25. Moody, J., 2004. Faculty Diversity—Problems and Solutions. Taylor and Francis.
26. National Academies, 2006. To Recruit and Advance: Women Students and Faculty in Science and Engineering. National Academies Press, Washington, DC.
27. National Academies, 2007. Beyond Bias and Barriers: Maximizing the Potential of Women in Academic Science and Engineering. National Academies Press, Washington, DC.
28. National Academy of Sciences, 1995. Reshaping the Graduate Education of Scientists and Engineers. National Academy Press, Washington, DC.
29. National Science Board, 2008. Science and Engineering Indicators, 2008. National Science Foundation (volume 1 NSB −08-01; volume 2 NSB-08-01A), Arlington, VA.
30. National Science Foundation, Division of Science Resources Statistics, 2007. Women, Minorities, and Persons with Disabilities in Science and Engineering. Available from: <http://nsf.gov/statistics/wmpd/> (accessed 26.02.15.).
31. National Science Foundation, Division of Science Resources Statistics, 2004. Gender Differences in the Careers of Academic Scientists and Engineers: A Literature Review, NSF 03–322. Available from: <http://www.nsf.gov/statistics/nsf03322/> (accessed 26.02.15.).
32. Nonnemaker, L., 2000. Women Physicians in Academic Medicine—New Insights from Cohort Studies. N. Engl. J. Med. 342, 399–405. Available from: <http://www.nejm.org/doi/full/10.1056/NEJM200002103420606> (accessed 26.02.15.).
33. NSF ADVANCE programs portal. Available from: <http://www.portal.advance.vt.edu/> (accessed 26.02.15.).
34. O'Bannon, D.J., Garavalia, L.S., Renz, D.O., McCarther, S.M., 2005. Advancing Women in STEM disciplines to Leadership Roles in Academe. ASEE Paper. 2005-294, Proceedings of the 2005 Annual ASEE Meeting, Portland, OR.

35. Preparing for an Academic Career in the Geosciences. Available from: <http://serc.carleton.edu/NAGTWorkshops/careerprep/index.html> (accessed 26.02.15.).

36. Preston, A., 2004. Leaving Science: Occupational Exit from Scientific Careers. Russell Sage Foundation, New York, NY. See <https://www.russellsage.org/publications/leaving-science> (accessed 26.02.15.).

37. Raphael, R., 2006. Academe Is Silent About Deaf Professors. Chron. High. Ed. Available from: http://chronicle.com/article/Academe-Is-Silent-About-Deaf/22785 (accessed 26.02.15.).

38. Rosser, S.V., 2004. The Science Glass Ceiling: Academic Women Scientists and the Struggle to Succeed. Rutledge, New York.

39. Kilminster, S., Hale, C., Lascelles, M., Morris, P., Roberts, T., Stark, P., et al., 2004. Learning for Real Life: Patient-Focused Interprofessional Workshops Offer Added Value. Med. Educ. 38, 717–726. Available from: <http://onlinelibrary.wiley.com/doi/10.1046/j.1365-2923.2004.01769.x/abstract> (accessed 26.02.15.).

40. SACNAS (Society for the Advancement of Chicanos and Native Americans in Science). Available from: <http://sacnas.org/> (accessed 26.02.15.).

41. Sandler, B., 1992. The Classroom Climate: Still a Chilly One for Women, in Women, Culture and Society: A Reader, Balliet and Humphreys, eds. Kendall Hunt Publishing, Dubuque, pp. 151–158.

42. Steele, C.M., Aronson, J., 1995. Stereotype Threat and the Intellectual Test Performance of African-Americans. J. Pers. Soc. Psychol. 69(5), 797–811.

43. Stewart, A.J., Malley J.E., LaVaque-Manty D., eds. 2007. Transforming Science and Engineering: Advancing Academic Women. University of Michigan Press, Ann Arbor.

44. The Leadership Alliance. Available from: <http://www.theleadershipalliance.org/matriarch/default.asp> (accessed 26.02.15.).

45. Trower, C.A., 2001. Women Without Tenure, Part 1. Available from: <http://sciencecareers.sciencemag.org/career_magazine/previous_issues/articles/2001_09_14/nodoi.10565480637185635938> (accessed 26.02.15.).

46. Trower, C.A., 2002. Women Without Tenure, Part II: The Gender Sieve. Available from: <http://sciencecareers.sciencemag.org/career_magazine/previous_issues/articles/2002_01_25/nodoi.7900867231599505905> (accessed 26.02.15.).

47. Trower, C.A., Bleak, J.L., 2004. Study of New Scholars. Gender: Statistical Report [Universities]. Harvard Graduate School of Education, Cambridge.

48. University of Oklahoma ADVANCE Project, 2008. Big 12 Workshop on Faculty Recruitment, Retention and Leadership. Available from: <http://www.ou.edu/advance/big12> (accessed 26.02.15.).
49. University of Oklahoma ADVANCE Project. Available from: <http://www.ou.edu/advance> (accessed 26.02.15.).
50. Valian, V., 1998. Why So Slow? The Advancement of Women. MIT Press, Cambridge, MA.
51. WELI, 2006. Women in Engineering Leadership Initiative (WELI). Available from: <http://www.weli.eng.iastate.edu/> (accessed 26.02.15.).
52. WEPAN, 2004. Route to 50/50: Shifting Gears for Inclusion, Proceedings from the WEPAN 2004 National Conference: Frehill & Hunt (Proceedings Co-Editors) "X-CD Technologies, Toronto.
53. WISELI, 2006. Study of Faculty Worklife at the University of Wisconsin-Madison. Available from: <http://wiseli.engr.wisc.edu/facworklife.php> (accessed 26.02.15.).
54. Wolf-Wendel, L., Twombly, S., Rice, S., 2003. The Two-Body Problem—Dual-Career-Couple Hiring Practices in Higher Education, Johns Hopkins University Press, Baltimore.

APPENDIX T: A DIALOGUE ON WORK/LIFE INTEGRATION

Work/Life Integration: Dramatic reading

Rachelle Heller and Julie Donovan (George Washington University) and Catherine Mavriplis (University of Ottawa)

Credit: FORWARD to Professorship, NSF Award #0930126

Contact: Rachelle Heller, sheller@gwu.edu

Work/life integration (it is not balance!) is a hot topic these days—whether work is merely a job or a career, and where life is defined as you want it to be—with a partner or not, with children or not, with hobbies and other interests or not—where a job is often hampered by the glass ceiling, where you can see the topmost reaches of the profession but there are few women there; or by glass cliffs, where women are appointed to lead organizational units that are in crisis and are not given the resources and support needed for success; or by glass walls, where you can see your male counterparts and know that you are earning 77 cents to every dollar they earn.

Most recently, the topic has been brought front and center in the popular press by Anne-Marie Slaughter,[2] who wrote in the *Atlantic* about women having it all. I differ with her on a few points, namely: It is not about balance, where sometimes work or family is on the heavy side and sometimes on the light side. And it is certainly not only about professional women resolving work and whether, when, and how to raise children. It is about integrating the work and a life. It is about having the full life you want.

The concept of work/life integration is so complex and so personal that it is not easily captured by studies or research. I therefore thought a fictional piece might be the best way of relating the issues to an audience. The following dramatic reading was inspired by the hundreds of stories we heard from FORWARD to Professorship participants over a 10-year period. The piece is appropriate for performance in contexts such as career or personal development workshops and has been tested on a variety of such audiences. Its performance provides a good departure point for group discussion.

Dramatic Reading

Setting: The anteroom of a university lecture hall. Here, the two main women in this scene are waiting to be led into the hall where they will participate in a roundtable discussion titled, "'Not Waving but Drowning'?: A Forum on Women's Careers in the University." They wear badges bearing their names. There is a table in the foreground with coffee, tea, juice and bagels, etc.

Shelly:	Caffeine! Hallelujah! Last night, my 3-year-old kept me up all night crying and wailing.
Judy:	Poor thing. Nothing serious, I hope?
Shelly:	She'll be fine—thanks. I think she may have an ear infection. My babysitter is taking her to the doctor today instead of me, as I had to get on an early plane from the East Coast to get here. I feel really guilty that I'm not taking her, but it would look so bad if I didn't show up to this forum.
Judy:	Well, considering this is a forum about women's position in the university, you not being able to attend because of your mothering responsibilities would be looked on very favorably, I think; it may even spark a constructive discussion.

[2]Slaughter, A., Why Women Still Can't Have It All. The Atlantic, July/August 2012. Available from <http://www.theatlantic.com/magazine/archive/2012/07/why-women-still-cant-have-it-all/309020/> (accessed 28.03.15.).

Shelly: Well, I'd like to think so, but women with excuses like mine are too often seen as a nuisance. I just don't have the confidence to say, "Look, I can't come—my child is sick."

Judy: And then there'd be men in the audience clueless at what the problem is—not because they never have sick children, but because it's never their problem.

Shelly: Sure. You know, I wish we were one big happy sisterhood, but other women with children aren't always the most sympathetic; in fact, I've found that other women are more sympathetic to men not being able to attend events due to kid commitments.

Judy: Perhaps women should help each other more. I have to remind myself now and then not to be exasperated when one of my female colleagues can't attend a university event because of her children. I know that it's not her problem, but the problem of the system within which she works. But I'm an associate professor at a small university in the South, and the only single woman in the department, so whenever there's an evening event, I'm the go-to woman asked to attend these things because every other woman has family obligations.

Shelly: That must grate on your nerves after a while. There's a point when you're not being asked as an honor, but as a lackey. I think that single women in the university must get fed up with the expectation that they can do anything just because they don't have a husband and children.

Judy: I used to be a pretty competent rock climber, but I'm way out of practice given all my work commitments. I feel superficial saying I can't attend an event because of a hobby, but then that's practically saying that I'll forgo my life and the things that make me happy to put a Band-Aid on a chronic problem: working mothers in the university don't get enough support, and a single woman is also asked (or effectively told) to represent the department on many committees because she is the only woman available.

Shelly: That's right. I also have the dubious distinction of being the go-to person for visiting female students. Honestly, I really enjoy doing a lot of these things, but after a while, the constant presumption that you're available is unfair.

Judy: I just wish the university would be fairer to everyone. It's bad enough being a single woman dealing with a potentially lascivious department chair who thinks I'm available! The last time I traveled to a conference with him, he called my room a few times late at night offering a drink. His tone was a bit suggestive.

Shelly: Are you serious? Did you report this? (Uncomfortable pause).

Judy: No, I decided that I was an adult and that I could handle this myself. I also couldn't face exposing myself by making a complaint, even though I was not at fault. I still feel really uneasy about the interaction, especially when I'm always advocating that students be aware of sexual harassment on campus. I'm embarrassed talking to you about it now.

Shelly: Well, it sounds as if this guy did not respect boundaries and acted really unprofessionally.

Judy: I've let this go for so long that I feel I can't make a fuss about it now.

Shelly: What if he tries it on with another faculty member or a student?

Judy: I know! It plagues my conscience that someone else might suffer because I haven't taken a stronger stand. Even though I made it clear to this individual that his behavior was inappropriate, have I also sent a message to him that it's okay to repeat the behavior?

Shelly: That's hard to know. In addition to more awareness about sexual harassment, it would be great if more universities would realize that providing more child-care support would increase faculty and staff productivity. Professors could get more teaching and research opportunities—those prestigious grants and fellowships that make universities look good. And for travel! To be honest, most of the time I don't even apply to go on conferences; it's just too much hassle and expense.

Judy: That's a shame. Conferences can help you get on. I find that they really inspire my research. Plus, they're a great way of meeting people and networking. And some conferences even have interested publishers who will publish selected conference papers, so you get a publication, on top of all the other benefits of going to a conference.

Shelly: Right. Then on top of not attending enough conferences or going to enough lectures, I'm pregnant again and thinking of taking tenure track delay; but I'm worried that I'll be compared with my male colleagues who did not take the extra year, but whose family grew during that time. And then there's those men who take parental leave and spend it writing more papers.

Judy: Oh, that's fantastic! When are you due?

Shelly: Well, summertime, of course! Because my university can't figure out how to replace me to teach my classes during the regular semesters. I was lucky enough to be able to plan that, but not everyone is. I surely didn't plan twins, though!

Judy: That's par for the course: multitask! But seriously, getting into a position to publish demands a mammoth amount of discipline and single-mindedness; it strikes me that no one can be so single-minded when they are trying to have a life. Eventually, I'll start writing, and that great moment when all the research comes together and makes sense happens.

Shelly: Yes, the classic dilemma is that you feel that you're neither doing the job of a professor nor being a full person properly. Men don't feel like this. My daughter is about to go to kindergarten, and I am about to have twins!

Judy: I bet that your husband will be having an entirely different conversation with his work colleagues when he announces the impending birth of the twins. They'll be all smiles and pats on the back, whereas a woman's work colleagues will be thinking, "What are you going to do about work?" You know that's true. People still view motherhood differently from fatherhood. Basically, kids are still a woman's "problem" rather than a shared responsibility and joy.

Shelly: The system has to change. Did you see the Olympics? The USA women have performed brilliantly, and they could not have done that without Title IX. They should have some kind of Title IX approach for working women.

Judy:	Right, and for all women—not just those with kids. I don't have kid issues, but I do have issues with my department and with the university administration where I work. I'm gay, but I find myself pretending that Sue, my partner, is just a roommate.
Shelly:	Surely most university workplaces support gay rights these days?
Judy:	I wish. I work at a small, conservative college, and my department chair has made a few snide comments showing that he has no idea about anything other than heterosexuality. I'm really apprehensive about how my department will view my sexuality when reviewing my promotion.
Shelly:	That's terrible, particularly since you work in the biology department. Surely biologists understand the nuances of gender?
Judy:	Not if those nuances interfere with ideology. Thankfully, my area of expertise is paleontology and the systematics of dinosaurs, so sexuality doesn't come up very directly! I also specialize in the field collection of Mesozoic vertebrates, so I can pretty much avoid controversial discussions about gay rights in that context too.
Shelly:	It's bound to come up in other aspects of your job, though.
Judy:	Sure. For example, I really want to volunteer for the LGBT community, perhaps even spearhead setting up an LGBT Resource Center in my university, similar to those already existing in many universities around the country. The problem is not only the nature of the volunteering I want to do, but also the fact that the men in my department see volunteering as less valuable than consulting.
Shelly:	Yes, although universities are becoming more aware of the value of volunteering and working with the community, the most prestigious thing is still publishing. Valuable research gets the glittering prizes. Consulting provides pay and networks. Volunteering gets you a pat on the head.
Judy:	I'm sure that we don't want to decry the value of research. That's what we all love to do. It's why we're here.
Shelly:	But a woman's life makes it harder to fulfill what the university rewards most.
Judy:	We all want academic rigor. We're here because that's what we practice and pursue. Yet I do think that women may have a more holistic approach to life. My lab research requires long hours and field work, which I relish; but I also see that there should be time for other opportunities—to have a life outside academia. When you are not in the lab, others question your commitment.
Shelly:	I think that the things women value are not valued by society in terms of pay and respect. The university is part of society and is bound to reflect its values unless it tries hard not to.
Judy:	Taking a career break is not an option for me right now, though I often feel overwhelmed and conflicted. When I mentioned job-sharing to my chair, he asked if I was really committed to science.

Shelly: No wonder women drop out of academia.

Judy: I do think that there's conscious discrimination in the department, but there's also a lot of unconscious discrimination against women in the university. Perhaps if there were more child-care options, improved mentoring for junior faculty to publish more, and an appreciation of why women don't progress through the ranks of academia in the same way men do, then we might get somewhere.

Shelly: You wonder how unconscious bias factors into the decisions of hiring committees.

Judy: Right—I wish we could have more of a discussion in the university about how we can address why career dynamics differ among genders, how women and men are equally well educated, but then, at some stage, a disparity arises whereby men start earning more than women.

Shelly: We should try and make allowances, I think, for career interruptions and the amount of hours that women can put into work. I think that these factors are behind gender differences in earnings across the years.

Judy: Sure, but how can the university get around the fact that women who take career breaks have less job experience than their male counterparts.

Shelly: Universities haven't gotten around the fact; that's an ongoing problem.

Judy: I also think that, at any level, women constantly second-guess themselves and their careers. I know a full professor who has traveled abroad on Fulbright scholarships. She served as chair of my department. Her husband, an academic, and she have worked well over the years as an academic team and as parents.

Shelly: Is her husband still working?

Judy: More than ever. He's been the president at our university for the last 2 years.

Shelly: It must be a nightmare job being the college president's wife; does she have to do hundreds of meet and greets—basically be charming and polite to order?

Judy: (*Laughs*) You know, she says she doesn't mind that; in fact, she enjoys it. It may sound superficial, but there's a civility in short exchanges that can be quite meaningful. It's exciting to know that she's part of a team in that sense. It's inspired her to want to become a college president as well.

Shelly: And take her husband's job?

Judy: (*Laughs*) I'm not sure if he's ready for that! Those two have partnered through academia by taking turns, as each put their career on hold while the other forged ahead. So far, they've passed the baton very well, but now that he's at the top of his game, I'm not sure if he'll want to pass that baton again.

Shelly: You have the dilemma of success but, as a woman, you feel that your luck may be running out—the glass ceiling?

Judy: Right. She's at a crossroads in her life. Their children are grown, and she'd like to make the move to apply to be a college president. You know, she's a pretty confident person, and I believe she has the credentials, but there's a voice inside of her saying that she's being too greedy and she should be thankful for what she's got. She also thinks that her husband's male ego needs the president position more than hers. I know this sounds defeatist, and that she's perpetuating the notion that women have to sacrifice themselves.

Shelly: Well, both of them could be college presidents.

Judy: Only unless they're prepared to carry on a marriage through Skype.

Shelly: That's a conundrum. Is there anything else she'd like to do?

Judy: One thing she mentioned is taking on the issue of parent care. Our parents aren't getting any younger, and they have health problems that could escalate pretty soon. Part of her wants to devote time to that, but she's worried she'd get sucked into a vortex. Her mother, especially, would hate it if she opted out of the president aspiration to look after her. She's always wanted her to forge ahead, in particular because she's a woman.

Shelly: I wonder where the moderator is—it is getting close to our forum time. By the way, the title of the forum we are about to do is "Not Waving but Drowning." I know that's a quote from a poem by Stevie Smith: "I was much too far out all my life/And not waving but drowning." It speaks to how women constantly feel that they're out of their depth, floundering, while society wants them to cheerily wave.

Direction: *Walk off and wave*

THE END
Opportunity for discussion

Index

Note: Page numbers followed by "*f*" and "*t*" refer to figures and tables, respectively.

A

AAAS. *See* American Association for the Advancement of Science (AAAS)
AAC&U. *See* Association of American Colleges and Universities (AAC&U)
AAUW. *See* American Association of University Women (AAUW)
ABD. *See* All but dissertation (ABD)
Academia, 3, 249
   shift in, 196
Academic career, 151, 154–155
   work/family balance, 160, 181, 248–249, 262
Academic toolkit
   balancing family and career, 156–158
   developing negotiation skills, 154–156
   effective mentoring and networking, 153–154
Academic women leaders, building programs for, 320–321
ACS. *See* American Chemical Society (ACS)
Active learning, 4, 11–12, 230, 257, 298, 323–324, 356
ADA. *See* Americans with Disabilities Act (ADA)
ADVANCE Center for Institutional Change, 379
ADVANCE program, 7–8, 20, 32, 74, 96, 130–131, 278–279, 349
Advancing Toward Professorship in Biology, Ecology, and Earth System Sciences workshop (ATP in BEESS workshop), 165, 339–340, 364–365. *See also* FORWARD Oklahoma State University workshop (FORWARD OSU workshop)
   advancing toward professorship in, 171*t*
   demographics, 171–172
   of ATPinBEESS workshop participants, 172*f*
   lessons learned, 180–182

work/life balance, 181–182
   logistical lessons, 173
      conference supplies, 174
      engaged participation, 173
      food and drink, 173–174
      institutional approval for survey, 175
      participant lodging and travel, 174
      publicity materials, 175
      securing venue, 174–175
   outcomes
      highlight on field work, 176–177
      mean effectiveness of personal network, 179*f*
      mean pre-workshop confidence, 178*f*
      perceptions through time, 177–180
      pre-workshop survey, 177
      qualitative successes, 175–176
      quantitative successes, 177
   post-workshop efforts, 182
   survey, 170
   time commitment, 172–173
AFOSR. *See* Air Force Office of Scientific Research (AFOSR)
Agboola, Isaac, 260–261, 261*f*
Air Force Office of Scientific Research (AFOSR), 24–25, 256–257
All but dissertation (ABD), 215
Alumnae community in leadership, 332–333
American Association for the Advancement of Science (AAAS), 3, 180, 339
American Association of University Women (AAUW), 79
American Astronomical Society Committee on the Status of Women, 380
American Chemical Society (ACS), 339
American Physical Society (APS), 200, 380
American Sign Language (ASL), 18, 224
   interpreters in scientific workshops, 240–242

Americans with Disabilities Act (ADA),
        226–227
Anita Borg Institute, 328–329, 379
APS. *See* American Physical Society (APS)
Arizona State University (ASU), 39, 63–64,
        274, 337–338, 378
Arizona team, 65
Army Research Office (ARO), 24–25,
        256–257
ARO. *See* Army Research Office (ARO)
ASL. *See* American Sign Language (ASL)
ASL Interpreters, 34, 240–242
Assessment, 4, 12, 34–35, 37, 84–86,
        99–100, 126, 139–141, 231, 356–357
Association for Women in Science (AWIS),
        69, 96, 274–275, 337–338, 374, 378
Association of American Colleges and
        Universities (AAC&U), 6
ASU. *See* Arizona State University (ASU)
ATP in BEESS workshop. *See* Advancing
        Toward Professorship in Biology,
        Ecology, and Earth System Sciences
        workshop (ATP in BEESS workshop)
AuD. *See* Audiology (AuD)
Audiology (AuD), 237
Audiovisual equipment (A/V
        equipment), 220
A/V equipment. *See* Audiovisual
        equipment (A/V equipment)
AWIS. *See* Association for Women in
        Science (AWIS)

B
Balancing family and career, 156–158
        exploring myth of work/family balance
        in academe, 160–162
Barry Oshry's Organization Workshop, 324
BEESS. *See* Biological, ecological, and earth
        systems sciences (BEESS)
BGSU. *See* Bowling Green State University
        (BGSU)
Biological, ecological, and earth systems
        sciences (BEESS), 167–168
        research within STEM disciplines,
        168–170
BNL. *See* Brookhaven National Laboratory
        (BNL)
Boston University, 54
Bowling Green State University
        (BGSU), 130
Brookhaven National Laboratory (BNL), 40,
        200, 369–371, 378

Brookhaven Women in Science (BWIS),
        200–201
Budgets, 125
Buzz, creating a, 358–359
BWIS. *See* Brookhaven Women in Science
        (BWIS)

C
Campus Climate Survey I (CCS-I), 153
Captioning Services (CART), 241–242
CARE 2012 organization, 202–203
CARE 2013A organization, 205
CARE 2013B organization, 207–208
Career Advancement in Research
        Environment 2012 workshop (CARE
        2012 workshop), 201, 369–370
        attendee job positions and affiliations, 203*t*
        organization, 202–203
        outcomes, 203–204
        topics, 201–202
Career Advancement in Research
        Environment 2013A workshop
        (CARE 2013A workshop), 204
        attendee job positions and affiliations, 205*t*
        organization, 205
        outcomes, 205–206
        poster, 205
        topics, 204–205
Career Advancement in Research
        Environment 2013B workshop
        (CARE 2013B workshop), 206
        outcomes, 207
        topics, 206
        workshop organization advice, 207–208
Career development, 296–297
Career plan development, 137
Career planning, 29, 31, 131, 135–137, 208,
        257
CART. *See* Captioning Services (CART)
Case Western Reserve University (CWRU),
        39, 129–130, 294*t*, 338, 350
        NSF ADVANCE initiative evolution,
        130–131
CCS-I. *See* Campus Climate Survey I
        (CCS-I)
Center for Research on Learning and
        Teaching (CRLT), 9, 27, 250
Center of Excellence Women and Science
        (CEWS), 41, 380
Central Connecticut State University, 40, 349
Central Connecticut University, 271,
        372–373, 379

CEWS. *See* Center of Excellence Women and Science (CEWS)
CFO. *See* Chief financial officer (CFO)
Challenges, 97
  operational, 98
  organizational, 97–98
  personal, 99
Character-related syndrome, 176–177
Chief financial officer (CFO), 329–330
Chin, Jean, 33–34, 258, 263
City Tech, 339. *See also* New York City College of Technology
City University of New York (CUNY), 185, 270
  full-time faculty, 189*t*
  New York City College of Technology, 194–195
Class assessment, within, 330–331
Cleveland State University (CSU), 130
COACh, 339
COACHE. *See* Collaborative on Academic Careers in Higher Education (COACHE)
COFA. *See* Compact of Free Association (COFA)
Collaborations, 200–201, 204, 206, 274–275, 332–333
Collaborative on Academic Careers in Higher Education (COACHE), 339
  faculty survey program, 11
College of Science and Mathematics at James Madison University, 380
Collegiality, level of, 19
Columbia University, 201
Committee on Status of Women in Physics (CSWP), 200
Communication, 33–35, 68*f*, 71–73, 83, 85, 96, 99–100, 100*t*, 126, 169–170, 174, 190, 207, 224, 241–242, 257, 263, 298, 313, 317, 330–331, 354
Compact of Free Association (COFA), 78
Competence, 158–160
Computing, 188–189
Conference supplies, 174
Conference-pooling, 379
Consciousness-raising groups, 6
Cornell University, 212–213
Cover letters, 378
Creation maturing, 359–362
Critical Conversations, 117
CRLT. *See* Center for Research on Learning and Teaching (CRLT)

Crow, Michael, 69
CSU. *See* Cleveland State University (CSU)
CSWP. *See* Committee on Status of Women in Physics (CSWP)
Cultural stereotypes, 167
CUNY. *See* City University of New York (CUNY)
Cu-SeeMe, 230–231
CWRU. *See* Case Western Reserve University (CWRU)

D

D/HoH. *See* Deaf and hard-of-hearing (D/HoH)
Daily formative workshop evaluations, 35–36
Deaf, 226–227
Deaf and hard-of-hearing (D/HoH), 224
  FORWARD on and GU, 234
  on "hearing" participants, 239–240
  Cargo, 239
  F2GS workshop, 235
  GU students, 236
  HCOP, 238
  personal career development, 237–238
  professional scientists, 237
  video interview, 235–236
  strategies for inclusion, 240–242
Demographics, 171–172
  of ATPinBEESS workshop participants, 172*f*
Dean(s), 18, 35, 83, 95–96, 132–133, 143, 247–249, 257, 262, 271, 296, 323, 327–328, 338, 347
Department Chairs, 162–163, 239–240, 248–249, 257, 275, 278–279, 296, 338
Department of Energy (DoE), 202, 274
Department of Science, Technology, and Mathematics (DSTM), 236
Development plan, 140
Dillehay, Deans Jane, 232, 260–261
Discipline specific, 339
Dissemination, 34–35, 130, 207, 290, 317, 340–343, 347–348
Diversity, 332–333
  diversity-effective organizations, 110–111
DoE. *See* Department of Energy (DoE)
Drexel University, 321–323, 326–327, 380
DSTM. *See* Department of Science, Technology, and Mathematics (DSTM)
Dual-career, 7–8, 28–29

E

Early career faculty, 211–212, 215
Earth Science Association (ESA), 340
Earth Sciences Women's Network (ESWN), 171–172
Ecological Society of America (ESA), 182
Ecology and earth systems sciences, 166–167
Effectiveness, 158–160
ELAM program. *See* Executive Leadership in Academic Medicine program (ELAM program)
ELATE program. *See* Executive Leadership in Academic Technology and Engineering program (ELATE program)
ELDers. *See* Experts in Leadership Development (ELDers)
Empowerment, 277–278
Engaged participation, 173
"Engaging Across Difference" workshop, 107
Engineering women faculty, pilot with, 327
ESA. *See* Earth Science Association (ESA); Ecological Society of America (ESA)
Ethnic groups, 340, 360–361
Evaluation forms, 35–36, 296–297, 300–301, 317
Executive coaching, 136, 143
Executive Leadership in Academic Medicine program (ELAM program), 6, 41, 321–323, 325–333, 380
Executive Leadership in Academic Technology and Engineering program (ELATE program), 319
  awareness about, 328–329
  building interest and recruiting for, 327–328
Exotic, 80
Experience, 158–160
Experiential program design, 323–326
Experimenting with and practicing new behaviors, 140
Experts in Leadership Development (ELDers), 41, 257–258, 290–292
  participants, 379–380
"Exploration-rich" activities, 110
Extended family, 79

F

F2GS. *See* FORWARD to Graduate School (F2GS)
F2GS workshop, 235

Faculty development, 1, 29–30, 131–132, 143, 337, 356
  ASU, 337–338
  challenges for, 344
  City Tech, 339
  CWRU, 338
  design issues for, 11–12
    challenges, 12
    handouts, 12
    Mind Tools website, 12
  Eugene Rice, 344–345
  FORWARD model workshops, 343
  FORWARD program, 341f
  future, 348–351
  historical stages, 4, 5t
  models evolving, 345–347
  online models, 347–348
  Pay It FORWARD program, 340–343
  program websites, 4–5
  role of faculty member, 4
  workshops, 353
Faculty Women's Association (FWA), 71, 337–338
"Family-friendly" policies, 181
Federated States of Micronesia (FSM), 78
Feedback, 49–50, 60
Female planetary scientists, 213
Final-day evaluation forms, 35–36
Focus on Reaching Women for Academics, Research, and Development (FORWARD), 8, 18, 65–66, 224. *See also* FORWARD to Graduate School; Pay It FORWARD program
  ADA, 226–227
  "BINGO", 386
  D/HOH into STEM, 227–228
  on D/HOH participants and GU, 234
  deaf, 226–227
  dialogue on work/life integration, 397–403
  duration of workshop in days, average number, 366
  evaluation questions, 386–387
  experts in leadership development for women, 379–381
  faculty development program, 337
  follow-up strategies, 375
  GU, 224
    origins, 228–229
    workshops at, 233–234
  handouts and resources, 376–377
  hard of hearing, 226–227

on "hearing" participants, 239–240
F2GS workshop, 235
GU students, 236
Health Careers Opportunity Program, 238
personal career development, 237–238
professional scientists, 237
video interview, 235–236
host institution, workshop title, target audience, 364–365
interactive activities, 375
M&M Icebreaker for Introductions, 385
mentoring, 375
model, 296–297
outreach and recruitment strategies, 374
panels and active sessions, 377–378
participant application/registration form, 373
Pay It FORWARD projects, 232–233
Pay It FORWARD trainee observation form, 382
photography release form, 374
planning, 376
to Professorship participant interviews, 383–385
to Professorship project, 232–233
resources, 376
list, 388–397
in SEM, 228–230
D/HoH community, 230
F2GS, 232
GRE tests, 232
scholarship award, 231
seminar course, 231
sustainability strategies, 378–379
team, 255–256
2-day workshop schedule, 369–370
2.5-day workshop schedule, 367–368
workshop sessions, 377
Follow-up, 3, 73–74, 98–99, 104, 186–187, 206, 208, 219–221, 233, 264, 300, 317, 338, 356
Follow-up Strategies, 375
Food and drink, 173–174
FORWARD. See Focus on Reaching Women for Academics, Research, and Development (FORWARD)
FORWARD Oklahoma State University workshop (FORWARD OSU workshop), 148. See also Biological, ecological, and earth systems sciences (BEESS)

analysis
experience, competence, effectiveness, and self-efficacy, 158–160
exploring myth of work/family balance in academe, 160–162
post-conference competence means and standard deviations, 162t
pre-conference survey, 158
self-efficacy means and standard deviations, 161t
teaching and research competence means and standard deviations, 159t
teaching and research experience means and standard deviations, 159t
balancing family and career, 156–158
developing negotiation skills, 154–156
effective mentoring and networking, 153–154
implications for future FORWARD workshops, 162–163
key areas, 150–151
as land-grant institution, 151–152
science, gender segregation, and land-grant mission, 152–153
FORWARD to Graduate School (F2GS), 232
FORWARD workshop organization, 276–277
FORWARDers (FWDers), 290, 292
Fouke, Janie, 271
FPBSON. See Frances Payne Bolton School of Nursing (FPBSON)
Frances Payne Bolton School of Nursing (FPBSON), 133–135
Freeland, Dr. Elizabeth, 251f, 260, 262
FSM. See Federated States of Micronesia (FSM)
Funding
National Institutes of Health (NIH), 21, 33–34, 94–95, 130, 202, 205–206, 256–258, 273, 331–332, 378, 391
National Science Foundation (NSF), 7–8, 18–20, 24–25, 32–34, 48, 74, 95, 108, 130, 132, 153–154, 166, 207, 227, 229–230, 238, 250, 256–257, 268, 328–329, 339, 380, 391, 395
Office of the Dean for Graduate Education (ODGE), 48, 57–59
Pay It FORWARD grant, 66, 71
program managers, 271
Funding agency program directors, 31
Future Workshop Developers (FWDers), 36–37, 39–40

FWA. *See* Faculty Women's Association (FWA)
FWDers. *See* FORWARDers (FWDers); Future Workshop Developers (FWDers)

G
Gallaudet Interpreting Service (GIS), 241–242
Gallaudet University (GU), 18, 130, 224–226, 224*f*, 258, 261*f*, 262, 280, 296, 348, 364–365
  to D/HoH, 224–225
  Daniel Lundberg, 239*f*
  FORWARD workshops at, 233–234
  IPEDS survey, 225*t*
  STEM programs at, 226
GCFs. *See* Graduate Community Fellows (GCFs)
Gender segregation, 151–153
George Washington University (GWU), 18, 228–229, 276, 285, 345, 364–365, 397
Georgetown University, 63–64
GIS. *See* Gallaudet Interpreting Service (GIS)
Goals, 4, 12, 20–21, 69, 122, 156–163
Gould, Dr. Elizabeth, 69
Grace Hopper Celebration for Women in Computing, 247, 379
Graduate Community Fellows (GCFs), 56
Graduate Record Examination (GRE), 18–19, 227–228
Graduate students, 6, 13, 21, 40, 48, 50, 56–57, 65, 67, 71, 94, 111–112, 123–124, 126–127, 148–149, 153, 157–160, 159*t*, 162, 169–170, 172–173, 186–187, 192–193, 201–202, 206, 215, 218, 225–226, 249, 251, 258, 272, 277, 299, 311–313, 315, 320, 339–340, 345–346
Graduate Student Government organization, 337–338
Graduate students as leaders, 56–57
Grant proposal writing, 4, 201–202, 204–206, 315
Grassroots actions, 268–270
Grass-roots community organization, 119
GRE. *See* Graduate Record Examination (GRE)
GU. *See* Gallaudet University (GU)
GU Interpreting Services (GIS), 241–242
GWU. *See* George Washington University (GWU)

H
Hampton University, 18, 229–230
Hard of hearing, 226–227
Harvard University, 55, 347–348, 393
HBCU. *See* Historically black college and university (HBCU)
Health Careers Opportunity Program (HCOP), 238
Heller, Rachelle S., 18, 31, 34–35, 84, 228–229, 276, 280
Herber, Dr. Joan, 69
Higher education, 4
  career in, 148
  and land-grant institutions, 151–152
  OSU workshop tools, 150–151
Highlight on field work, 176–177
Historically black college and university (HBCU), 18
History, 3–4, 34–35, 38, 71–72, 80, 111, 148, 261
Holman, Scott, 72
Honoraria, 39, 41, 260, 358
Hood College, 18, 229–230, 235, 256
How To Say No, 25
HR. *See* Human resources (HR)
Human resources (HR), 202

I
IAPs. *See* Institutional Action Projects (IAPs)
Icebreaker activity, 23
ICELA. *See* International Center for Executive Leadership in Academics (ICELA)
Idaho State University, 74
IDEA. *See* Individuals with Disability Act (IDEA)
IDEAL. *See* Institutions Developing Excellence in Academic Leadership (IDEAL)
"Ideal Self", 138–139
Impact, 37, 95, 104, 117, 140, 201–202, 233–234, 272, 290–292, 297–298, 300, 303, 311, 329, 331–332, 346, 353
Individuals with Disability Act (IDEA), 226–227
Influence, 137
Informal peer networks (IPNs), 179
Institution-centered workshop, 55–56
Institutional Action Projects (IAPs), 325–326
Institutional approval for survey, 175

Institutional leadership, 57
Institutional Review Board (IRB), 175
Institutional support, 154—155, 305—306, 323, 339, 349—350
Institutionalized financial support, 57
Institutions Developing Excellence in Academic Leadership (IDEAL), 130—131
  objectives, 131
Integrated Post-secondary Data System (IPEDS), 225*t*
Intellectual outcomes, 280—281
Intentional change models, 138, 139*f*, 143
  developing trust relationships, 140
  development plan, 140
  experimenting with and practicing new behaviors, 140
  "Ideal Self", 138—139
  Learning Agenda, 140
  "Real Self", 139—140
  role-playing, 140
Interactive activities, 375
Interdisciplinary research, 168, 170
International Center for Executive Leadership in Academics (ICELA), 321—323, 328
  alumnae community in leadership, 332—333
  diversity, collaboration, 332—333
  at Drexel Leadership Learning Cycle, 324*f*
  guide improvement of leadership development programs, 330
    within class assessment, 330—331
    evaluation of outcomes, 331—332
    program review and process improvement, 331
  for national leaders in engineering and science
    awareness about ELATE, 328—329
    building interest and recruiting for ELATE, 327—328
    interviews, 326—327
    leaders in engineering and technology, 326
    lessons from first class, 329—330
    pilot with engineering women faculty, 327
  program design evolution, 321—323
Inverso, Dr. Yell, 33—35, 237
IPEDS. *See* Integrated Post-secondary Data System (IPEDS)

IPNs. *See* Informal peer networks (IPNs)
IRB. *See* Institutional Review Board (IRB)

J
James Madison University, 380
Jamieson, Leah, 271
Jumpstarting STEM careers (JSC), 63—64, 69—70, 73
  creating program, 65—66
  event feedback, 73—74
  "leaky pipeline" studies, 64—65
  organizing team, 65
  STEM professionals, 64
  symposium
    Business of Science, 72
    communication, 71—72
  workshop, 67, 69—70
    AWIS, 69
    format, 70—71
    FORWARD team, 69
    modules, 68*f*
    STEM disciplines, 67*f*
    timeline guide, 68*f*
    USDA, 70

K
Kent State University (KSU), 130
Keynote, 24, 32, 69—70, 170, 171*t*
Keynote speakers, 32, 248—249
Keynote speech, 23
Kimmel, Karen, 260—261
Klawe, Maria, 248, 257, 260, 263
Kornelson, Drs. Keri, 259, 262—264
Koster, Janet, 70

L
Lake, Kari, 71—72
Land-grant institution, 151—152
Land-grant mission, 152—153
LC. *See* Learning community (LC)
Lea, Tracy, 72
Leaders, strategies for developing community of
  building programs for academic women leaders, 320—321
  experiential program design, 323—326
  ICELA program design evolution, 321—323
Leadership, 276—277, 333, 378
Leadership development, 290—292
  caucus role, 379
    ELDer participants, 379—380
    ELDers' recommendations, 380—381

"Leaky pipeline" studies, 64–65
Learning, 273–274
  Learning Agenda, 140
  learning-focused conflict, 112
Learning community (LC), 325
Linked-in, 252–253, 360, 375
Listservs, 32, 299
Logistical lessons, 173
  conference supplies, 174
  engaged participation, 173
  food and drink, 173–174
  institutional approval for survey, 175
  participant lodging and travel, 174
  publicity materials, 175
  securing venue, 174–175
Logistics, 143
Lundberg, Daniel, Dr, 239f

M
Mandel School of Applied Social Sciences
  (MSASS), 133–135
Mann, Henrietta, Dr, 148, 149f
Massachusetts Institute of Technology
  (MIT), 20, 48, 273, 337–338
Mathematics, 188–189
Madsen, Lynette, 256–257, 261–262,
  275–276
Mann, Dr. Henrietta, 148, 149f
Medical University of Ohio, 92
Mentoring, 153–154, 157, 272, 375
Merits, 200
Metrics, 98
Michigan State University, 346–347
Michigan Technical University, 285
Micronesia, 77–78, 87
Mind Tools website, 12
Minorities, 32, 38, 67, 104, 130–131, 150,
  153–154, 157, 162–163, 166,
  200–201, 208, 225–226, 232–234,
  237, 255–257, 271, 308–311, 318
Minority women
  respondents, 308–309
  STEM, 290, 293
MIT. See Massachusetts Institute of
  Technology (MIT)
MIT Report, 20
Models, 3–4, 6, 11–12, 321, 337–338, 345
Monetary, 378
Moving FORWARD in SPACE 2012
  Budget, 372
Moving FORWARD in SPACE Application,
  373

Moving FORWARD in Space workshop, 212
  design and implementation, 213–214
  faculty mentors at first workshop, 215f
  follow-up, 220–221
  participant feedback, 219
  schedule for multiple day workshop,
    216t
  schedule for single day workshop, 217t
  settings and demographics, 214–219
  team, 339
MSASS. See Mandel School of Applied
  Social Sciences (MSASS)
Multicultural/multiethnic group, 94
Multiple-day workshop, 215–218
  on-site workshops, 218
  schedule for, 216t

N
Nahrgang, Dr. Jennifer, 72
NASA. See National Aeronautics and Space
  Administration (NASA)
National Aeronautics and Space
  Administration (NASA), 74, 219, 339
National Center for Education Statistics
  (NCES), 225t
National Center for Faculty Development
  and Diversity, 348
National Center for Health Statistics
  (NCHS), 226
National Institutes of Health (NIH), 21,
  33–34, 94–95, 130, 202, 205–206,
  256–258, 273, 331–332, 378, 391
National Institutes of Health/National
  Institute of General Medical Sciences
  (NIH/NIGMS), 202
National model workshop, 367–368, 374
  adaptations
    format and schedule, 298–299
    recruitment, 299
  "BINGO", 386
  M&M Icebreaker for Introductions, 385
National Ocean and Atmospheric
  Administration (NOAA), 349–350
National Postdoctoral Association (NPA),
  380
National Science Foundation (NSF), 7–8,
  18–20, 24–25, 32–34, 48, 74, 95, 108,
  130, 132, 153–154, 166, 207, 227,
  229–230, 238, 250, 256–257, 268,
  328–329, 339, 380, 391, 395
National Society of Black Engineers
  (NSBE), 38

National Technical Institute for Deaf
(NTID), 18, 229–230
Natural affinities for collaboration, 168
Natural Sciences and Engineering
Council of Canada
(NSERC), 9–10
NCES. *See* National Center for Education
Statistics (NCES)
NCHS. *See* National Center for Health
Statistics (NCHS)
Near-peers (mentoring), 21–23, 26–28, 29f
NEASC. *See* New England Association of
Schools and Colleges (NEASC)
Negative perception, 281–282
Negotiation, 157
salary, 27–28, 178f, 314, 377–378
skills, 154–156, 311, 311t
space and support, 27–28, 54–55,
154–155
speakers, 31
start-up packages, 69–70, 154–155, 311t
travel, 21, 247
Networking, 153–154, 196, 274–275
New England Association of Schools and
Colleges (NEASC), 49
New York City College of Technology,
194–195
NGOs. *See* Nongovernmental organizations
(NGOs)
NIH. *See* National Institutes of Health
(NIH)
NIH/NIGMS. *See* National Institutes of
Health/National Institute of General
Medical Sciences (NIH/NIGMS)
NOAA. *See* National Ocean and
Atmospheric Administration
(NOAA)
Nongovernmental organizations
(NGOs), 180
Norfolk State University, 111, 271, 273–274,
280
North Carolina State University, 96
Northern Arizona University, 170
NPA. *See* National Postdoctoral Association
(NPA)
NSBE. *See* National Society of Black
Engineers (NSBE)
NSERC. *See* Natural Sciences and
Engineering Council of Canada
(NSERC)
NSF. *See* National Science Foundation
(NSF)

NSF ADVANCE program
evolution, 130–131
OSU program, 153–154
NTID. *See* National Technical Institute for
Deaf (NTID)

O
Observation, 24, 42, 121, 176–177, 293, 324,
330–331, 360
Observer, 37, 40, 42
ODGE. *See* Office of the Dean for Graduate
Education (ODGE)
Office of Management and Budget (OMB),
349–350
Office of Naval Research (ONR), 24–25,
256–257
Office of the Dean for Graduate Education
(ODGE), 48, 57–59
Ohio State University, 40, 343
Oklahoma State University (OSU), 39, 147,
167–168, 274, 276, 278–279
OMB. *See* Office of Management and
Budget (OMB)
Online faculty development model,
347–348
ONR. *See* Office of Naval Research (ONR)
Operational challenges, 98
Oregon State University (OSU), 40,
167–168, 340, 349
Organizational challenges, 97–98
Organizational skills development, 276–277
OSU. *See* Oregon State University (OSU)
Outcomes, 38, 43, 49–50, 81, 101–103,
141–142, 203–207, 264, 325,
330–332, 353–354
Outreach and Recruitment Strategies, 374
Overcommitment, 84

P
P&T process. *See* Promotion and tenure
process (P&T process)
Panelists, 148–149
Panels and active sessions, 377–378
Participant activities, 248–250
Participant expectations, 248
Participant experience
during conference, 248
institutions round-table discussions, 249
Marie Curie, 251f
negotiation skills, 250
post-conference, 251–252
pre-conference, 248

Participant experience (*Continued*)
two-body problem, 246
women, 245
workshops for women, 246–247
Participant lodging and travel, 174
Participants
charged, 136
Passive lectures, 214
Path of Professorship, 49, 51, 54
Pay It FORWARD award (2011), 130, 374
Pay It FORWARD grant, 66, 71
Pay It FORWARD program, 36, 290
career progression, 310*f*
design, 36–37
competition for seed funding and
training, 38–39
FWDers, 37
training program, 37–38
ELDers, 41
evaluation methods, 300
FORWARD workshop model, 296–297
FWDer teams, 39–40
lessons learning through evaluation
process, 317
logic model, 290–292, 291*f*
national model workshop adaptations
format and schedule, 298–299
recruitment, 299
participation percentage by career
stage, 309*t*
percentage of representation of ethnic
diversity in, 307*t*
project, 232–233, 268, 340
questionnaire respondents, 316*t*
results, 43
check-in interviews, 301–303
formative feedback, 300–301
participant experiences, 303–304
results from follow-up questionnaire,
307–313
snapshot of participant group, 313–316
workshop leader efficacy, 304–307
2010 and 2011 training programs, 42–43
variation in disciplines, 308*t*
workshop, 339
component rating percentage, 312*t*
workshop leadership team training, 292
FORWARD to professorship workshop
session, 294*t*
FWDer teams, 296
FWDers, 292
on-site observations, 293

Pennisi, Elizabeth, 69
People with disabilities in STEM, 226–227,
234, 237, 241–242
Perceptions through time, 177–180
"Permanent white water", 320–321
Personal career plan, 249
Personal challenges, 99
Personal network, 271
Personalized plan session, 29, 84
PFF. *See* Preparing Future
Faculty (PFF)
Photography release form, 374
Pipeline model, 321
PKAL. *See* Project Kaleidoscope (PKAL)
Planetary science, 211–212
Planning group, 111
Politics, 137
Post-conference, 251–252
Power, 137
"Power of Persuasion", 339–340
POWRE. *See* Professional Opportunities for
Women in Research and Education
(POWRE)
Pre-conference, 248
Pre-conference survey, 158
Preparation, 6, 18–19, 64, 70–71, 95,
152–153, 182, 235, 239, 277, 330–331,
345–346, 381
Preparing Future Faculty (PFF), 6
Presenters vs speakers, 258
Pre-tenure STEM faculty, 132, 138
Pre-workshop
survey, 177
work, 114–115
Pre-Workshop Activities, 383
Princeton University, 257, 392
Process improvement, 331
Professional development, 49, 51, 55–56,
93, 95, 186–187, 192. *See also* Faculty
development
Professional Opportunities for Women in
Research and Education (POWRE),
7–8, 20
Professors
lecturers, 214
part-time, 311–313, 315, 316*t*
Program design evolution, 321–323
Program managers, 202, 204–206, 208, 271,
273
Program review, 331
Project competence, 176–177
Project Kaleidoscope (PKAL), 380

Promotion and tenure process (P&T process), 175–176
Publicity materials, 175
Purdue University, 262, 271

Q
Qualitative successes, 175–176
Quantitative successes, 177

R
R1 institutions. *See* Research 1 institutions (R1 institutions)
"Real Self", 139–140
Reappointment, promotion, and tenure processes (RPT processes), 148–149
Recruitment, 10, 32–33, 63–64, 72, 186–187, 230–231, 290–292, 299, 307–308, 327–328, 358–360
Recycle materials and handouts, 379
Regional, 36–37, 194, 268
Regional learning community, 133–135
Requests for Proposal (RFP), 38
Research/grant writing, 85
Research collaborations, 186–187
opportunities for, 188–189, 194
Research 1 institutions (R1 institutions), 234–235, 249
Research Statements, 25–26, 38, 377–378
Resources, 376
development, 8–9
COACHE faculty survey program, 11
CRLT, 9
NSERC, 9–10
WinSETT, 10
RFP. *See* Requests for Proposal (RFP)
RIT. *See* Rochester Institute of Technology (RIT)
Rochester Institute of Technology (RIT), 18, 229–230
Role-playing, 140
RPT processes. *See* Reappointment, promotion, and tenure processes (RPT processes)

S
SACNAS. *See* Society for Advancement of Hispanics/Chicanos and Native Americans in Science (SACNAS)
San Jose State University, 345–346
SBU. *See* Stony Brook University (SBU)
School of Dental Medicine (SDM), 133–135
Science, 148, 152–153

Science, Engineering, and Mathematics (SEM), 18, 224
Science, technology, engineering, and mathematics (STEM), 2, 18, 48, 63–64, 77–78, 130, 200–201, 255–256, 268, 290, 339, 354, 374
early programs and movements, 5
ADVANCE program, 7–8
consciousness-raising groups and meetings, 6
FORWARD program, 8
NSF, 7
POWRE, 7
SWE, 5–6
WEPAN, 6
OSU workshop and, 151
programs for advancing women in, 5–8
women, 313–316
beyond workshops, 13–14
Science, technology, engineering, mathematics, and medicine (STEMM), 92, 320
Science Education Resource Center at Carleton College (SERC), 212
SDM. *See* School of Dental Medicine (SDM)
Second-tier workshops, 290
Securing venue, 174–175
Self-awareness, 136
Self-care, 93, 97–98
Self-efficacy, 158–160, 161*t*
SEM. *See* Science, Engineering, and Mathematics (SEM)
SERC. *See* Science Education Resource Center at Carleton College (SERC)
Service
overcommitment, 34, 84–85
sessions, 31
SHPE. *See* Society of Hispanic Professional Engineers (SHPE)
Single day workshop
conference workshop, 218–219
schedule for, 217*t*
Skill building, 137
and learning, 272–273
Skype, 214, 253, 379
SMART goals. *See* Specific, measureable, attainable, realistic, time-bound goals (SMART goals)
Smith College, 18, 229–230
Snyder, David, 18, 31, 34–35, 227–229, 235, 237–239
Social entrepreneurship and advocacy, 270

Society for Advancement of Hispanics/
    Chicanos and Native Americans in
    Science (SACNAS), 35
Society of Hispanic Professional Engineers
    (SHPE), 38
Society of Women Engineers (SWE), 5–6, 38
Sorensen, Charlene, 18, 31, 34–35, 228–229,
    235–239, 280
Speakers, 27, 31–32, 34, 38–39, 49–50,
    53–54, 60, 66–67, 68f, 69–70, 72–73,
    84, 194, 201–202, 205–206, 208,
    213–214, 218, 237, 241, 246, 250,
    255–256, 271, 273–274, 280, 296,
    376–377, 379, 381, 387
  choosing, 30–32, 358
    administrators, 32
    funding agency program directors, 31
    issues of STEM higher education, 31
    keynote speakers, 32
    negotiation speakers, 31
    teaching session, 31
    writing and service sessions, 31
  career planning send-off session, 257
  eager speakers, 258
    GU, 258, 260–261
    MIT FORWARD workshop, 259–260
    two-body problem, 259
  FORWARD team, 255–257
  invited speakers, 297, 301, 361
  keynote speaker, 297–298
  unanticipated impact on presenters, 261
    FORWARD seminars, 262
    personal stories, 264
Specific, measureable, attainable, realistic,
    time-bound goals (SMART goals),
    136, 141
Springboard, 279–280
Stanford University, 344, 346–347
STEM. See Science, technology,
    engineering, and mathematics
    (STEM)
STEMM. See Science, technology,
    engineering, mathematics, and
    medicine (STEMM)
Stereotype threat, strategies to face,
    156–158
Stony Brook University (SBU), 200–201,
    369–371
Stress Management, 29, 257
Student leadership model
    challenges and responses, 58–59
    graduate students as leaders, 56–57

impact on attendees and organizers, 50,
    50t
    2012 survey of MIT alumni, 50–51
    benefits to speakers and attendees,
        53–54
    former planning team members, 52–53
    mentorship lessons, 53
    number of women at MIT, 51, 52f
    Path of Professorship, 51, 54
    valuable networking opportunity, 53
  institution-centered workshop, 55–56
  institutional leadership, 57
  institutionalized financial support, 57
  lessons learned, 60
  origin and goals, 48
  revisions, 59–60
  successes and outcomes, 49–50
  workshop sessions, 54–55
Sustainability, 282, 378–379
SWE. See Society of Women Engineers
    (SWE)

T
Teaching, 4, 12, 24, 30, 68f, 69–70, 155, 159t,
    180, 188, 194–196, 230, 311–313, 315,
    345–346
    session, 31
Teaching statements, 25–26, 38, 159t, 162t,
    377–378
Team building, 353
Team diversity, 354
Team player, 155–156
Team-nag, 355
Temple University, 40, 211, 271, 294t, 372,
    379
Tenure, 48, 54
    tenure-line faculty member, 195–196
    track, 168, 171–172, 212–213
The Faculty Meeting, 250
Time budgeting, 29–30
Time commitment, 172–173
Time management, 54
Time requirements, 281
Timekeeper, 355
Timeline, 13, 67, 68f, 201–202, 272, 340, 355,
    361, 380
To Tenure and Beyond (TT&B), 130.
    See also Science, technology,
    engineering, and mathematics
    (STEM)
    challenges and efforts, 142–144
    evaluation and outcomes, 141–142, 142t

female non-STEM faculty participation, 134*t*
female STEM faculty participation, 132*t*, 133*t*, 134*t*
intentional change models, 138, 139*f*
 Developing Trust Relationships, 140
 development plan, 140
 Experimenting with and Practicing New Behaviors, 140
 Ideal Self, 138–139
 Learning Agenda, 140
 Real Self, 139–140
 role-playing, 140
modules and customization development, 135–137
 career plan development, 137
 power, politics, and influence, 137
 self-awareness, 136
NSF ADVANCE initiative evolution at CWRU, 130–131
 objectives, 131–132
 recruitment of participants, 132–135
 TT&B West, 133
Training high-quality personnel, 272
Trust Relationships, 140
TT&B. *See* To Tenure and Beyond (TT&B)
Tufts University, 226–227
Two-body problem, 259

U
U.Va. *See* University of Virginia (U.Va.)
UA. *See* University of Akron (UA)
Under-represented, 109, 169
University of Akron (UA), 130
University of Arizona, 274
University of California, 167
University of Connecticut, 190
University of Florida, 271
University of Guam, 39, 77, 270, 294*t*
University of Guam project, 77
 AAUW, 79
 difficult way, 87–89
 individual programs, 81–82
 map of region of Western Pacific, 78*f*
 objective, 77–78
 Pacific Island traditions, 79–80
 project evaluation–challenges and criticism, 86–87
 project evaluation–successes, 82–83
 feedback, 84
 management team, 85–86
 participant responses, 83–84

participants, 83
 "Personalized Plan" segment, 84
 presentation and sessions, 84
 project's effectiveness, 84
 STEM fields, 86
 strategies, 85
 WLI, 83
 workshop, 83, 270
 STEM programs, 81–82
 2-day workshop series, 81
 women, 79
 workshop, 81
University of Kansas Medical Center, 345
University of Maryland, 235
University of Massachusetts, 346, 351
University of Michigan, 5*t*, 9, 27, 250, 315
University of Minnesota, 285
University of Montana, 346–347
University of New Haven Press, 8–9
University of Oklahoma, 259, 397
University of Oregon, 339
University of Ottawa, 190, 397
University of Toledo (UT), 39–40, 92, 130, 274–275, 294*t*, 343, 349
University of Toronto, 31
University of Virginia (U.Va.), 39–40, 108–109, 271, 273–274, 276, 278–280, 294*t*, 338, 350–351
University of Washington, 226–227
University of Wisconsin, 31, 392, 397
University presidents, 326–327, 329–330
University Press of Colorado, 391
US Department of Agriculture (USDA), 70
UT. *See* University of Toledo (UT)

V
Venues, 174–175, 190, 192, 194, 241, 339–340
Verchot Dr. Jeanmarie, 274, 279
Video, 9–10, 137, 208, 235–236, 241, 252, 347–348, 374
Virginia Commonwealth University, 111, 271, 273–274, 278–280, 338
Visiting Professorships for Women (VPW), 7, 20

W
Walk on the Moon, 18, 31
Washington University, 130, 212–213
Wayne State University, 95
Weatherhead School of Management (WSOM), 133–135

WEPAN. *See* Women in Engineering
　　Programs and Advocates Network
　　(WEPAN)
Werb, Dr. Zena, 70
"When and Where I Enter. . .." workshop, 91
　challenges, 97
　　operational challenges, 98
　　organizational challenges, 97–98
　　personal challenges, 99
　description
　　attendee application and profiles, 94
　　day 1 of workshop, 95–96
　　day 2 of workshop, 96–97
　　dinner, 96
　　funding, 97
　　lunch period, 96
　　opening dinner, 94–95
　　organizing committee, 94
　evaluations, 99–101
　　challenges identified by workshop
　　　attendees, 100*t*
　　job description of workshop
　　　attendees, 99*t*
　　take-home messages from
　　　participants, 101*t*
　goals, 93–94
　lessons learned, 103–104
　outcomes and successes, 101–103
WHOI. *See* Woods Hole Oceanographic
　　Institute (WHOI)
WinSETT. *See* Women in Science,
　　Engineering, Trades and Technology
　　(WinSETT)
WISE. *See* Women in Science and
　　Engineering (WISE)
WLI. *See* Women's Leadership Initiative
　　(WLI)
Women
　of color, 92–94
　in science, 167
　scientists, 246–248
　in STEM academia, 20, 293, 300, 302
　workshops for, 246–247
Women in Engineering Programs and
　　Advocates Network (WEPAN), 6, 35,
　　328–329
Women in Science, Engineering, Trades
　　and Technology (WinSETT), 10
Women in Science and Engineering (WISE),
　　200–201
Women's Leadership Initiative
　　(WLI), 83

Woods Hole Oceanographic Institute
　　(WHOI), 349
Work/life balance, 70–71, 181–182
Work/life integration, 28–29
Workshop, 354
　buzz, creating a, 358–359
　creation guidance, 12
　core principles and strategies, 111–112
　　application information, 114
　　faculty member at research
　　　institution, 114
　　faculty member at teaching
　　　institution, 113
　　high level of interaction, 112
　　narrative-based and dialogue-based
　　　work, 112–113
　　PhD candidate, 114
　　planning process, 112
　　postdoctoral scientist, 114
　creation mature, 359–362
　design for diversity and dialogue, 108
　　conceptual and intellectual framework,
　　　110–111
　　facilitation perspective, 121–124
　　participants' perspective, 119–120
　　planning group, 111
　　practical lessons learned, 124–125
　　pre-workshop work, 114–115
　　recommendations, 125–126
　　starting with story, 108–110
　devil, 356–358
　follow-up survey, 193–194
　goals, 18–20
　　and design, 20–22
　good team planning, 355
　hosting, 355–356
　implementation, 22–35
　　choosing the speakers, 30–32
　　funding, 33–34
　　management team, 34–35
　　recruitment, 32–33
　　setting the program, 23–30
　　setting, 33
　institutional history and importance,
　　194–196
　interactive format, 115–116
　　Community and Connectivity,
　　　117–118
　　conventional workshop practice, 116
　　Critical Conversations, 117
　　morning sessions, 116
　　panel moderator, 118

panelists, 119
participants, 116–117
wall of network drawings, 118–119
lessons learned, 192
looking back at the workshop series,
192–193
Pay It FORWARD program. *See* Pay It
FORWARD program
relevance to other institutions, 196
results, 35–36
sessions, 54–55
suggestions for group planning, 194
team diversity, 354–355
timekeeper, 355
women in mathematics and computer
science across NYC, 189–191
workshop flyer, 191*f*
Workshop activities, 67, 99, 237, 240–241
classroom management, 24, 250, 367–368
How to Say No, 25
negotiation, 27–29, 31, 38, 85, 96,
100–102, 137, 154–156, 158–159,
247, 250, 253, 257–258, 262–263,
311–314, 378
communication, 13–14, 29, 33, 68*f*,
71–73, 79–80, 87, 100, 169, 174, 190,
207, 240–241
service, 14, 19, 23, 25, 29–31, 34, 93,
100–101, 155–156, 173–174,
195–196, 224, 281–282, 311–313,
354–355
stress management, 29, 257, 377
teaching, 4, 12, 24, 30–31, 68*f*, 69–70,
155, 159*t*, 180, 188, 194–196, 230,
311–313, 315, 345–346
writing, 13–14, 23, 25–26, 26*f*, 31, 64, 68*f*,
95–96, 98, 158–159, 194, 204–206,
240–241, 247, 257, 263, 297–298, 348
Workshop leadership team training, 292
FWDers, 292, 296

on-site observations, 293
Workshop organizers
benefits
collaboration, 274–275
empowerment, 277–278
gratitude, 275
improving climate, 278–279
intellectual outcomes, 280–281
leadership, 276–277
learning, 273–274
networking, 274–275
organizational skills development,
276–277
satisfaction, 275
springboard, 279–280
visibility, 275–276
drawbacks and difficulties
difficulties and concerns, 282–283
negative perception, 281–282
sustainability, 282
time requirements, 281
FORWARD, 268
mentoring literature, 269
motivations, 269
mentoring, 272
personal network, 271
skills building and learning, 272–273
social entrepreneurship and advocacy,
270
training high-quality personnel, 272
Writing
cover letters, 25–26, 367–368, 378
grant proposal writing, 4, 201–202,
204–206, 315
teaching statements, 25–26, 159*t*, 162*t*
research statement, 25–26, 159*t*, 162*t*
Writing sessions, 31
WSOM. *See* Weatherhead School of
Management (WSOM)

Printed and bound by CPI Group (UK) Ltd, Croydon, CR0 4YY

08/05/2025

01864997-0001